⑫

Love&Lies

LOVE and LIES by MUSAWO

The Misaki Ending

CONTENTS

Chapter 45: Protected by a Lie

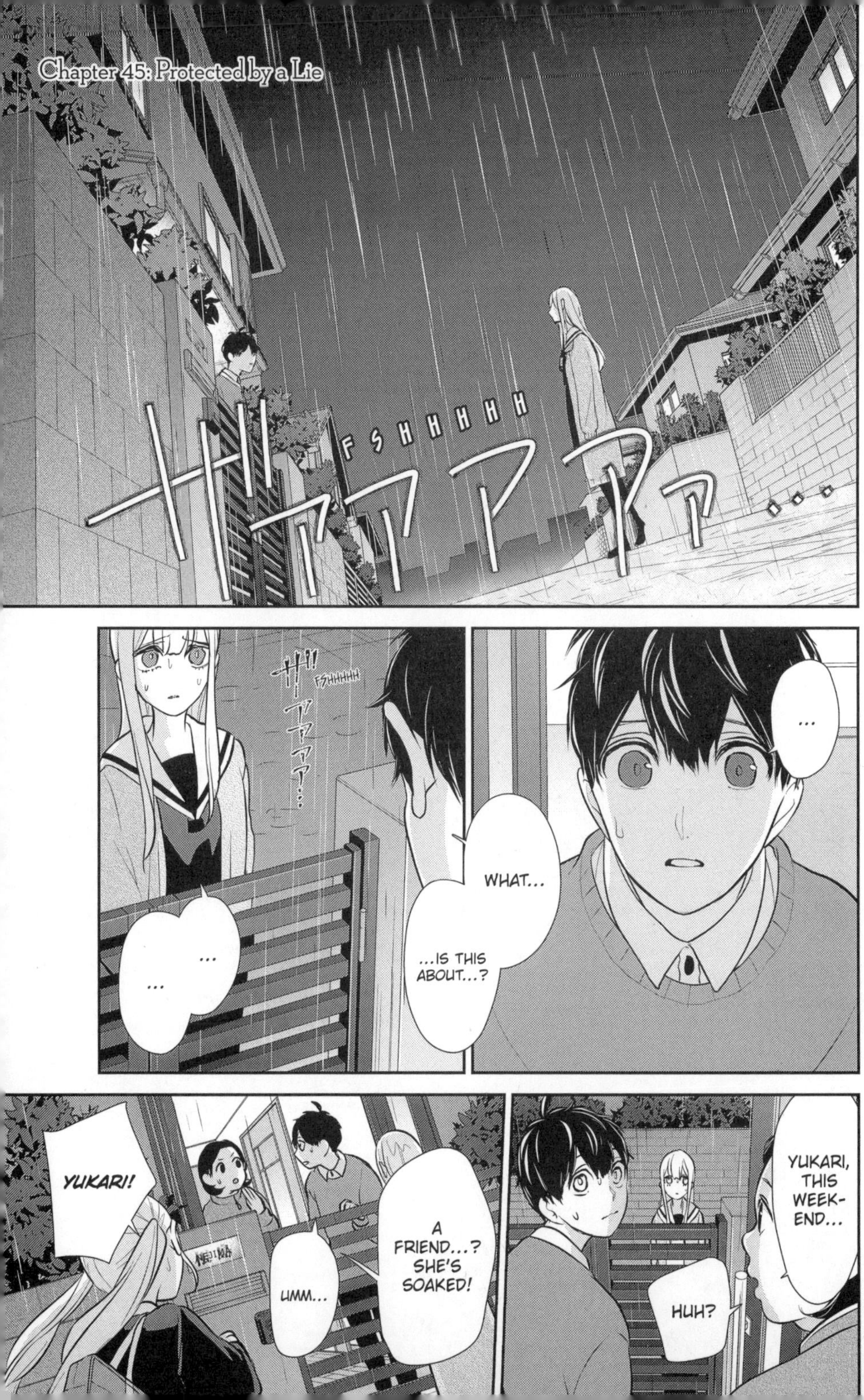
FSHHHHHH
...
WHAT...
...IS THIS ABOUT...?
FSHHHHH
...
...
YUKARI, THIS WEEK-END...
HUH?
A FRIEND...? SHE'S SOAKED!
UMM...
YUKARI!

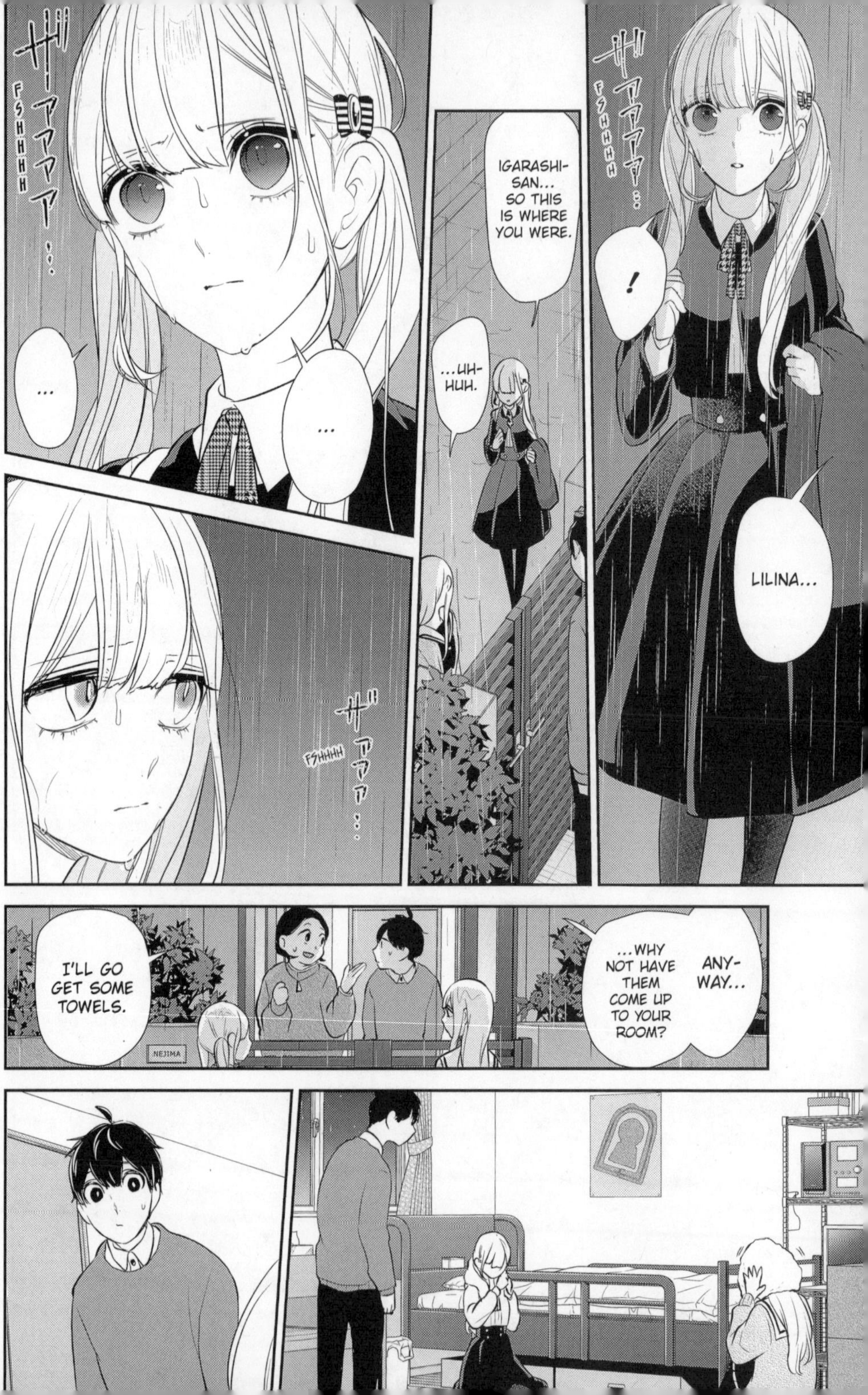
FSHHHHH
!
LILINA...
IGARASHI-SAN... SO THIS IS WHERE YOU WERE.
...UH-HUH.
FSHHHHH
...
...
FSHHHH
ANY-WAY...
...WHY NOT HAVE THEM COME UP TO YOUR ROOM?
I'LL GO GET SOME TOWELS.
NEJIMA

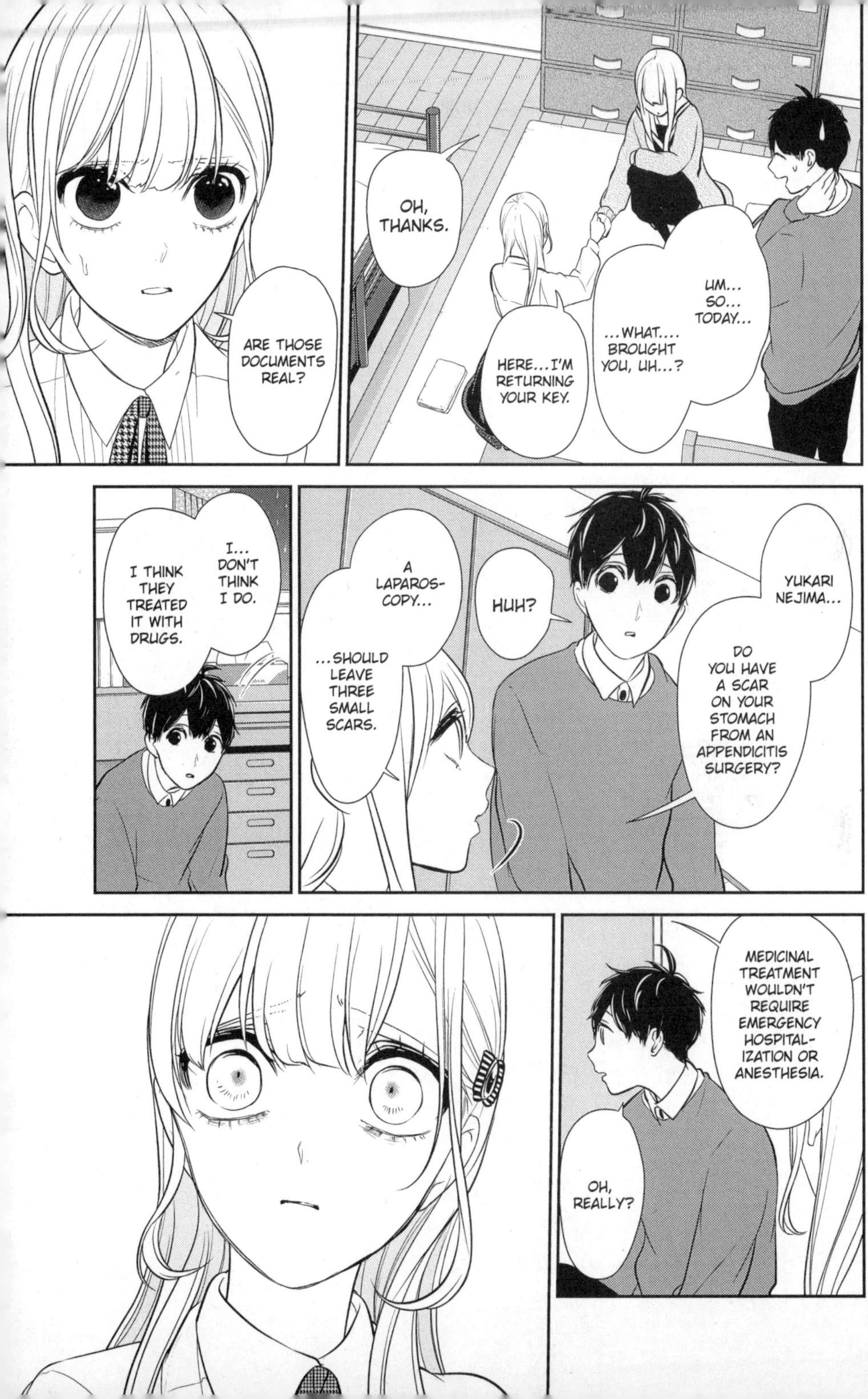
HERE...I'M RETURNING YOUR KEY.
OH, THANKS.
UM... SO... TODAY...
...WHAT.... BROUGHT YOU, UH...?
ARE THOSE DOCUMENTS REAL?
YUKARI NEJIMA...
DO YOU HAVE A SCAR ON YOUR STOMACH FROM AN APPENDICITIS SURGERY?
HUH?
A LAPAROS-COPY...
...SHOULD LEAVE THREE SMALL SCARS.
I... DON'T THINK I DO.
I THINK THEY TREATED IT WITH DRUGS.
MEDICINAL TREATMENT WOULDN'T REQUIRE EMERGENCY HOSPITAL-IZATION OR ANESTHESIA.
OH, REALLY?

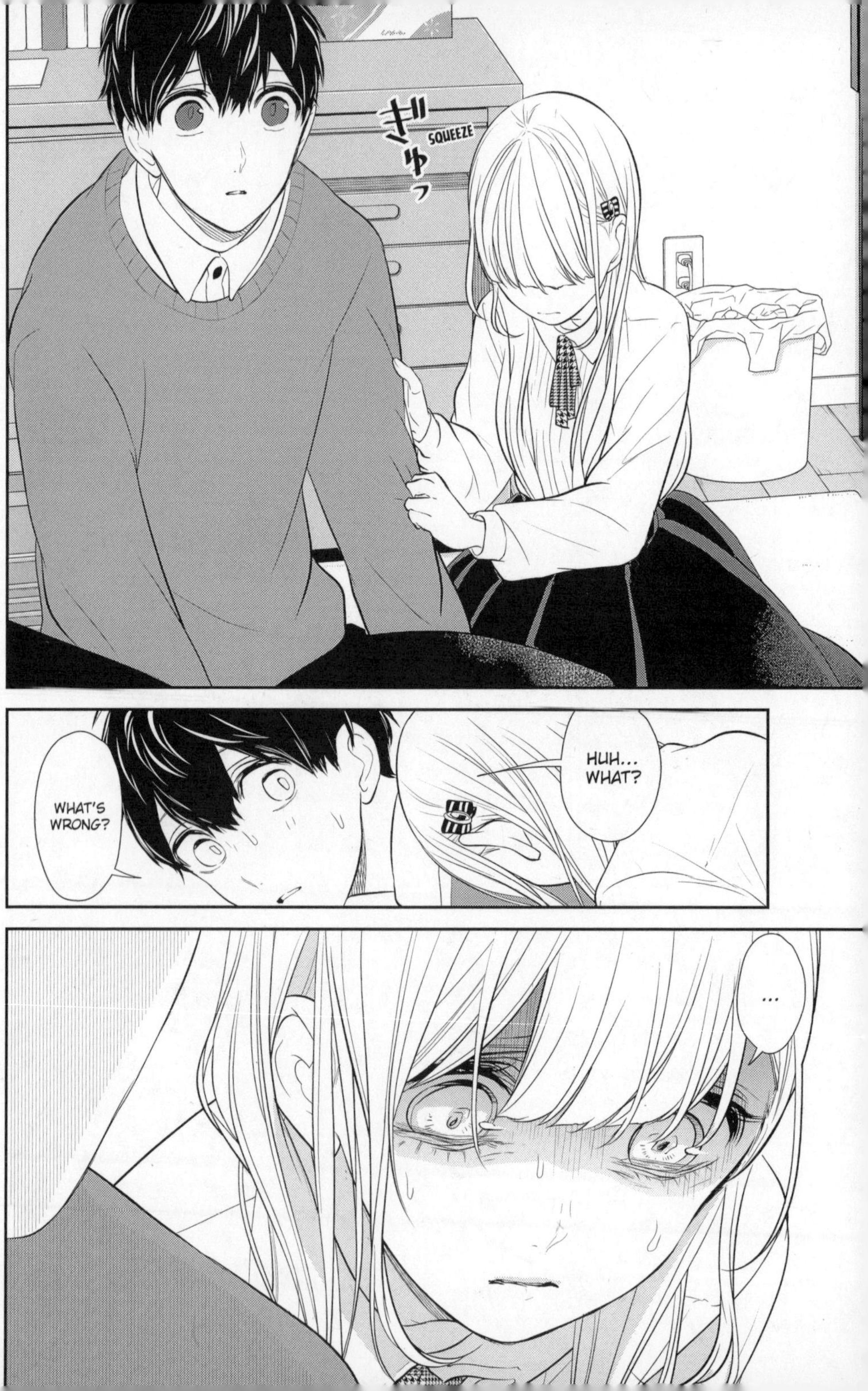
ギュッ
SQUEEZE
HUH... WHAT?
WHAT'S WRONG?
...

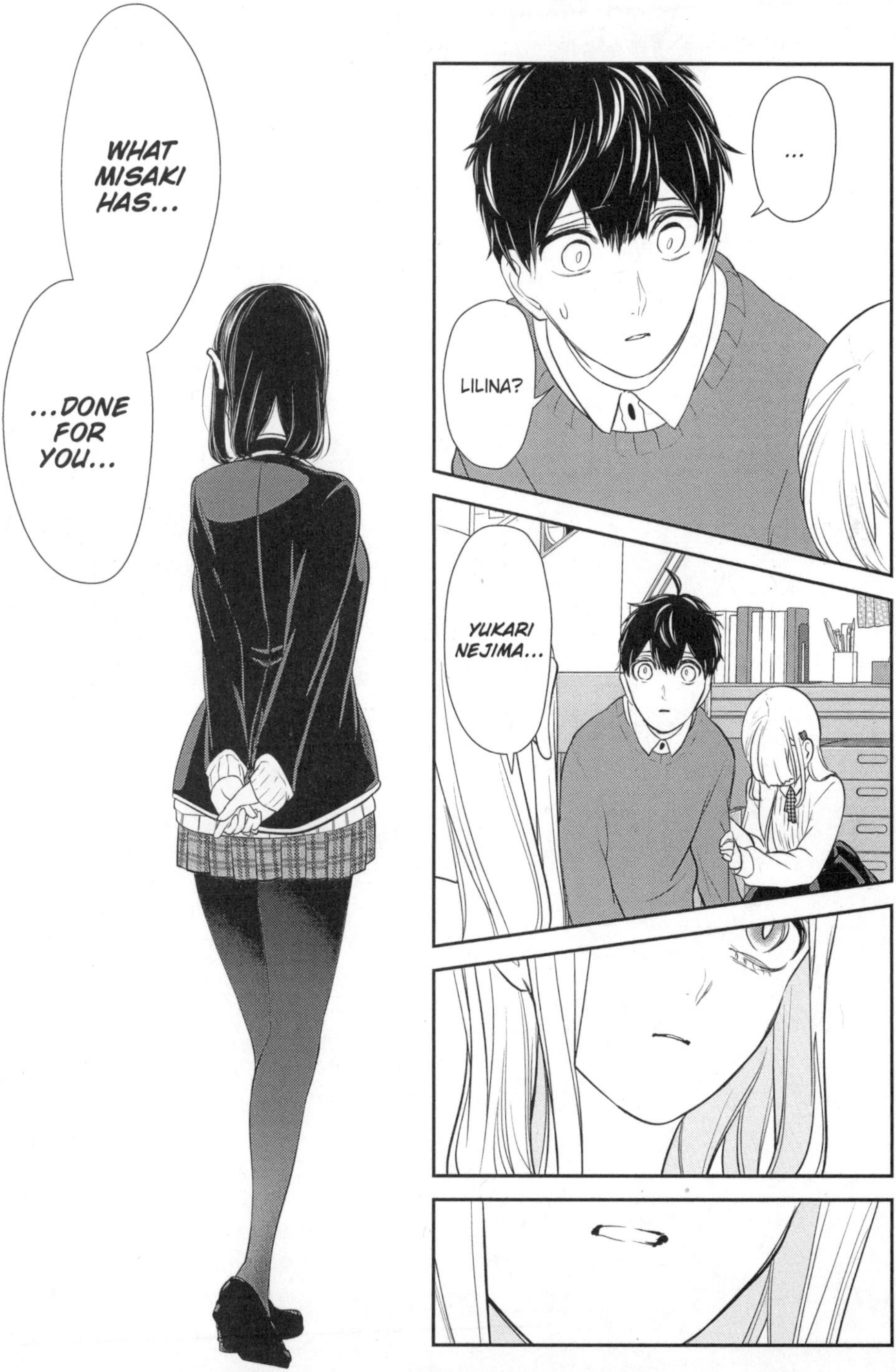
...
LILINA?
YUKARI NEJIMA...
WHAT MISAKI HAS...
...DONE FOR YOU...

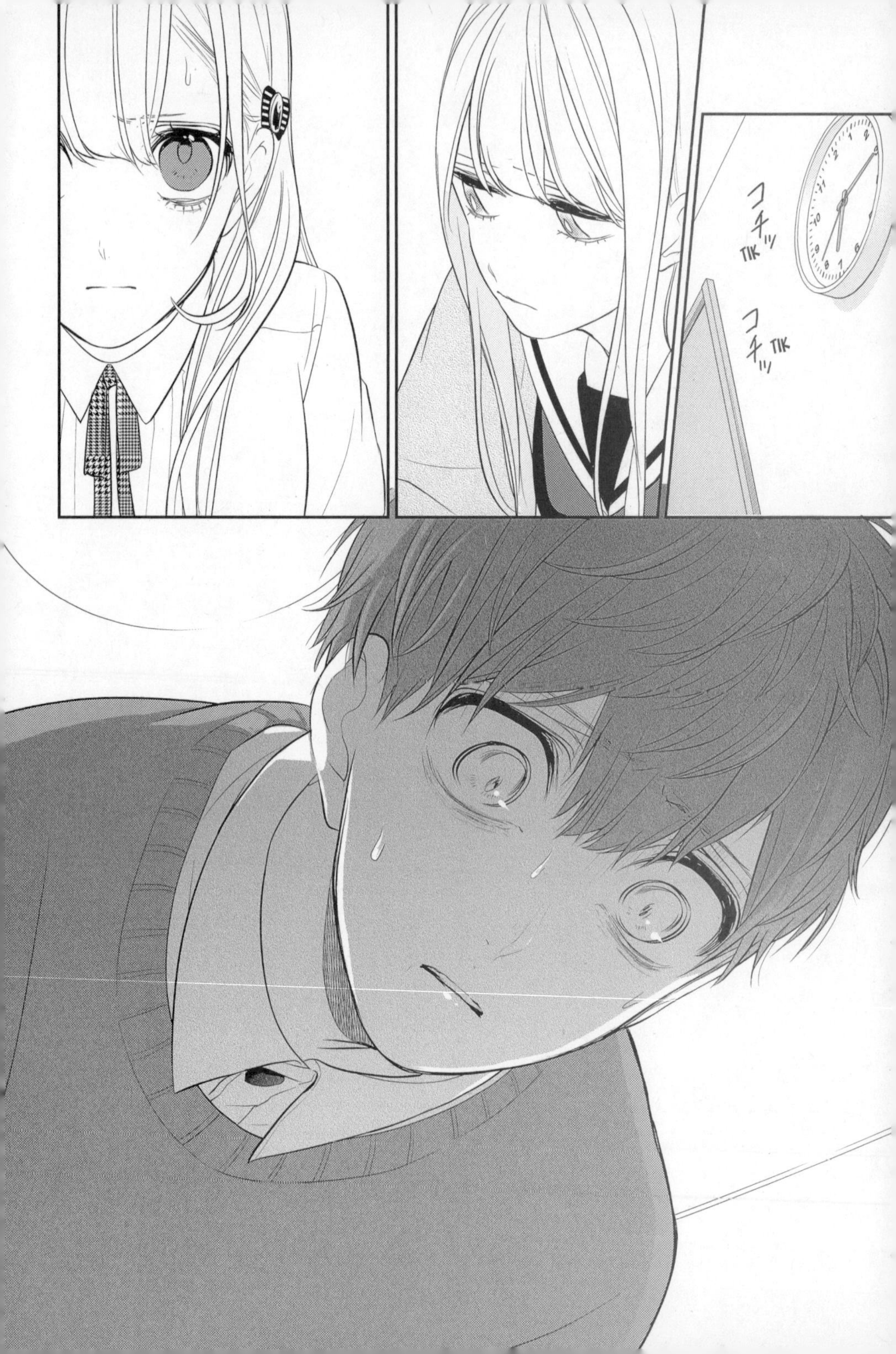
コチッ
TIK
コチッ
TIK

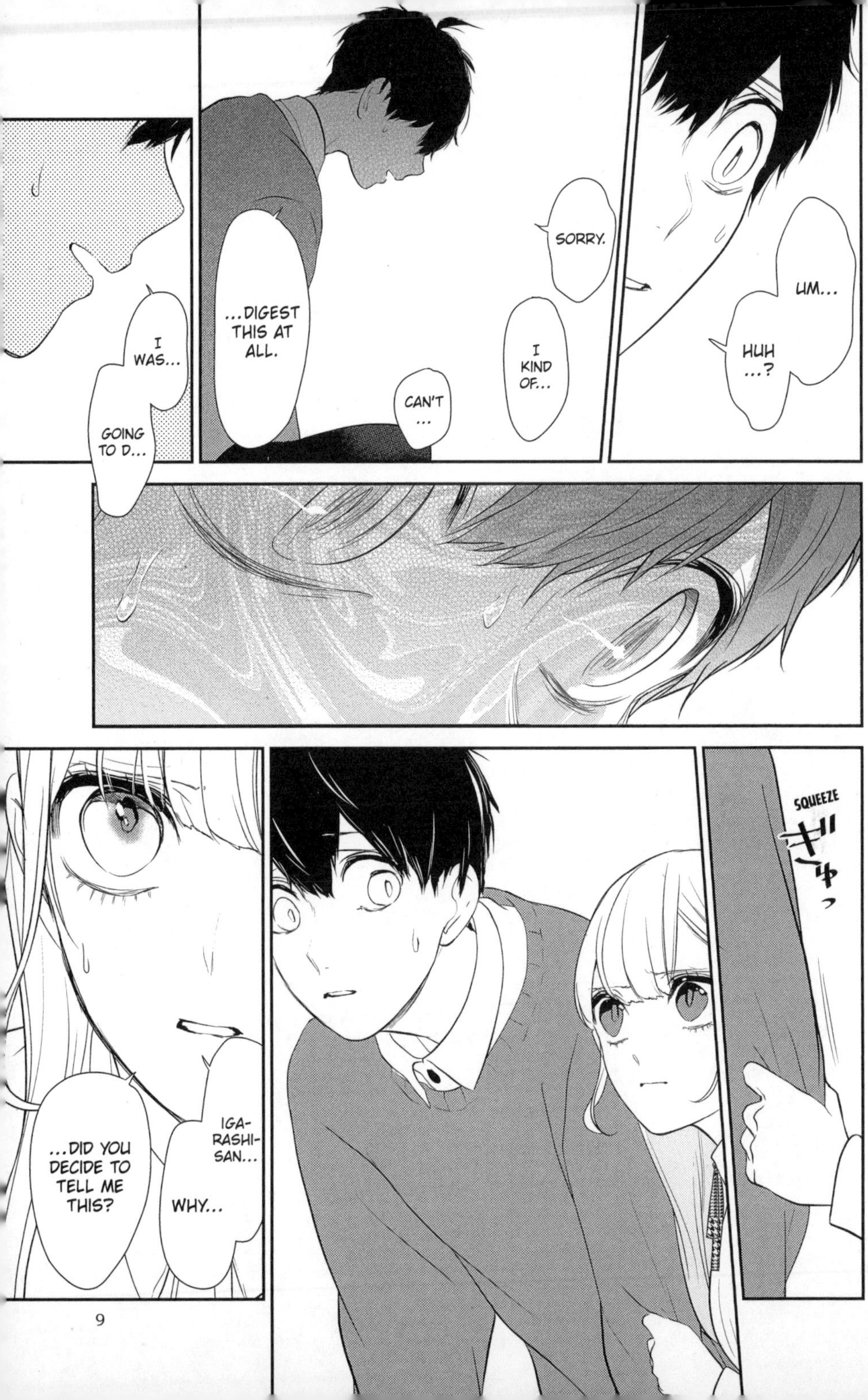
UM...
HUH ...?
SORRY.
I KIND OF...
CAN'T ...
...DIGEST THIS AT ALL.
I WAS...
GOING TO D...
SQUEEZE
ギュッ
IGA-RASHI-SAN...
WHY...
...DID YOU DECIDE TO TELL ME THIS?

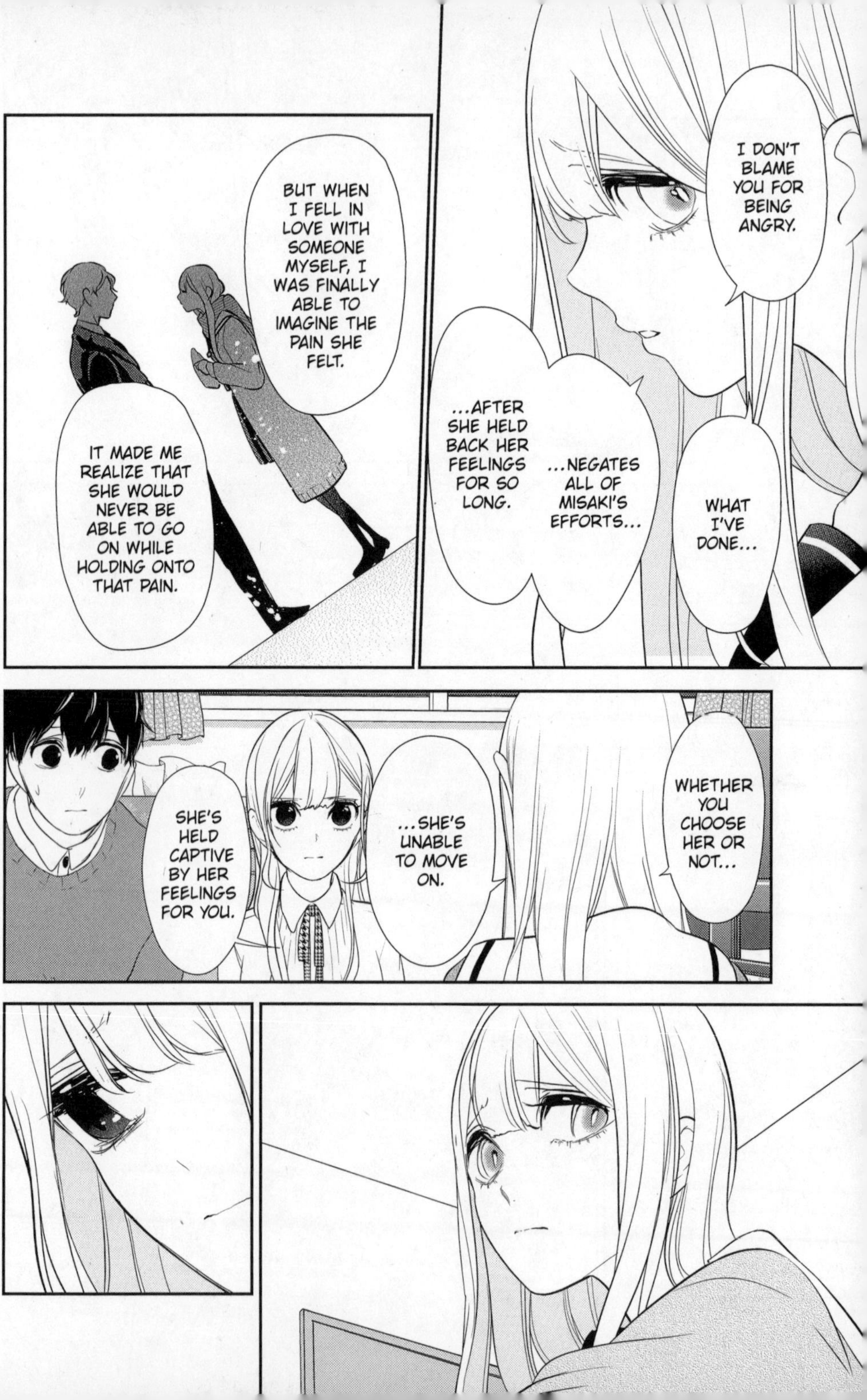
I DON'T BLAME YOU FOR BEING ANGRY.
WHAT I'VE DONE...
...NEGATES ALL OF MISAKI'S EFFORTS...
...AFTER SHE HELD BACK HER FEELINGS FOR SO LONG.
BUT WHEN I FELL IN LOVE WITH SOMEONE MYSELF, I WAS FINALLY ABLE TO IMAGINE THE PAIN SHE FELT.
IT MADE ME REALIZE THAT SHE WOULD NEVER BE ABLE TO GO ON WHILE HOLDING ONTO THAT PAIN.
WHETHER YOU CHOOSE HER OR NOT...
...SHE'S UNABLE TO MOVE ON.
SHE'S HELD CAPTIVE BY HER FEELINGS FOR YOU.

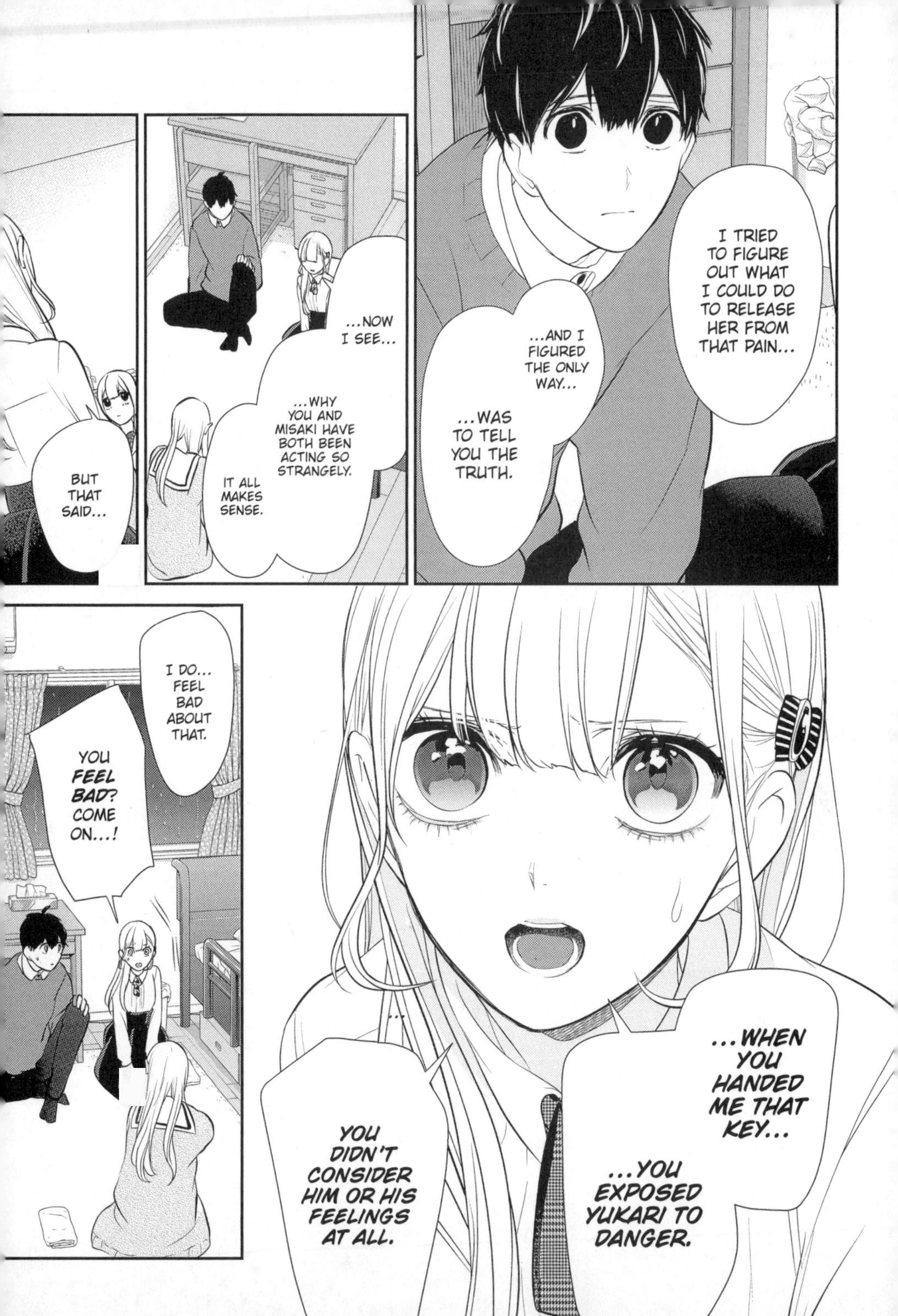
I TRIED TO FIGURE OUT WHAT I COULD DO TO RELEASE HER FROM THAT PAIN...
...AND I FIGURED THE ONLY WAY...
...WAS TO TELL YOU THE TRUTH.
...NOW I SEE...
...WHY YOU AND MISAKI HAVE BOTH BEEN ACTING SO STRANGELY.
IT ALL MAKES SENSE.
BUT THAT SAID...
...WHEN YOU HANDED ME THAT KEY...
...YOU EXPOSED YUKARI TO DANGER.
YOU DIDN'T CONSIDER HIM OR HIS FEELINGS AT ALL.
I DO... FEEL BAD ABOUT THAT.
YOU FEEL BAD? COME ON...!

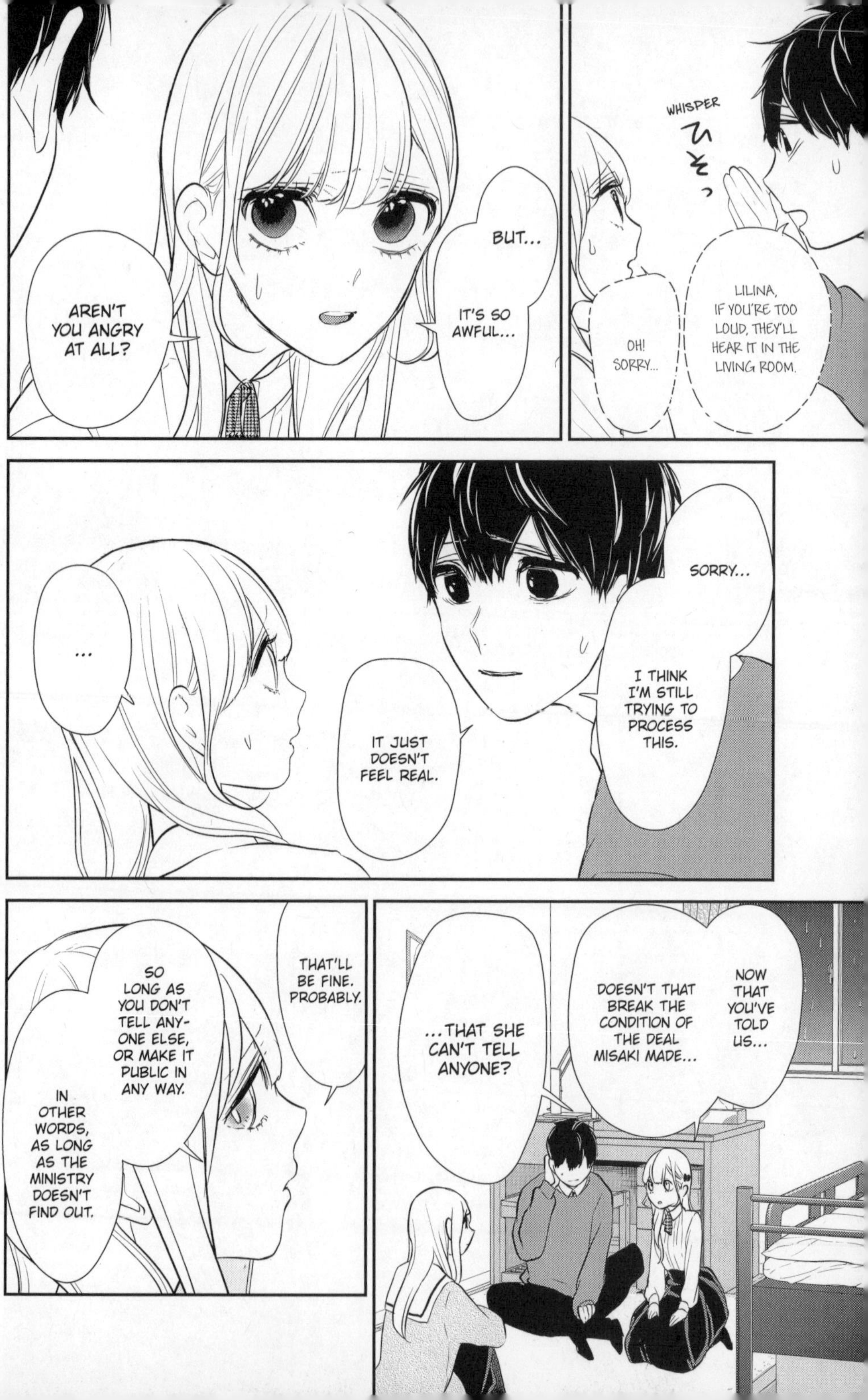
WHISPER
ひそっ
LILINA, IF YOU'RE TOO LOUD, THEY'LL HEAR IT IN THE LIVING ROOM.
OH! SORRY...
BUT...
IT'S SO AWFUL...
AREN'T YOU ANGRY AT ALL?
SORRY...
I THINK I'M STILL TRYING TO PROCESS THIS.
IT JUST DOESN'T FEEL REAL.
...
NOW THAT YOU'VE TOLD US...
DOESN'T THAT BREAK THE CONDITION OF THE DEAL MISAKI MADE...
...THAT SHE CAN'T TELL ANYONE?
THAT'LL BE FINE. PROBABLY.
SO LONG AS YOU DON'T TELL ANY-ONE ELSE, OR MAKE IT PUBLIC IN ANY WAY.
IN OTHER WORDS, AS LONG AS THE MINISTRY DOESN'T FIND OUT.

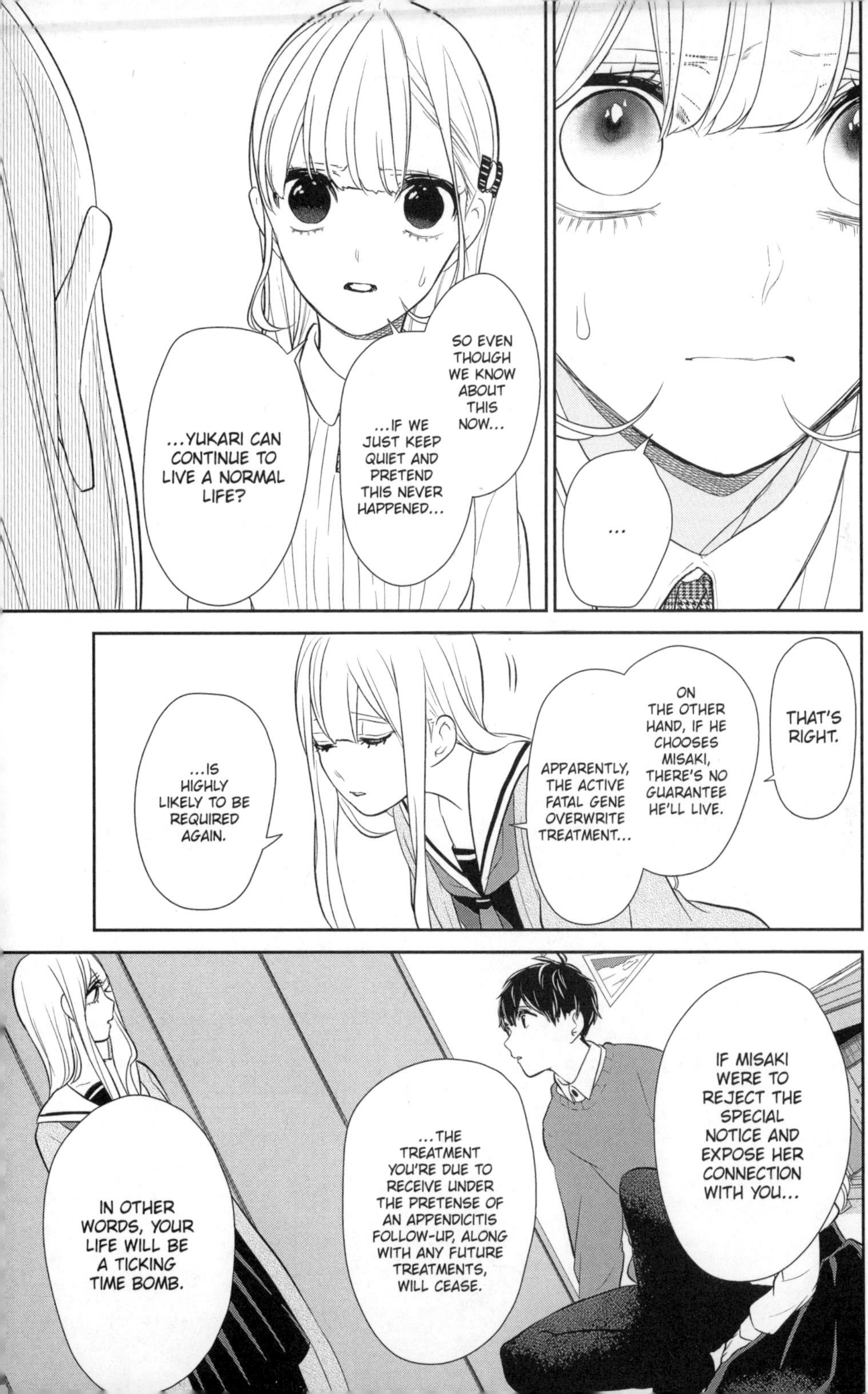
…
SO EVEN THOUGH WE KNOW ABOUT THIS NOW…
…IF WE JUST KEEP QUIET AND PRETEND THIS NEVER HAPPENED…
…YUKARI CAN CONTINUE TO LIVE A NORMAL LIFE?
THAT'S RIGHT.
ON THE OTHER HAND, IF HE CHOOSES MISAKI, THERE'S NO GUARANTEE HE'LL LIVE.
APPARENTLY, THE ACTIVE FATAL GENE OVERWRITE TREATMENT…
…IS HIGHLY LIKELY TO BE REQUIRED AGAIN.
IF MISAKI WERE TO REJECT THE SPECIAL NOTICE AND EXPOSE HER CONNECTION WITH YOU…
…THE TREATMENT YOU'RE DUE TO RECEIVE UNDER THE PRETENSE OF AN APPENDICITIS FOLLOW-UP, ALONG WITH ANY FUTURE TREATMENTS, WILL CEASE.
IN OTHER WORDS, YOUR LIFE WILL BE A TICKING TIME BOMB.

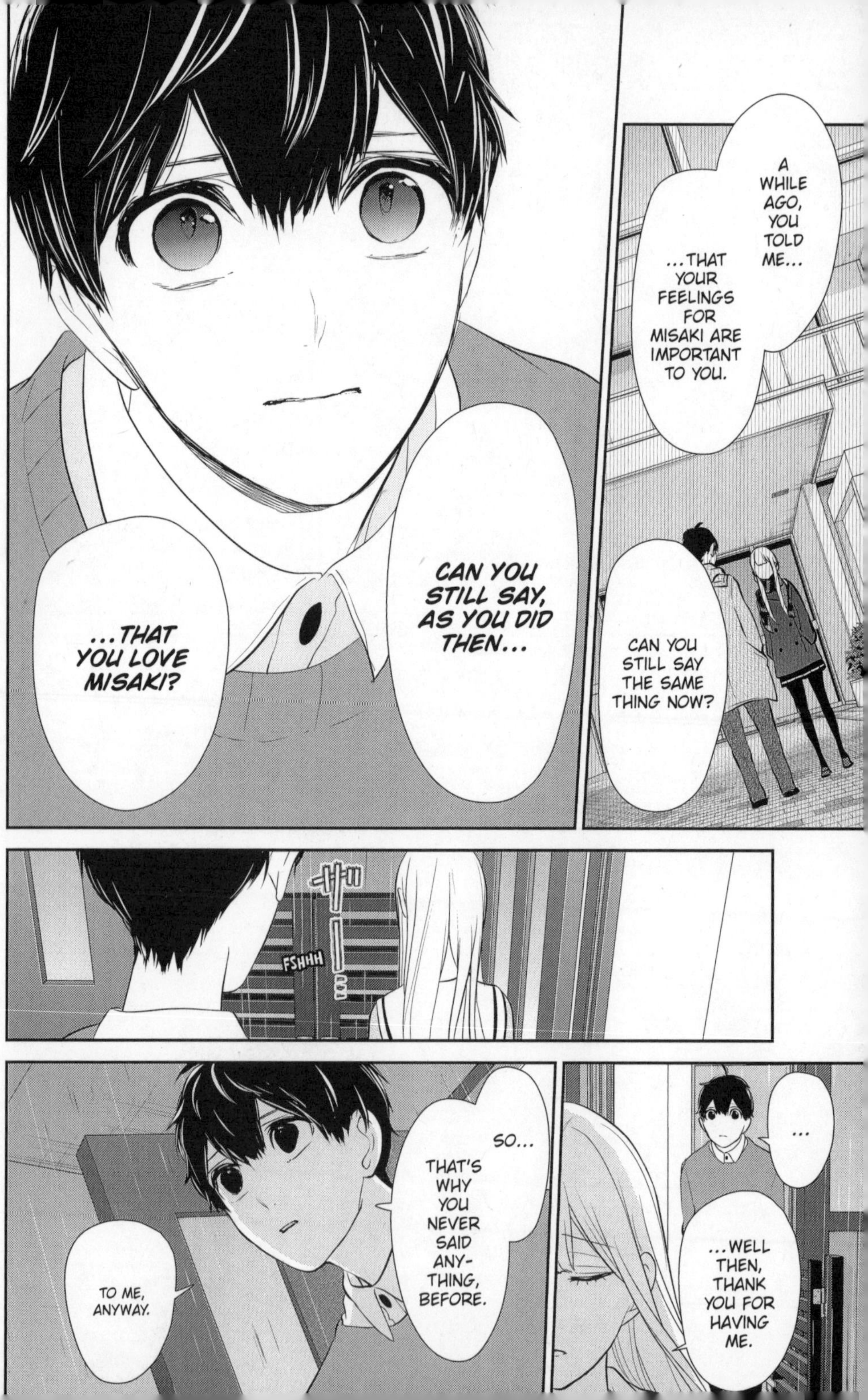
A WHILE AGO, YOU TOLD ME...
...THAT YOUR FEELINGS FOR MISAKI ARE IMPORTANT TO YOU.
CAN YOU STILL SAY THE SAME THING NOW?
CAN YOU STILL SAY, AS YOU DID THEN...
...THAT YOU LOVE MISAKI?
FSHHH
...
...WELL THEN, THANK YOU FOR HAVING ME.
SO...
THAT'S WHY YOU NEVER SAID ANY-THING, BEFORE.
TO ME, ANYWAY.

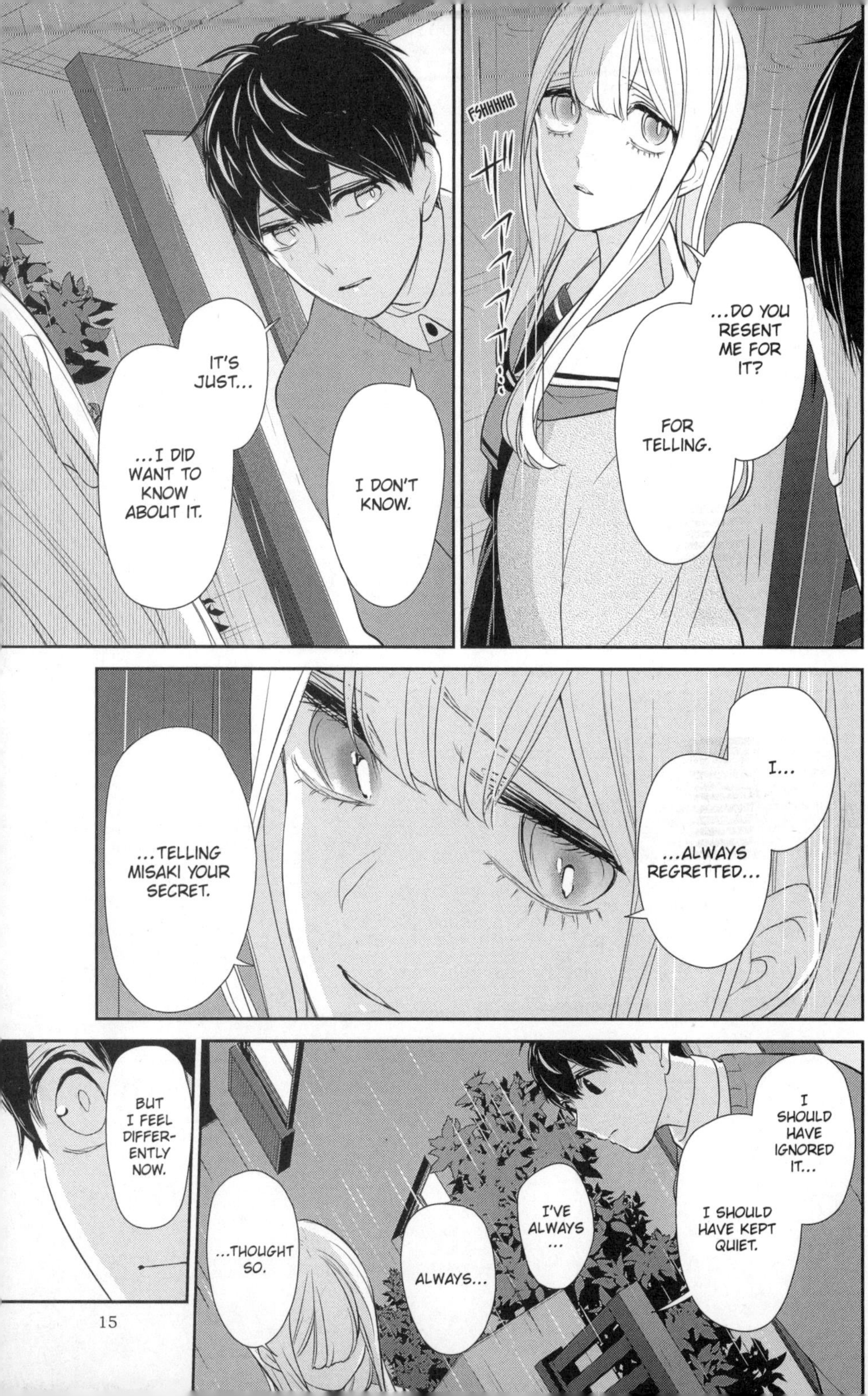
FSHHHHH
...DO YOU RESENT ME FOR IT?
FOR TELLING.
I DON'T KNOW.
IT'S JUST...
...I DID WANT TO KNOW ABOUT IT.
I...
...ALWAYS REGRETTED...
...TELLING MISAKI YOUR SECRET.
I SHOULD HAVE IGNORED IT...
I SHOULD HAVE KEPT QUIET.
I'VE ALWAYS ...
ALWAYS...
...THOUGHT SO.
BUT I FEEL DIFFERENTLY NOW.

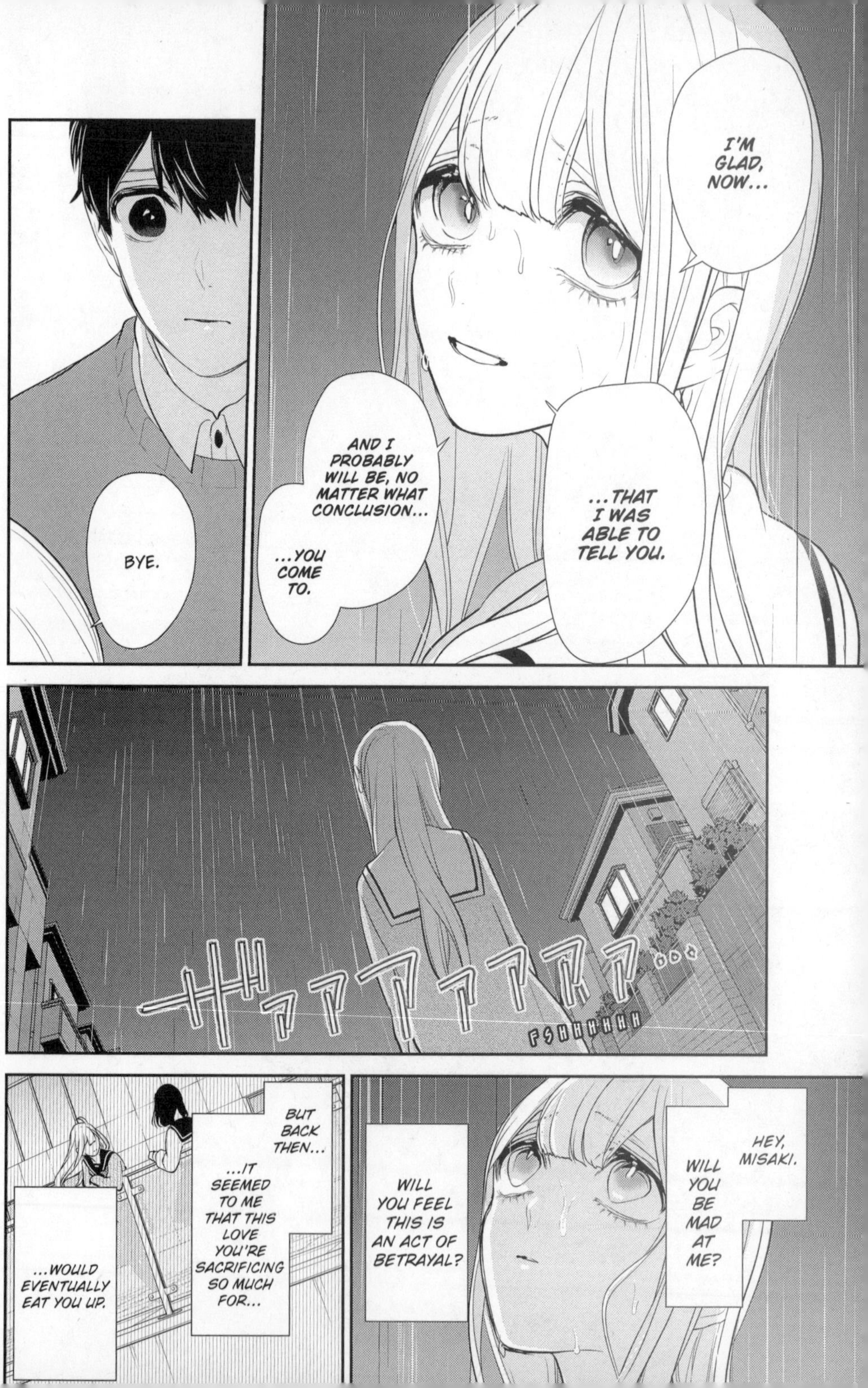
I'M GLAD, NOW...
...THAT I WAS ABLE TO TELL YOU.
AND I PROBABLY WILL BE, NO MATTER WHAT CONCLUSION...
...YOU COME TO.
BYE.
FSHHHHHH
HEY, MISAKI.
WILL YOU BE MAD AT ME?
WILL YOU FEEL THIS IS AN ACT OF BETRAYAL?
BUT BACK THEN...
...IT SEEMED TO ME THAT THIS LOVE YOU'RE SACRIFICING SO MUCH FOR...
...WOULD EVENTUALLY EAT YOU UP.

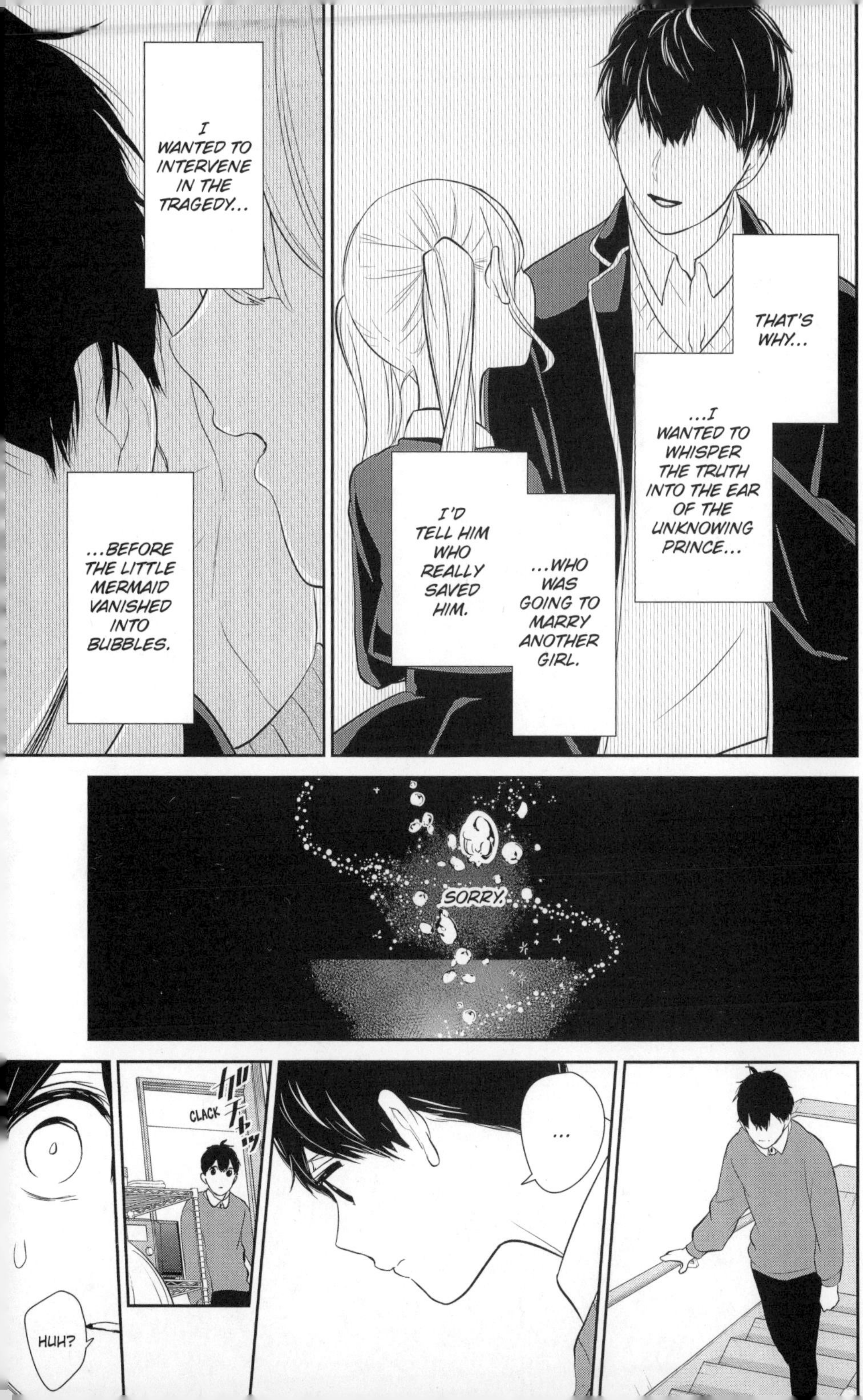
THAT'S WHY...
...I WANTED TO WHISPER THE TRUTH INTO THE EAR OF THE UNKNOWING PRINCE...
...WHO WAS GOING TO MARRY ANOTHER GIRL.
I'D TELL HIM WHO REALLY SAVED HIM.
I WANTED TO INTERVENE IN THE TRAGEDY...
...BEFORE THE LITTLE MERMAID VANISHED INTO BUBBLES.
SORRY.
...
CLACK
HUH?

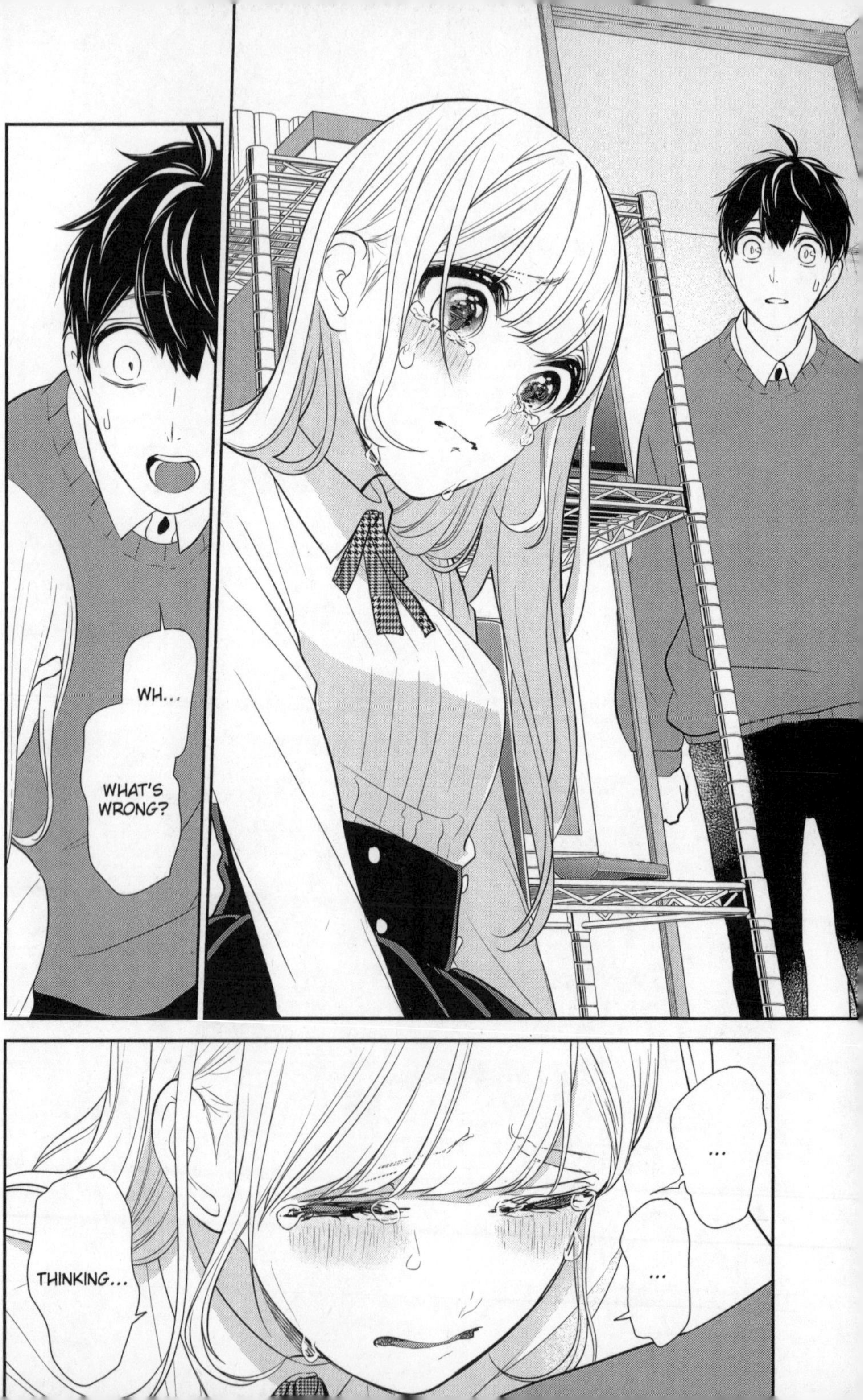
WH...
WHAT'S WRONG?
...
...
THINKING...

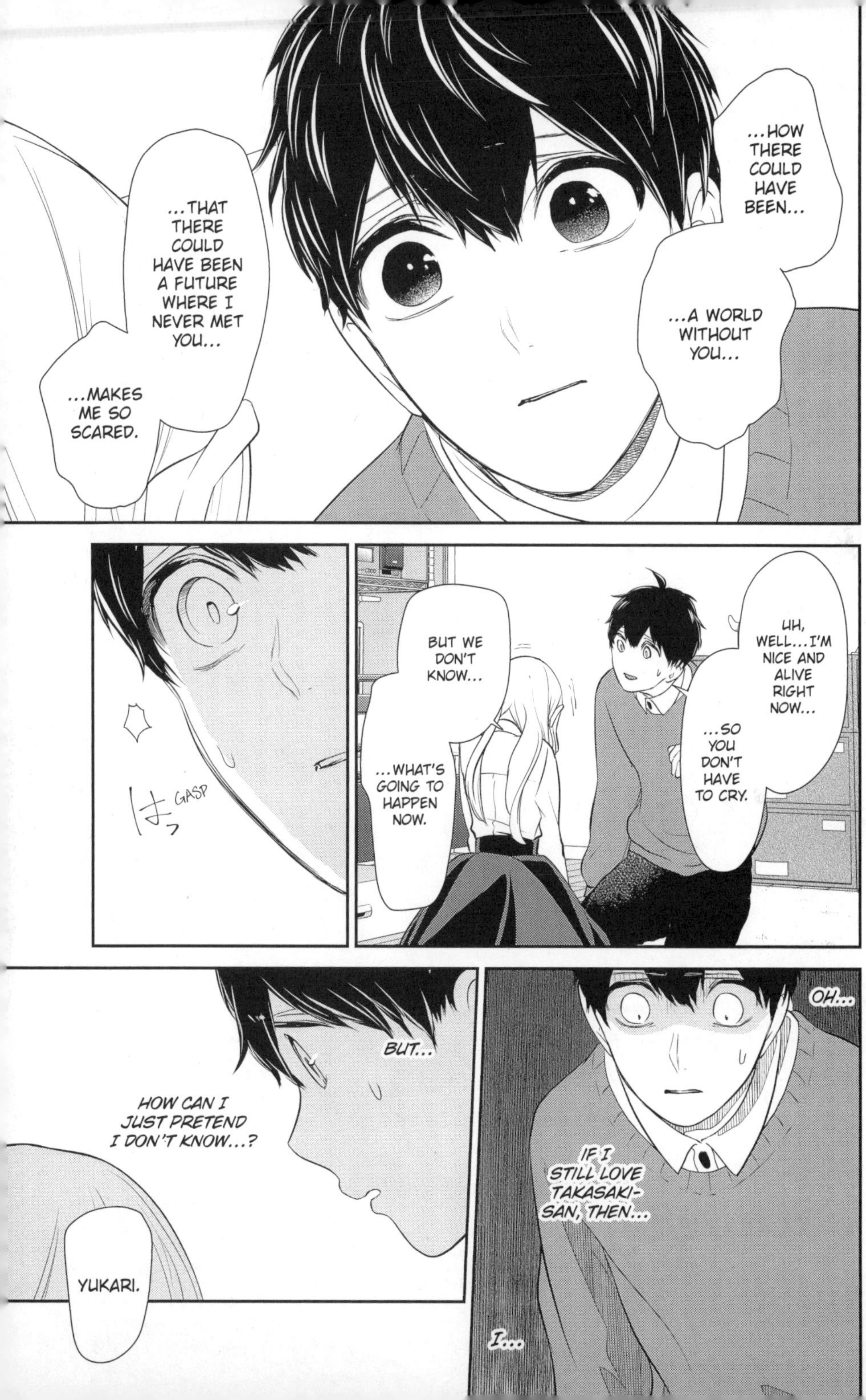
...HOW THERE COULD HAVE BEEN...
...A WORLD WITHOUT YOU...
...THAT THERE COULD HAVE BEEN A FUTURE WHERE I NEVER MET YOU...
...MAKES ME SO SCARED.
UH, WELL...I'M NICE AND ALIVE RIGHT NOW...
...SO YOU DON'T HAVE TO CRY.
BUT WE DON'T KNOW...
...WHAT'S GOING TO HAPPEN NOW.
は GASP
OH...
IF I STILL LOVE TAKASAKI-SAN, THEN...
I...
BUT...
HOW CAN I JUST PRETEND I DON'T KNOW...?
YUKARI.

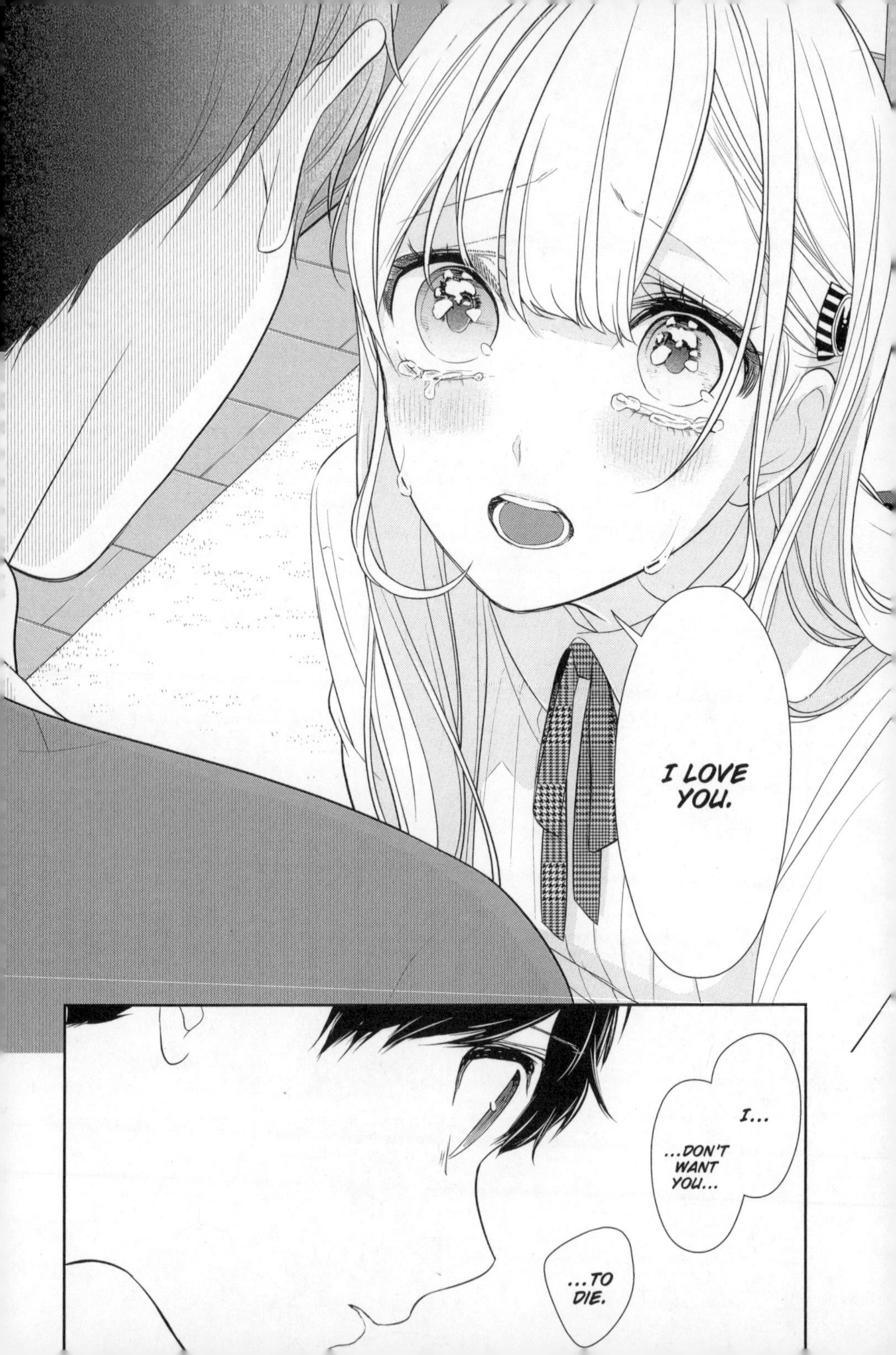
I LOVE YOU.
I...
...DON'T WANT YOU...
...TO DIE.

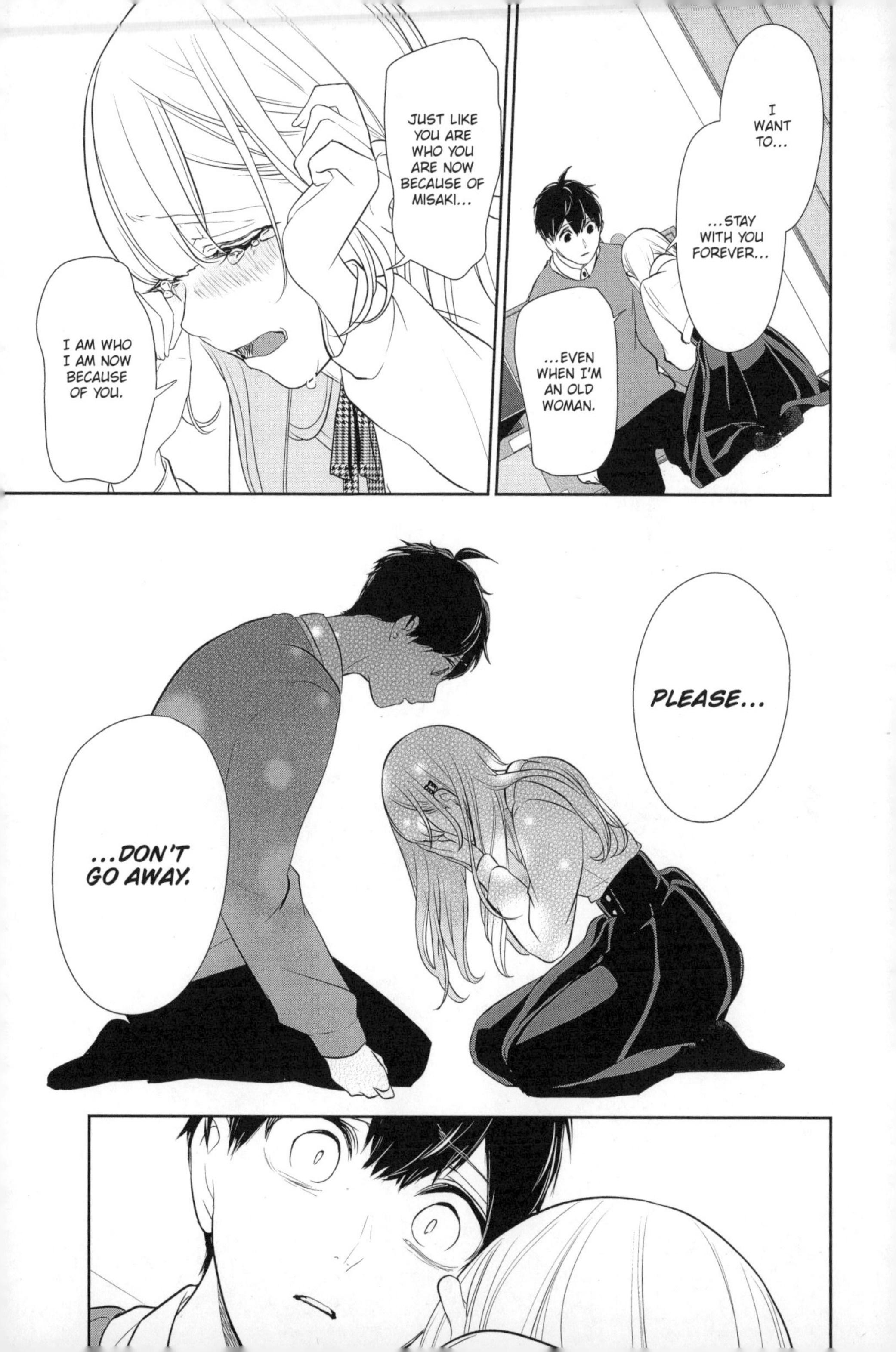
I WANT TO...
...STAY WITH YOU FOREVER...
...EVEN WHEN I'M AN OLD WOMAN.
JUST LIKE YOU ARE WHO YOU ARE NOW BECAUSE OF MISAKI...
I AM WHO I AM NOW BECAUSE OF YOU.
PLEASE...
...DON'T GO AWAY.

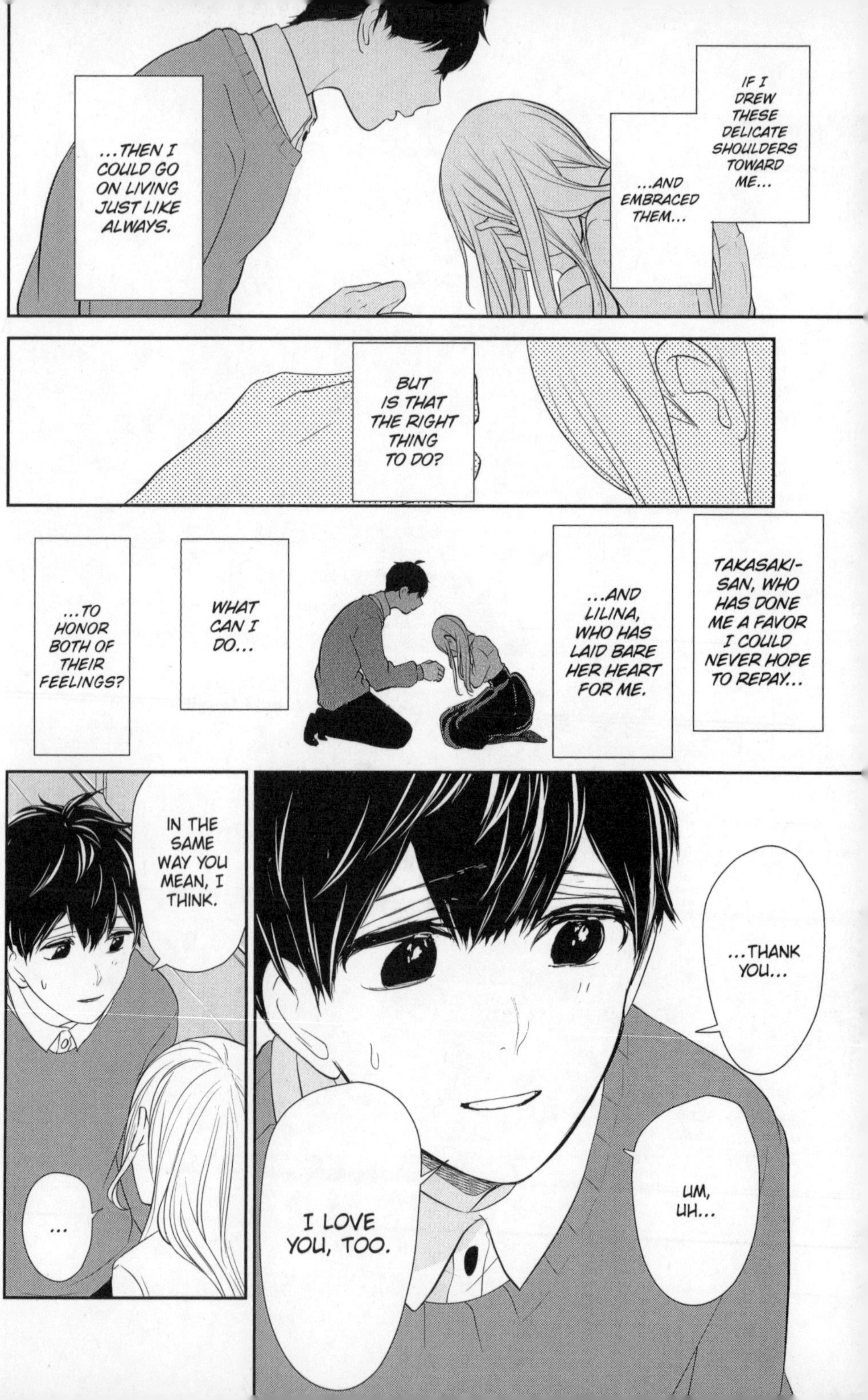
IF I DREW THESE DELICATE SHOULDERS TOWARD ME…
…AND EMBRACED THEM…
…THEN I COULD GO ON LIVING JUST LIKE ALWAYS.
BUT IS THAT THE RIGHT THING TO DO?
TAKASAKI-SAN, WHO HAS DONE ME A FAVOR I COULD NEVER HOPE TO REPAY…
…AND LILINA, WHO HAS LAID BARE HER HEART FOR ME.
WHAT CAN I DO…
…TO HONOR BOTH OF THEIR FEELINGS?
…THANK YOU…
UM, UH…
I LOVE YOU, TOO.
IN THE SAME WAY YOU MEAN, I THINK.
…

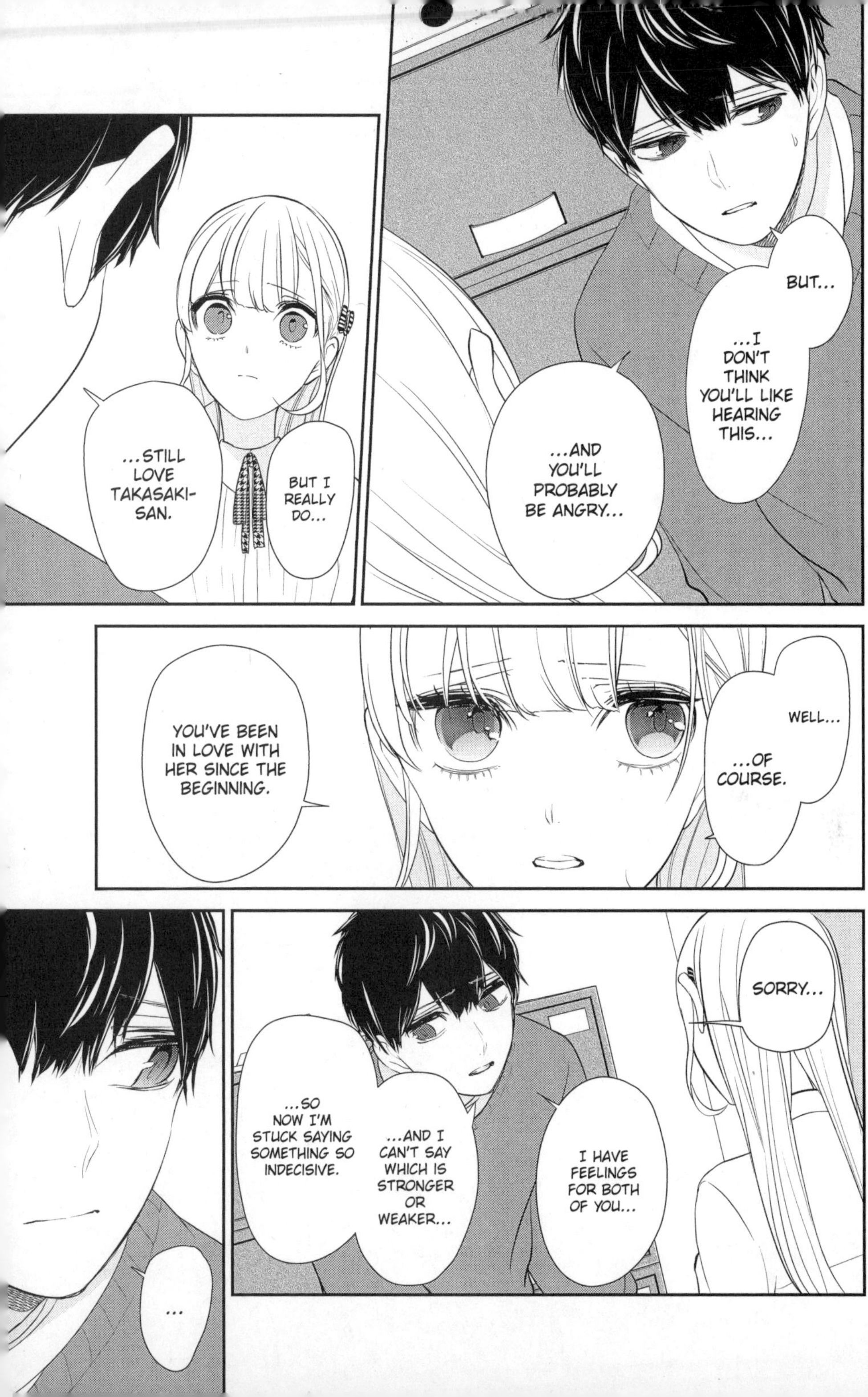
BUT...
...I DON'T THINK YOU'LL LIKE HEARING THIS...
...AND YOU'LL PROBABLY BE ANGRY...
BUT I REALLY DO...
...STILL LOVE TAKASAKI-SAN.
WELL...
...OF COURSE.
YOU'VE BEEN IN LOVE WITH HER SINCE THE BEGINNING.
SORRY...
I HAVE FEELINGS FOR BOTH OF YOU...
...AND I CAN'T SAY WHICH IS STRONGER OR WEAKER...
...SO NOW I'M STUCK SAYING SOMETHING SO INDECISIVE.
...

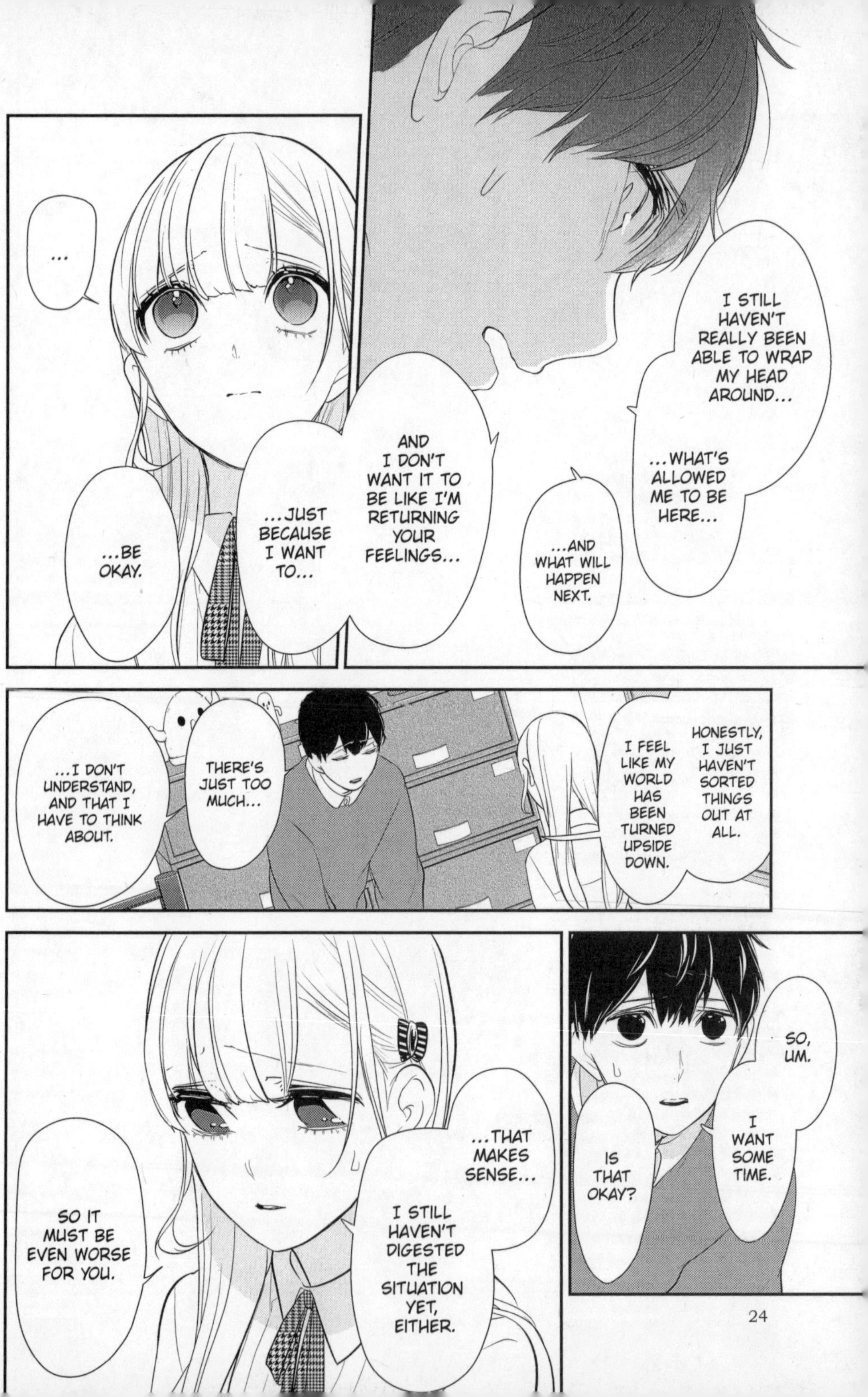
I STILL HAVEN'T REALLY BEEN ABLE TO WRAP MY HEAD AROUND...
...WHAT'S ALLOWED ME TO BE HERE...
...AND WHAT WILL HAPPEN NEXT.
AND I DON'T WANT IT TO BE LIKE I'M RETURNING YOUR FEELINGS...
...JUST BECAUSE I WANT TO...
...BE OKAY.
...
HONESTLY, I JUST HAVEN'T SORTED THINGS OUT AT ALL.
I FEEL LIKE MY WORLD HAS BEEN TURNED UPSIDE DOWN.
THERE'S JUST TOO MUCH...
...I DON'T UNDERSTAND, AND THAT I HAVE TO THINK ABOUT.
SO, UM.
I WANT SOME TIME.
IS THAT OKAY?
...THAT MAKES SENSE...
I STILL HAVEN'T DIGESTED THE SITUATION YET, EITHER.
SO IT MUST BE EVEN WORSE FOR YOU.

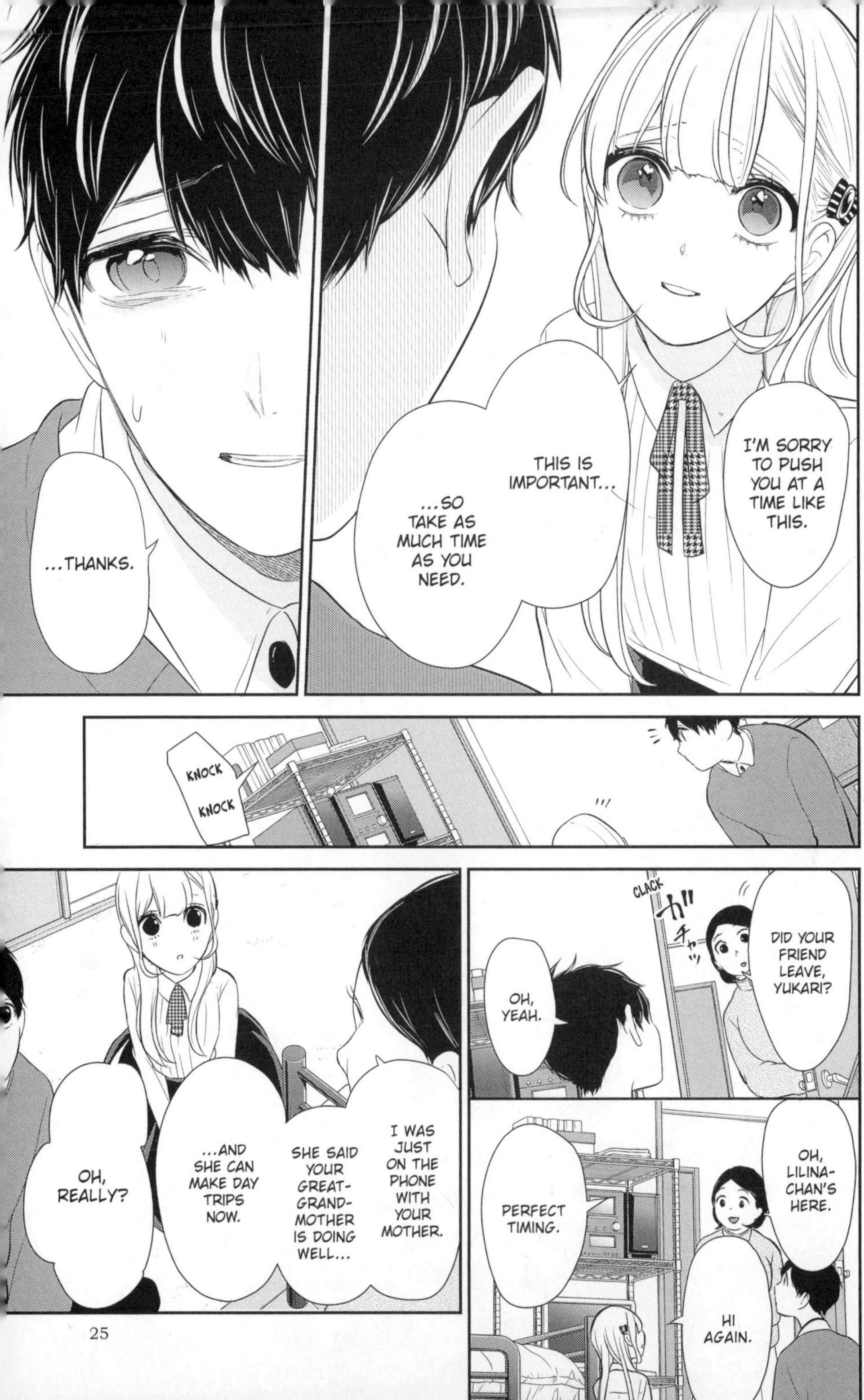
I'M SORRY TO PUSH YOU AT A TIME LIKE THIS.
THIS IS IMPORTANT...
...SO TAKE AS MUCH TIME AS YOU NEED.
...THANKS.
KNOCK KNOCK
CLACK
ガチャッ
DID YOUR FRIEND LEAVE, YUKARI?
OH, YEAH.
OH, LILINA-CHAN'S HERE.
HI AGAIN.
PERFECT TIMING.
I WAS JUST ON THE PHONE WITH YOUR MOTHER.
SHE SAID YOUR GREAT-GRANDMOTHER IS DOING WELL...
...AND SHE CAN MAKE DAY TRIPS NOW.
OH, REALLY?

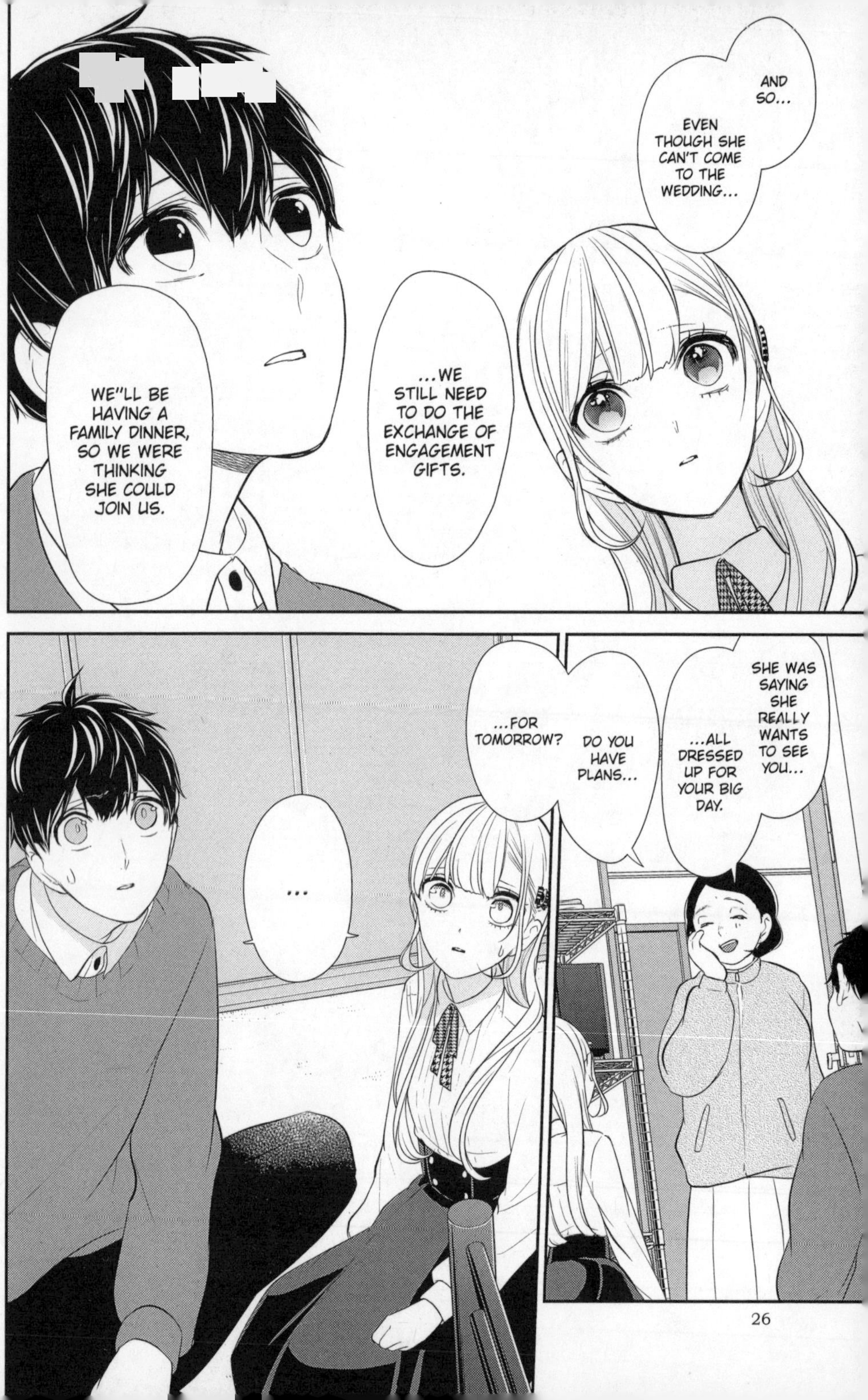
AND SO...
EVEN THOUGH SHE CAN'T COME TO THE WEDDING...
...WE STILL NEED TO DO THE EXCHANGE OF ENGAGEMENT GIFTS.
WE'LL BE HAVING A FAMILY DINNER, SO WE WERE THINKING SHE COULD JOIN US.
SHE WAS SAYING SHE REALLY WANTS TO SEE YOU...
...ALL DRESSED UP FOR YOUR BIG DAY.
DO YOU HAVE PLANS...
...FOR TOMORROW?
...

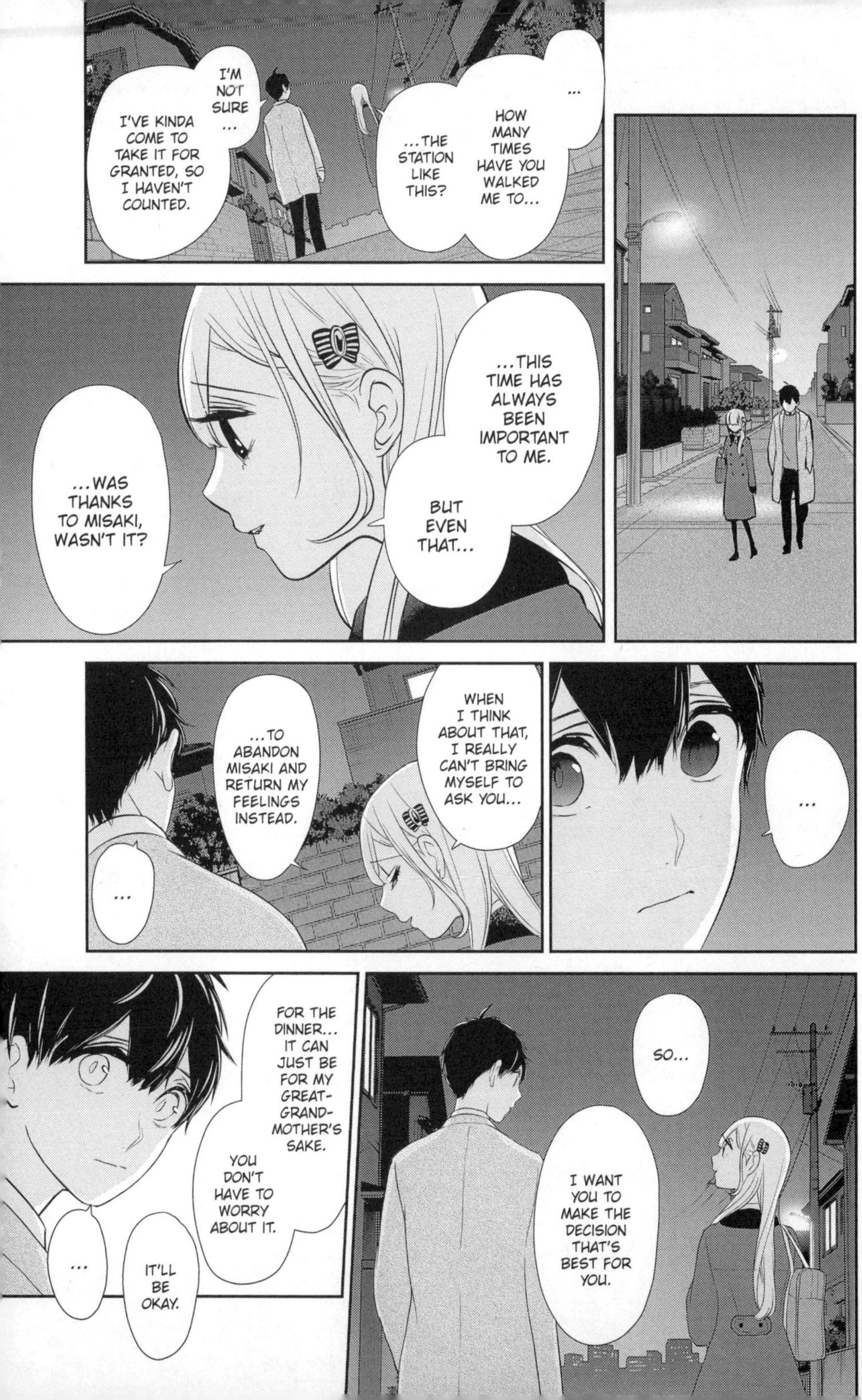
...
HOW MANY TIMES HAVE YOU WALKED ME TO...
...THE STATION LIKE THIS?
I'M NOT SURE...
I'VE KINDA COME TO TAKE IT FOR GRANTED, SO I HAVEN'T COUNTED.
...THIS TIME HAS ALWAYS BEEN IMPORTANT TO ME.
BUT EVEN THAT...
...WAS THANKS TO MISAKI, WASN'T IT?
...
WHEN I THINK ABOUT THAT, I REALLY CAN'T BRING MYSELF TO ASK YOU...
...TO ABANDON MISAKI AND RETURN MY FEELINGS INSTEAD.
...
SO...
I WANT YOU TO MAKE THE DECISION THAT'S BEST FOR YOU.
FOR THE DINNER... IT CAN JUST BE FOR MY GREAT-GRANDMOTHER'S SAKE.
YOU DON'T HAVE TO WORRY ABOUT IT.
IT'LL BE OKAY.
...

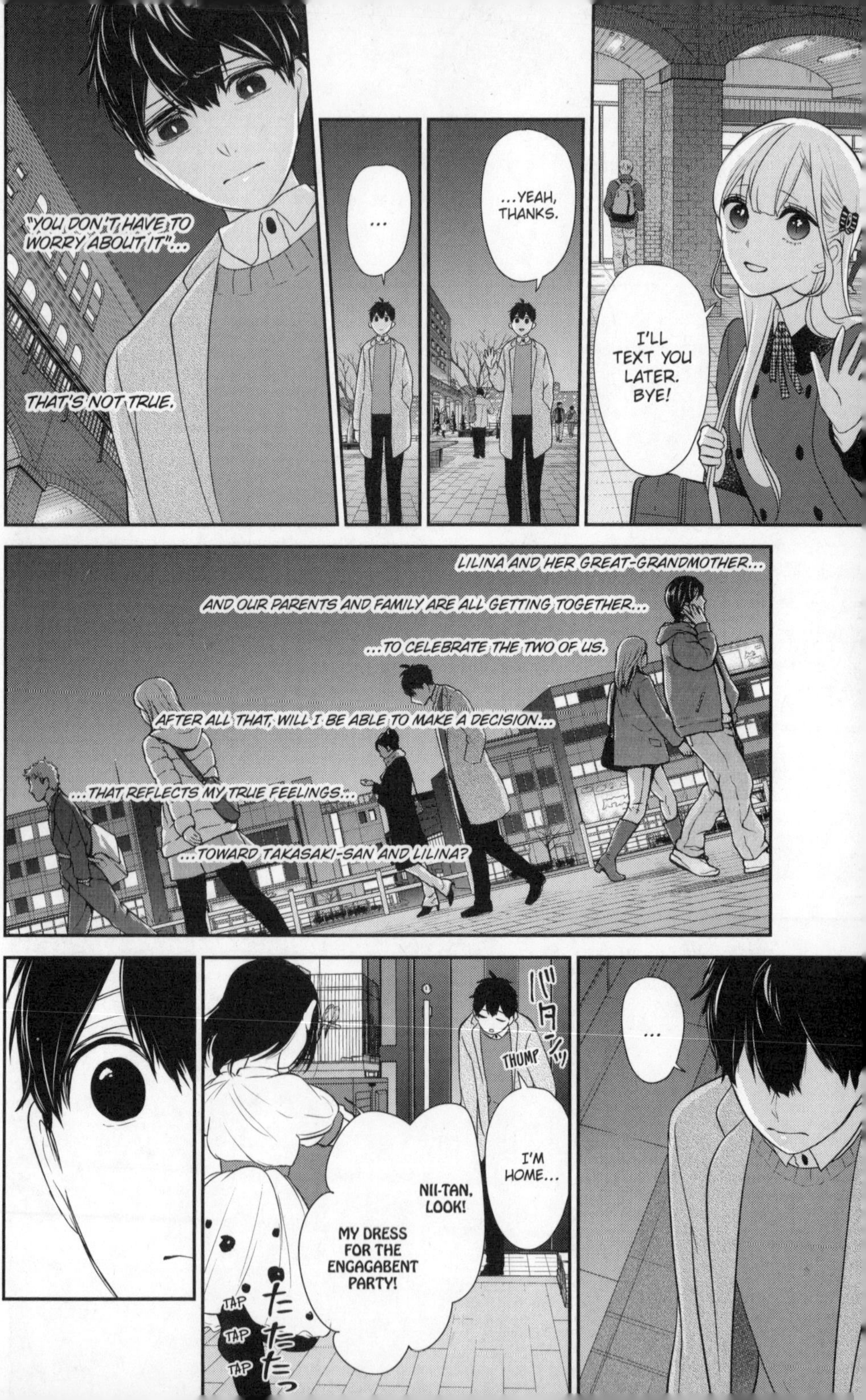
I'LL TEXT YOU LATER. BYE!
...YEAH, THANKS.
...
"YOU DON'T HAVE TO WORRY ABOUT IT"...
THAT'S NOT TRUE.
LILINA AND HER GREAT-GRANDMOTHER...
AND OUR PARENTS AND FAMILY ARE ALL GETTING TOGETHER...
...TO CELEBRATE THE TWO OF US.
AFTER ALL THAT, WILL I BE ABLE TO MAKE A DECISION...
...THAT REFLECTS MY TRUE FEELINGS...
...TOWARD TAKASAKI-SAN AND LILINA?
...
バタンッ
THUMP
I'M HOME...
NII-TAN, LOOK!
MY DRESS FOR THE ENGAGABENT PARTY!
たたたっ
TAP
TAP
TAP

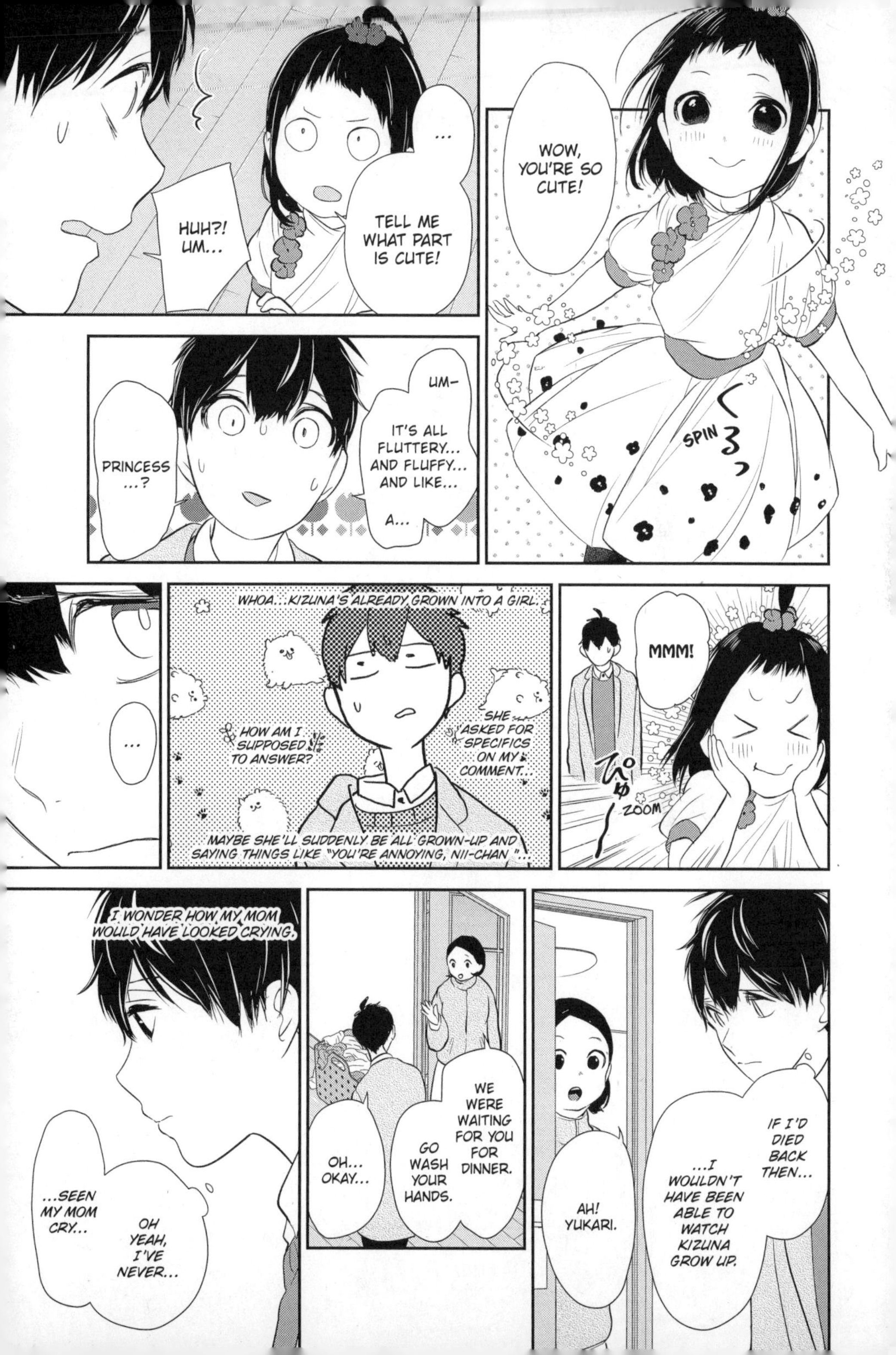
WOW, YOU'RE SO CUTE!
SPIN
...
TELL ME WHAT PART IS CUTE!
HUH?! UM...
UM-
IT'S ALL FLUTTERY... AND FLUFFY... AND LIKE...
A...
PRINCESS ...?
MMM!
ZOOM
WHOA...KIZUNA'S ALREADY GROWN INTO A GIRL.
SHE ASKED FOR SPECIFICS ON MY COMMENT...
HOW AM I SUPPOSED TO ANSWER?
MAYBE SHE'LL SUDDENLY BE ALL GROWN-UP AND SAYING THINGS LIKE "YOU'RE ANNOYING, NII-CHAN"...
...
IF I'D DIED BACK THEN...
...I WOULDN'T HAVE BEEN ABLE TO WATCH KIZUNA GROW UP.
AH! YUKARI.
WE WERE WAITING FOR YOU FOR DINNER.
GO WASH YOUR HANDS.
OH... OKAY...
I WONDER HOW MY MOM WOULD HAVE LOOKED CRYING.
OH YEAH, I'VE NEVER...
...SEEN MY MOM CRY...

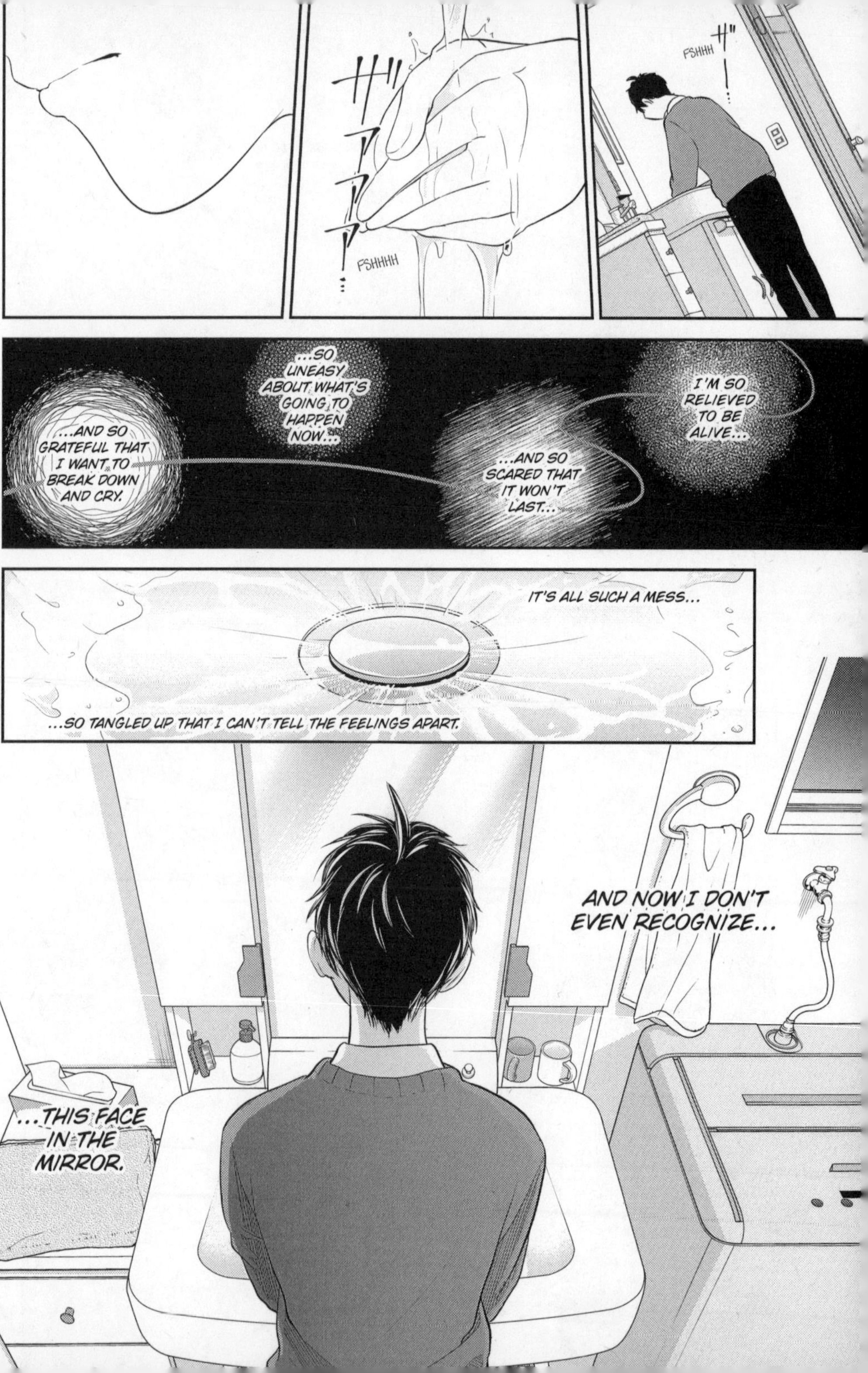
FSHHH
FSHHH
I'M SO RELIEVED TO BE ALIVE...
...AND SO SCARED THAT IT WON'T LAST...
...SO UNEASY ABOUT WHAT'S GOING TO HAPPEN NOW...
...AND SO GRATEFUL THAT I WANT TO BREAK DOWN AND CRY.
IT'S ALL SUCH A MESS...
...SO TANGLED UP THAT I CAN'T TELL THE FEELINGS APART.
AND NOW I DON'T EVEN RECOGNIZE...
...THIS FACE IN THE MIRROR.

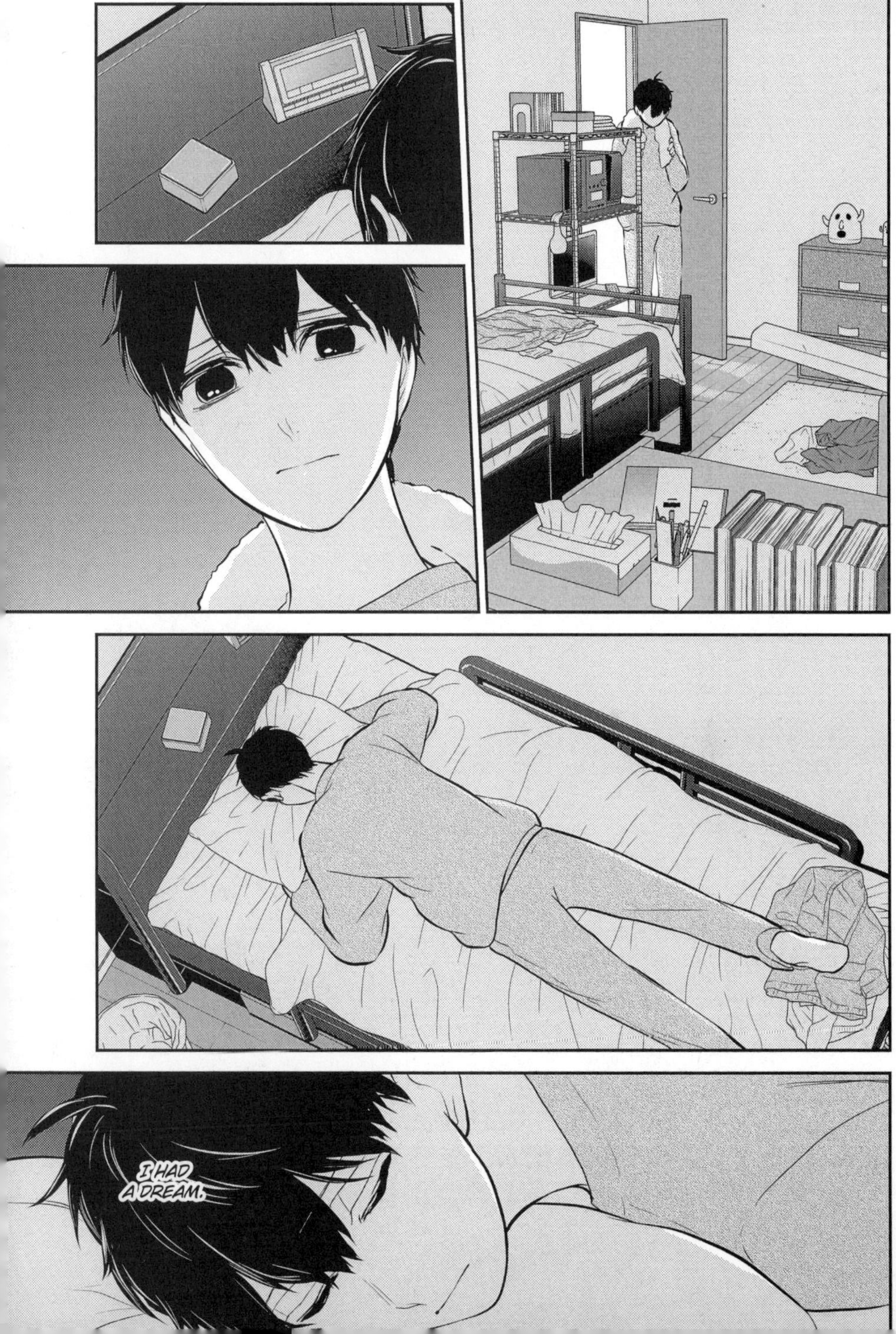
I HAD A DREAM.

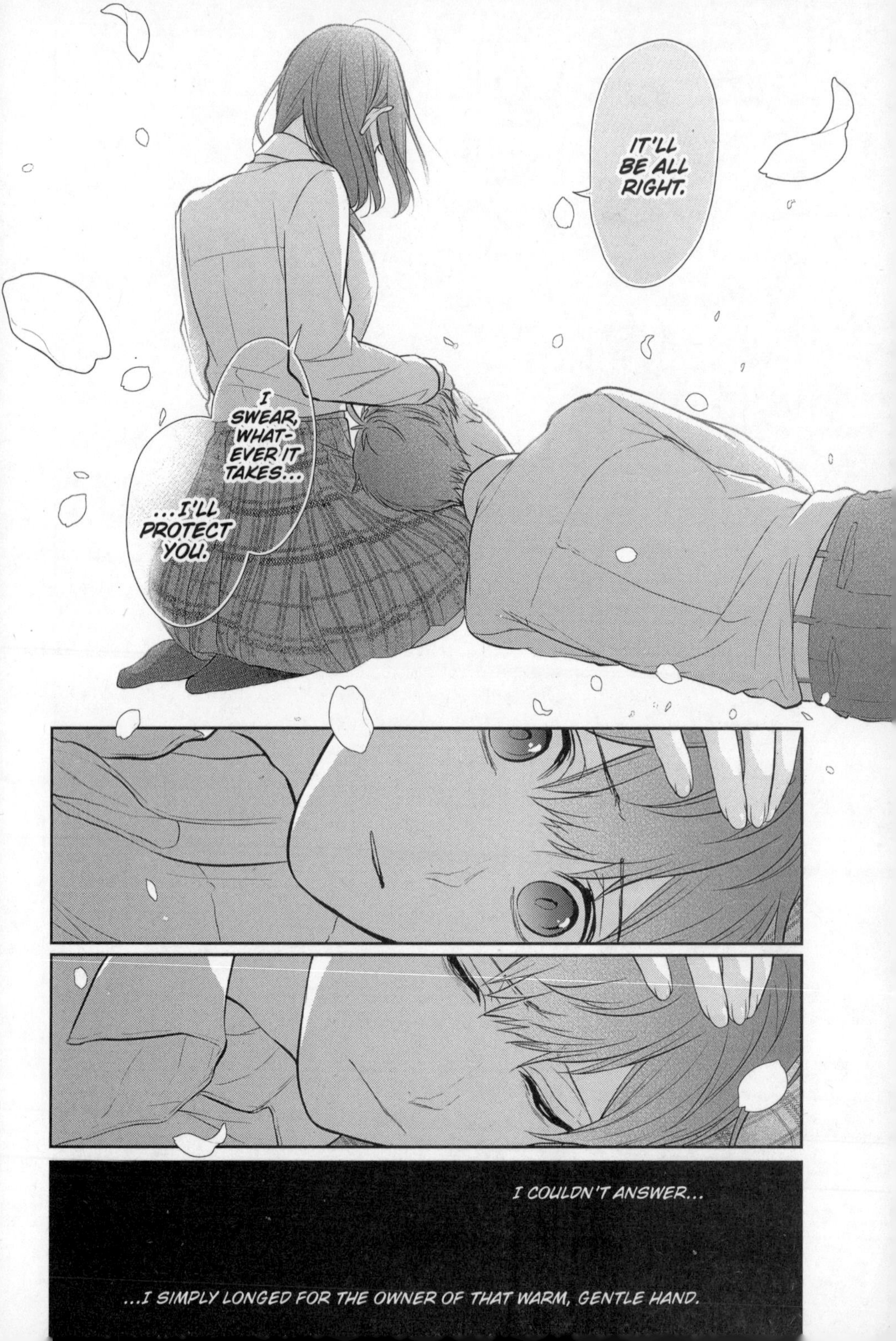
IT'LL BE ALL RIGHT.
I SWEAR, WHAT-EVER IT TAKES... ...I'LL PROTECT YOU.
I COULDN'T ANSWER...
...I SIMPLY LONGED FOR THE OWNER OF THAT WARM, GENTLE HAND.

Love&Lies

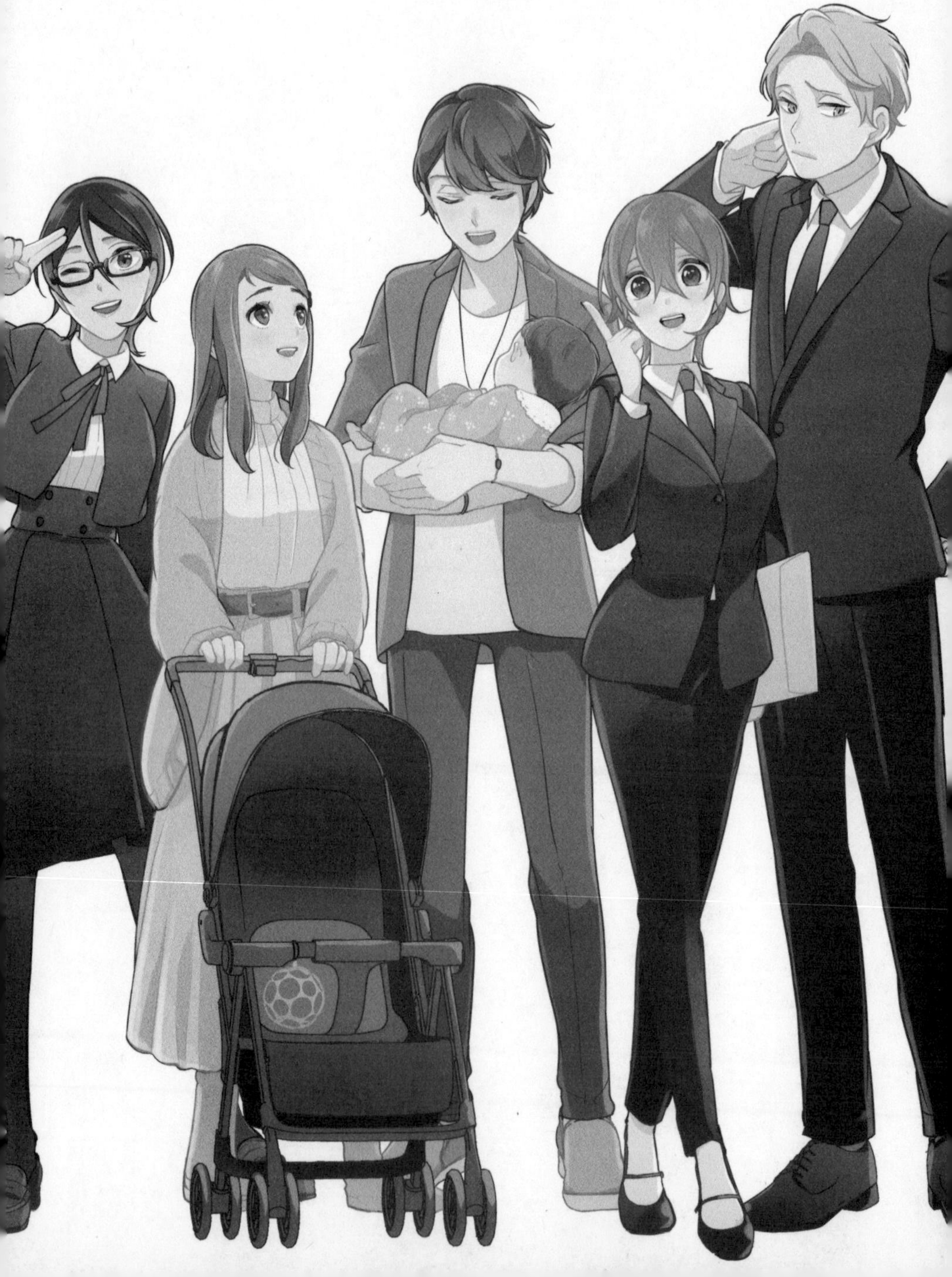

Chapter 46: Given by Love

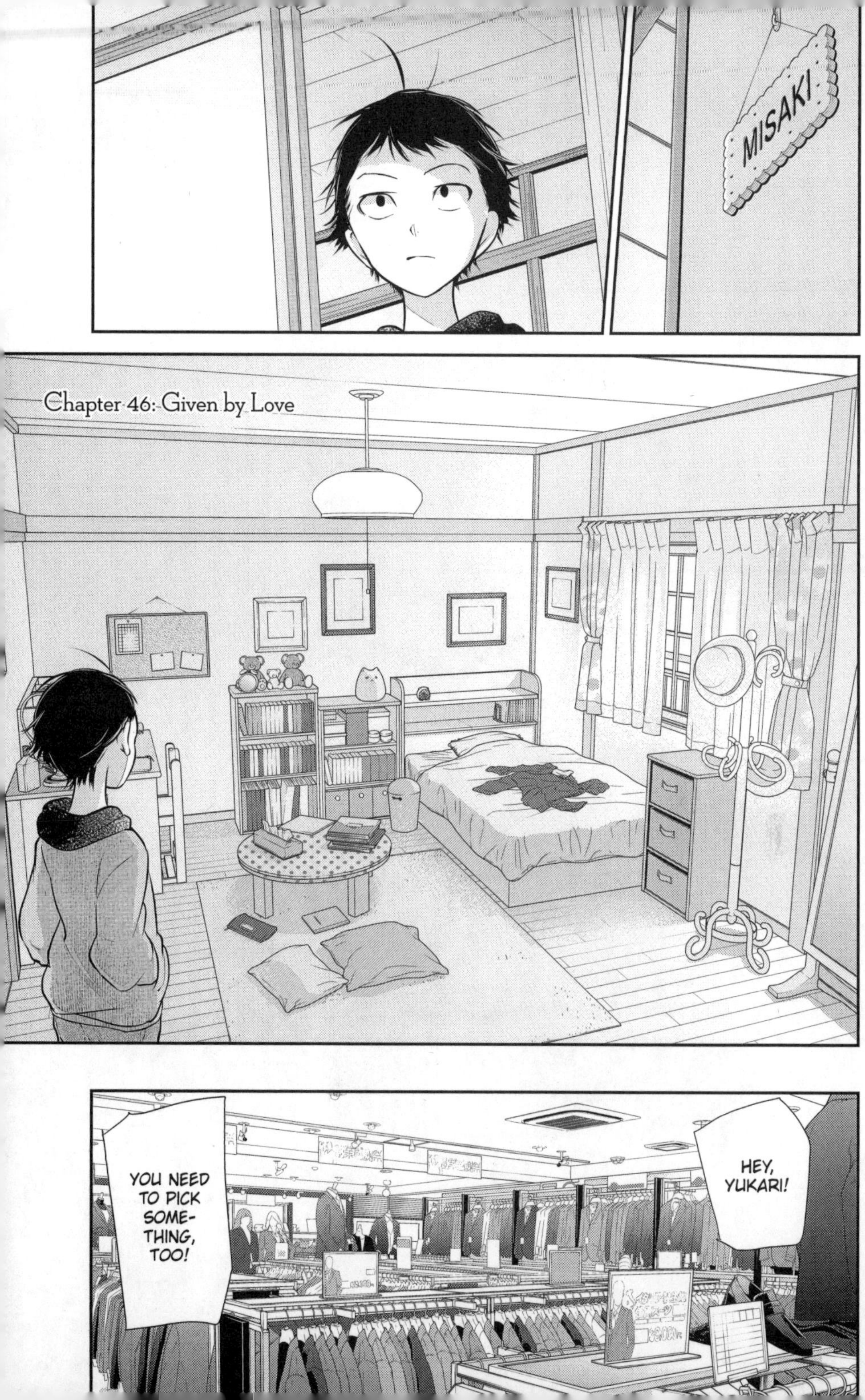
MISAKI
HEY, YUKARI!
YOU NEED TO PICK SOME-THING, TOO!

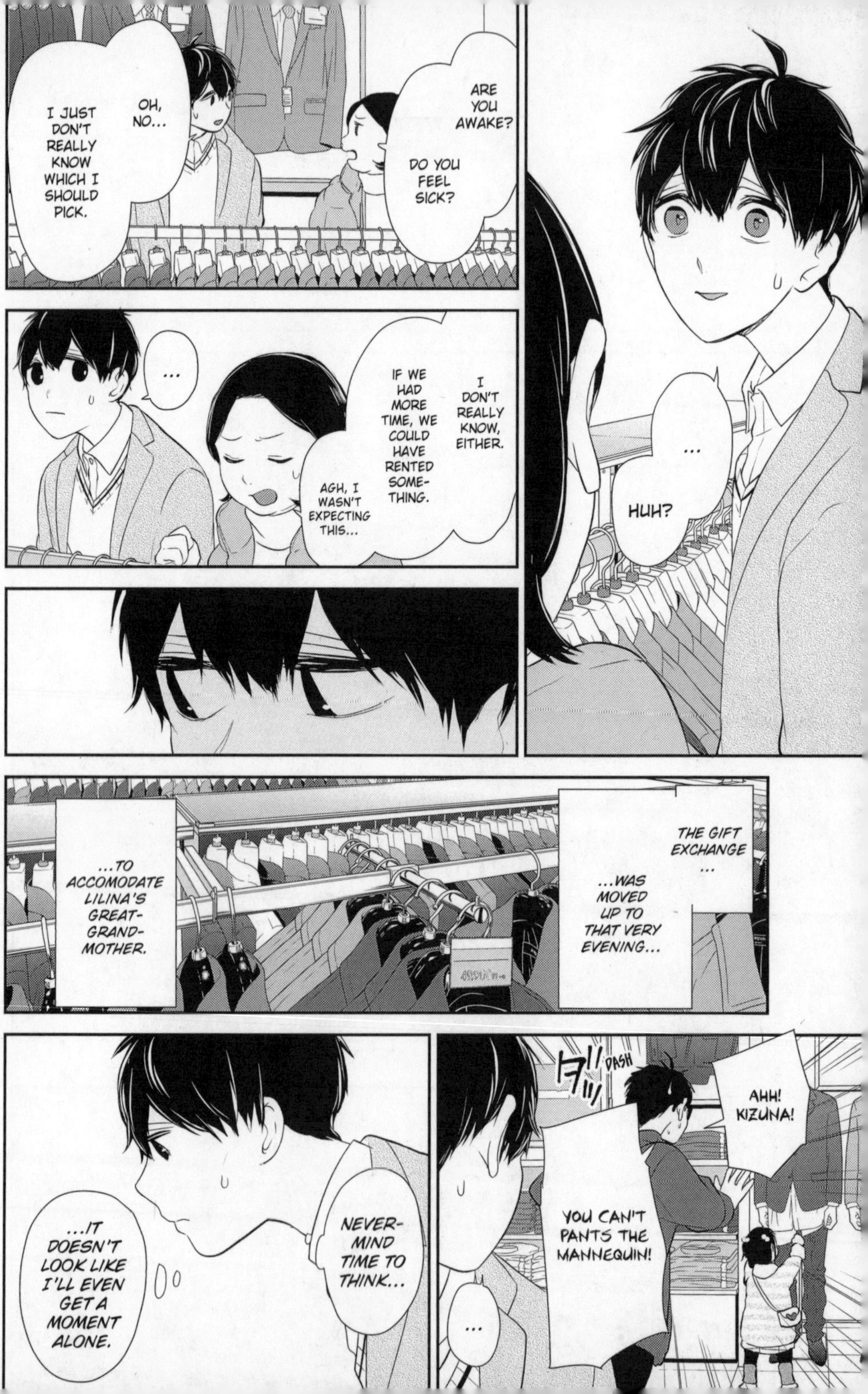
...
HUH?
ARE YOU AWAKE?
DO YOU FEEL SICK?
OH, NO...
I JUST DON'T REALLY KNOW WHICH I SHOULD PICK.
I DON'T REALLY KNOW, EITHER.
IF WE HAD MORE TIME, WE COULD HAVE RENTED SOMETHING.
AGH, I WASN'T EXPECTING THIS...
...
THE GIFT EXCHANGE...
...WAS MOVED UP TO THAT VERY EVENING...
...TO ACCOMODATE LILINA'S GREAT-GRANDMOTHER.
DASH
AHH! KIZUNA!
YOU CAN'T PANTS THE MANNEQUIN!
...
NEVER-MIND TIME TO THINK...
...IT DOESN'T LOOK LIKE I'LL EVEN GET A MOMENT ALONE.

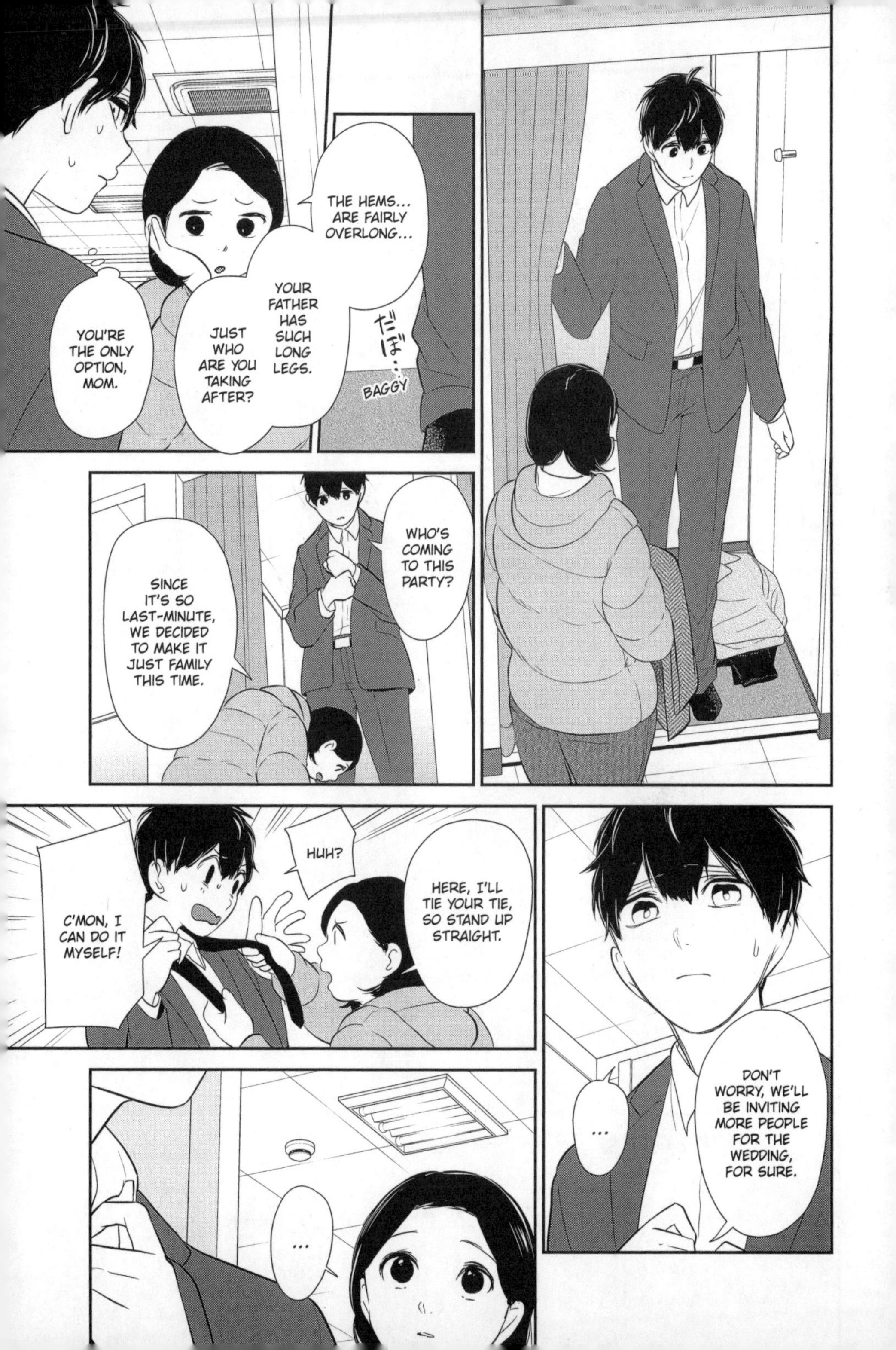
THE HEMS... ARE FAIRLY OVERLONG...
だぼ…
BAGGY
YOUR FATHER HAS SUCH LONG LEGS.
JUST WHO ARE YOU TAKING AFTER?
YOU'RE THE ONLY OPTION, MOM.
WHO'S COMING TO THIS PARTY?
SINCE IT'S SO LAST-MINUTE, WE DECIDED TO MAKE IT JUST FAMILY THIS TIME.
DON'T WORRY, WE'LL BE INVITING MORE PEOPLE FOR THE WEDDING, FOR SURE.
...
HERE, I'LL TIE YOUR TIE, SO STAND UP STRAIGHT.
HUH?
C'MON, I CAN DO IT MYSELF!
...

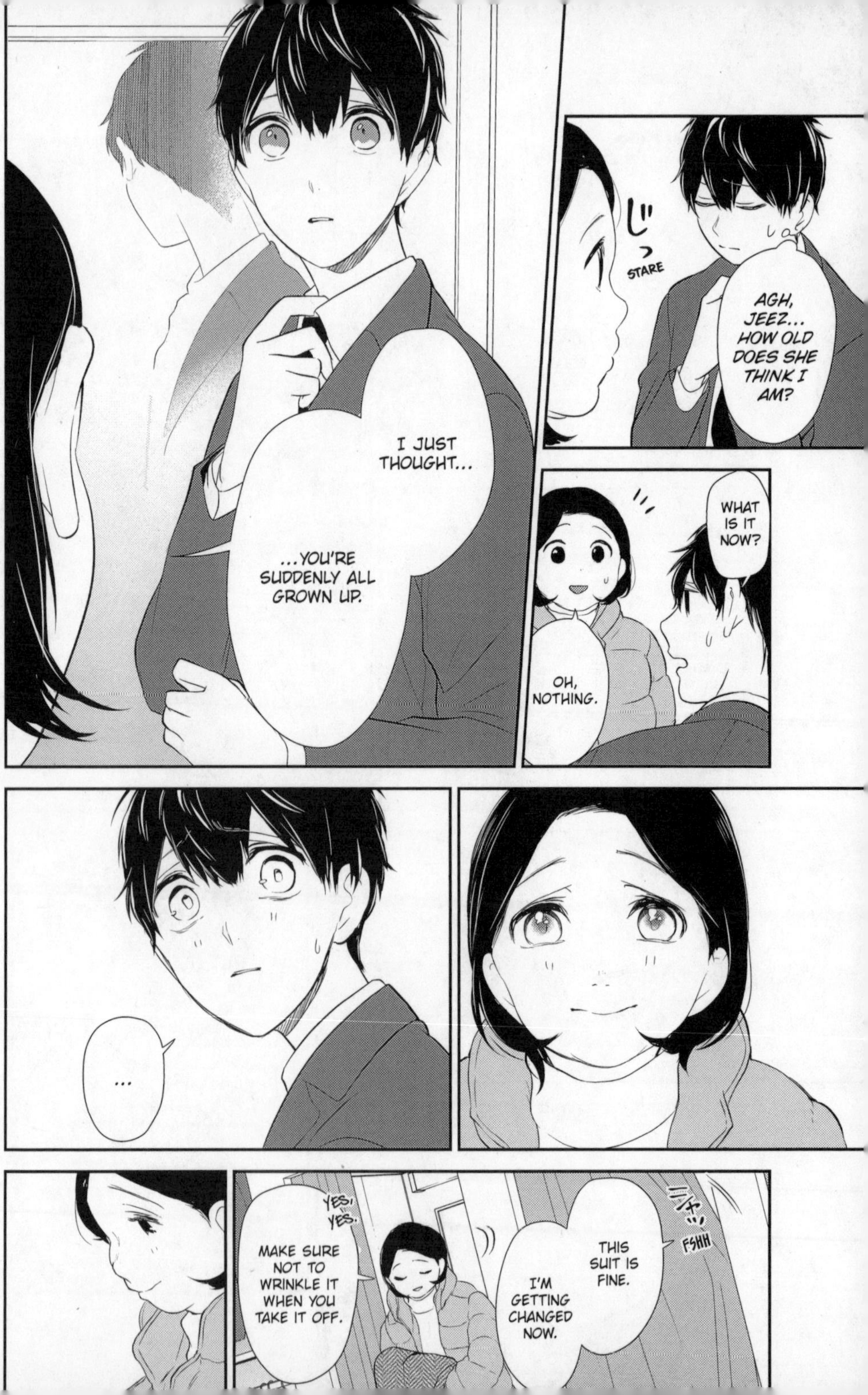
じっ
STARE
AGH, JEEZ... HOW OLD DOES SHE THINK I AM?
WHAT IS IT NOW?
OH, NOTHING.
I JUST THOUGHT...
...YOU'RE SUDDENLY ALL GROWN UP.
...
FSHH
THIS SUIT IS FINE.
I'M GETTING CHANGED NOW.
YES, YES.
MAKE SURE NOT TO WRINKLE IT WHEN YOU TAKE IT OFF.

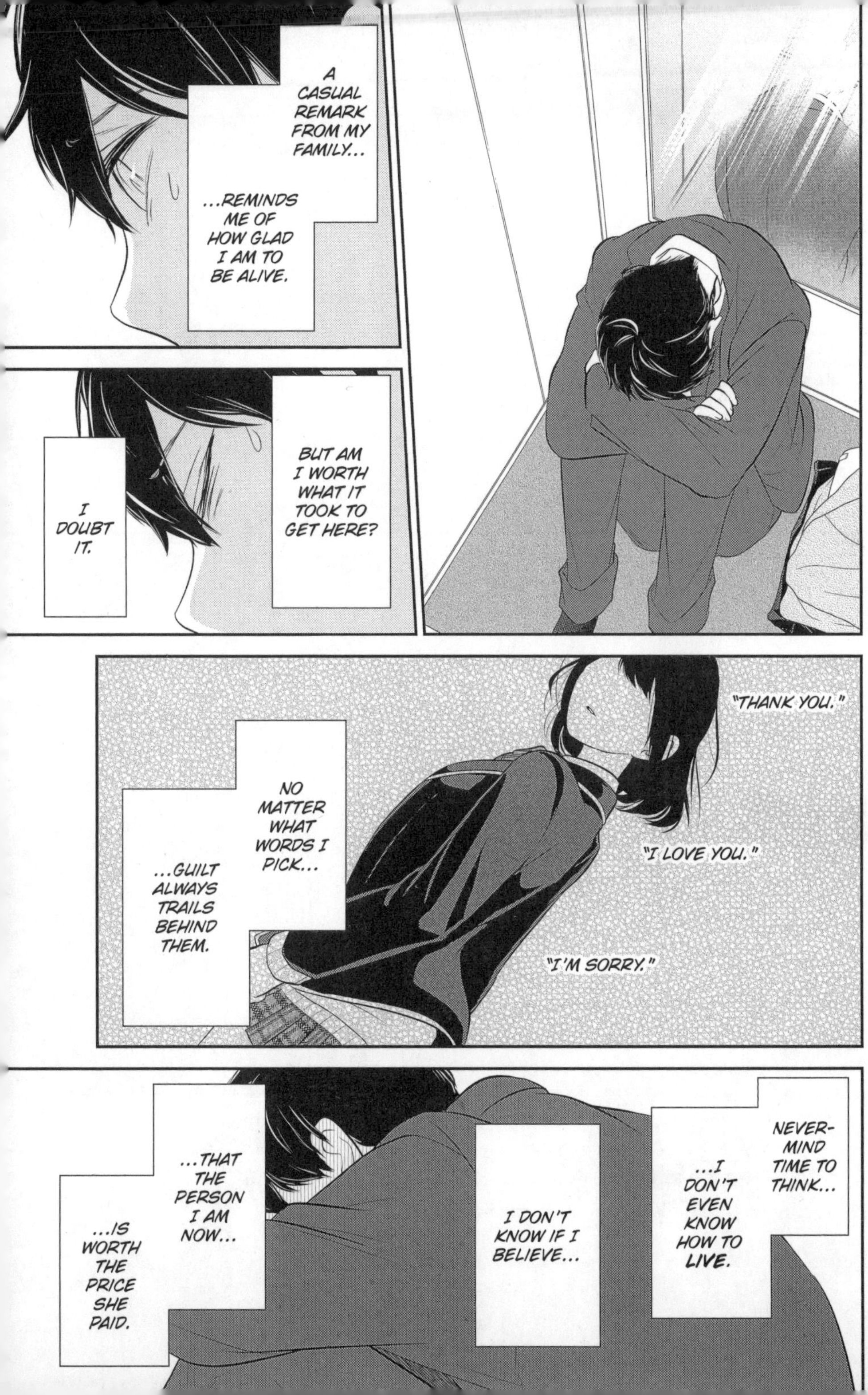
A CASUAL REMARK FROM MY FAMILY...
...REMINDS ME OF HOW GLAD I AM TO BE ALIVE.
BUT AM I WORTH WHAT IT TOOK TO GET HERE?
I DOUBT IT.
"THANK YOU."
"I LOVE YOU."
"I'M SORRY."
NO MATTER WHAT WORDS I PICK...
...GUILT ALWAYS TRAILS BEHIND THEM.
NEVER-MIND TIME TO THINK...
...I DON'T EVEN KNOW HOW TO **LIVE**.
I DON'T KNOW IF I BELIEVE...
...THAT THE PERSON I AM NOW...
...IS WORTH THE PRICE SHE PAID.

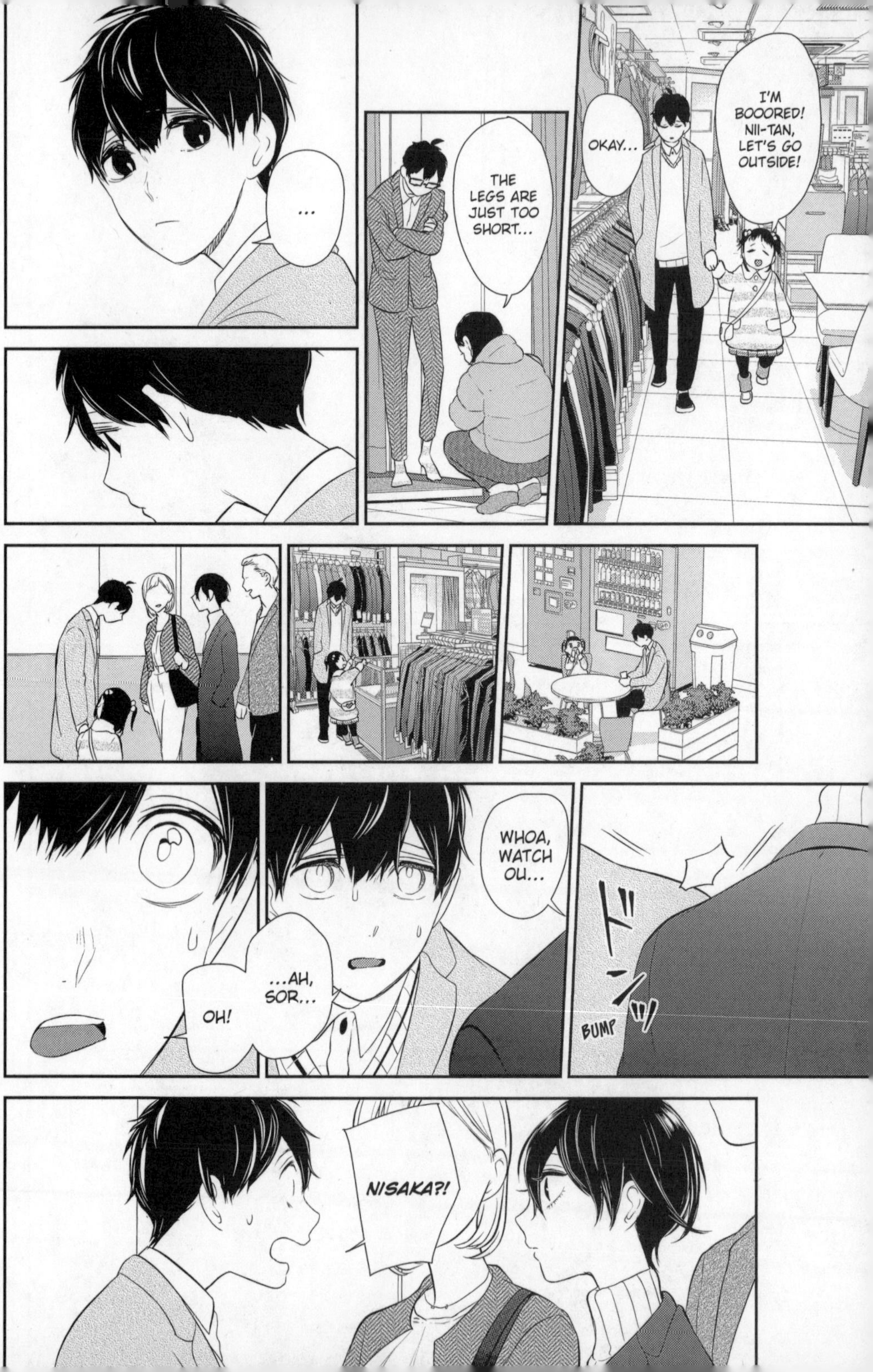
I'M BOOORED! NII-TAN, LET'S GO OUTSIDE!
OKAY...
THE LEGS ARE JUST TOO SHORT...
...
WHOA, WATCH OU...
BUMP
...AH, SOR...
OH!
NISAKA?!

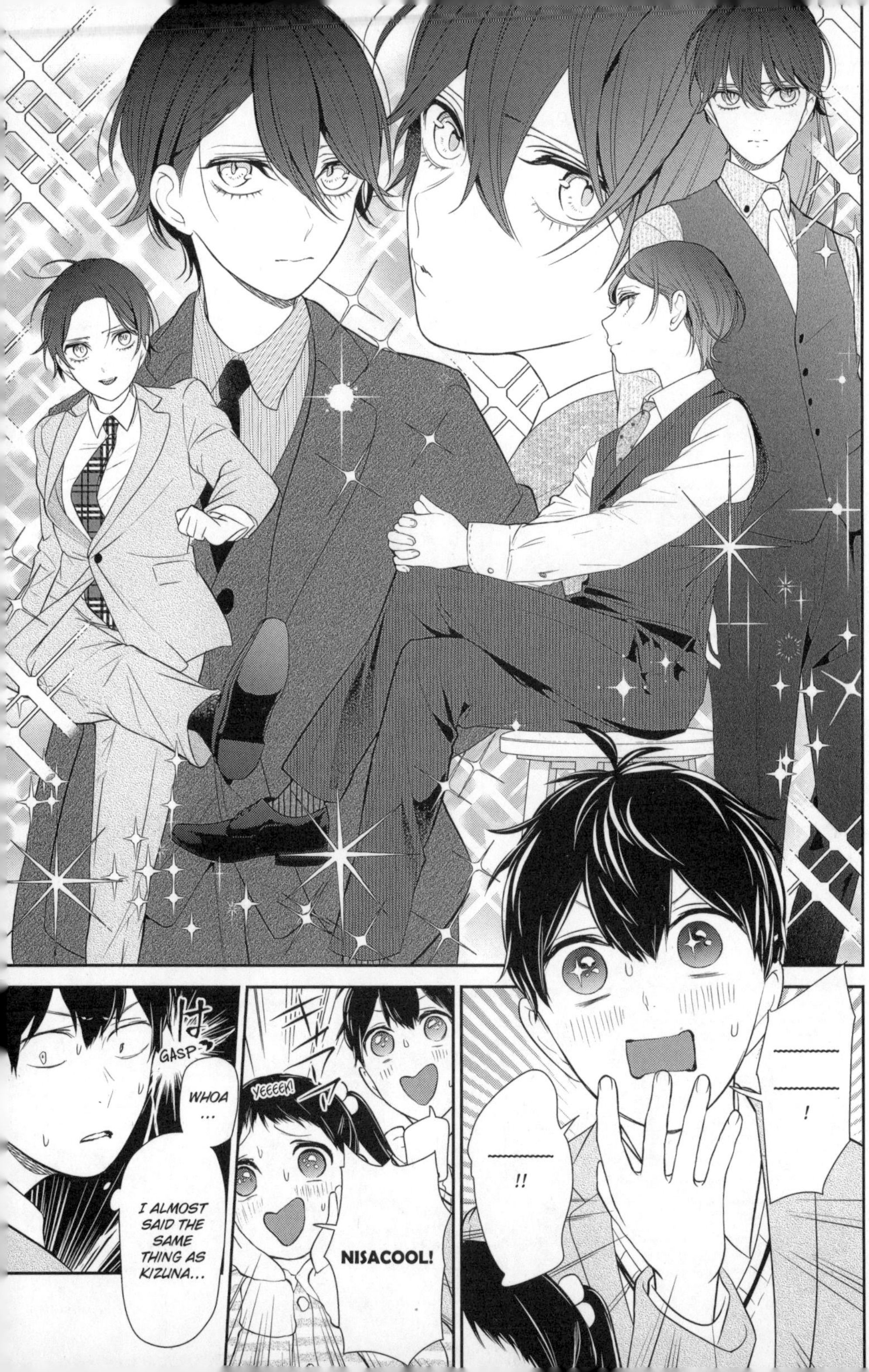
——!
——!!
YEEEEK!
NISACOOL!
GASP
WHOA...
I ALMOST SAID THE SAME THING AS KIZUNA...

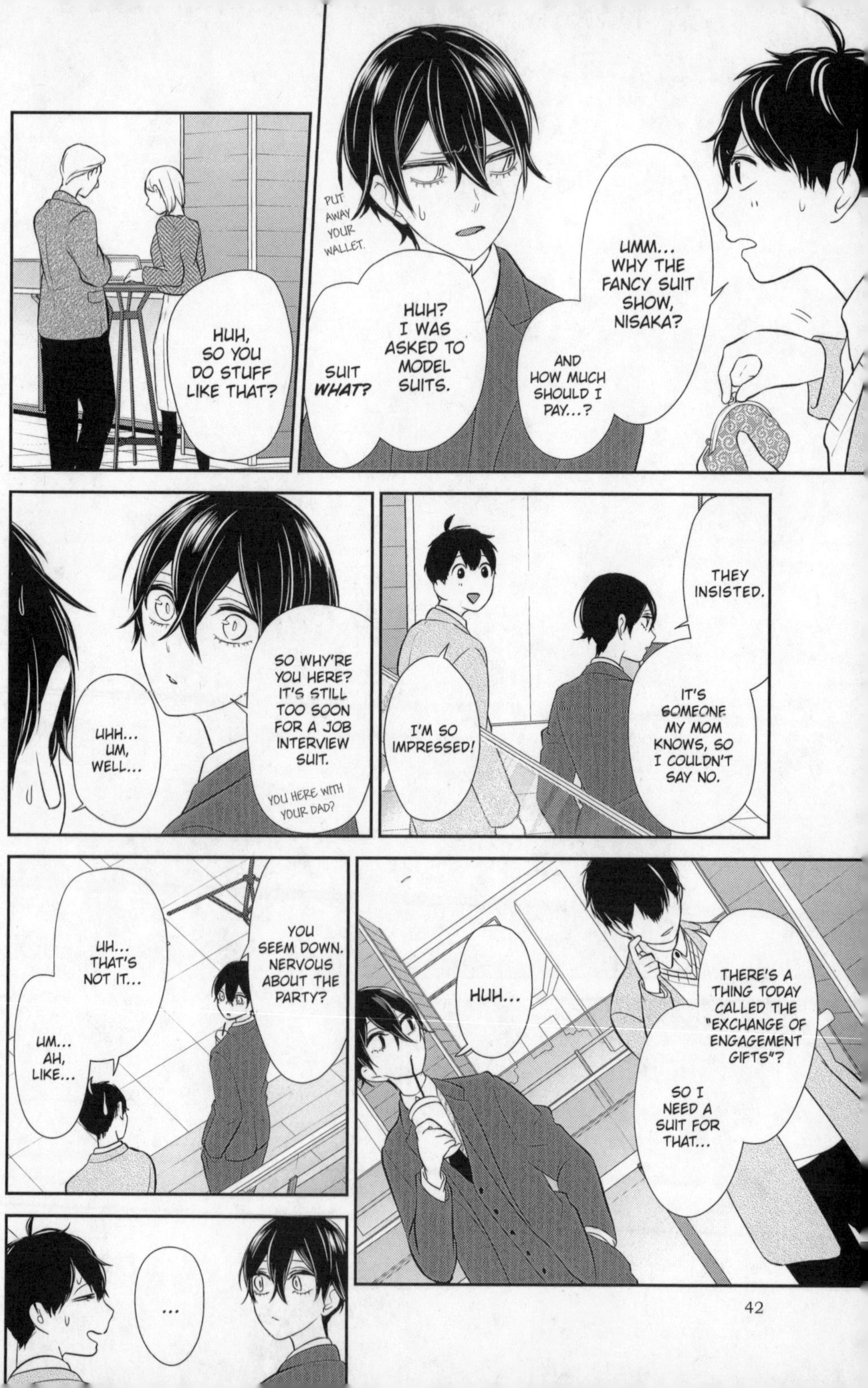
UMM... WHY THE FANCY SUIT SHOW, NISAKA?
AND HOW MUCH SHOULD I PAY...?
HUH? I WAS ASKED TO MODEL SUITS.
SUIT *WHAT?*
PUT AWAY YOUR WALLET.
HUH, SO YOU DO STUFF LIKE THAT?
THEY INSISTED.
IT'S SOMEONE MY MOM KNOWS, SO I COULDN'T SAY NO.
I'M SO IMPRESSED!
SO WHY'RE YOU HERE? IT'S STILL TOO SOON FOR A JOB INTERVIEW SUIT.
YOU HERE WITH YOUR DAD?
UHH... UM, WELL...
THERE'S A THING TODAY CALLED THE "EXCHANGE OF ENGAGEMENT GIFTS"?
SO I NEED A SUIT FOR THAT...
HUH...
YOU SEEM DOWN. NERVOUS ABOUT THE PARTY?
UH... THAT'S NOT IT...
UM... AH, LIKE...
...

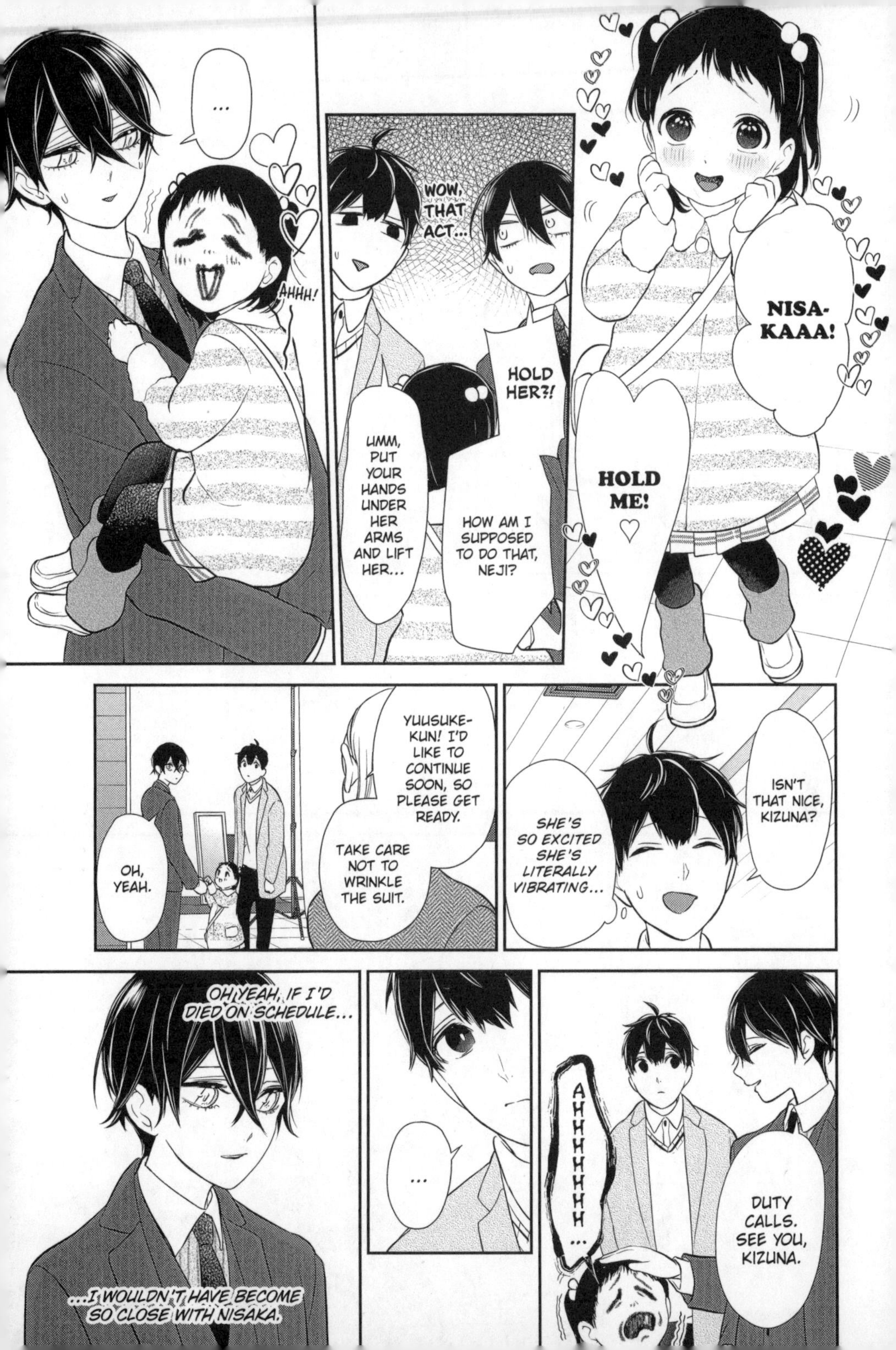
NISA-KAAA!
HOLD ME!
WOW, THAT ACT...
HOLD HER?!
HOW AM I SUPPOSED TO DO THAT, NEJI?
UMM, PUT YOUR HANDS UNDER HER ARMS AND LIFT HER...
...
AHHH!
ISN'T THAT NICE, KIZUNA?
SHE'S SO EXCITED SHE'S LITERALLY VIBRATING...
YUUSUKE-KUN! I'D LIKE TO CONTINUE SOON, SO PLEASE GET READY.
TAKE CARE NOT TO WRINKLE THE SUIT.
OH, YEAH.
DUTY CALLS. SEE YOU, KIZUNA.
AHHHHHHH...
...
OH YEAH, IF I'D DIED ON SCHEDULE...
...I WOULDN'T HAVE BECOME SO CLOSE WITH NISAKA.

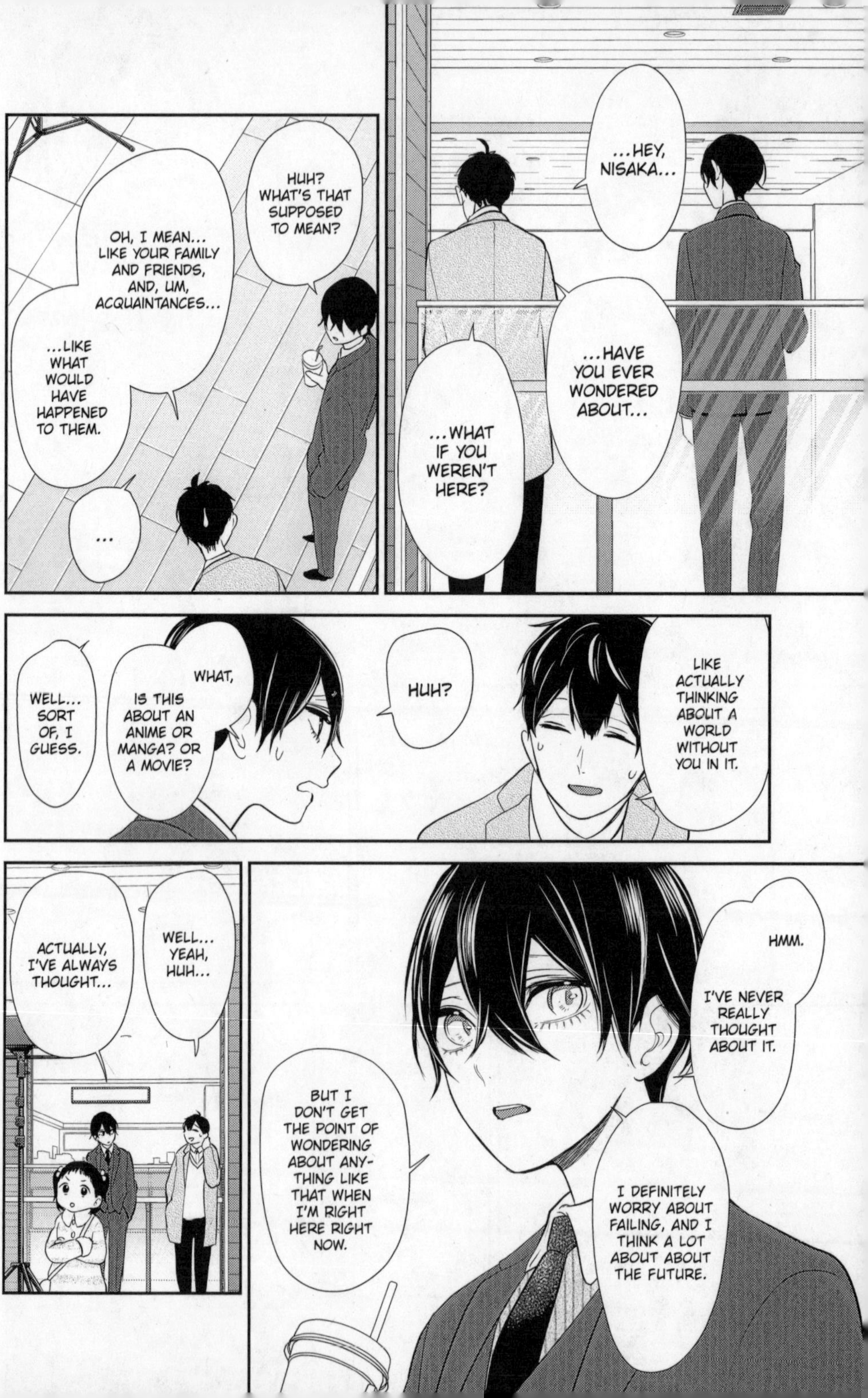
...HEY, NISAKA...
...HAVE YOU EVER WONDERED ABOUT...
...WHAT IF YOU WEREN'T HERE?
HUH? WHAT'S THAT SUPPOSED TO MEAN?
OH, I MEAN... LIKE YOUR FAMILY AND FRIENDS, AND, UM, ACQUAINTANCES...
...LIKE WHAT WOULD HAVE HAPPENED TO THEM.
...
LIKE ACTUALLY THINKING ABOUT A WORLD WITHOUT YOU IN IT.
HUH?
WHAT, IS THIS ABOUT AN ANIME OR MANGA? OR A MOVIE?
WELL... SORT OF, I GUESS.
HMM.
I'VE NEVER REALLY THOUGHT ABOUT IT.
I DEFINITELY WORRY ABOUT FAILING, AND I THINK A LOT ABOUT ABOUT THE FUTURE.
BUT I DON'T GET THE POINT OF WONDERING ABOUT ANY-THING LIKE THAT WHEN I'M RIGHT HERE RIGHT NOW.
WELL... YEAH, HUH...
ACTUALLY, I'VE ALWAYS THOUGHT...

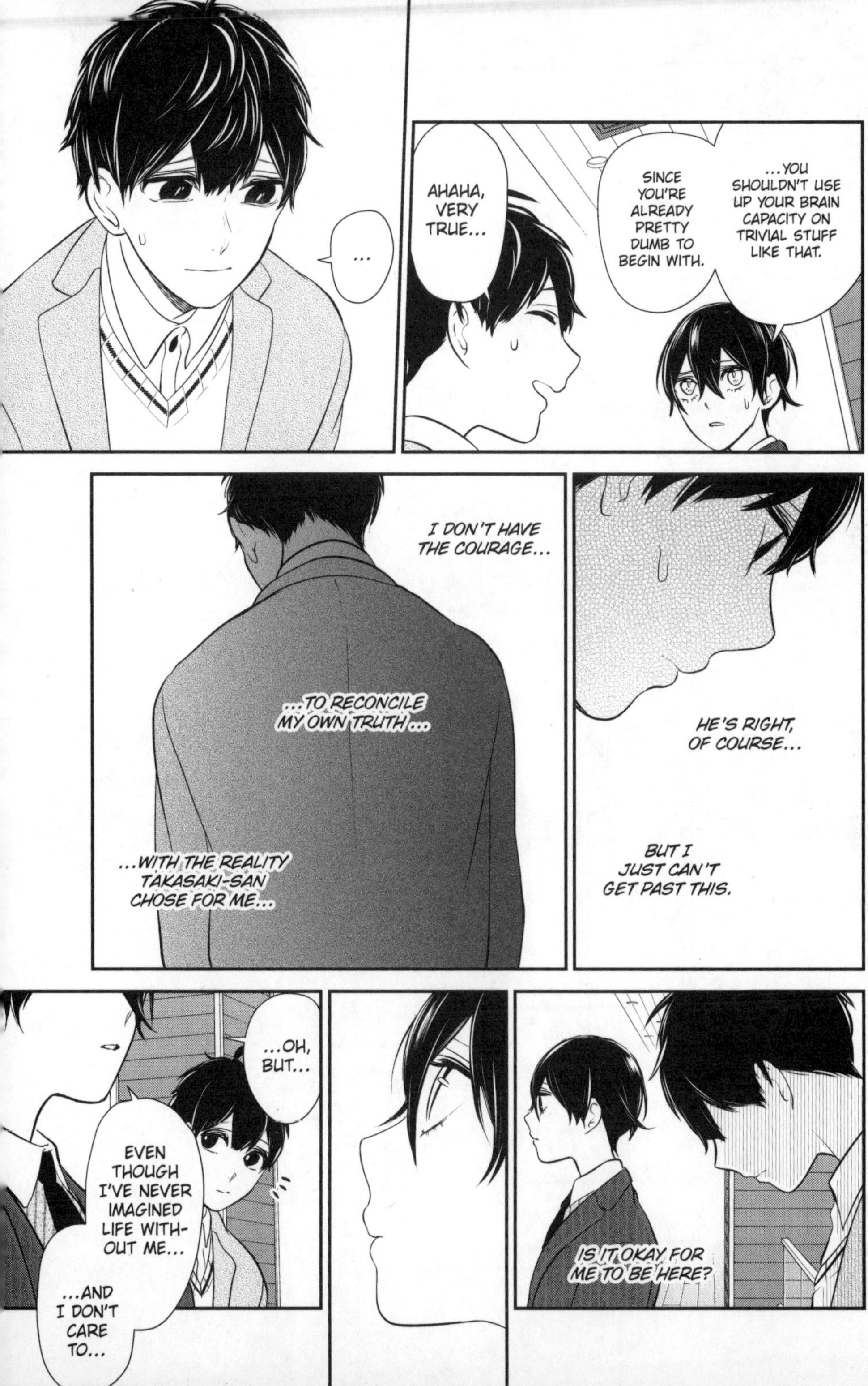
...YOU SHOULDN'T USE UP YOUR BRAIN CAPACITY ON TRIVIAL STUFF LIKE THAT.
SINCE YOU'RE ALREADY PRETTY DUMB TO BEGIN WITH.
AHAHA, VERY TRUE...
...
HE'S RIGHT, OF COURSE...
BUT I JUST CAN'T GET PAST THIS.
I DON'T HAVE THE COURAGE...
...TO RECONCILE MY OWN TRUTH...
...WITH THE REALITY TAKASAKI-SAN CHOSE FOR ME...
IS IT OKAY FOR ME TO BE HERE?
...OH, BUT...
EVEN THOUGH I'VE NEVER IMAGINED LIFE WITH-OUT ME...
...AND I DON'T CARE TO...

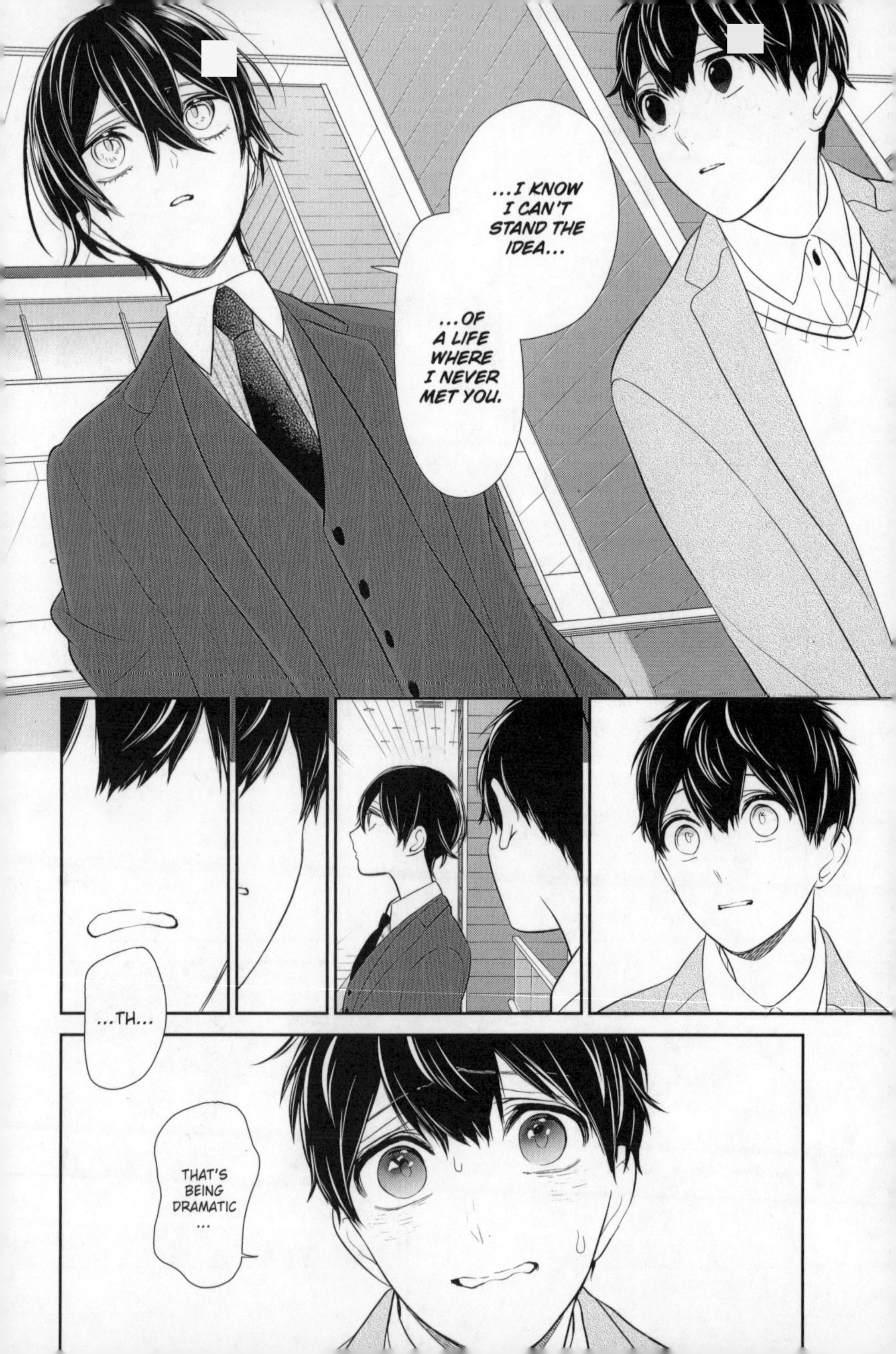
...I KNOW I CAN'T STAND THE IDEA...
...OF A LIFE WHERE I NEVER MET YOU.
...TH...
THAT'S BEING DRAMATIC ...

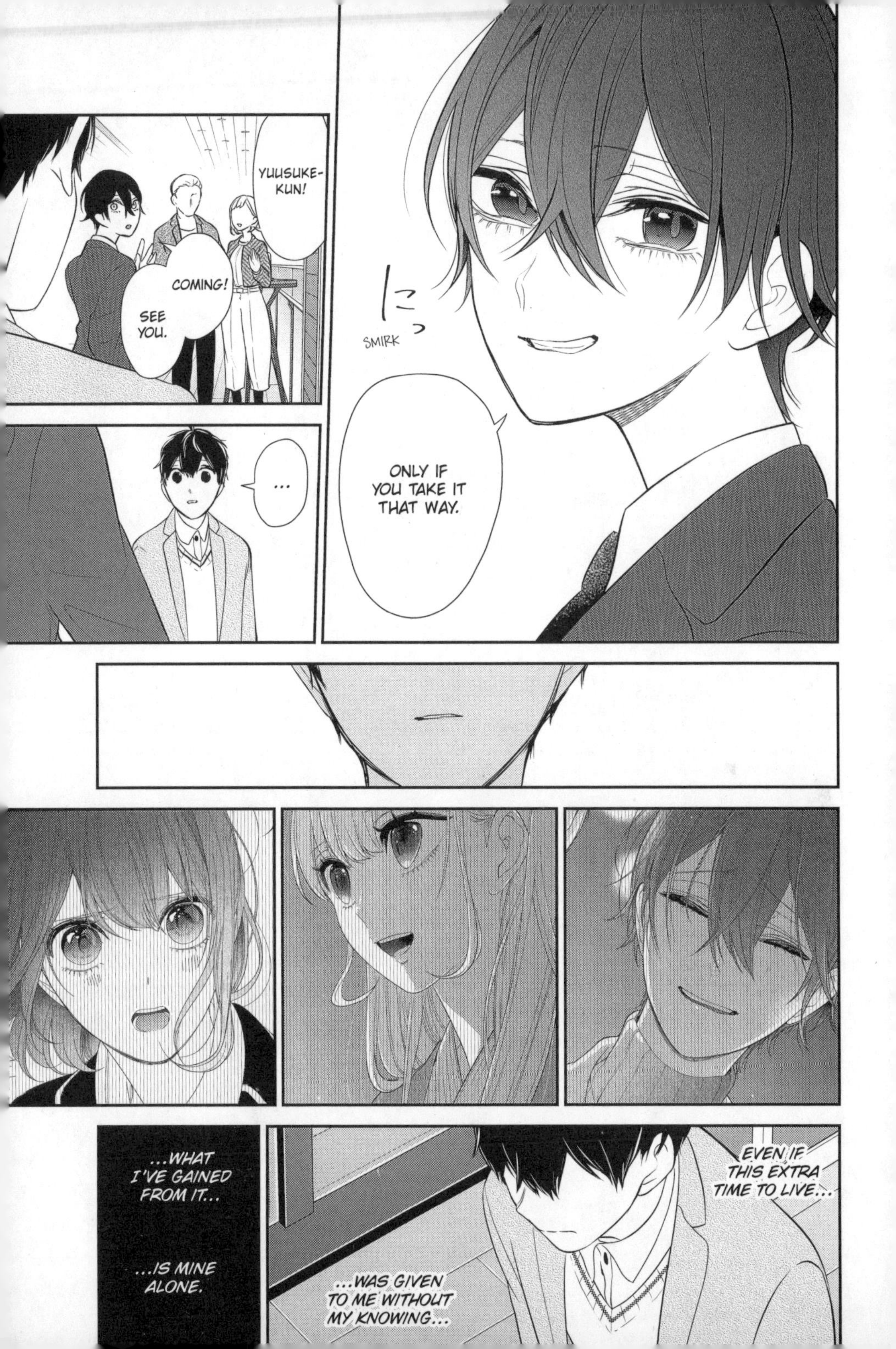
にっ
SMIRK
ONLY IF YOU TAKE IT THAT WAY.
YUUSUKE-KUN!
COMING!
SEE YOU.
...
EVEN IF THIS EXTRA TIME TO LIVE...
...WAS GIVEN TO ME WITHOUT MY KNOWING...
...WHAT I'VE GAINED FROM IT...
...IS MINE ALONE.

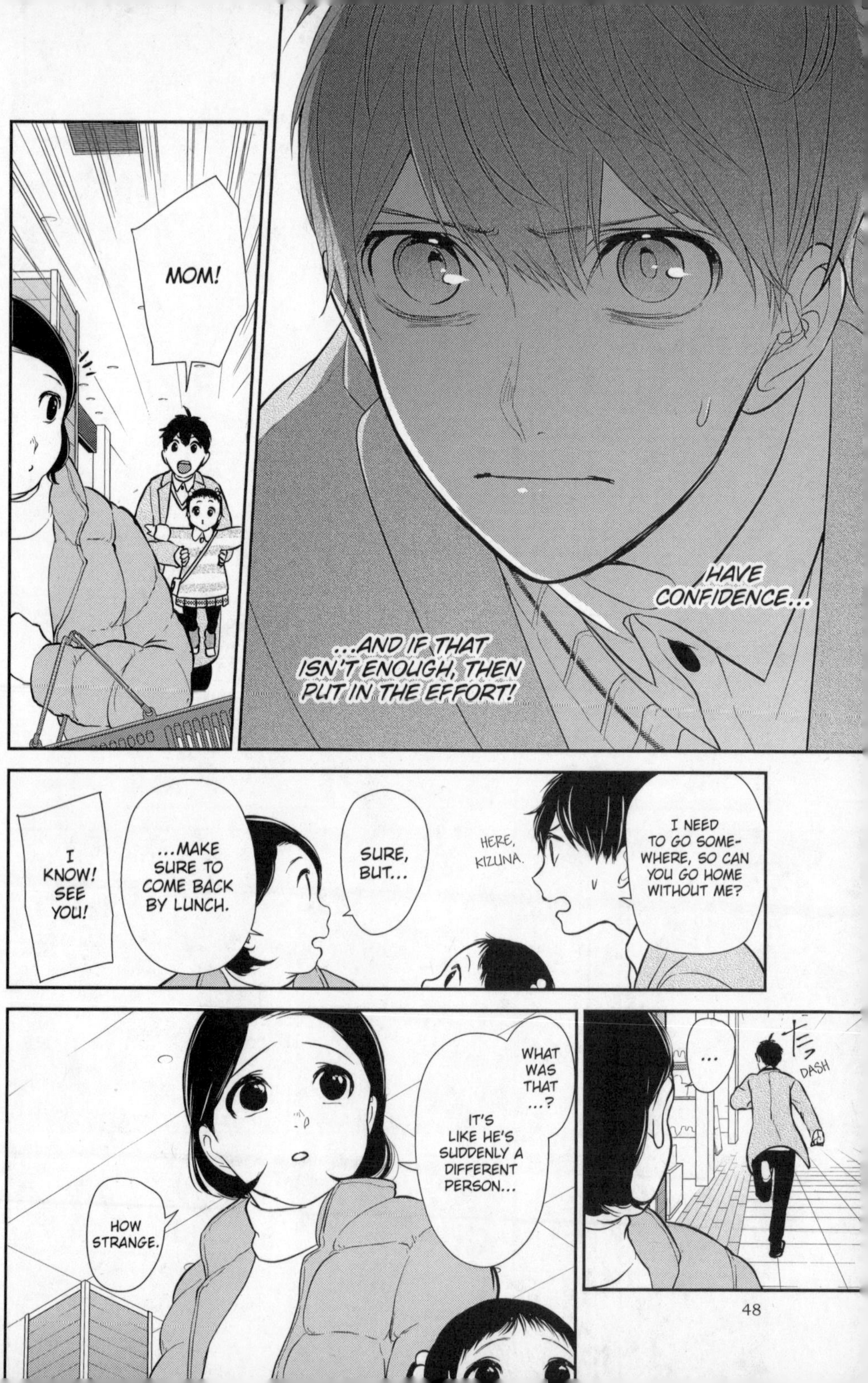
HAVE CONFIDENCE...
...AND IF THAT ISN'T ENOUGH, THEN PUT IN THE EFFORT!
MOM!
I NEED TO GO SOME-WHERE, SO CAN YOU GO HOME WITHOUT ME?
HERE, KIZUNA.
SURE, BUT...
...MAKE SURE TO COME BACK BY LUNCH.
I KNOW! SEE YOU!
...
DASH
WHAT WAS THAT ...?
IT'S LIKE HE'S SUDDENLY A DIFFERENT PERSON...
HOW STRANGE.

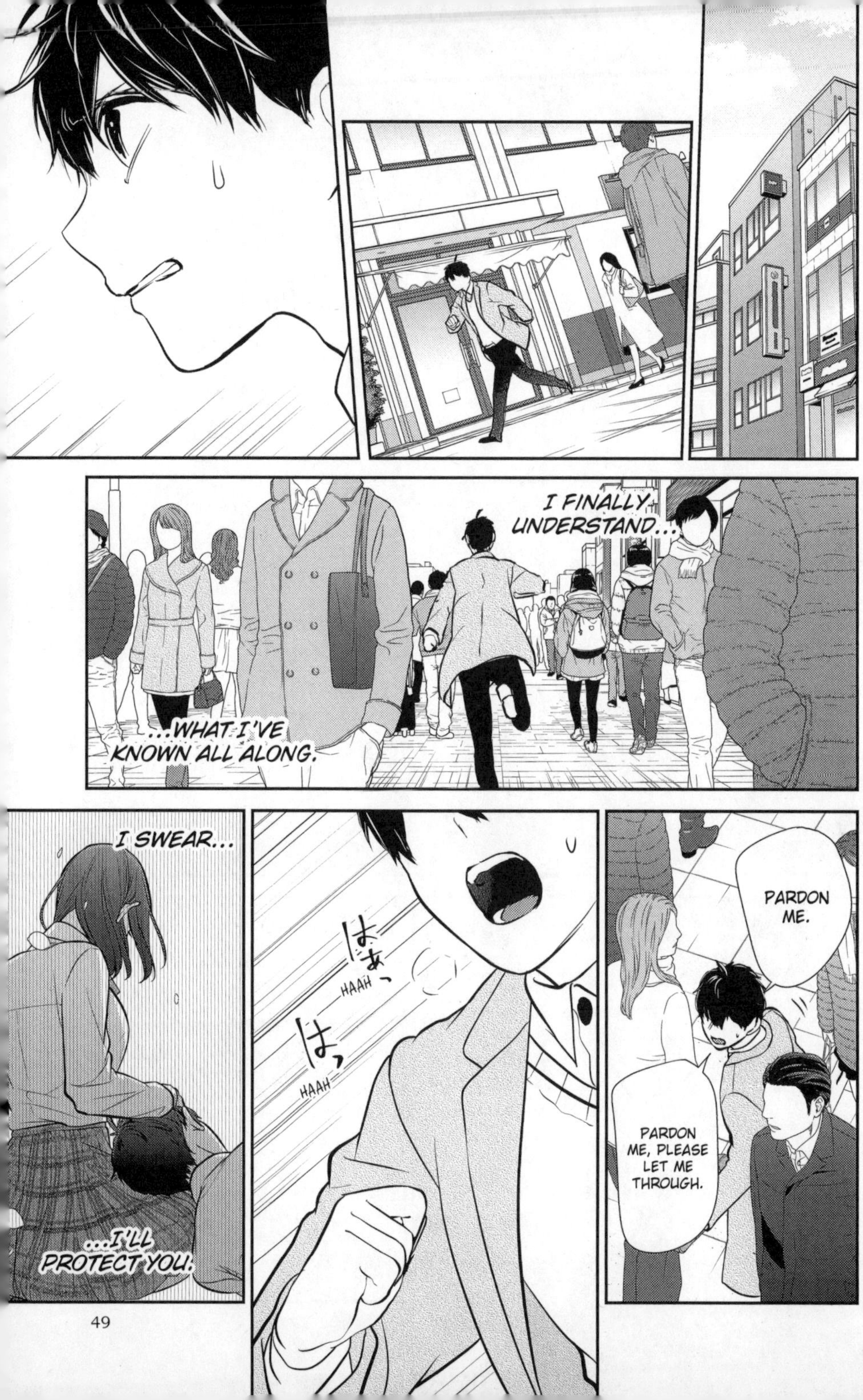
I FINALLY UNDERSTAND...
...WHAT I'VE KNOWN ALL ALONG.
PARDON ME.
PARDON ME, PLEASE LET ME THROUGH.
はぁ、
HAAH
はっ
HAAH
I SWEAR...
...I'LL PROTECT YOU.

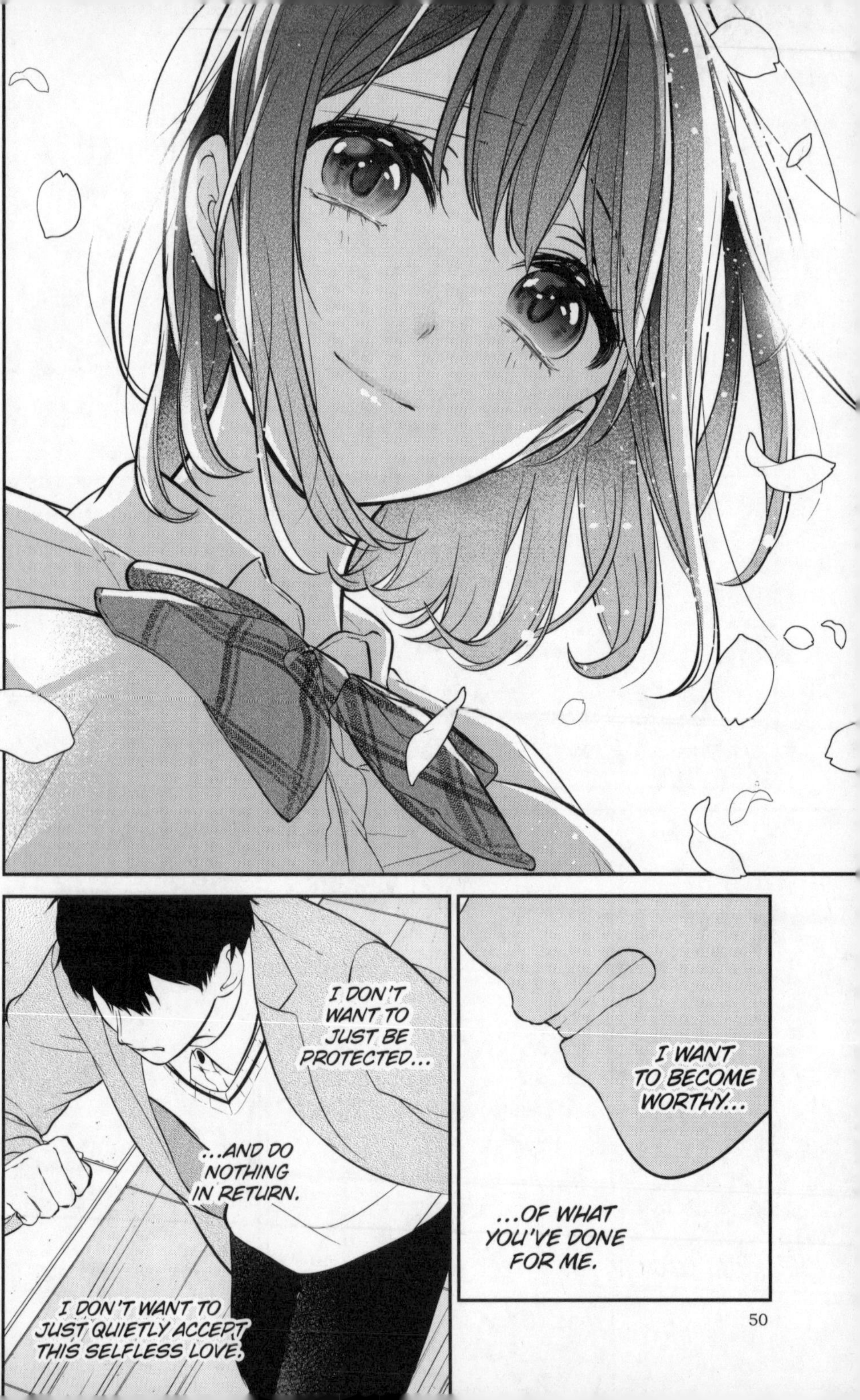
I WANT TO BECOME WORTHY...
...OF WHAT YOU'VE DONE FOR ME.
I DON'T WANT TO JUST BE PROTECTED...
...AND DO NOTHING IN RETURN.
I DON'T WANT TO JUST QUIETLY ACCEPT THIS SELFLESS LOVE.

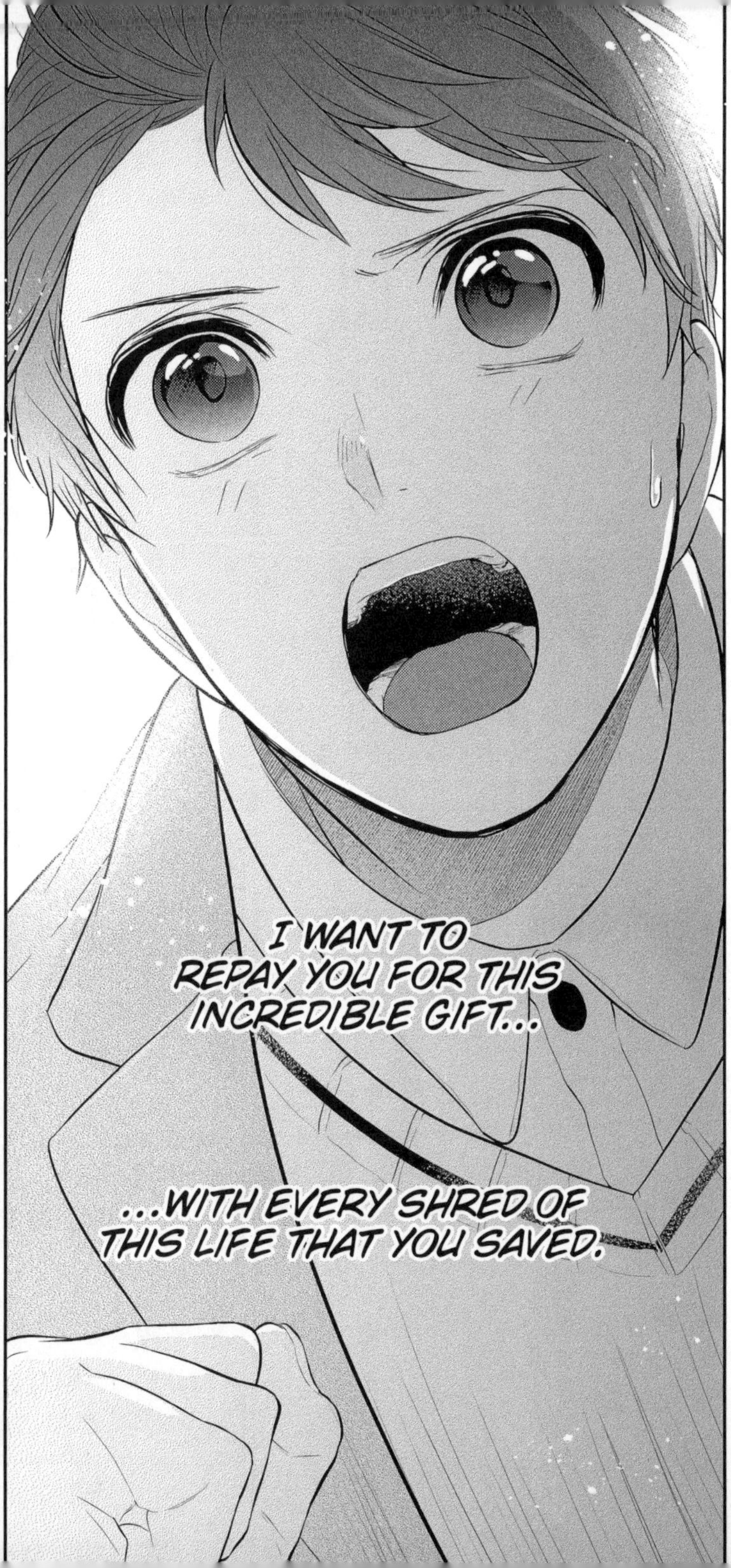
I WANT TO REPAY YOU FOR THIS INCREDIBLE GIFT...
...WITH EVERY SHRED OF THIS LIFE THAT YOU SAVED.
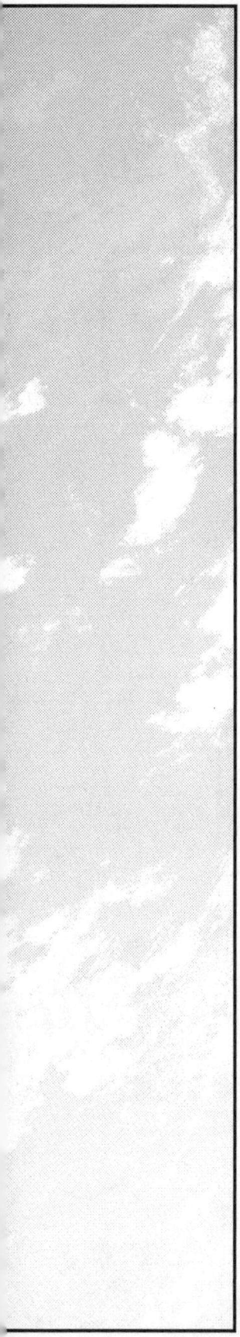

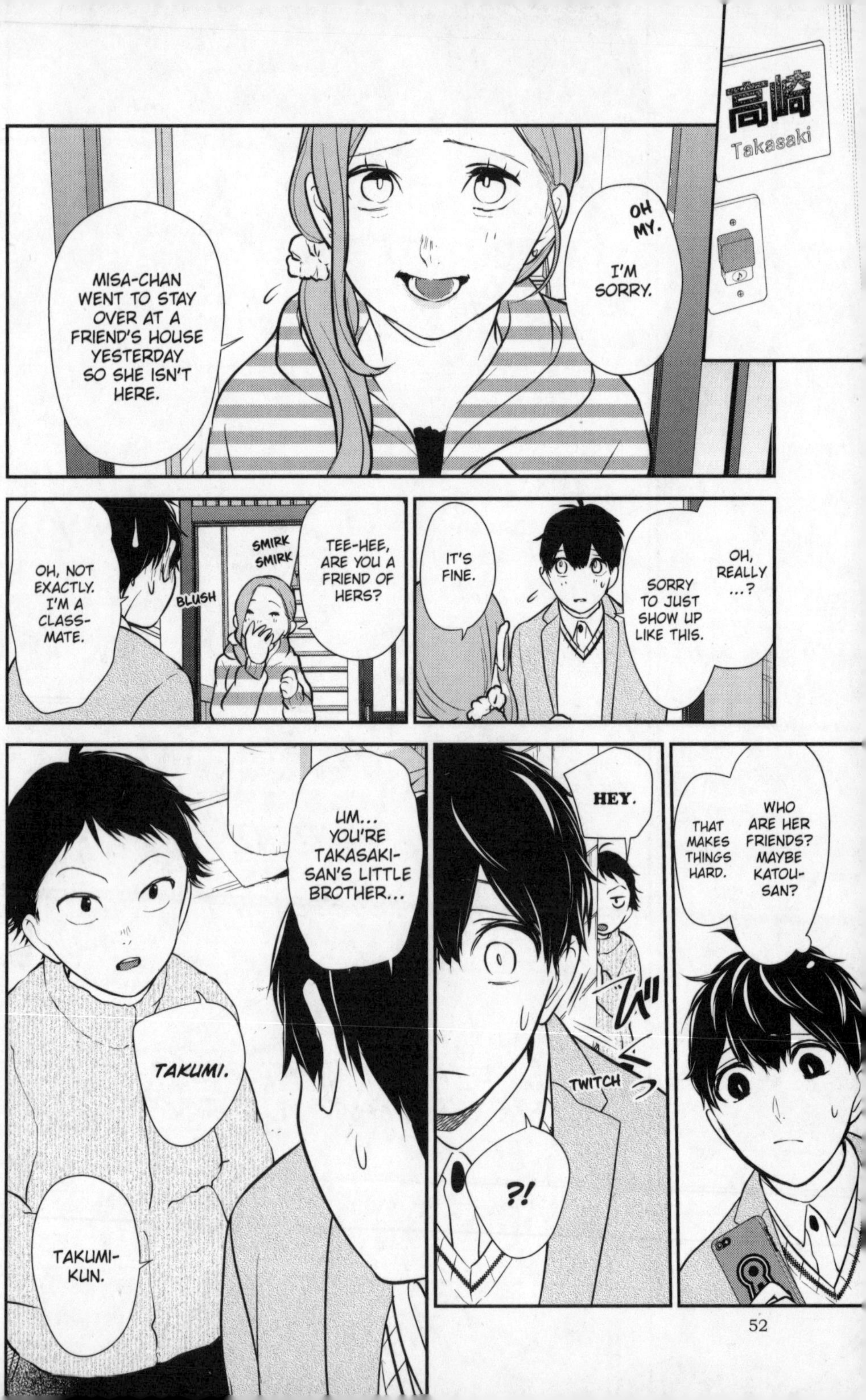
高崎
Takasaki
OH MY.
I'M SORRY.
MISA-CHAN WENT TO STAY OVER AT A FRIEND'S HOUSE YESTERDAY SO SHE ISN'T HERE.
OH, REALLY ...?
SORRY TO JUST SHOW UP LIKE THIS.
IT'S FINE.
TEE-HEE, ARE YOU A FRIEND OF HERS?
SMIRK SMIRK
BLUSH
OH, NOT EXACTLY. I'M A CLASSMATE.
WHO ARE HER FRIENDS? MAYBE KATOU-SAN?
THAT MAKES THINGS HARD.
HEY.
TWITCH
?!
UM... YOU'RE TAKASAKI-SAN'S LITTLE BROTHER...
TAKUMI.
TAKUMI-KUN.

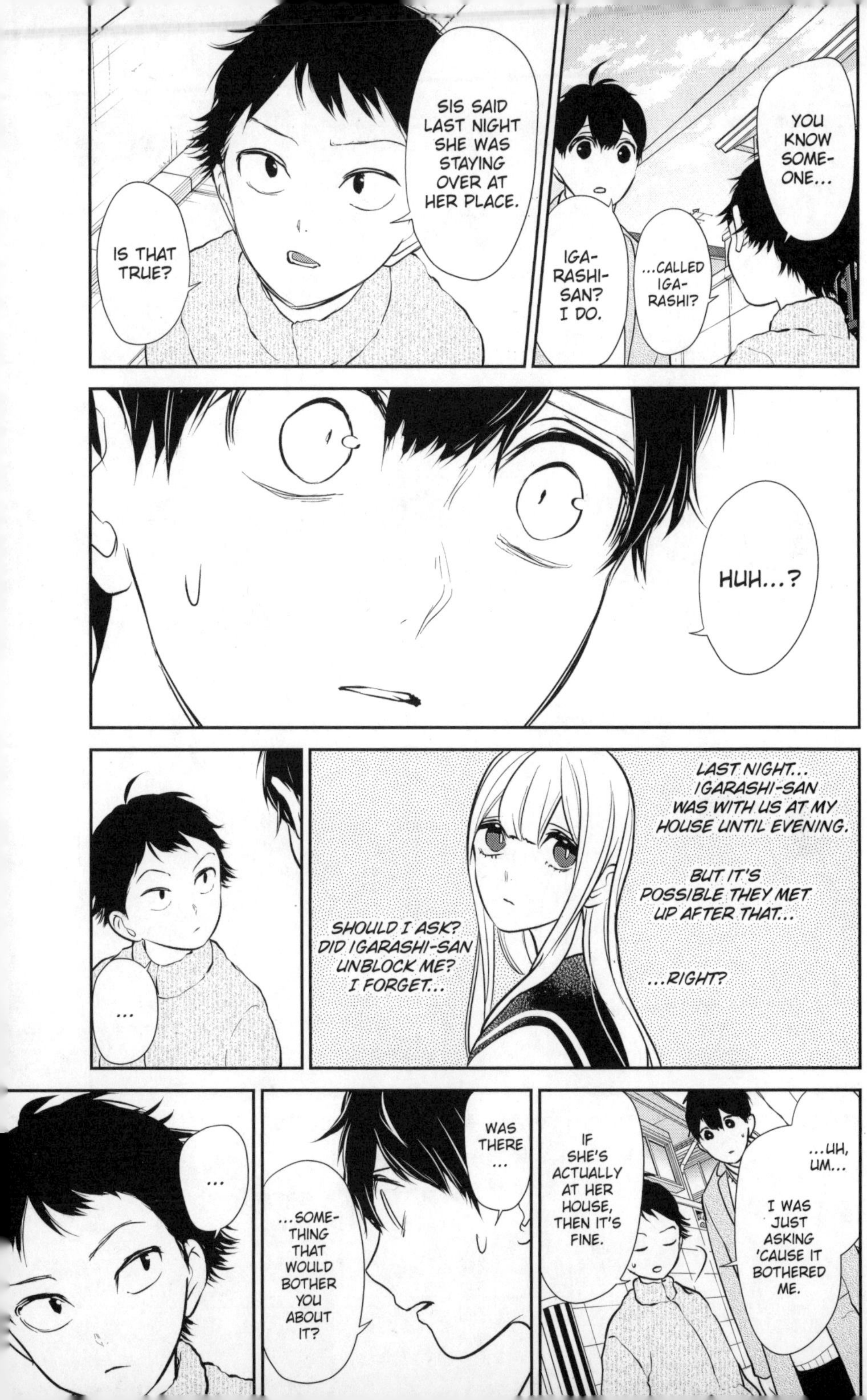
YOU KNOW SOMEONE...
...CALLED IGARASHI?
IGARASHI-SAN? I DO.
SIS SAID LAST NIGHT SHE WAS STAYING OVER AT HER PLACE.
IS THAT TRUE?
HUH...?
LAST NIGHT... IGARASHI-SAN WAS WITH US AT MY HOUSE UNTIL EVENING.
BUT IT'S POSSIBLE THEY MET UP AFTER THAT...
...RIGHT?
SHOULD I ASK? DID IGARASHI-SAN UNBLOCK ME? I FORGET...
...
...UH, UM...
I WAS JUST ASKING 'CAUSE IT BOTHERED ME.
IF SHE'S ACTUALLY AT HER HOUSE, THEN IT'S FINE.
WAS THERE...
...SOMETHING THAT WOULD BOTHER YOU ABOUT IT?
...

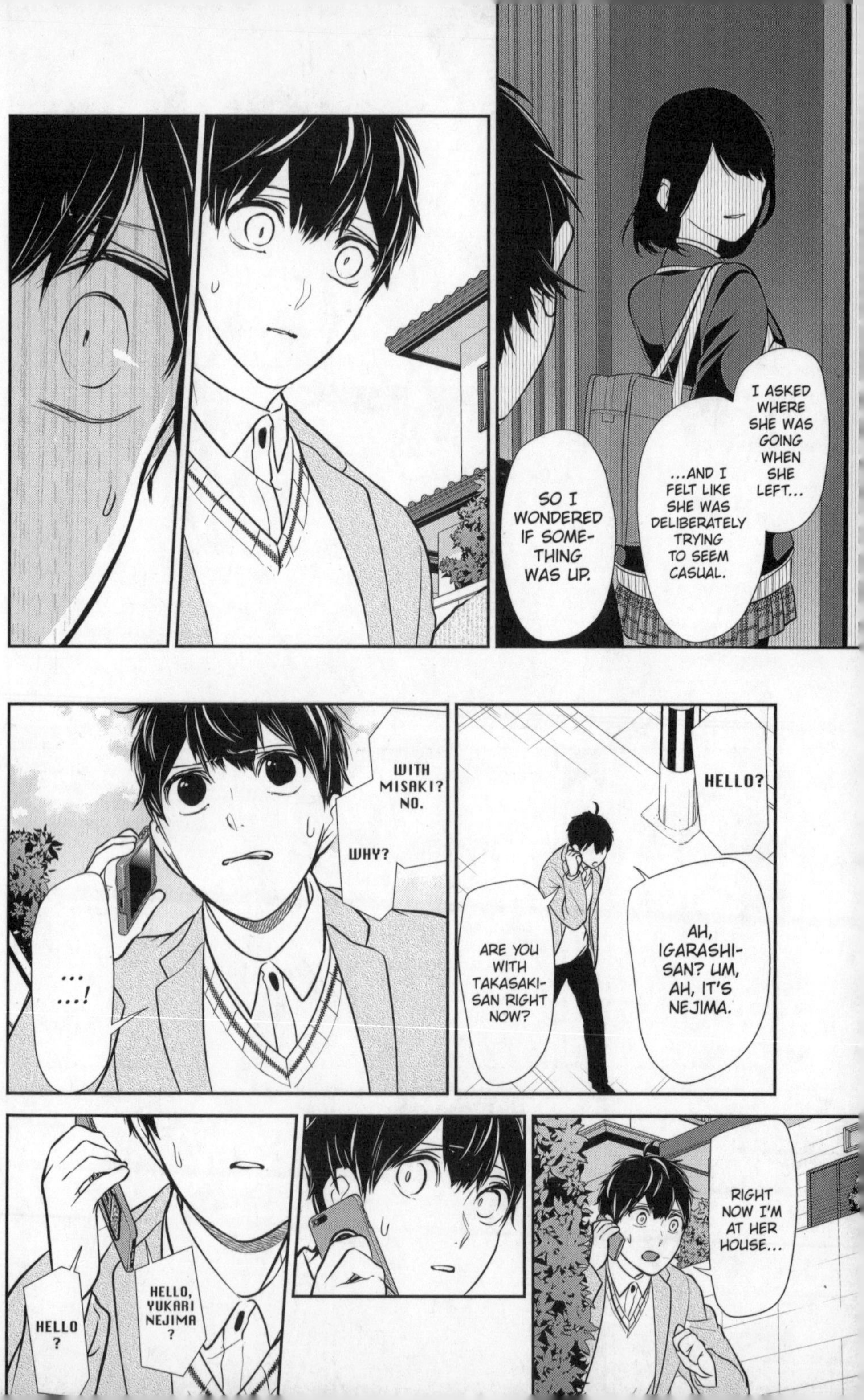
I ASKED WHERE SHE WAS GOING WHEN SHE LEFT...
...AND I FELT LIKE SHE WAS DELIBERATELY TRYING TO SEEM CASUAL.
SO I WONDERED IF SOME-THING WAS UP.
HELLO?
AH, IGARASHI-SAN? UM, AH, IT'S NEJIMA.
ARE YOU WITH TAKASAKI-SAN RIGHT NOW?
WITH MISAKI? NO.
WHY?
... ...!
RIGHT NOW I'M AT HER HOUSE...
HELLO, YUKARI NEJIMA?
HELLO?

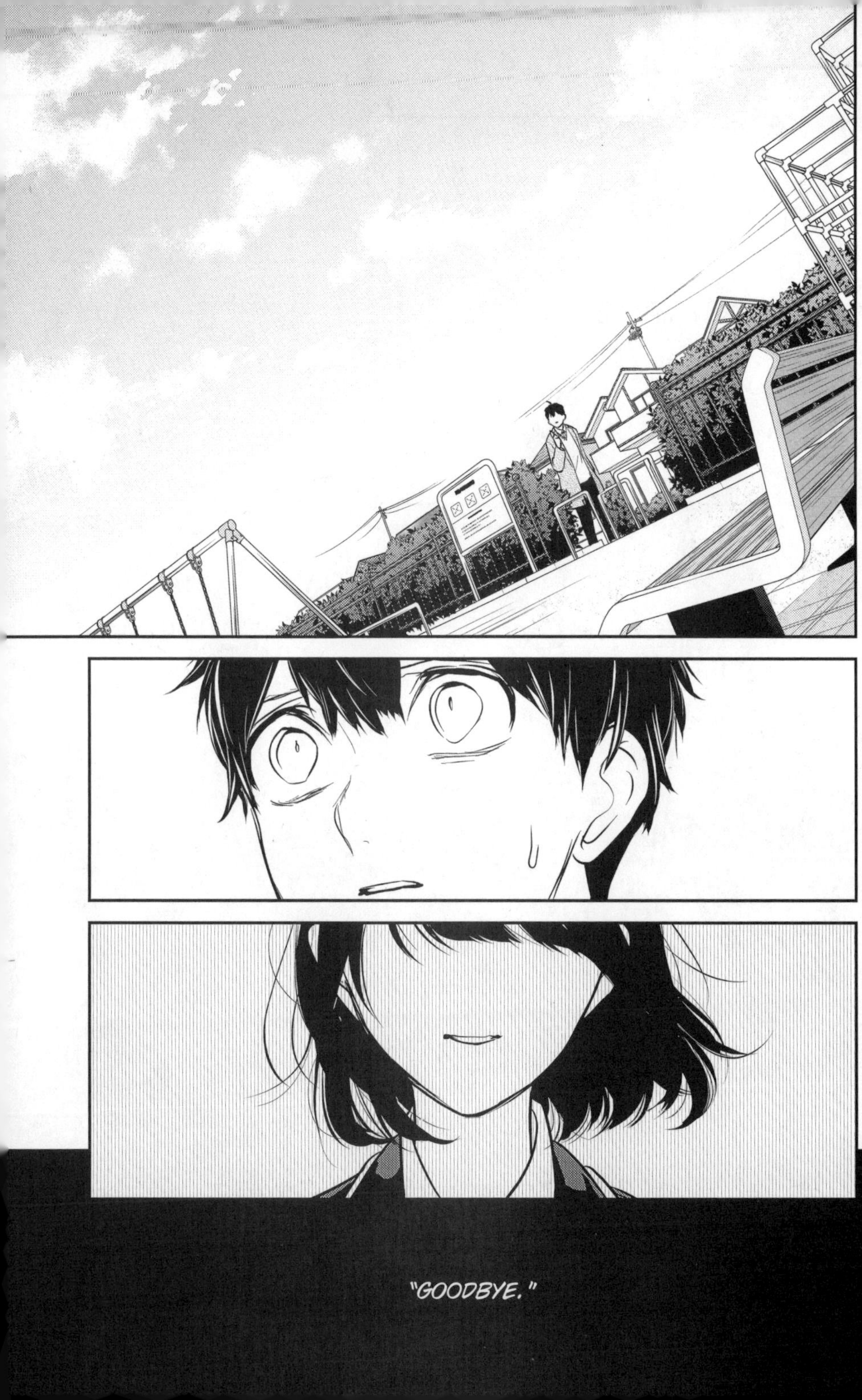
"GOODBYE."

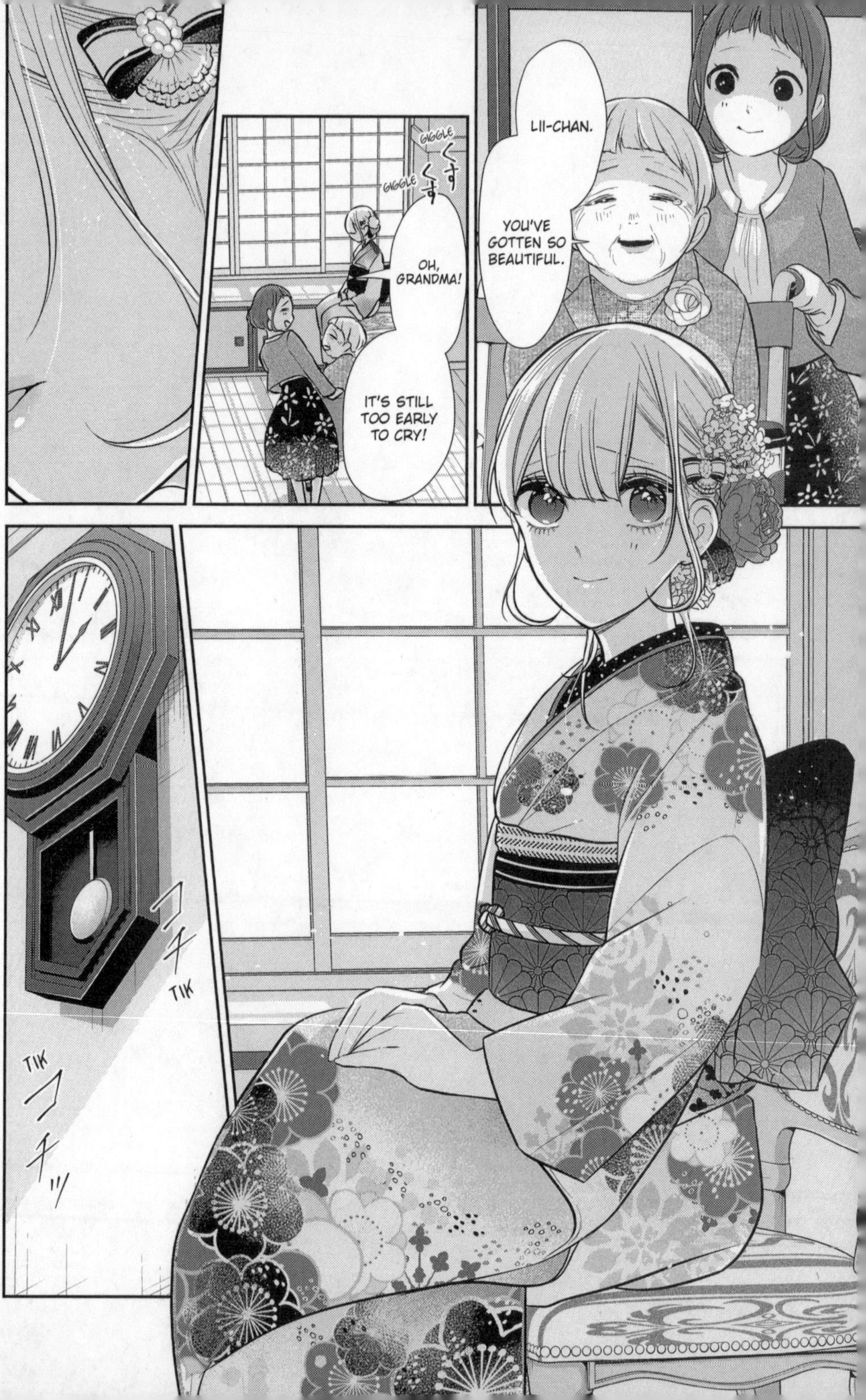
LII-CHAN.
YOU'VE GOTTEN SO BEAUTIFUL.
GIGGLE くす
GIGGLE くす
OH, GRANDMA!
IT'S STILL TOO EARLY TO CRY!
コチ
TIK
TIK
コチッ

Love & Lies

Love & Lies

Chapter 47: Facing Love and Lies

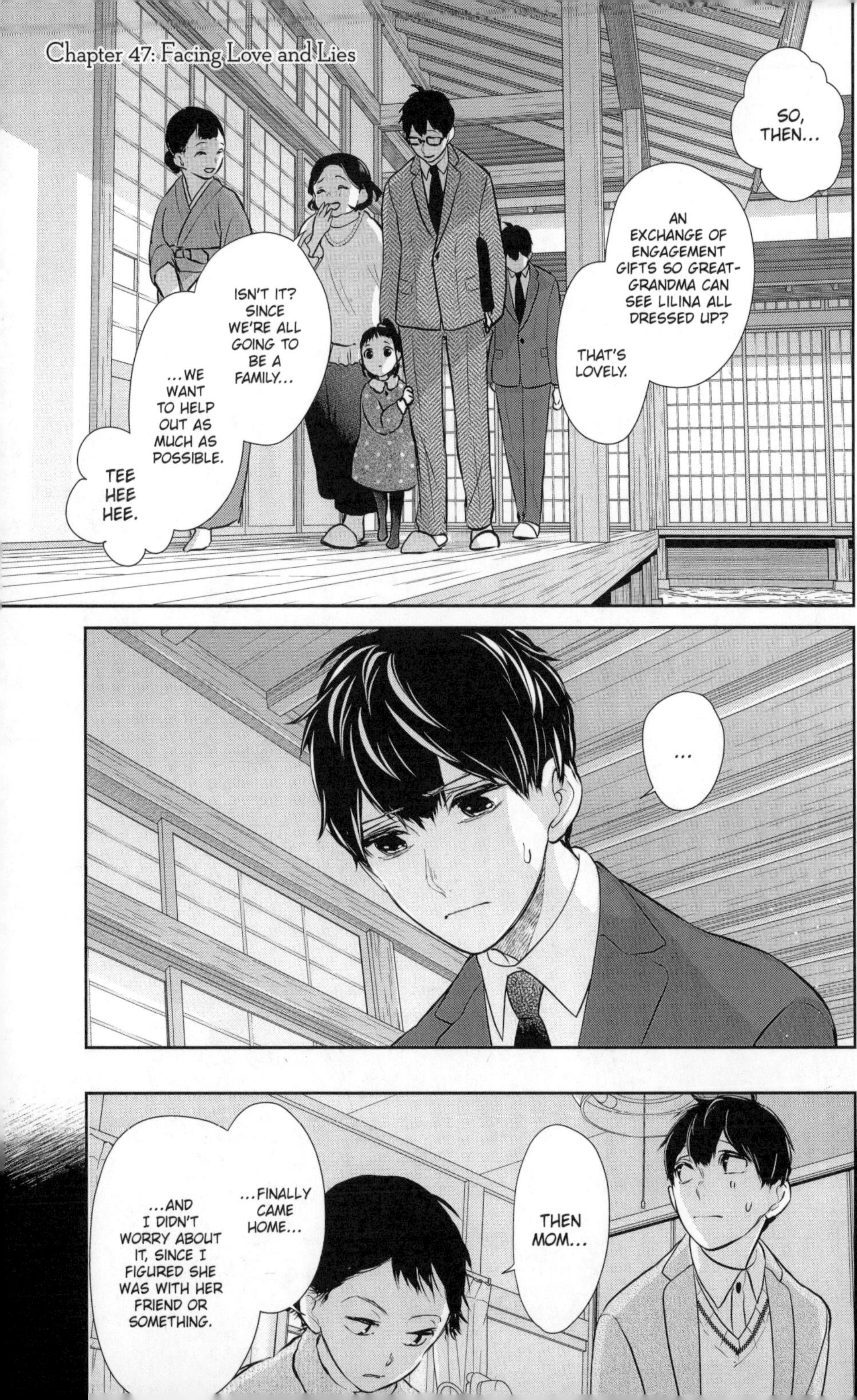

SO, THEN...
AN EXCHANGE OF ENGAGEMENT GIFTS SO GREAT-GRANDMA CAN SEE LILINA ALL DRESSED UP?
THAT'S LOVELY.
ISN'T IT? SINCE WE'RE ALL GOING TO BE A FAMILY...
...WE WANT TO HELP OUT AS MUCH AS POSSIBLE.
TEE HEE HEE.
...
THEN MOM...
...FINALLY CAME HOME...
...AND I DIDN'T WORRY ABOUT IT, SINCE I FIGURED SHE WAS WITH HER FRIEND OR SOMETHING.

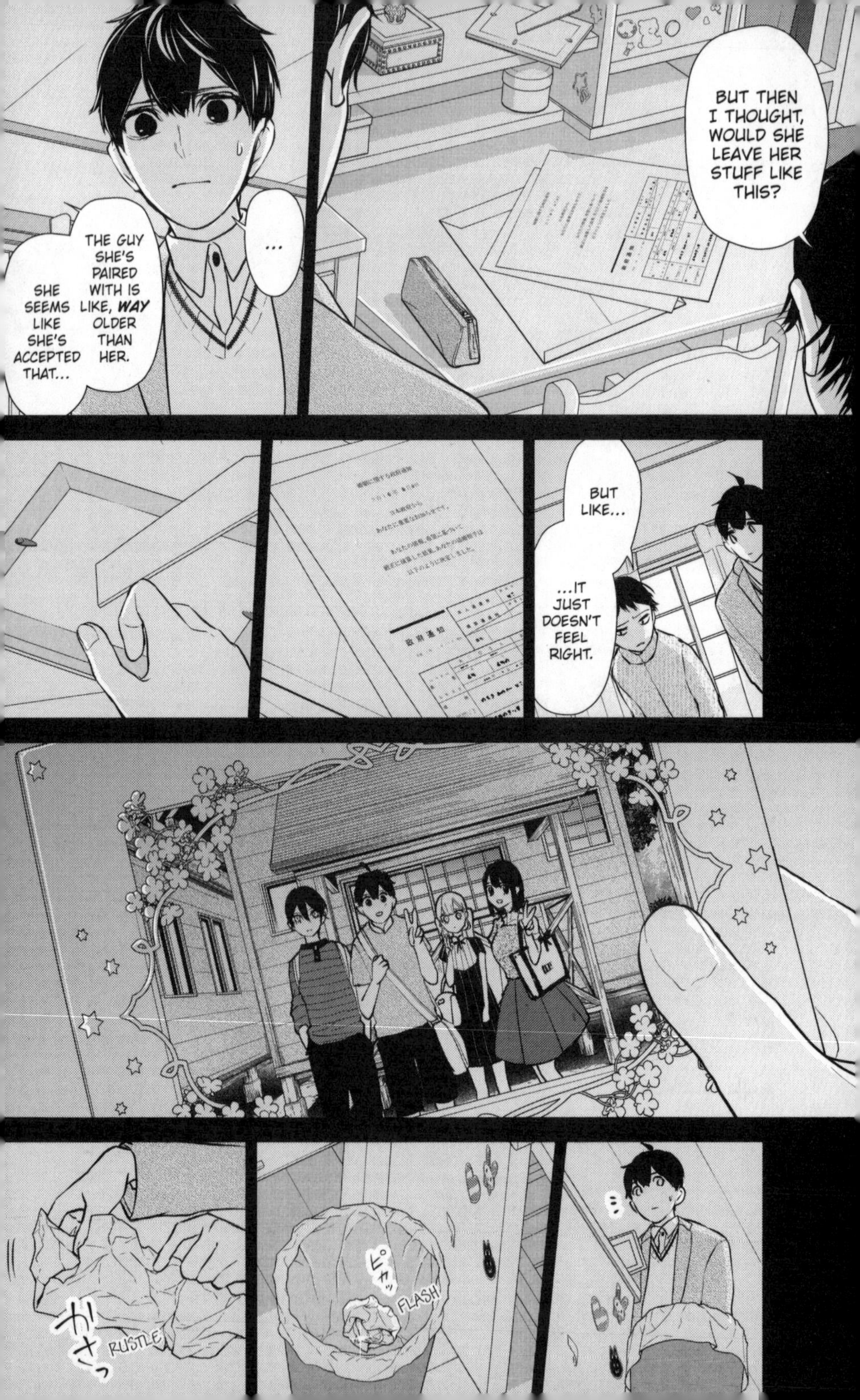
BUT THEN I THOUGHT, WOULD SHE LEAVE HER STUFF LIKE THIS?
...
THE GUY SHE'S PAIRED WITH IS LIKE, *WAY* OLDER THAN HER.
SHE SEEMS LIKE SHE'S ACCEPTED THAT...
BUT LIKE...
...IT JUST DOESN'T FEEL RIGHT.
...
ピカッ
FLASH
がさっ
RUSTLE

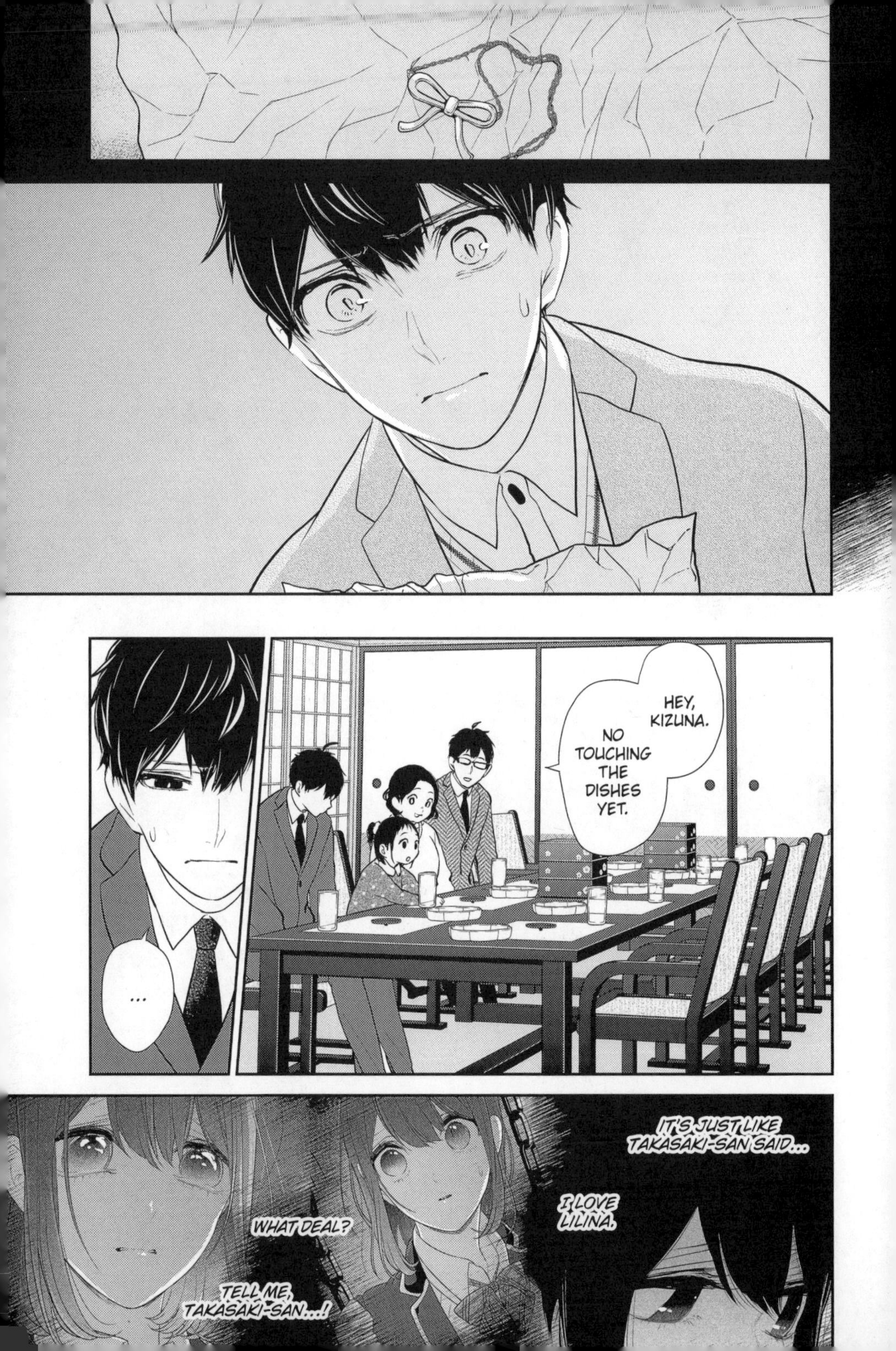
HEY, KIZUNA.
NO TOUCHING THE DISHES YET.
...
IT'S JUST LIKE TAKASAKI-SAN SAID...
I LOVE LILINA.
WHAT DEAL?
TELL ME, TAKASAKI-SAN...!

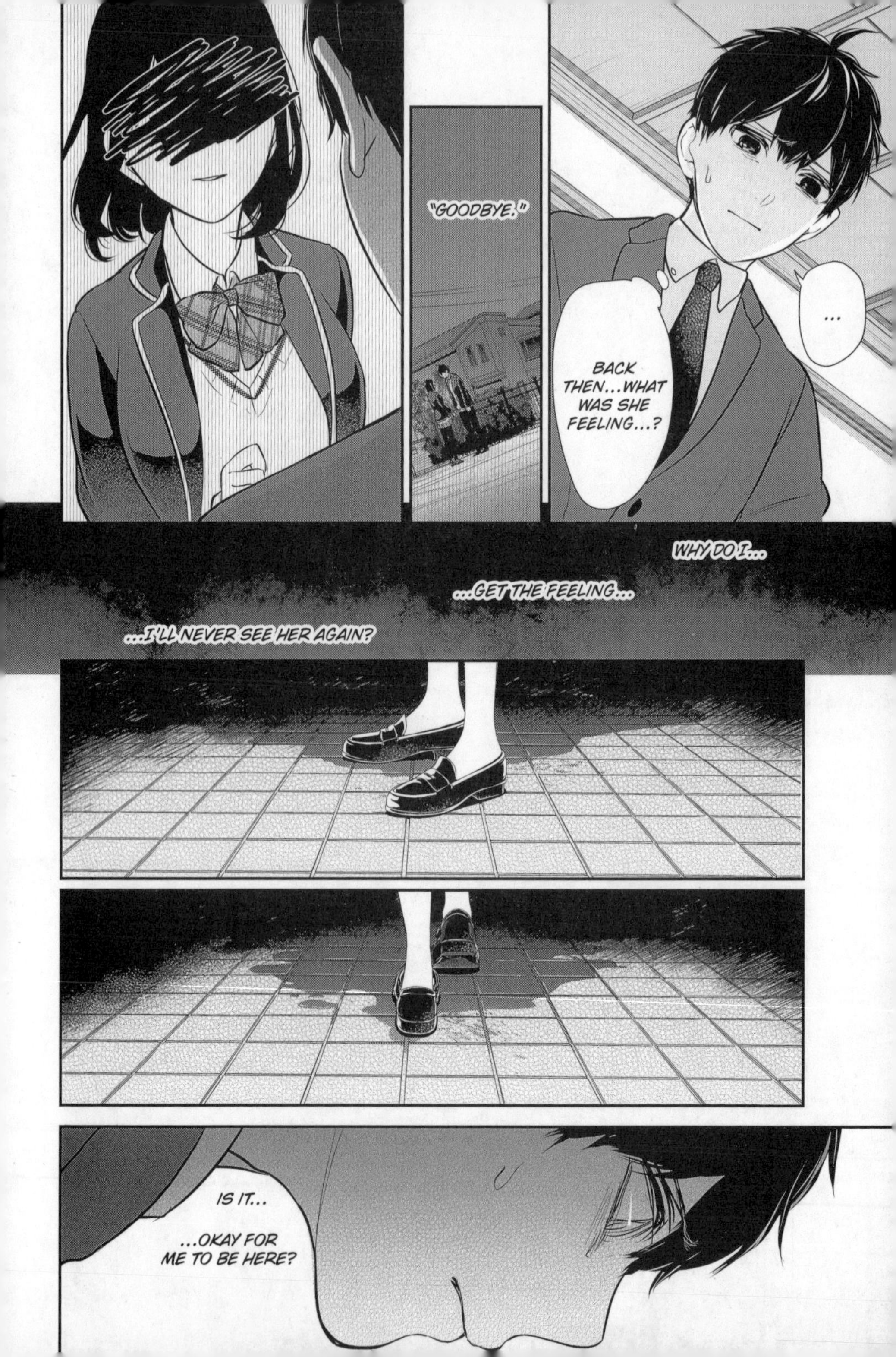
...
BACK THEN...WHAT WAS SHE FEELING...?
"GOODBYE."
WHY DO I...
...GET THE FEELING...
...I'LL NEVER SEE HER AGAIN?
IS IT...
...OKAY FOR ME TO BE HERE?

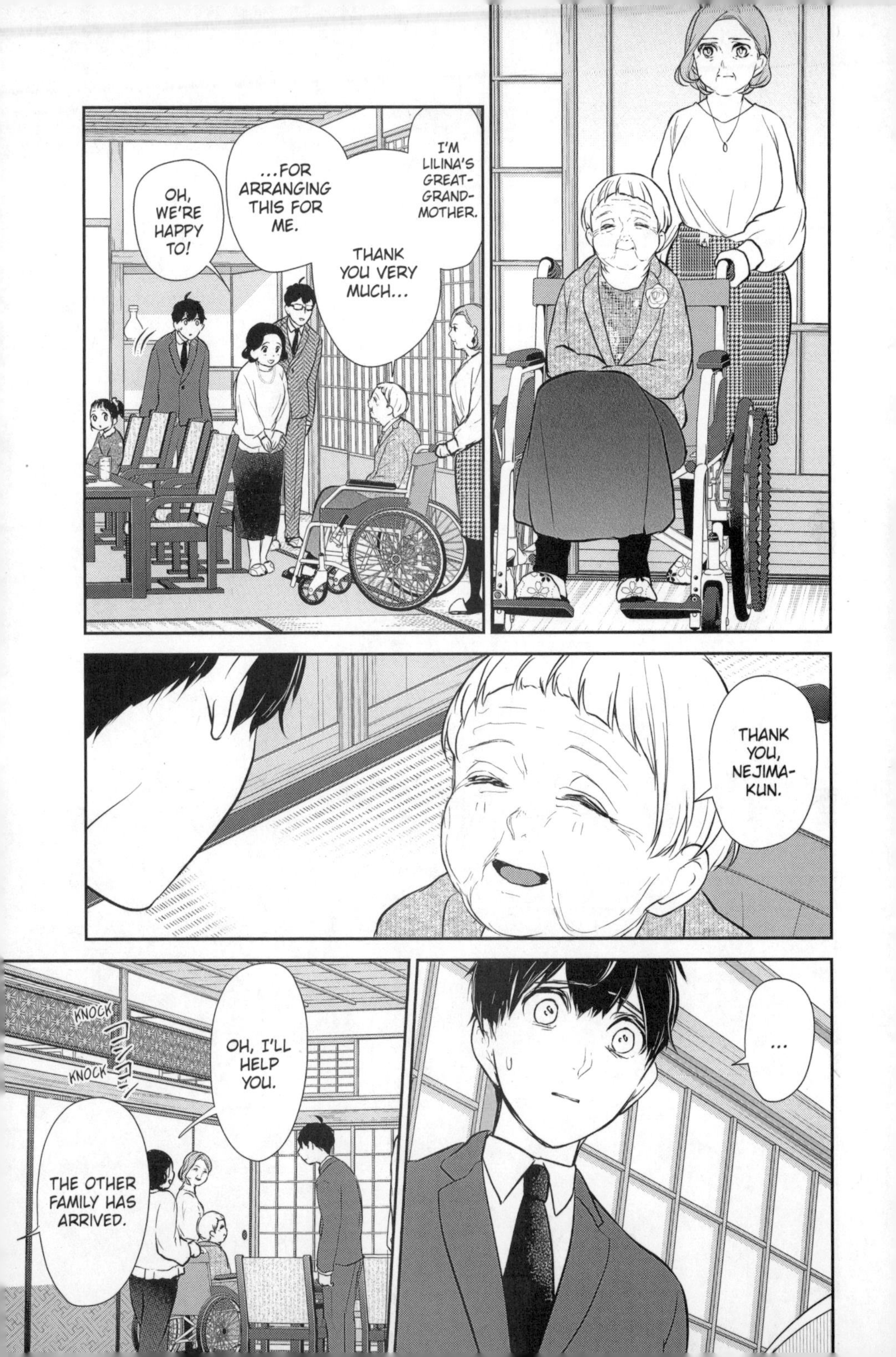
I'M LILINA'S GREAT-GRANDMOTHER.
THANK YOU VERY MUCH...
...FOR ARRANGING THIS FOR ME.
OH, WE'RE HAPPY TO!
THANK YOU, NEJIMA-KUN.
...
OH, I'LL HELP YOU.
KNOCK
KNOCK
THE OTHER FAMILY HAS ARRIVED.

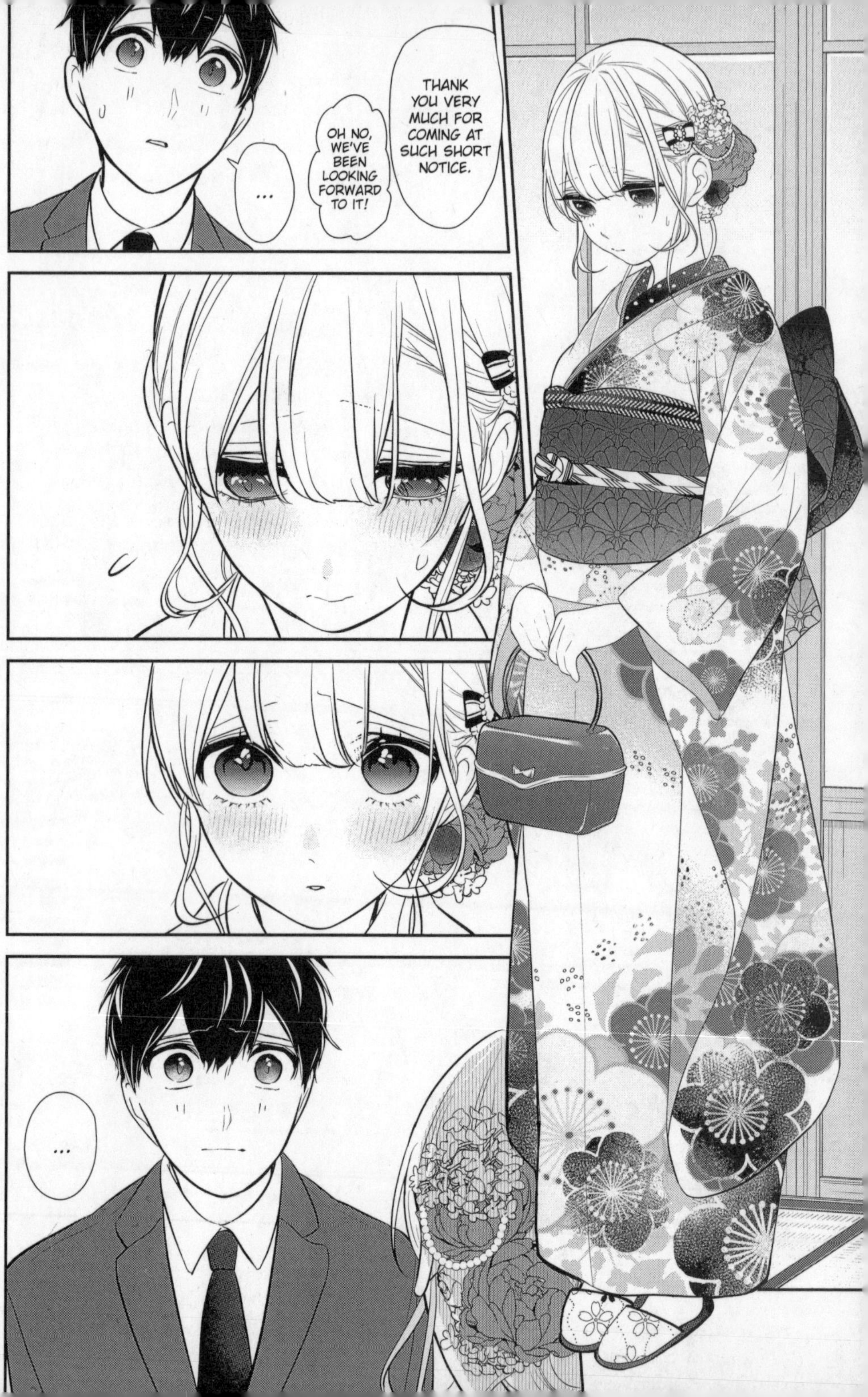
THANK YOU VERY MUCH FOR COMING AT SUCH SHORT NOTICE.
OH NO, WE'VE BEEN LOOKING FORWARD TO IT!
...
...

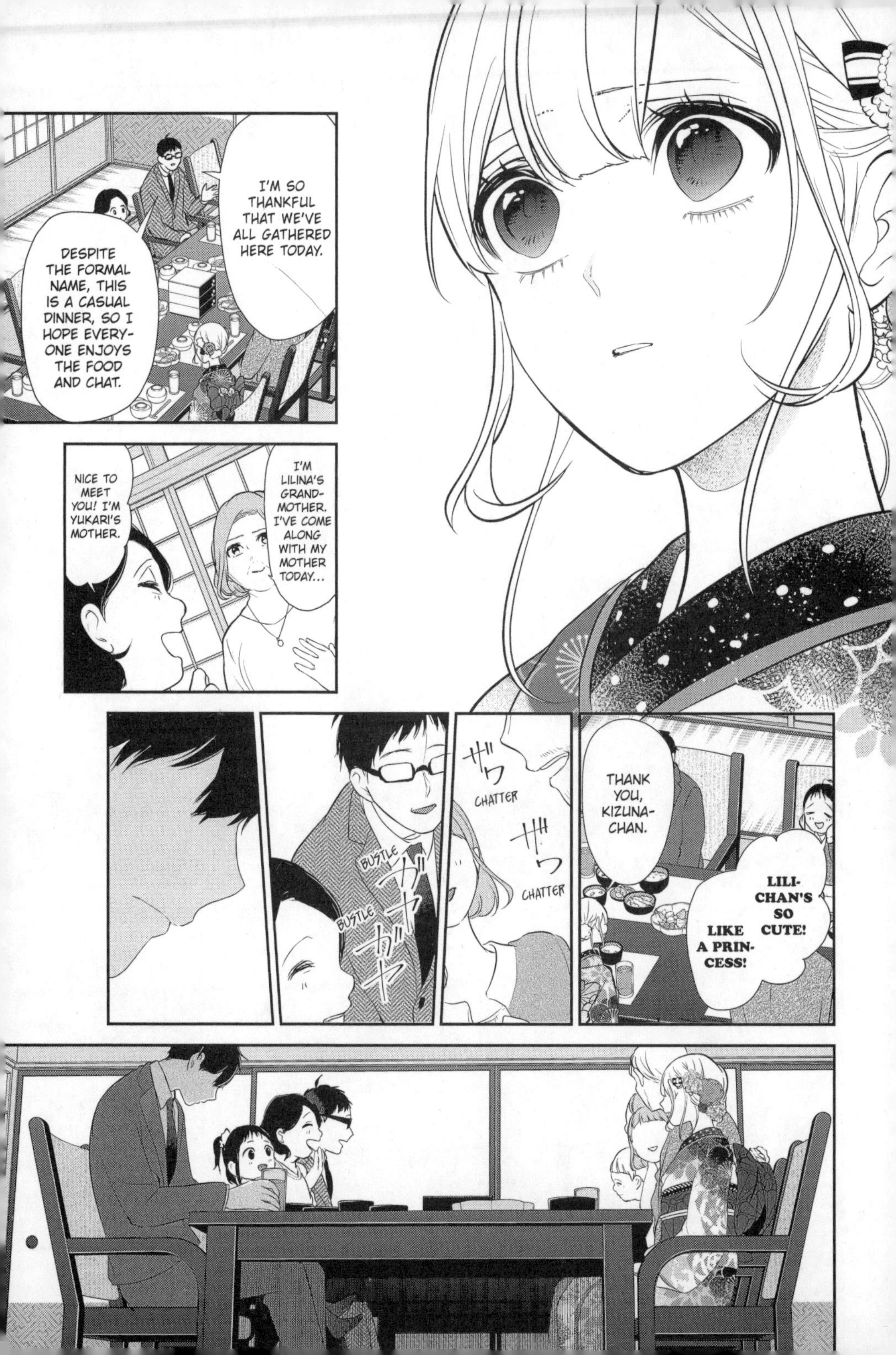
I'M SO THANKFUL THAT WE'VE ALL GATHERED HERE TODAY.
DESPITE THE FORMAL NAME, THIS IS A CASUAL DINNER, SO I HOPE EVERY-ONE ENJOYS THE FOOD AND CHAT.
I'M LILINA'S GRAND-MOTHER. I'VE COME ALONG WITH MY MOTHER TODAY...
NICE TO MEET YOU! I'M YUKARI'S MOTHER.
THANK YOU, KIZUNA-CHAN.
LILI-CHAN'S SO CUTE!
LIKE A PRIN-CESS!
ザワ CHATTER
ザワ CHATTER
BUSTLE ガヤ
BUSTLE ガヤ

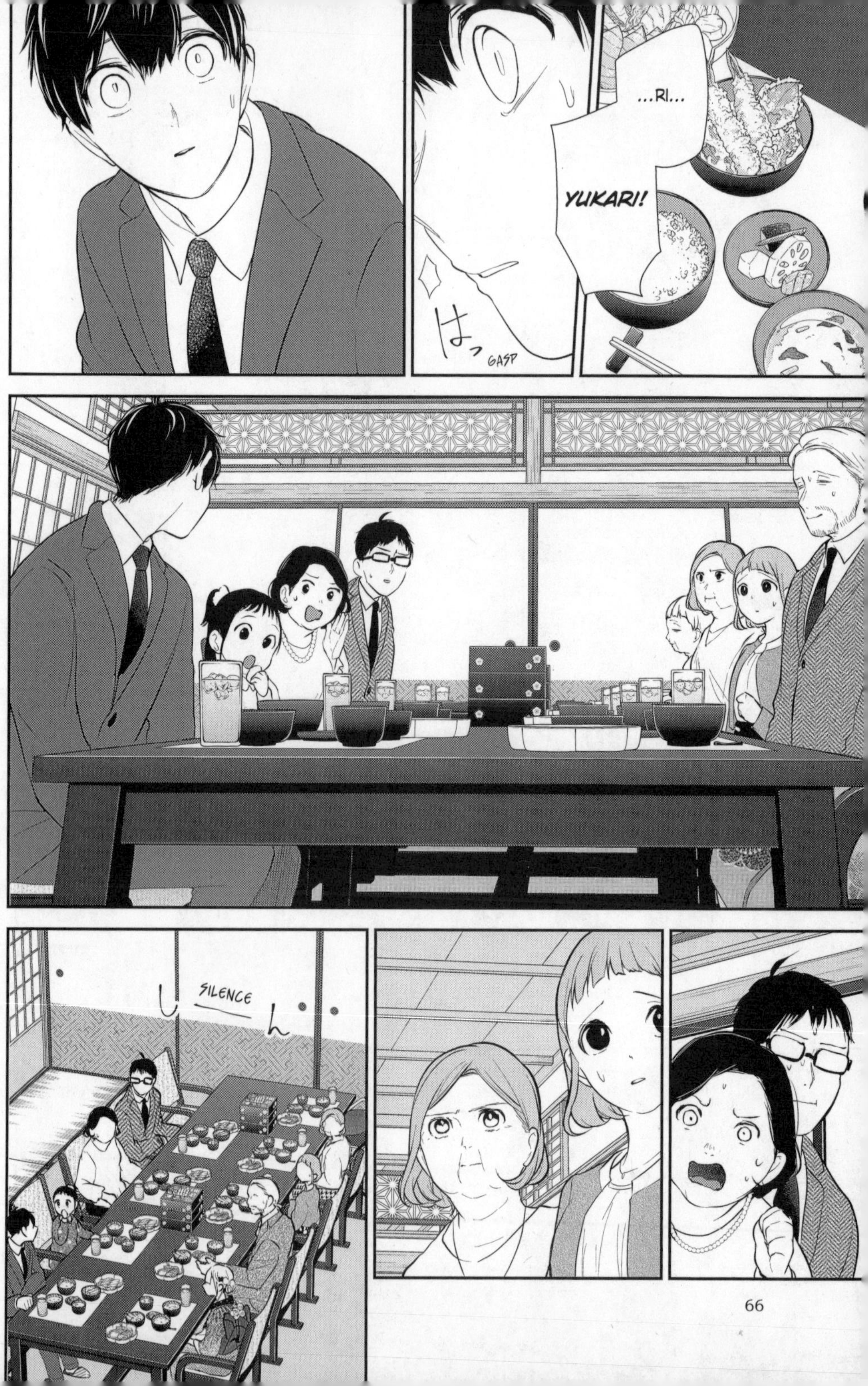
...RI...
YUKARI!
はっ
GASP
しーん
SILENCE

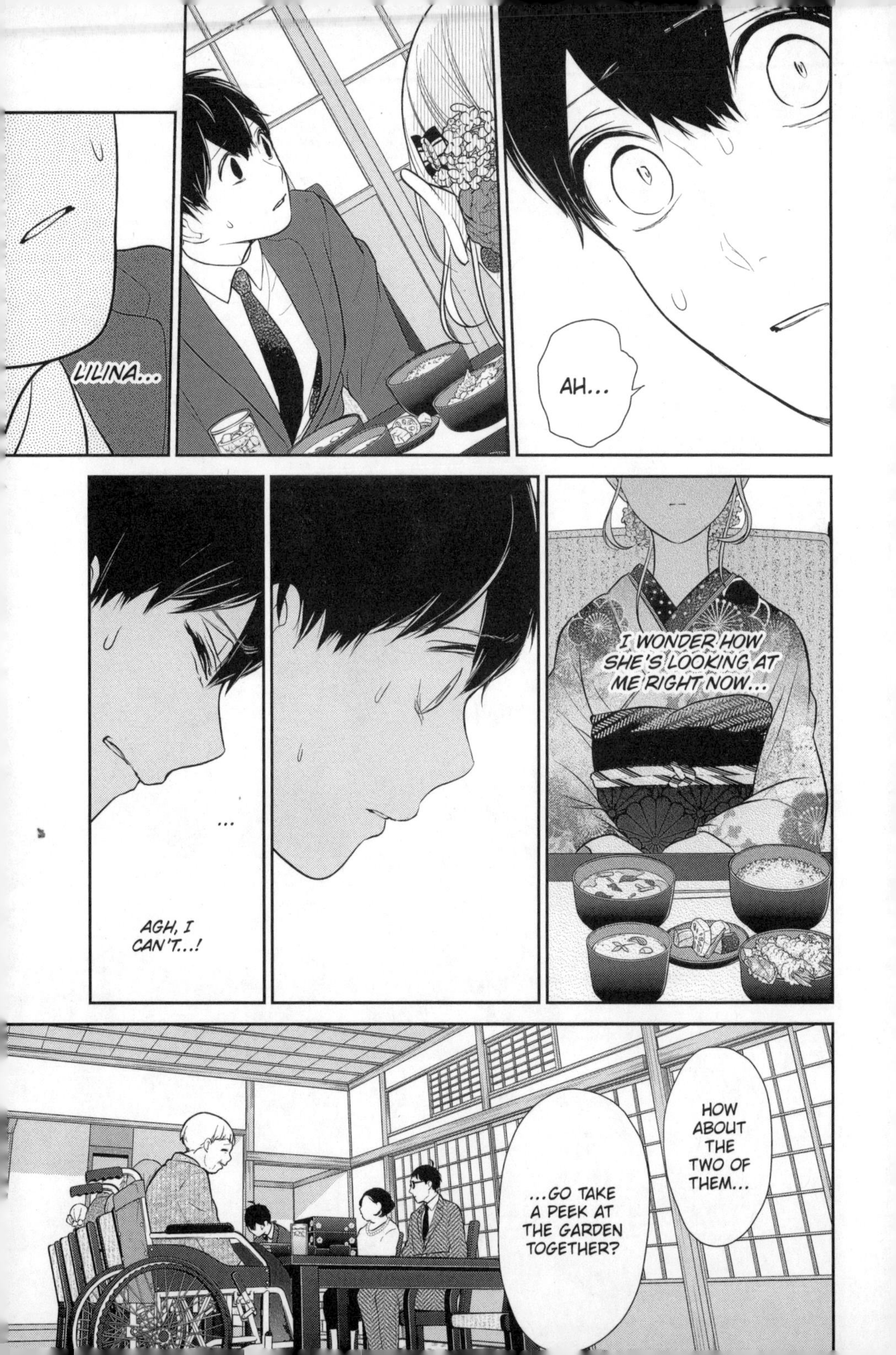
AH…
LILINA…
I WONDER HOW SHE'S LOOKING AT ME RIGHT NOW…
…
AGH, I CAN'T…!
HOW ABOUT THE TWO OF THEM…
…GO TAKE A PEEK AT THE GARDEN TOGETHER?

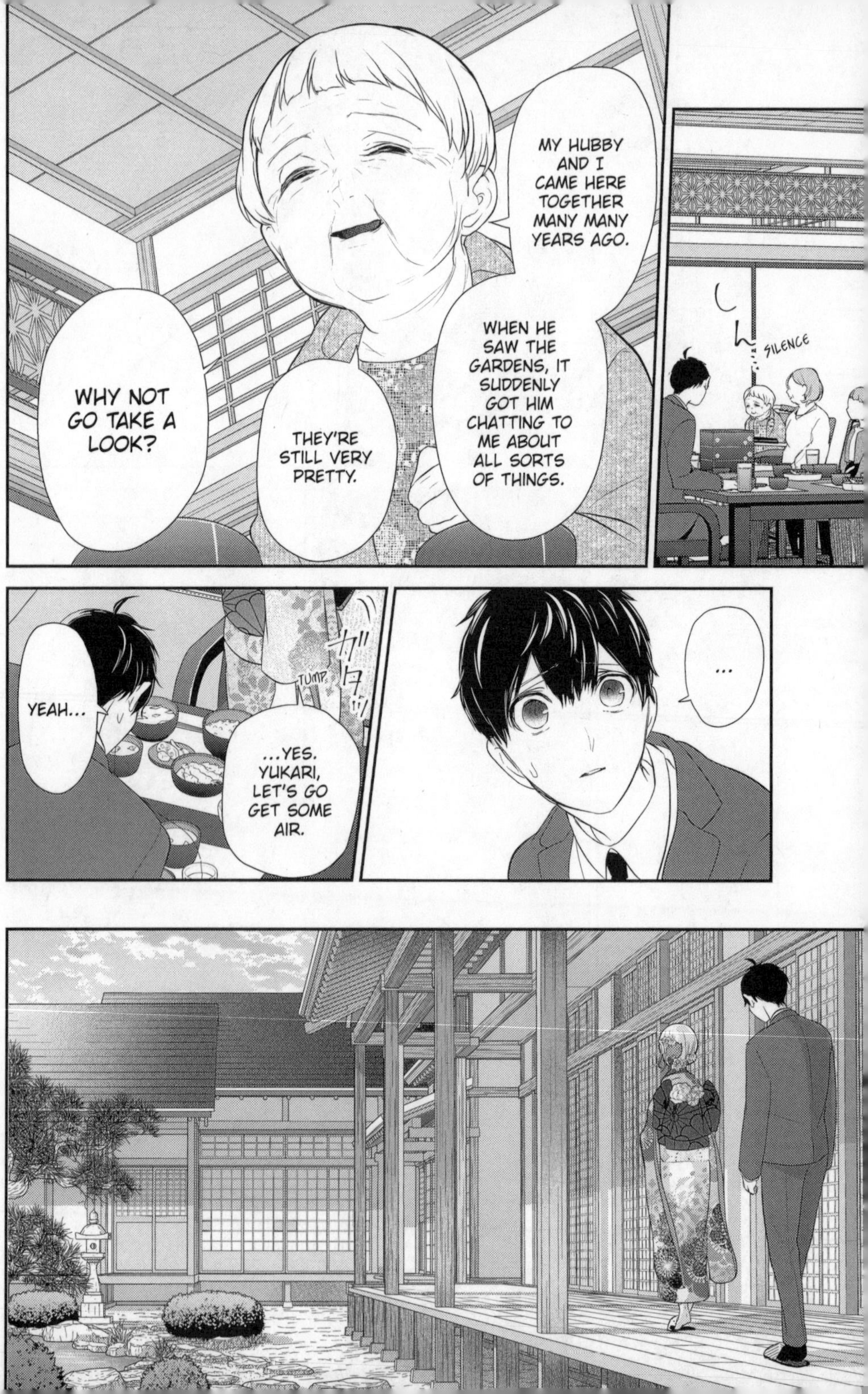
SILENCE
MY HUBBY AND I CAME HERE TOGETHER MANY MANY YEARS AGO.
WHEN HE SAW THE GARDENS, IT SUDDENLY GOT HIM CHATTING TO ME ABOUT ALL SORTS OF THINGS.
THEY'RE STILL VERY PRETTY.
WHY NOT GO TAKE A LOOK?
...
TUMP
...YES. YUKARI, LET'S GO GET SOME AIR.
YEAH...

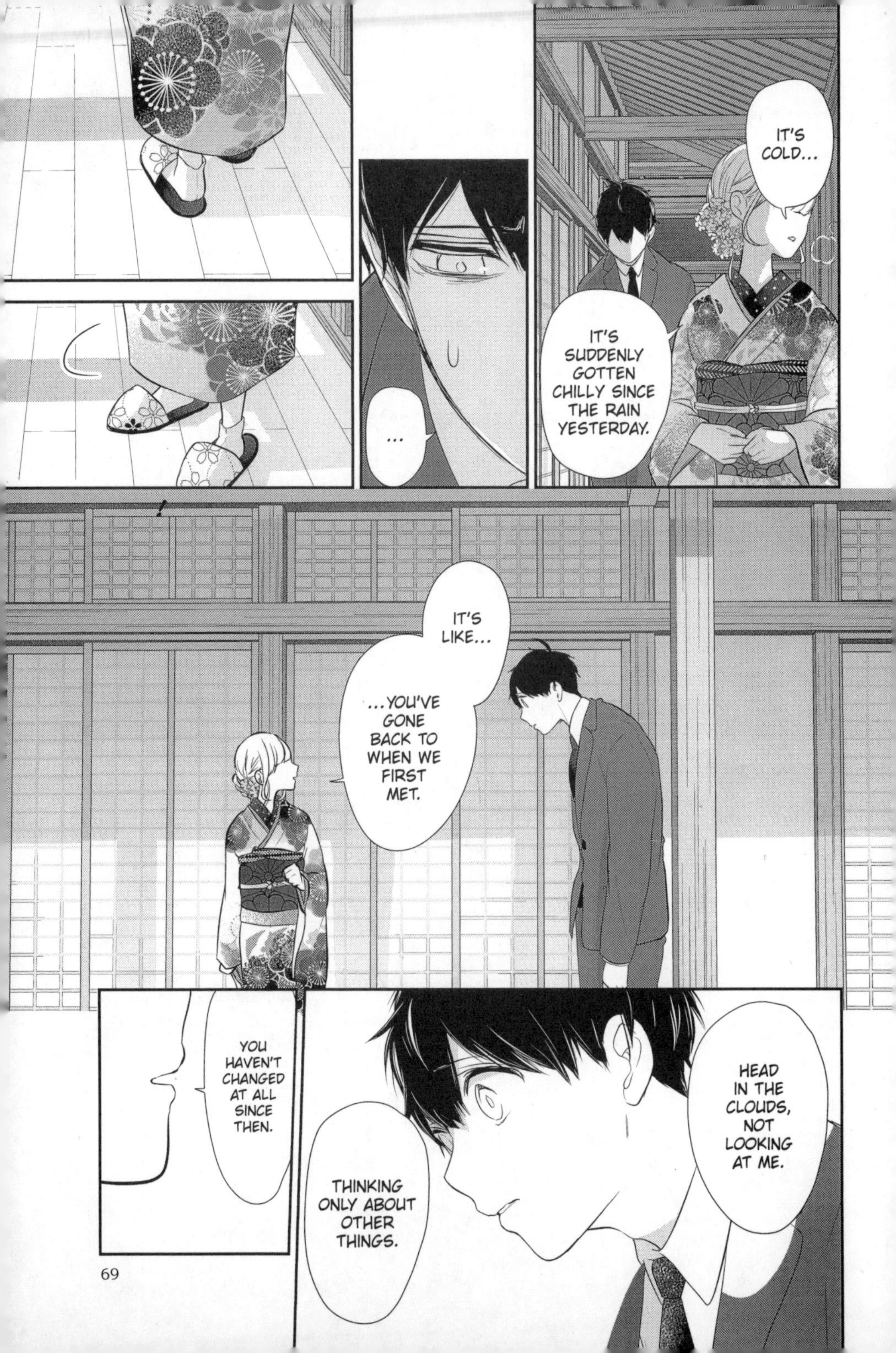
IT'S COLD...
IT'S SUDDENLY GOTTEN CHILLY SINCE THE RAIN YESTERDAY.
...
IT'S LIKE...
...YOU'VE GONE BACK TO WHEN WE FIRST MET.
HEAD IN THE CLOUDS, NOT LOOKING AT ME.
THINKING ONLY ABOUT OTHER THINGS.
YOU HAVEN'T CHANGED AT ALL SINCE THEN.

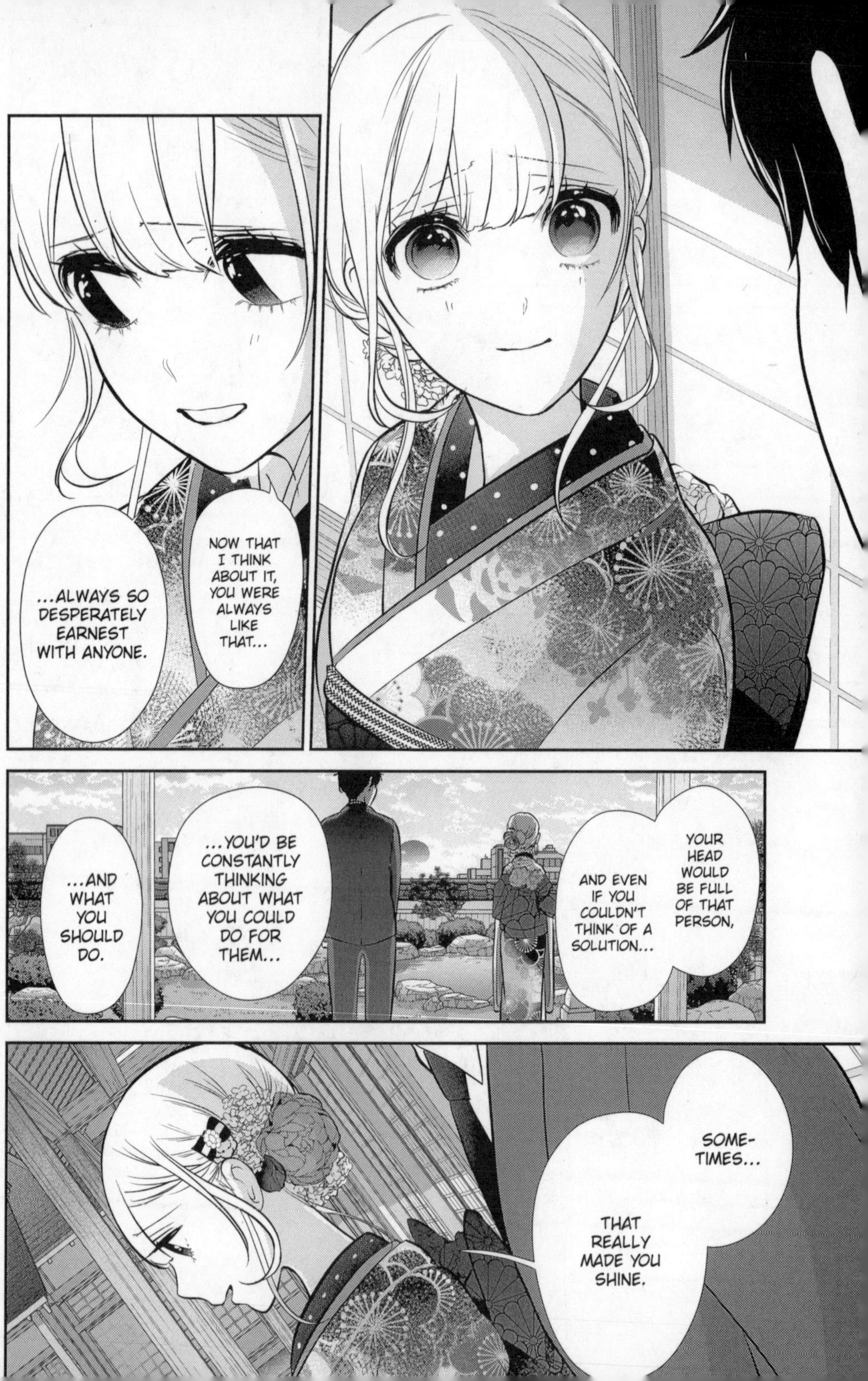
NOW THAT I THINK ABOUT IT, YOU WERE ALWAYS LIKE THAT...
...ALWAYS SO DESPERATELY EARNEST WITH ANYONE.
YOUR HEAD WOULD BE FULL OF THAT PERSON,
AND EVEN IF YOU COULDN'T THINK OF A SOLUTION...
...YOU'D BE CONSTANTLY THINKING ABOUT WHAT YOU COULD DO FOR THEM...
...AND WHAT YOU SHOULD DO.
SOME-TIMES...
THAT REALLY MADE YOU SHINE.

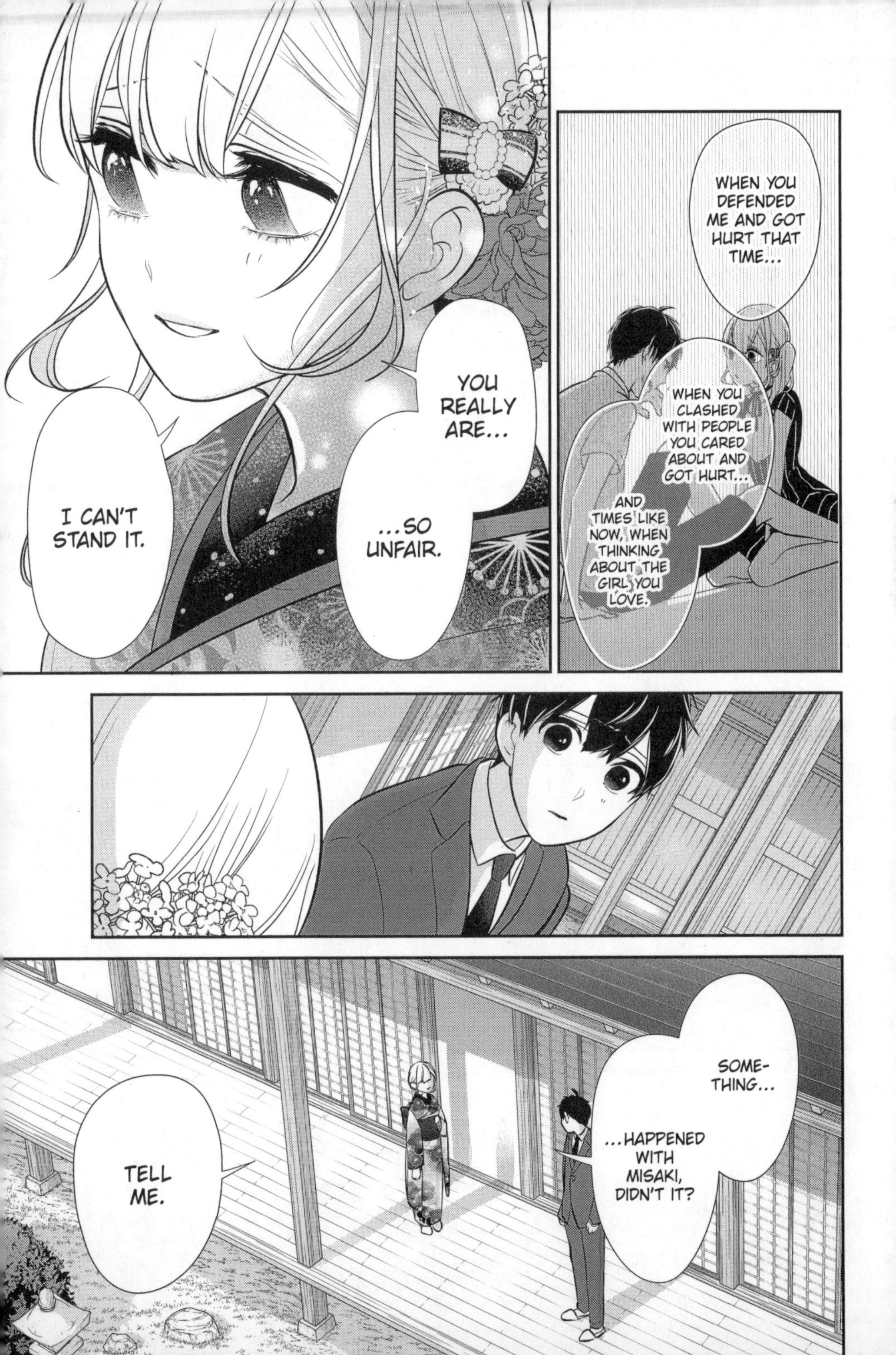
WHEN YOU DEFENDED ME AND GOT HURT THAT TIME...
WHEN YOU CLASHED WITH PEOPLE YOU CARED ABOUT AND GOT HURT...
AND TIMES LIKE NOW, WHEN THINKING ABOUT THE GIRL YOU LOVE.
YOU REALLY ARE...
...SO UNFAIR.
I CAN'T STAND IT.
SOME-THING...
...HAPPENED WITH MISAKI, DIDN'T IT?
TELL ME.

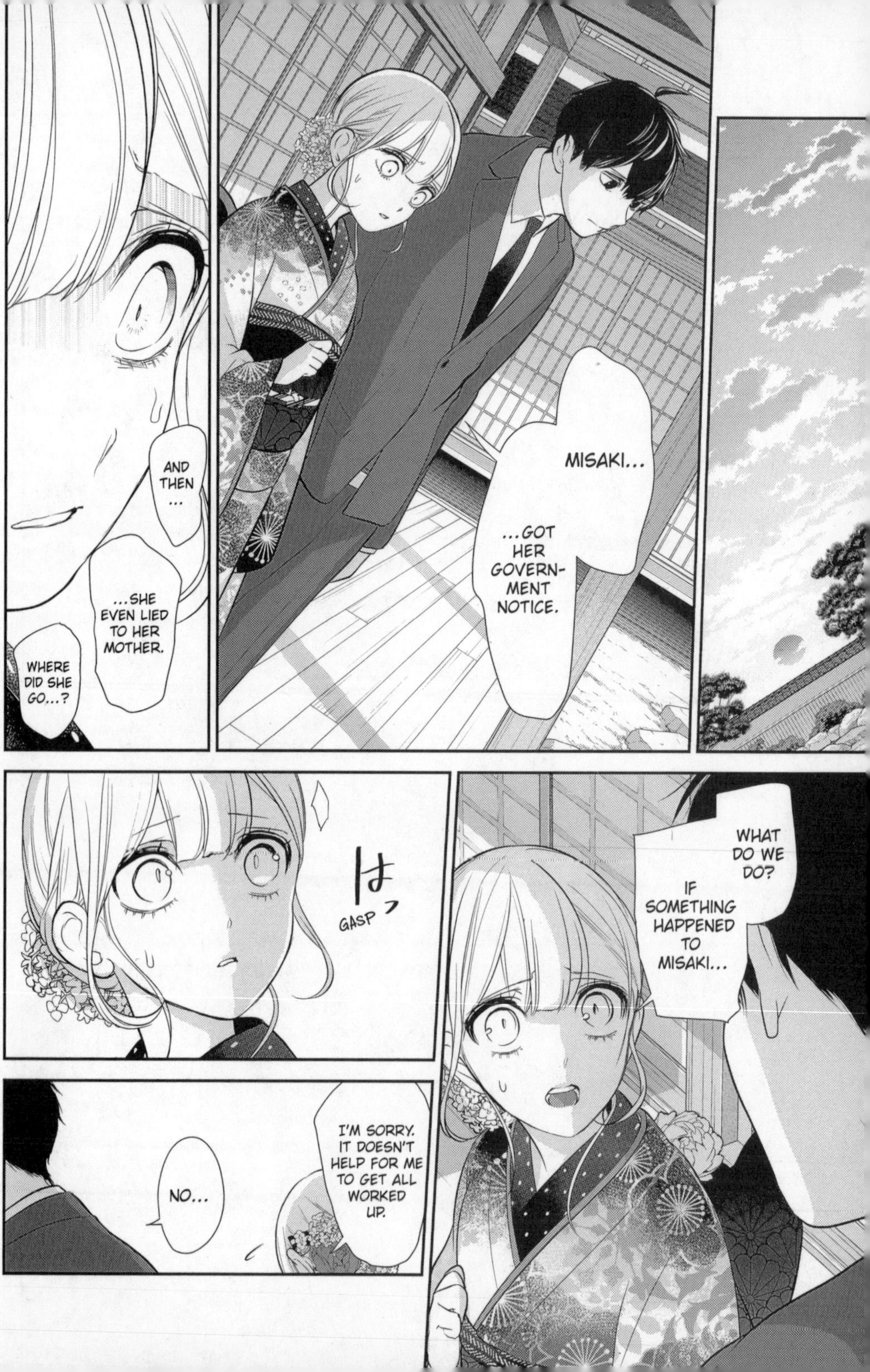
MISAKI...
...GOT HER GOVERNMENT NOTICE.
AND THEN ...
...SHE EVEN LIED TO HER MOTHER.
WHERE DID SHE GO...?
WHAT DO WE DO?
IF SOMETHING HAPPENED TO MISAKI...
は
GASP
I'M SORRY. IT DOESN'T HELP FOR ME TO GET ALL WORKED UP.
NO...

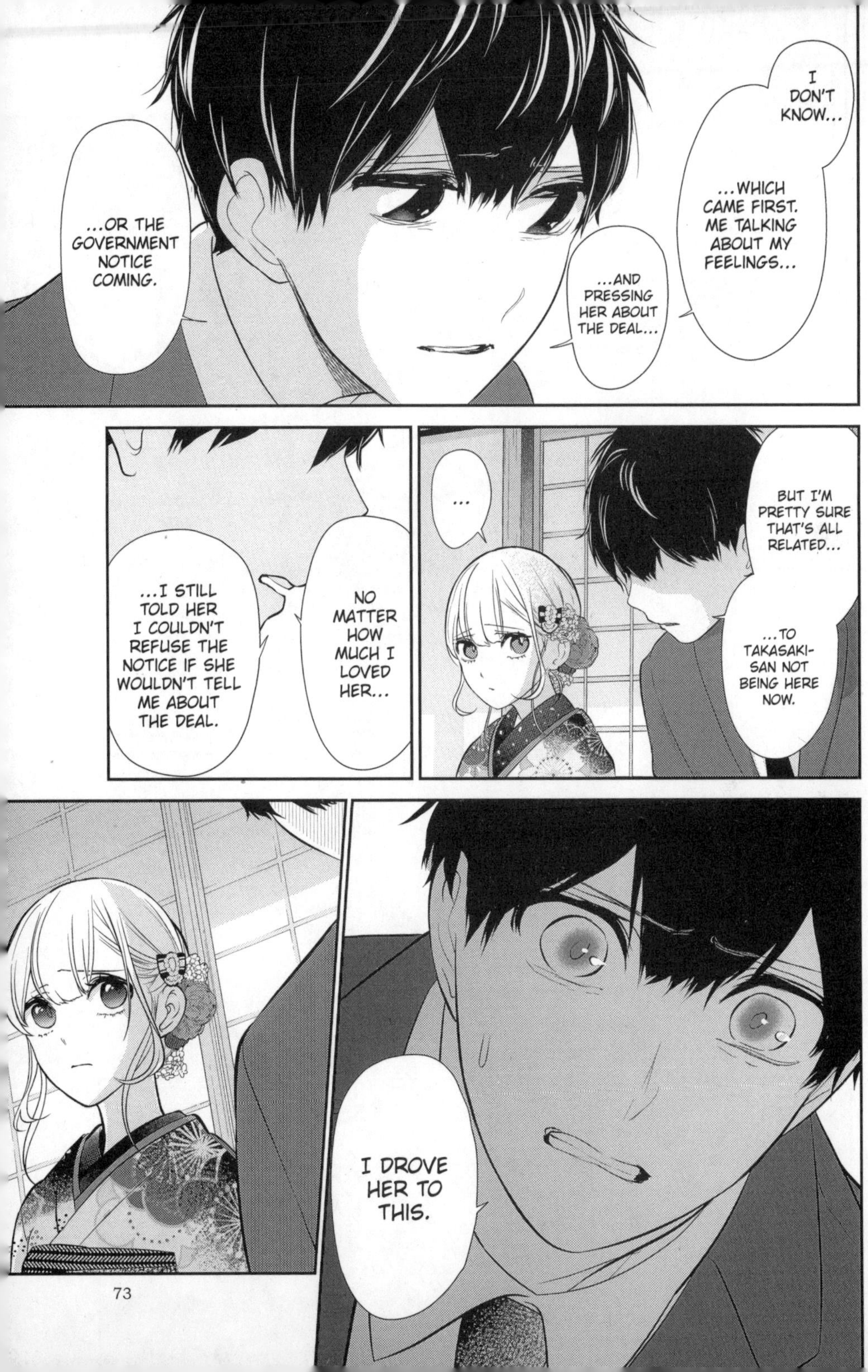
I DON'T KNOW…
…WHICH CAME FIRST. ME TALKING ABOUT MY FEELINGS…
…AND PRESSING HER ABOUT THE DEAL…
…OR THE GOVERNMENT NOTICE COMING.
BUT I'M PRETTY SURE THAT'S ALL RELATED…
…TO TAKASAKI-SAN NOT BEING HERE NOW.
…
NO MATTER HOW MUCH I LOVED HER…
…I STILL TOLD HER I COULDN'T REFUSE THE NOTICE IF SHE WOULDN'T TELL ME ABOUT THE DEAL.
I DROVE HER TO THIS.

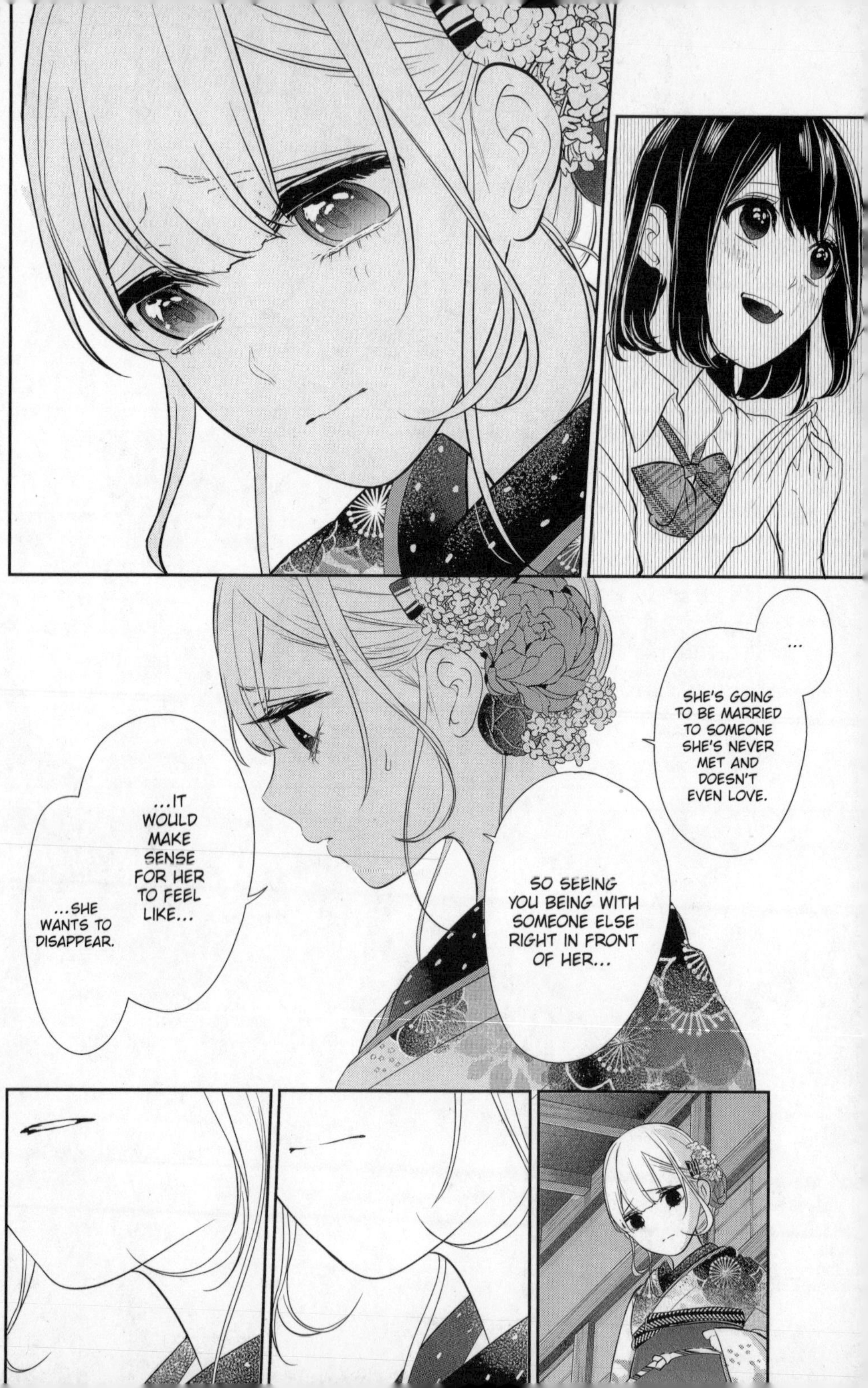
...
SHE'S GOING TO BE MARRIED TO SOMEONE SHE'S NEVER MET AND DOESN'T EVEN LOVE.
SO SEEING YOU BEING WITH SOMEONE ELSE RIGHT IN FRONT OF HER...
...IT WOULD MAKE SENSE FOR HER TO FEEL LIKE...
...SHE WANTS TO DISAPPEAR.

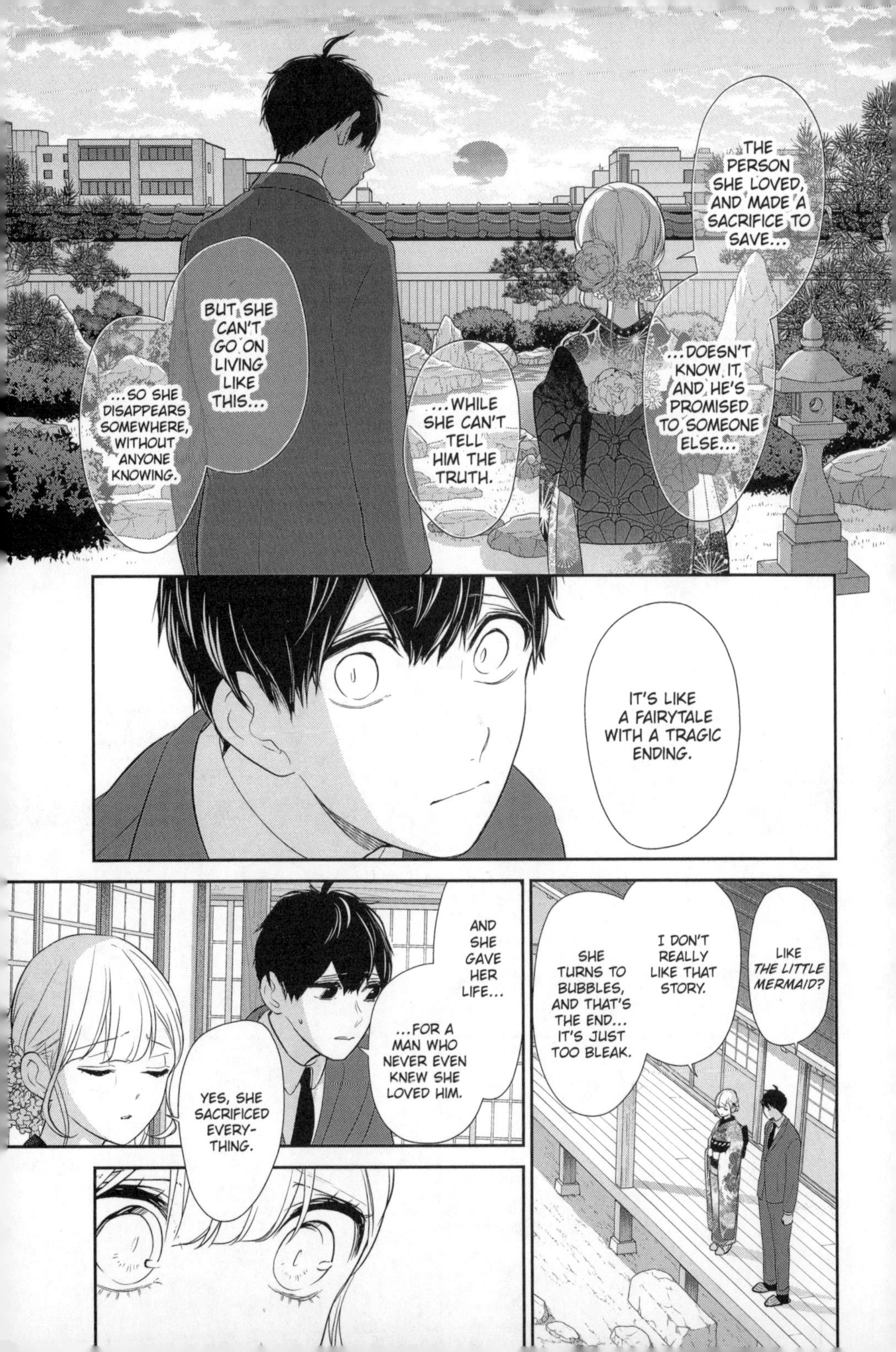
THE PERSON SHE LOVED, AND MADE A SACRIFICE TO SAVE...
...DOESN'T KNOW IT, AND HE'S PROMISED TO SOMEONE ELSE...
...WHILE SHE CAN'T TELL HIM THE TRUTH.
BUT SHE CAN'T GO ON LIVING LIKE THIS...
...SO SHE DISAPPEARS SOMEWHERE, WITHOUT ANYONE KNOWING.
IT'S LIKE A FAIRYTALE WITH A TRAGIC ENDING.
LIKE *THE LITTLE MERMAID?*
I DON'T REALLY LIKE THAT STORY.
SHE TURNS TO BUBBLES, AND THAT'S THE END... IT'S JUST TOO BLEAK.
AND SHE GAVE HER LIFE...
...FOR A MAN WHO NEVER EVEN KNEW SHE LOVED HIM.
YES, SHE SACRIFICED EVERY-THING.

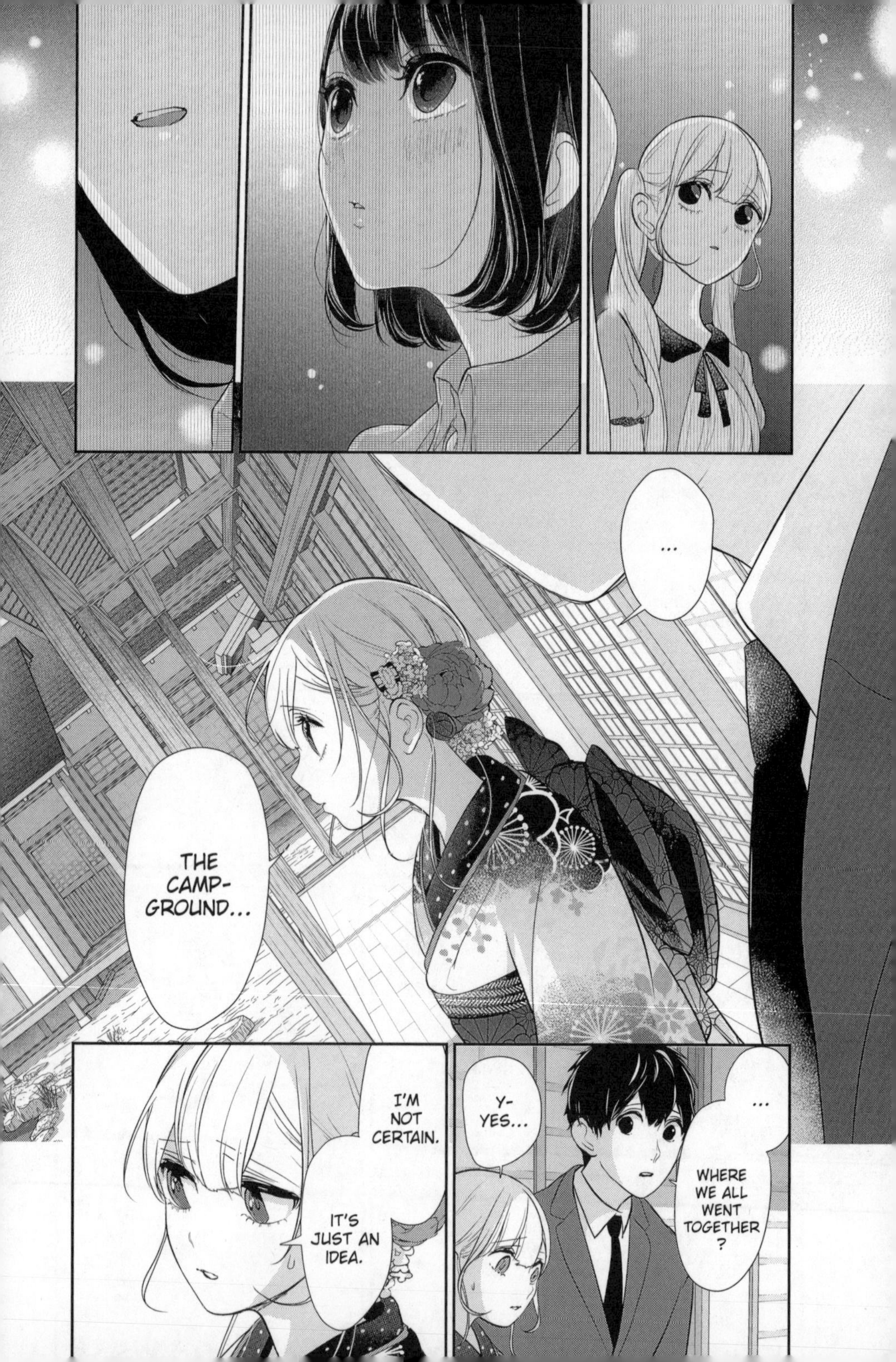
...
THE CAMP-GROUND...
...
WHERE WE ALL WENT TOGETHER?
Y-YES...
I'M NOT CERTAIN.
IT'S JUST AN IDEA.

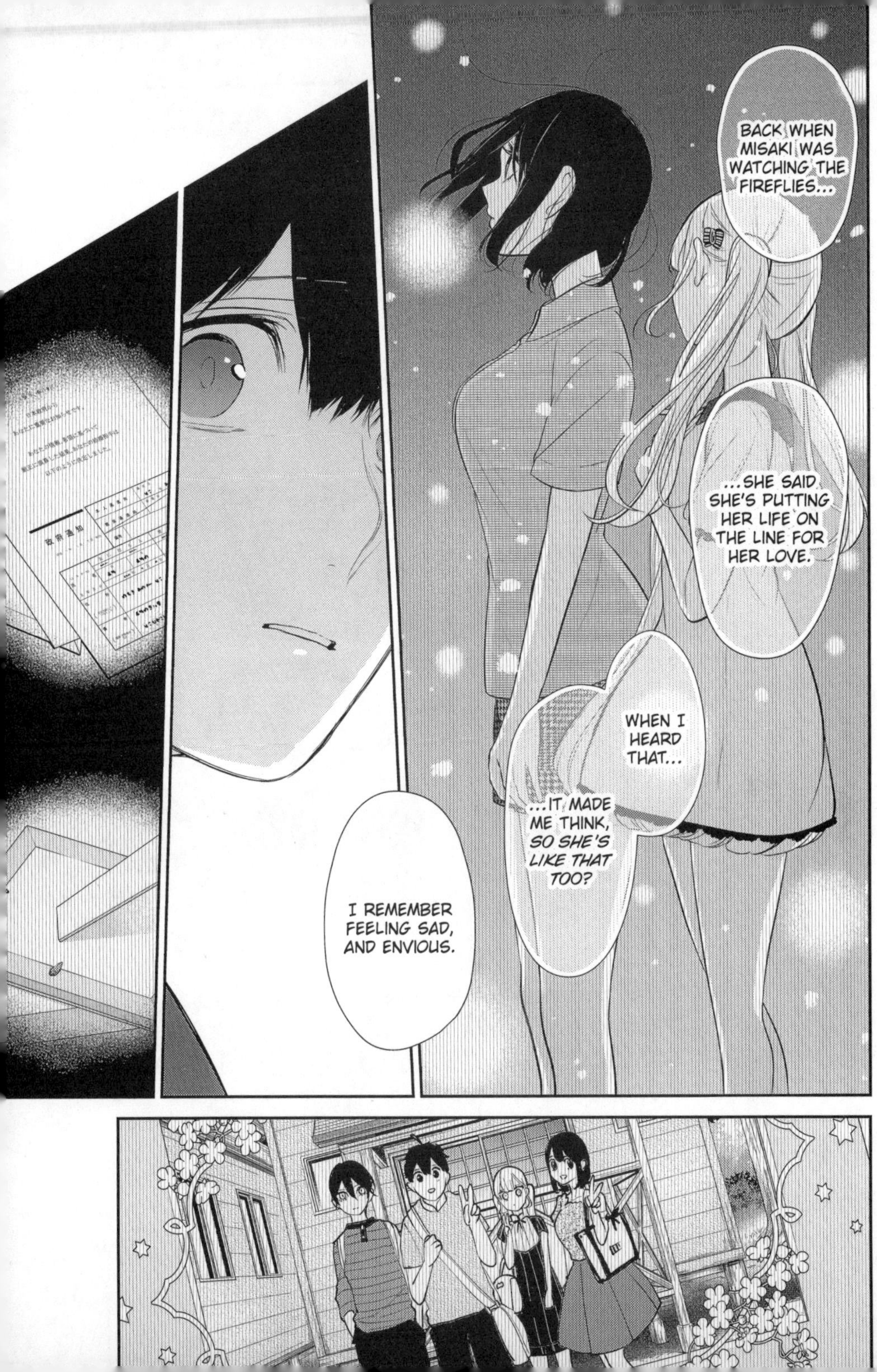
BACK WHEN MISAKI WAS WATCHING THE FIREFLIES...
...SHE SAID SHE'S PUTTING HER LIFE ON THE LINE FOR HER LOVE.
WHEN I HEARD THAT...
...IT MADE ME THINK, SO SHE'S LIKE THAT TOO?
I REMEMBER FEELING SAD, AND ENVIOUS.

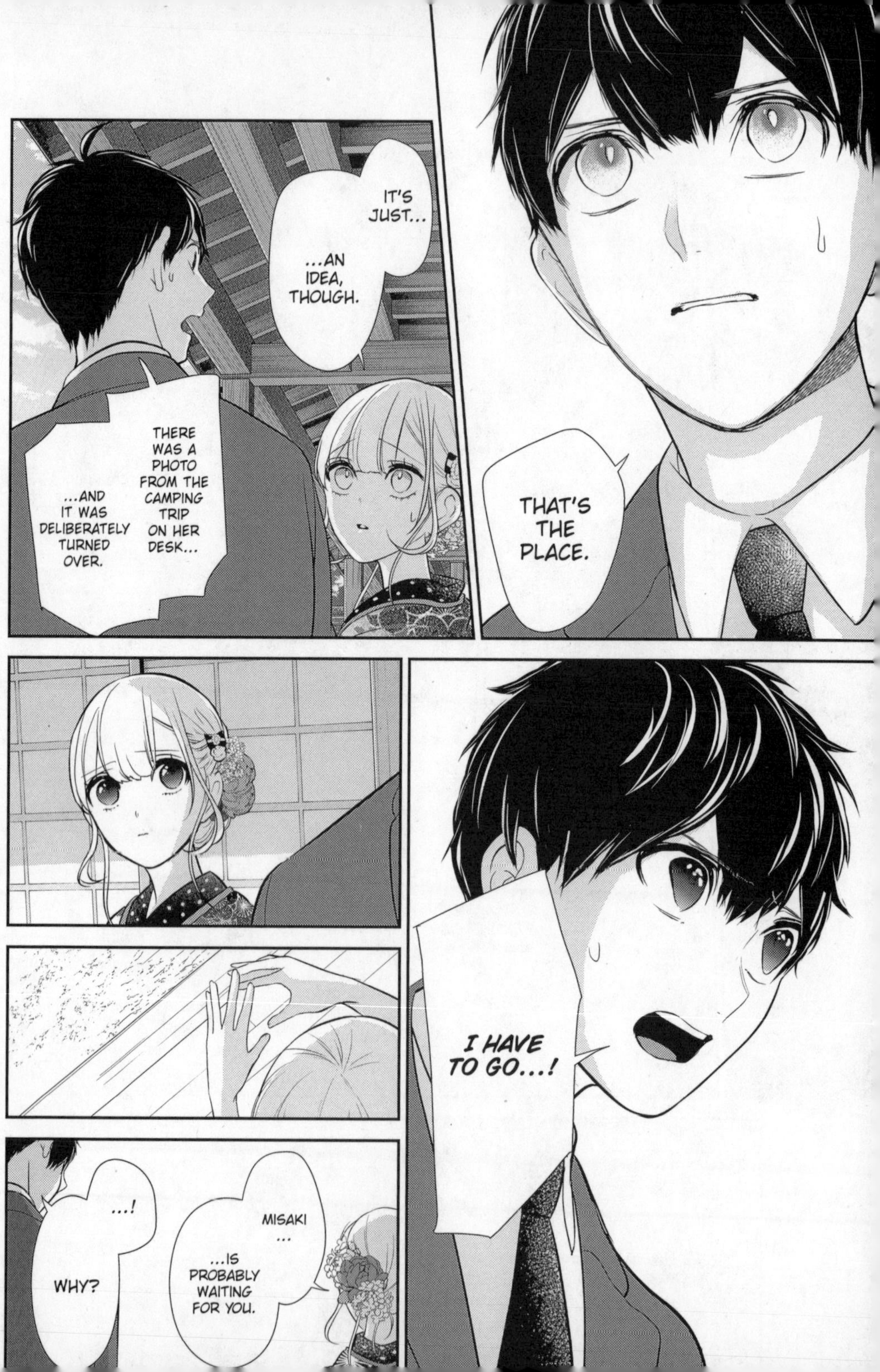
THAT'S THE PLACE.
IT'S JUST...
...AN IDEA, THOUGH.
THERE WAS A PHOTO FROM THE CAMPING TRIP ON HER DESK...
...AND IT WAS DELIBERATELY TURNED OVER.
I HAVE TO GO...!
MISAKI ...
...IS PROBABLY WAITING FOR YOU.
...!
WHY?

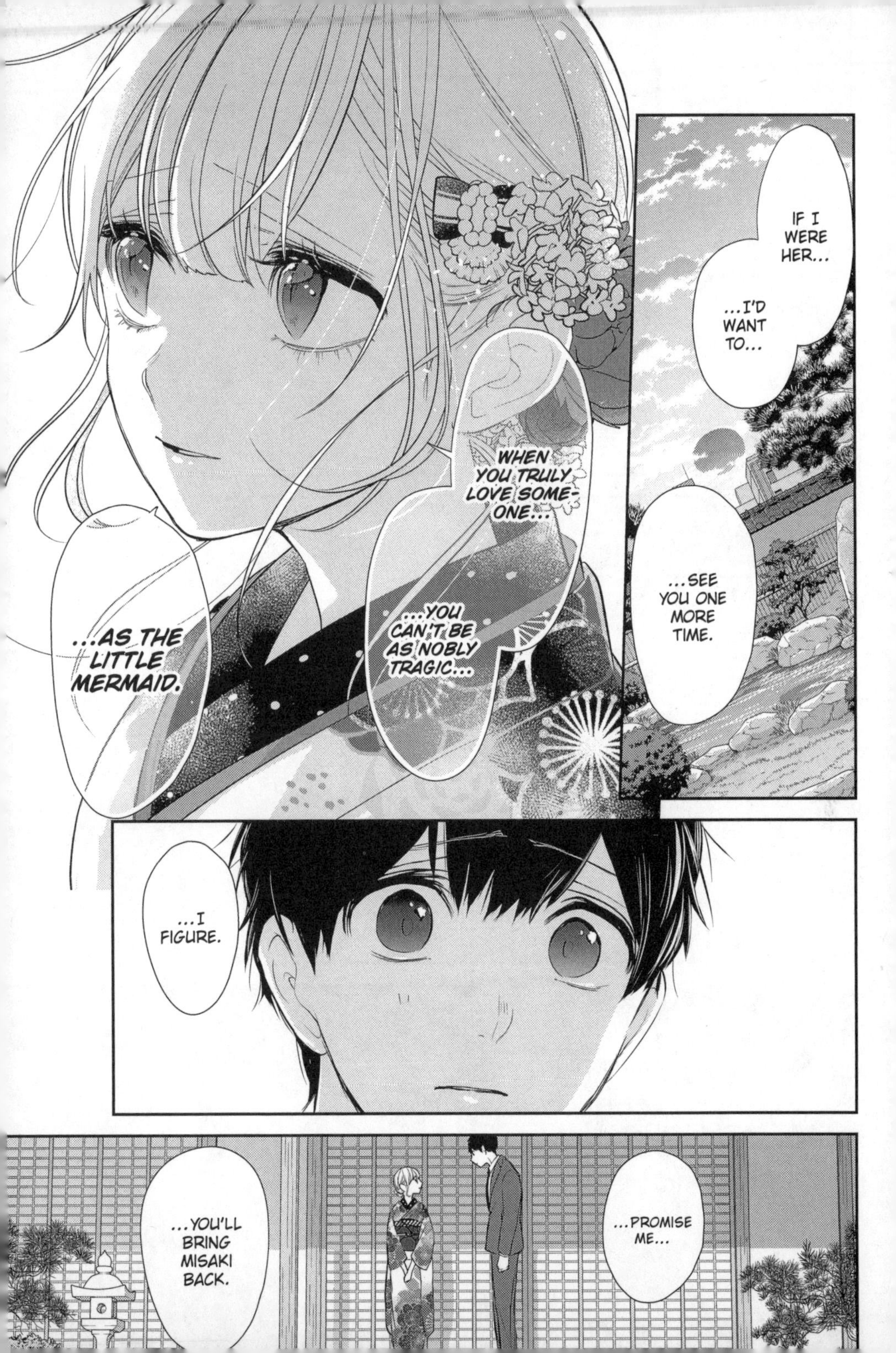
IF I WERE HER...
...I'D WANT TO...
...SEE YOU ONE MORE TIME.
WHEN YOU TRULY LOVE SOME-ONE...
...YOU CAN'T BE AS NOBLY TRAGIC...
...AS THE LITTLE MERMAID.
...I FIGURE.
...PROMISE ME...
...YOU'LL BRING MISAKI BACK.

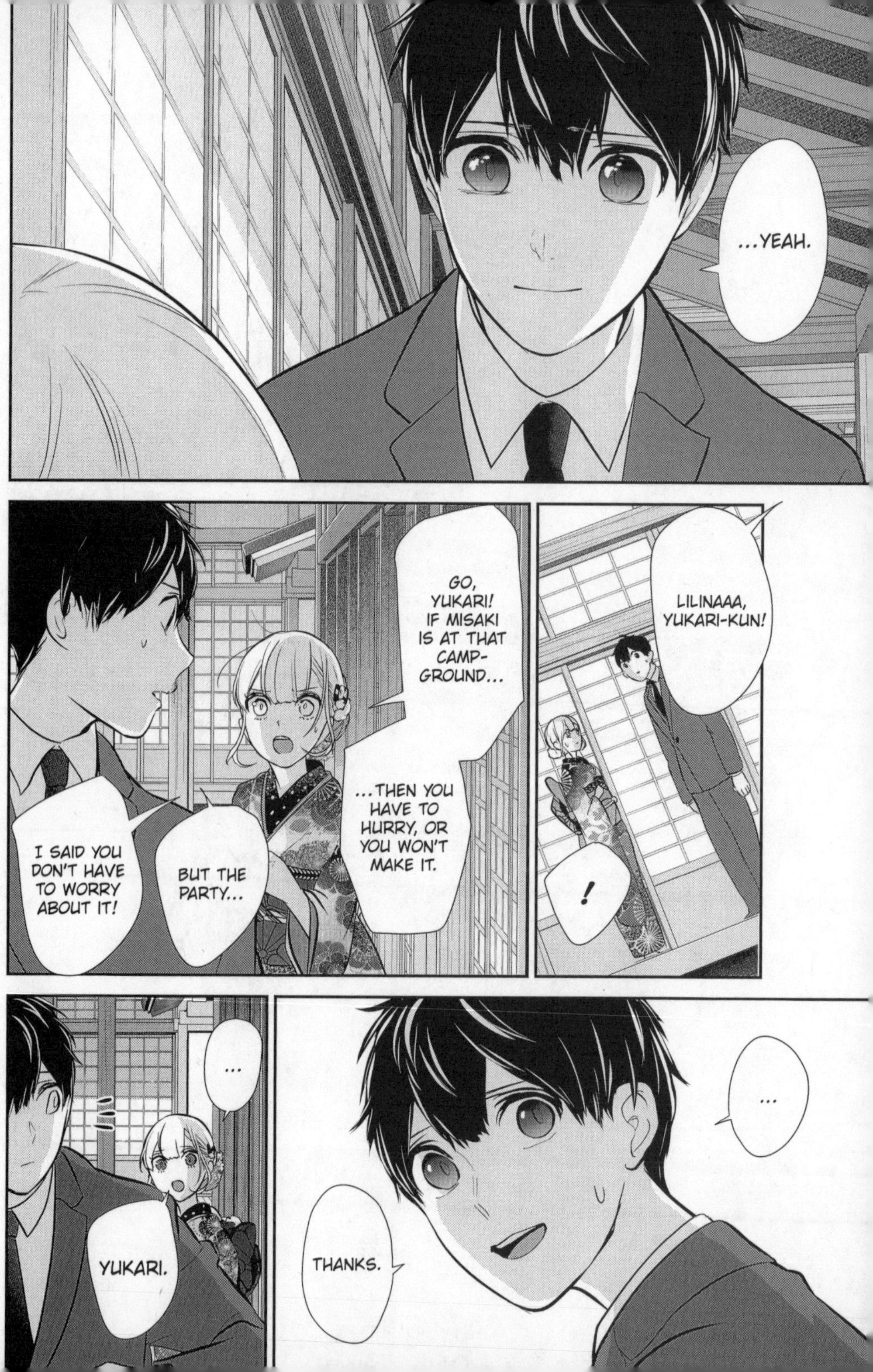
...YEAH.
LILINAAA, YUKARI-KUN!
!
GO, YUKARI! IF MISAKI IS AT THAT CAMP-GROUND...
...THEN YOU HAVE TO HURRY, OR YOU WON'T MAKE IT.
BUT THE PARTY...
I SAID YOU DON'T HAVE TO WORRY ABOUT IT!
...
THANKS.
...
YUKARI.

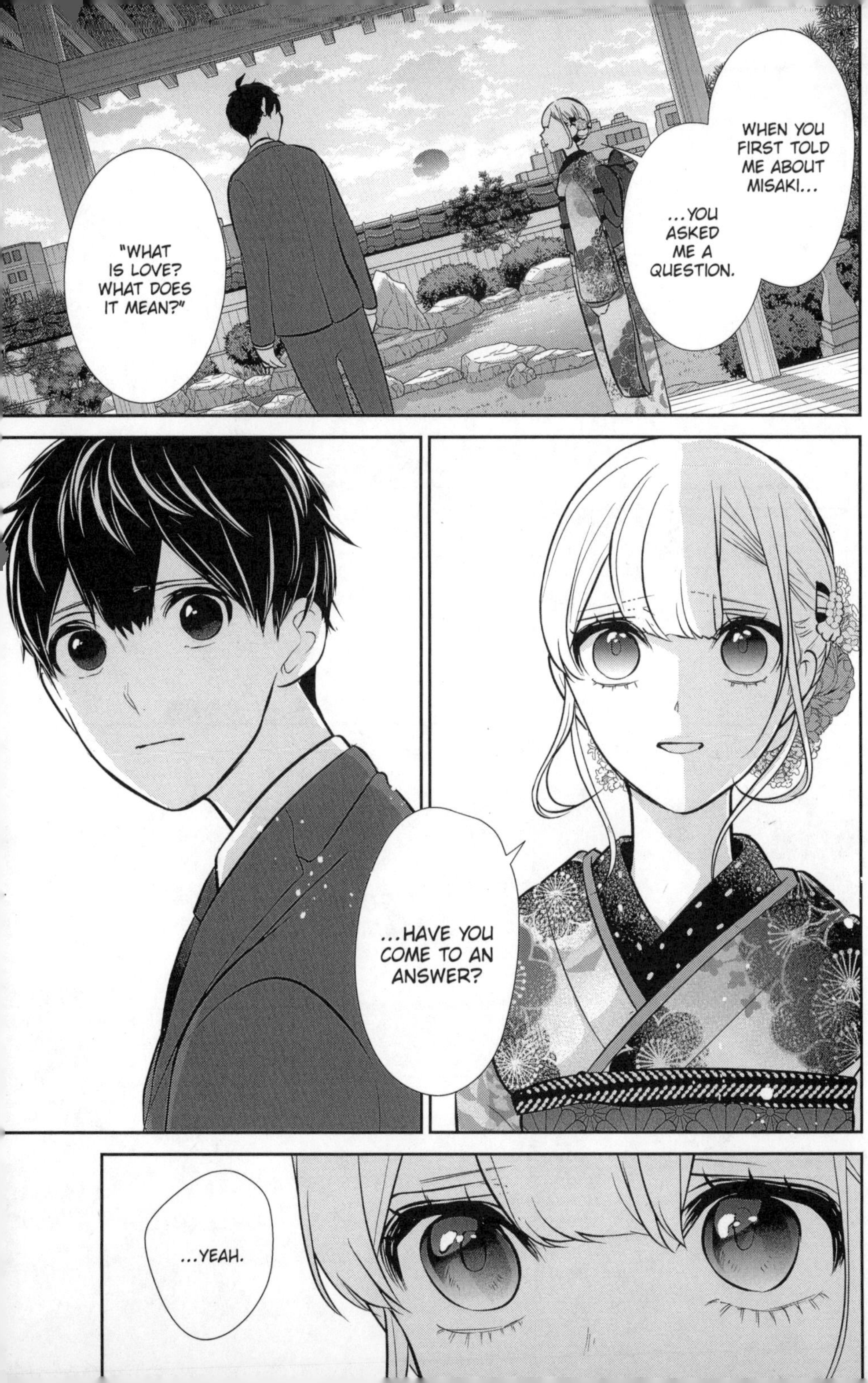
WHEN YOU FIRST TOLD ME ABOUT MISAKI...
...YOU ASKED ME A QUESTION.
"WHAT IS LOVE? WHAT DOES IT MEAN?"
...HAVE YOU COME TO AN ANSWER?
...YEAH.

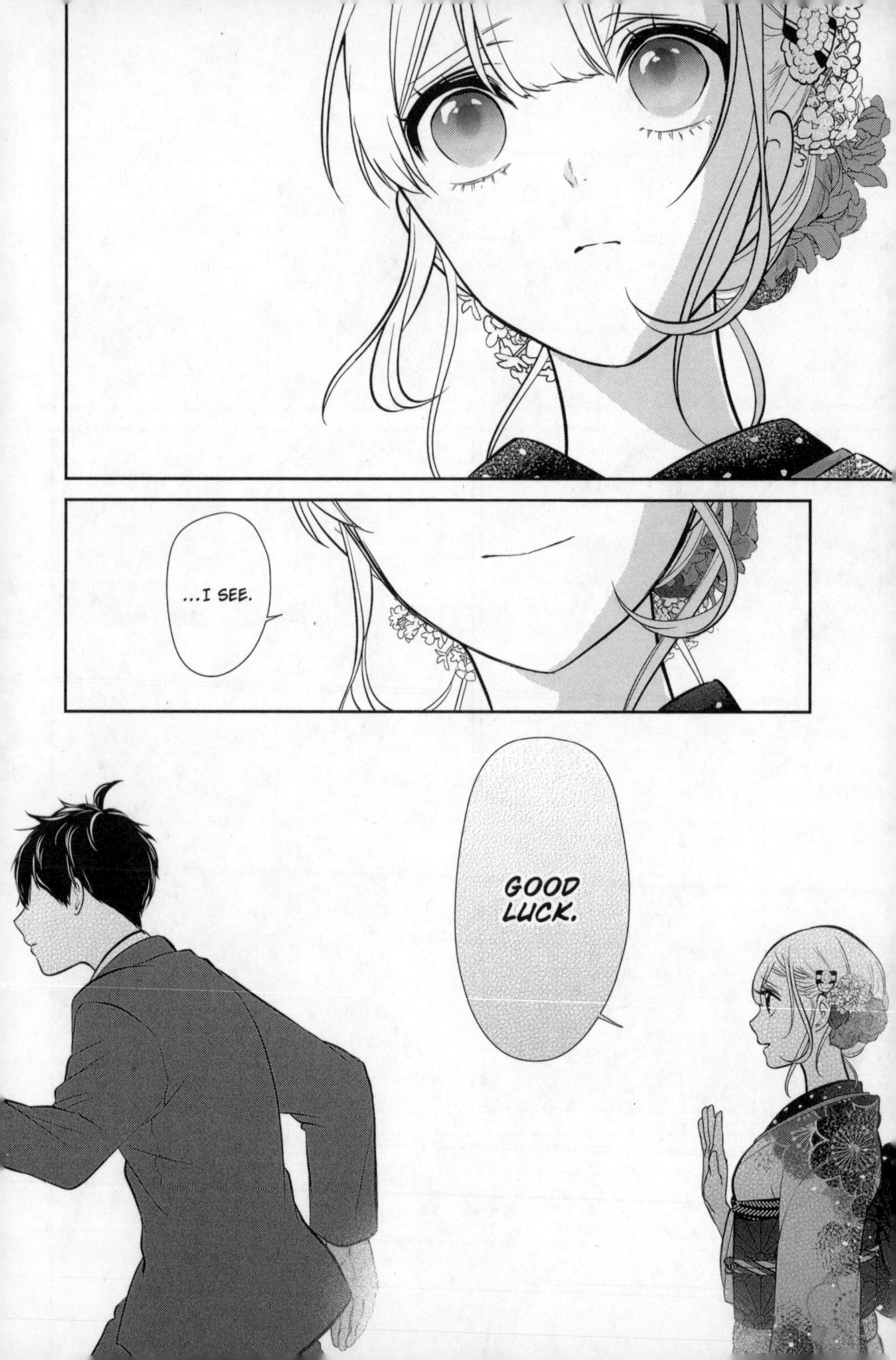
...I SEE.
GOOD LUCK.

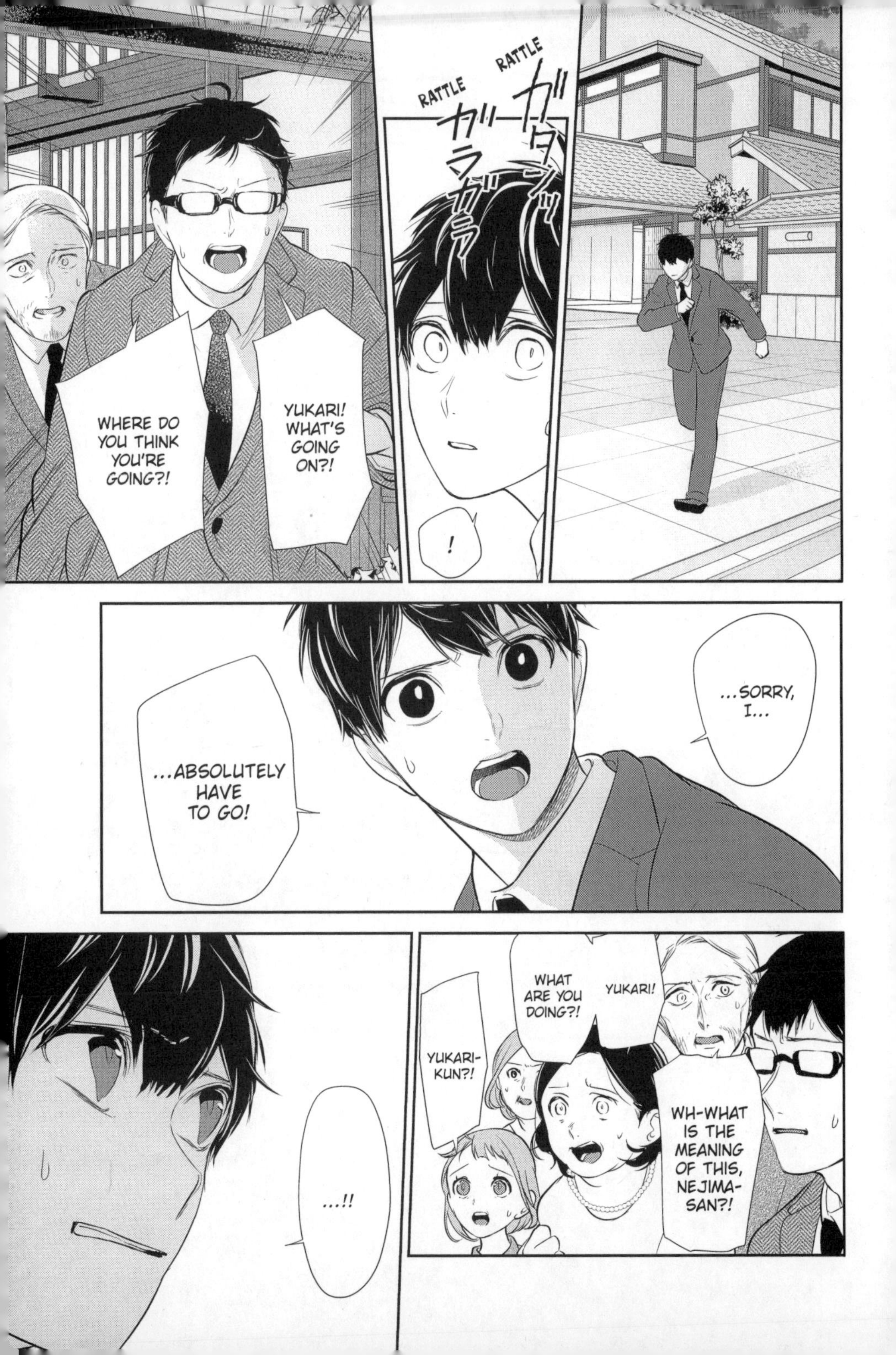
RATTLE
RATTLE
ガラガラ
!
YUKARI! WHAT'S GOING ON?!
WHERE DO YOU THINK YOU'RE GOING?!
...SORRY, I...
...ABSOLUTELY HAVE TO GO!
YUKARI!
WHAT ARE YOU DOING?!
YUKARI-KUN?!
WH-WHAT IS THE MEANING OF THIS, NEJIMA-SAN?!
...!!

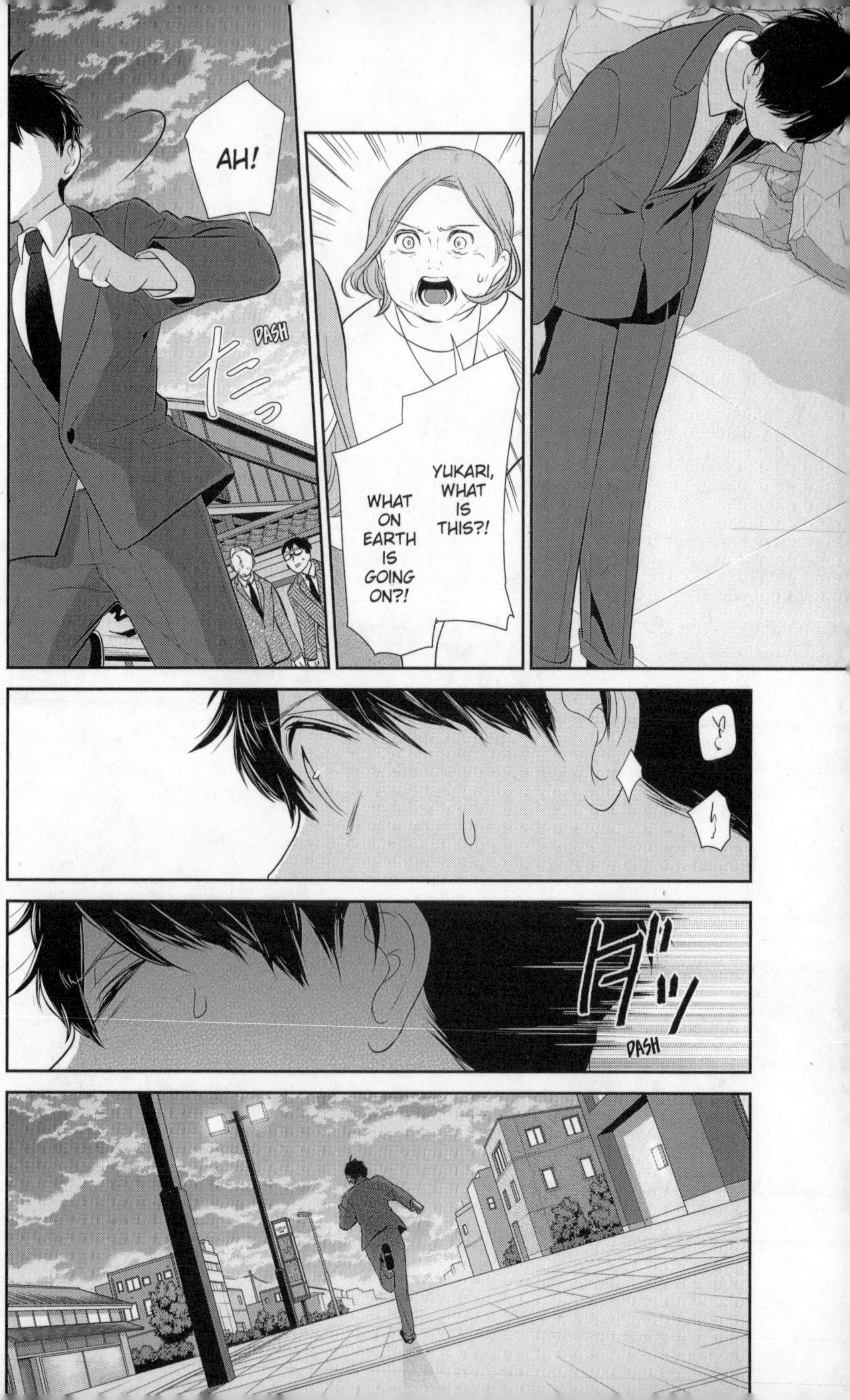
YUKARI, WHAT IS THIS?!
WHAT ON EARTH IS GOING ON?!
AH!
DASH
DASH

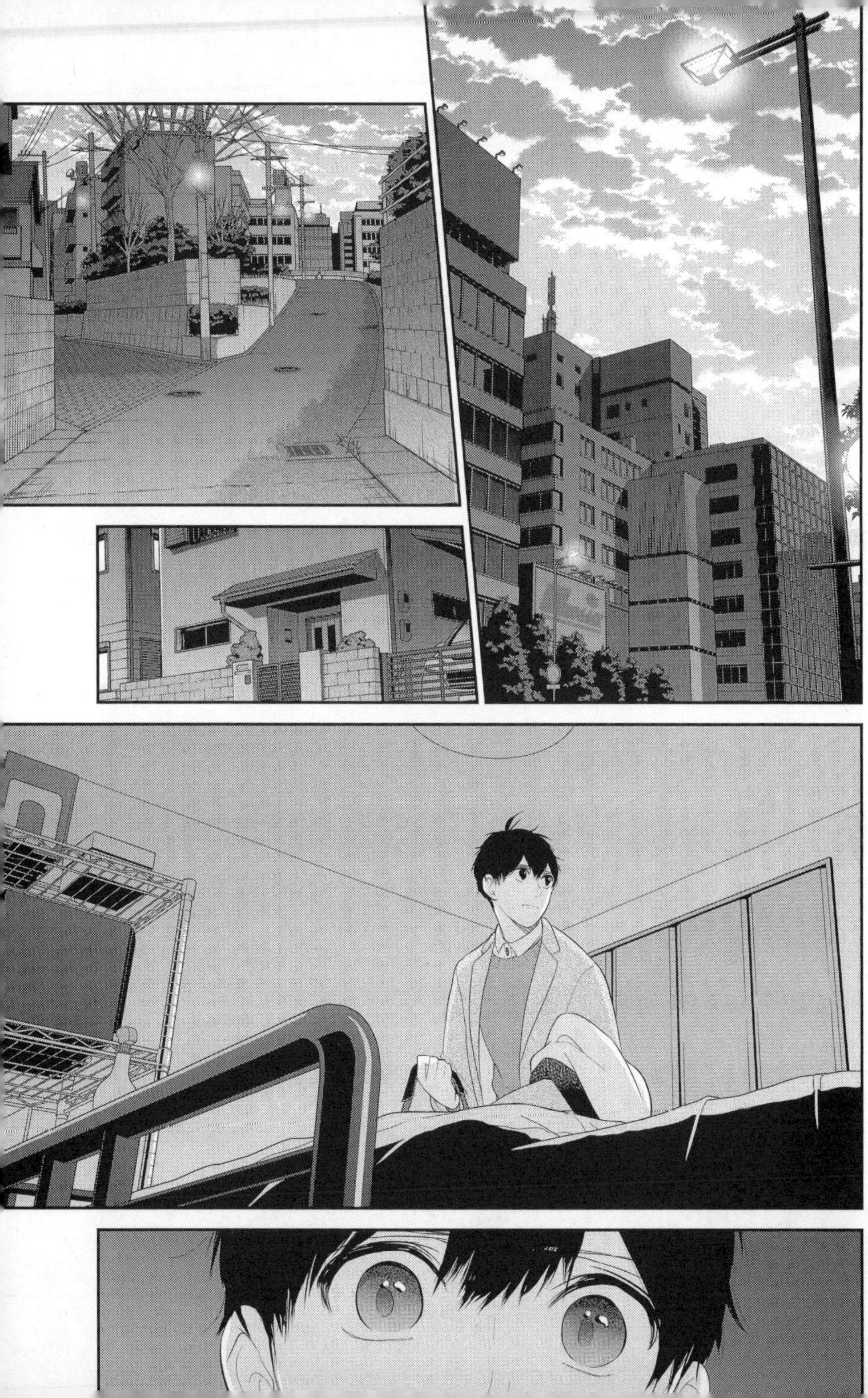

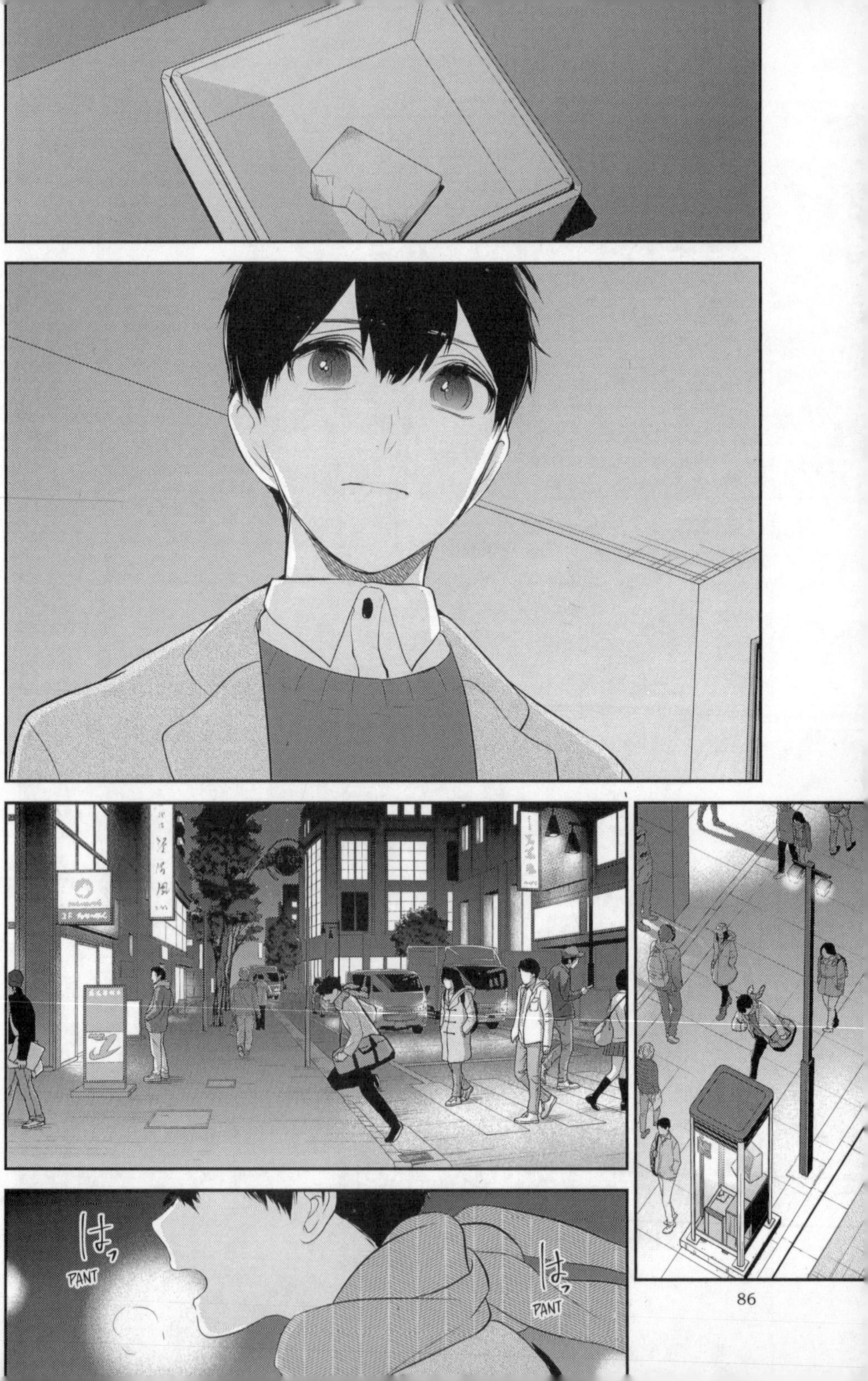
はっ
PANT
はっ
PANT

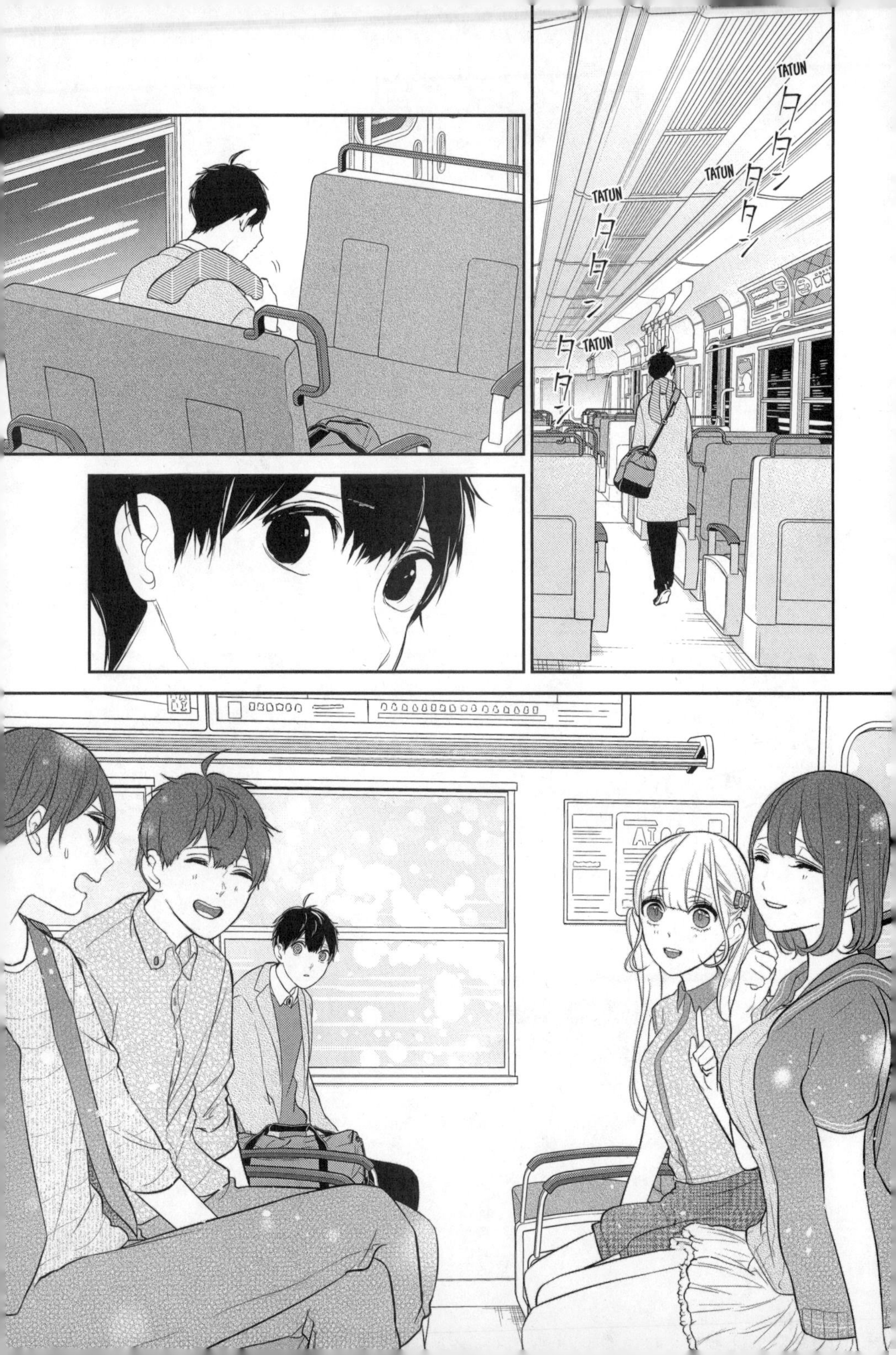
TATUN
タタン
TATUN
タタン
TATUN
タタン
TATUN
タタン

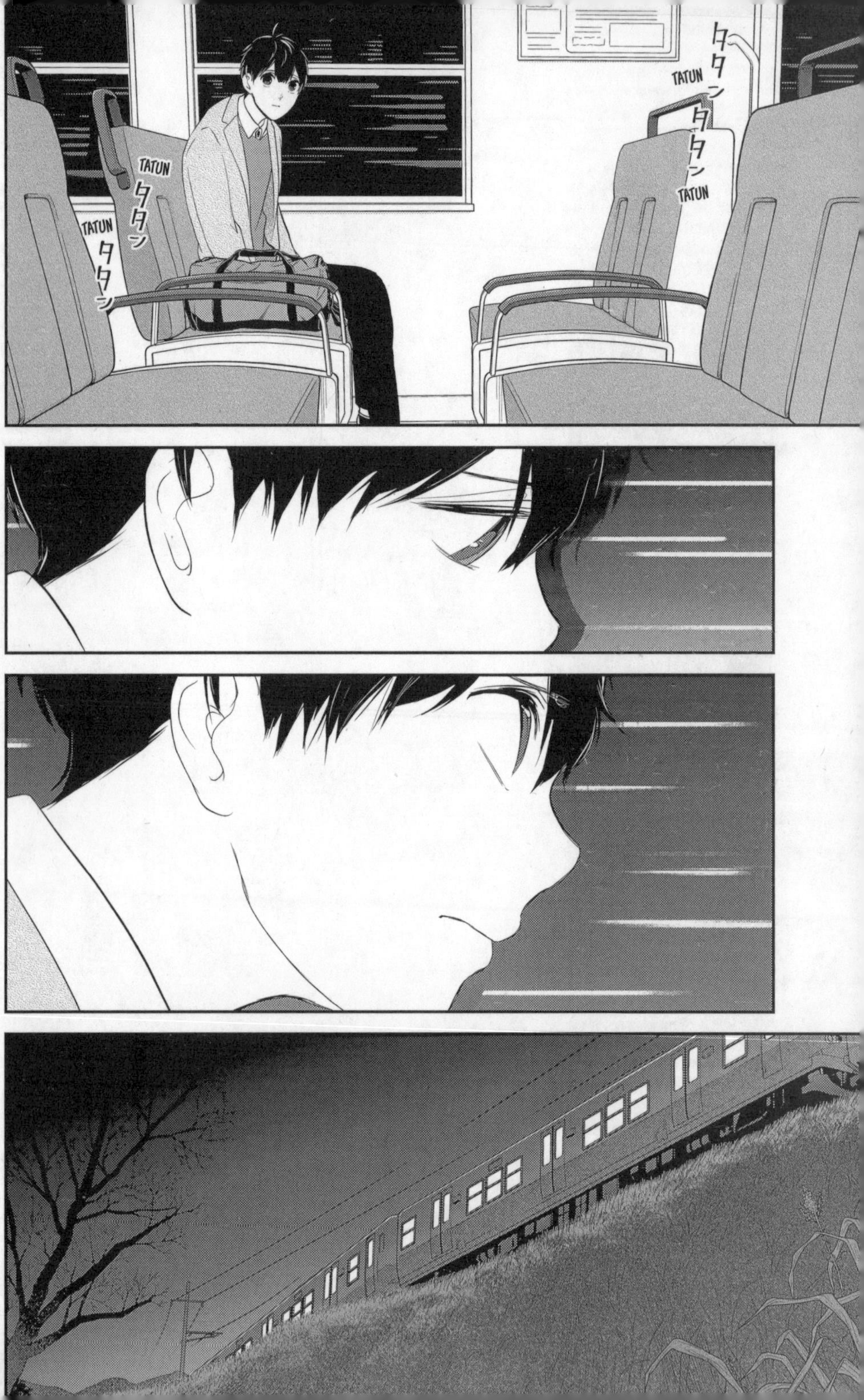

タタン
TATUN
タタン
TATUN
TATUN
タタン
TATUN
タタン

Love&Lies

Love & Lies

Chapter 48: Staking My Life

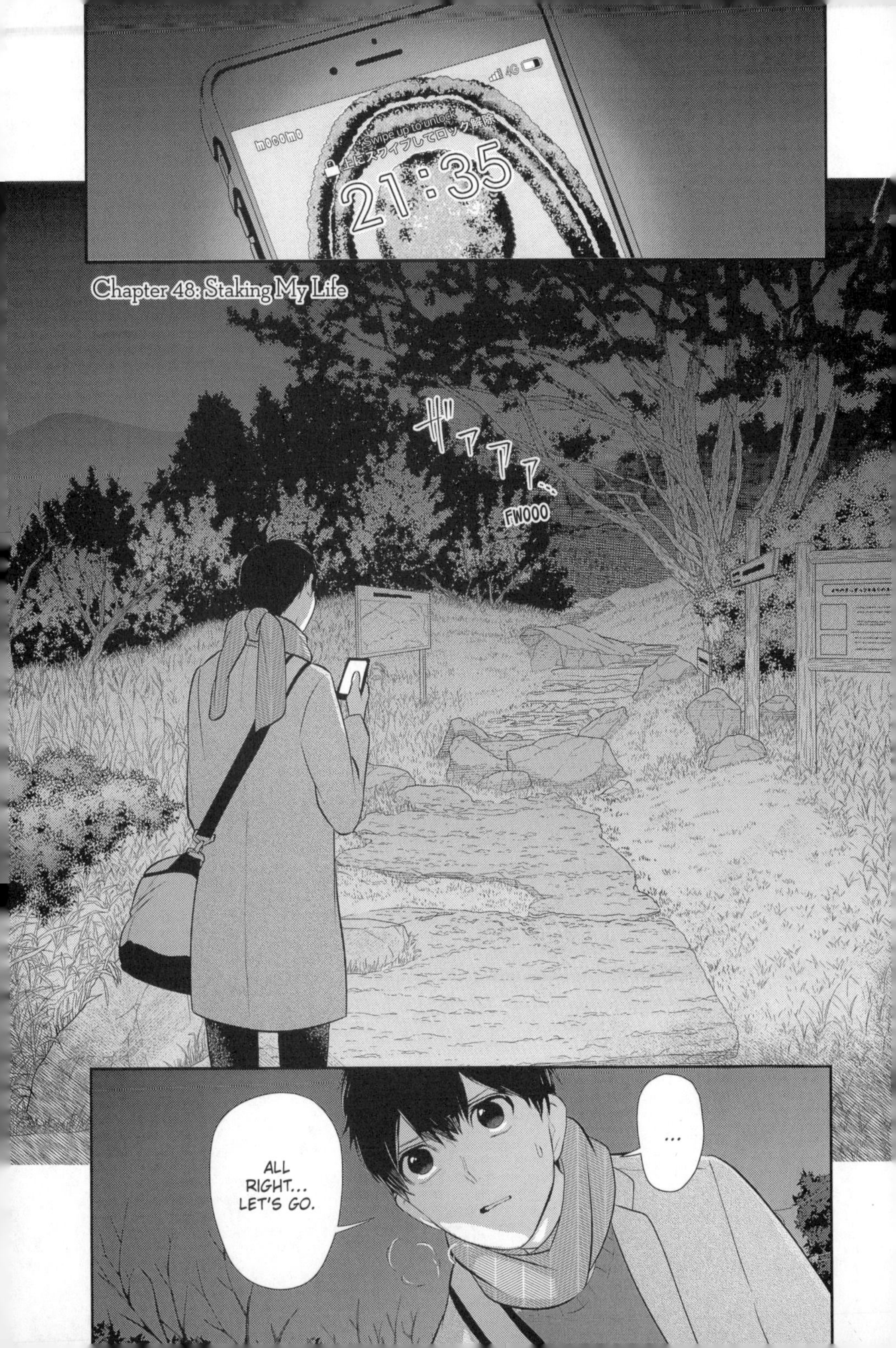
mocomo
4G
*Swipe up to unlock
上にスワイプしてロック解除
21:35
ザァァァ…
FWOOO
...
ALL RIGHT... LET'S GO.

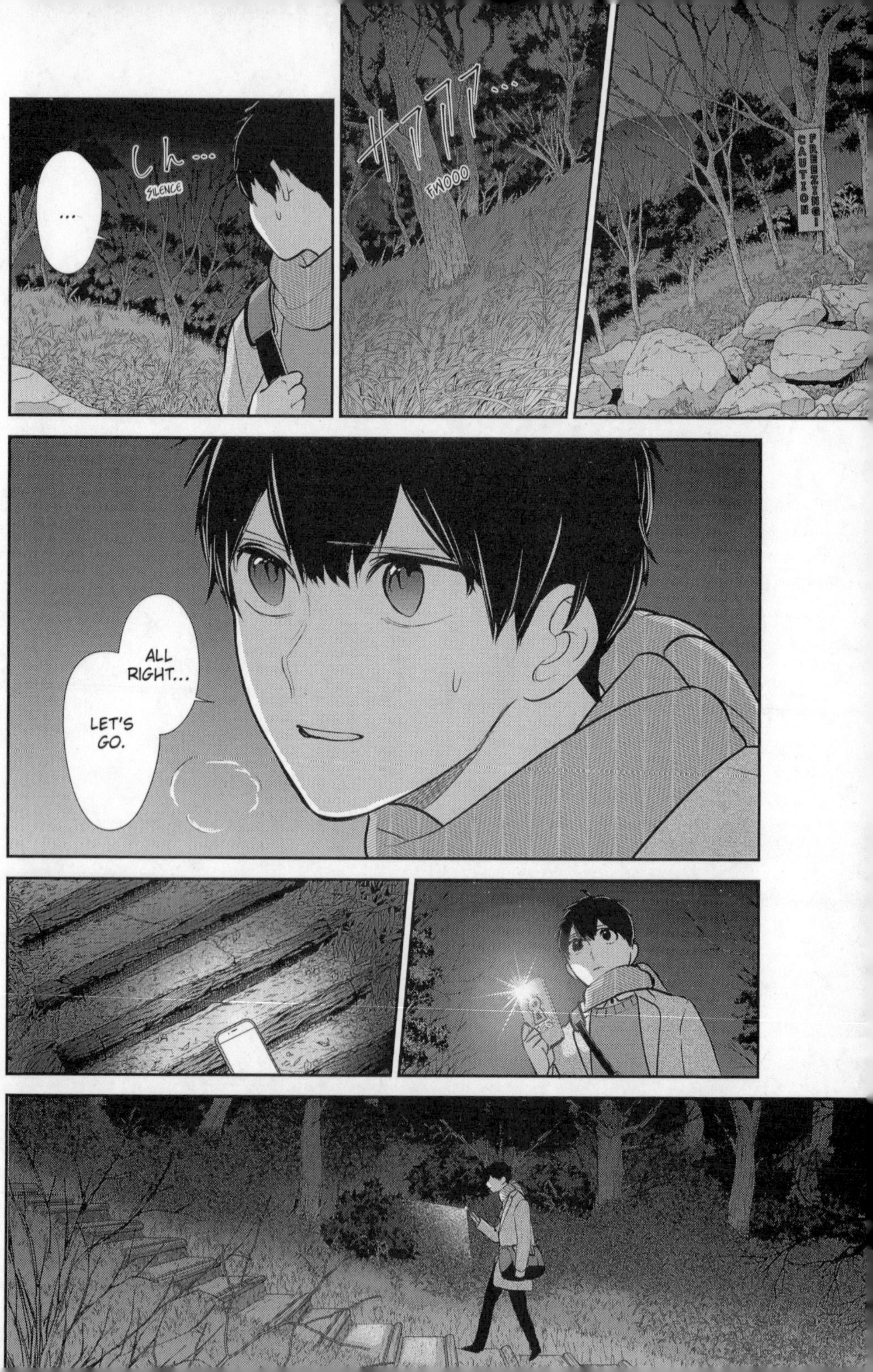
CAUTION
FREEZING!
サァァァ…
FWOOO
しん…
SILENCE
…
ALL RIGHT…
LET'S GO.

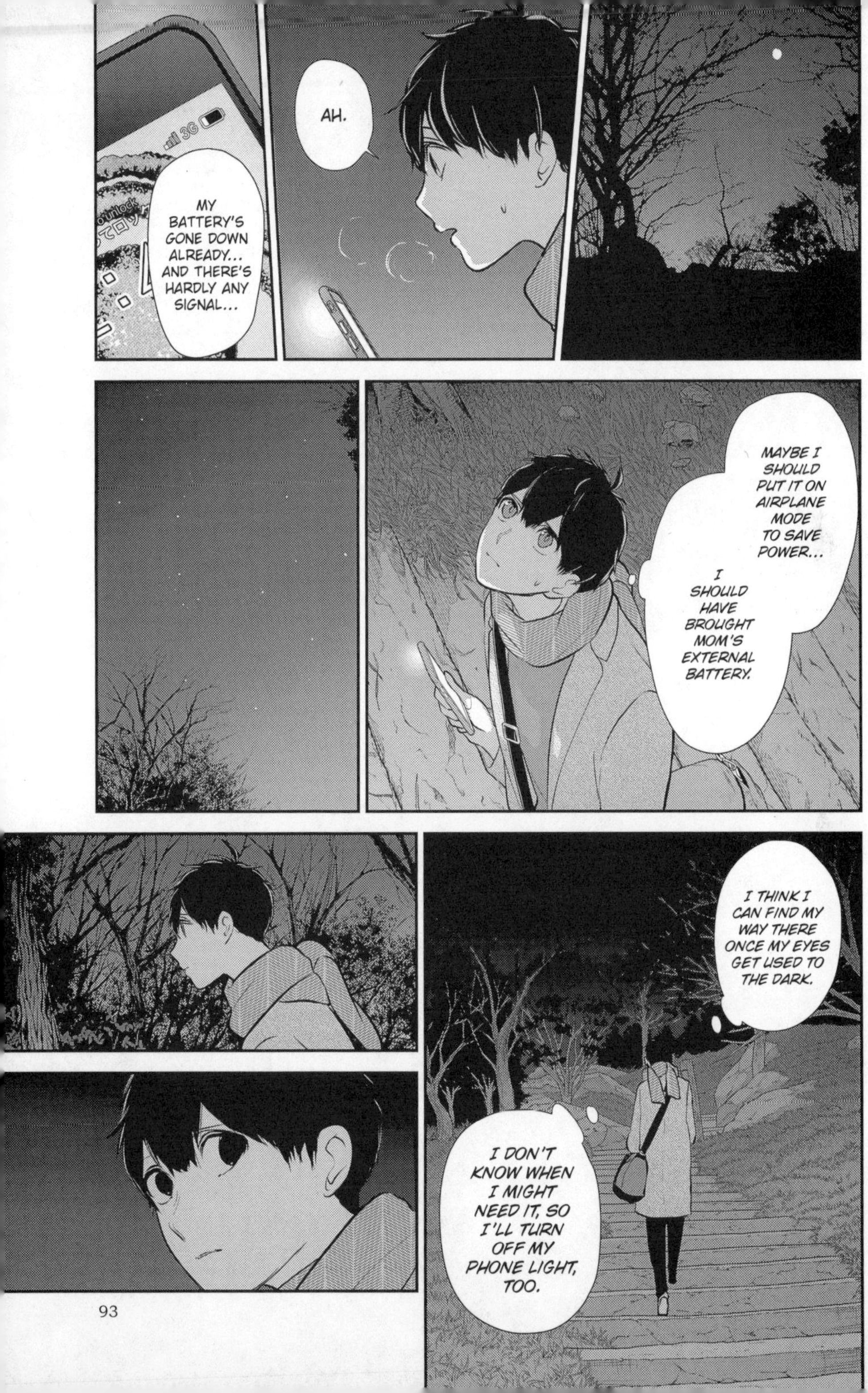
AH.
MY BATTERY'S GONE DOWN ALREADY... AND THERE'S HARDLY ANY SIGNAL...
MAYBE I SHOULD PUT IT ON AIRPLANE MODE TO SAVE POWER...
I SHOULD HAVE BROUGHT MOM'S EXTERNAL BATTERY.
I THINK I CAN FIND MY WAY THERE ONCE MY EYES GET USED TO THE DARK.
I DON'T KNOW WHEN I MIGHT NEED IT, SO I'LL TURN OFF MY PHONE LIGHT, TOO.

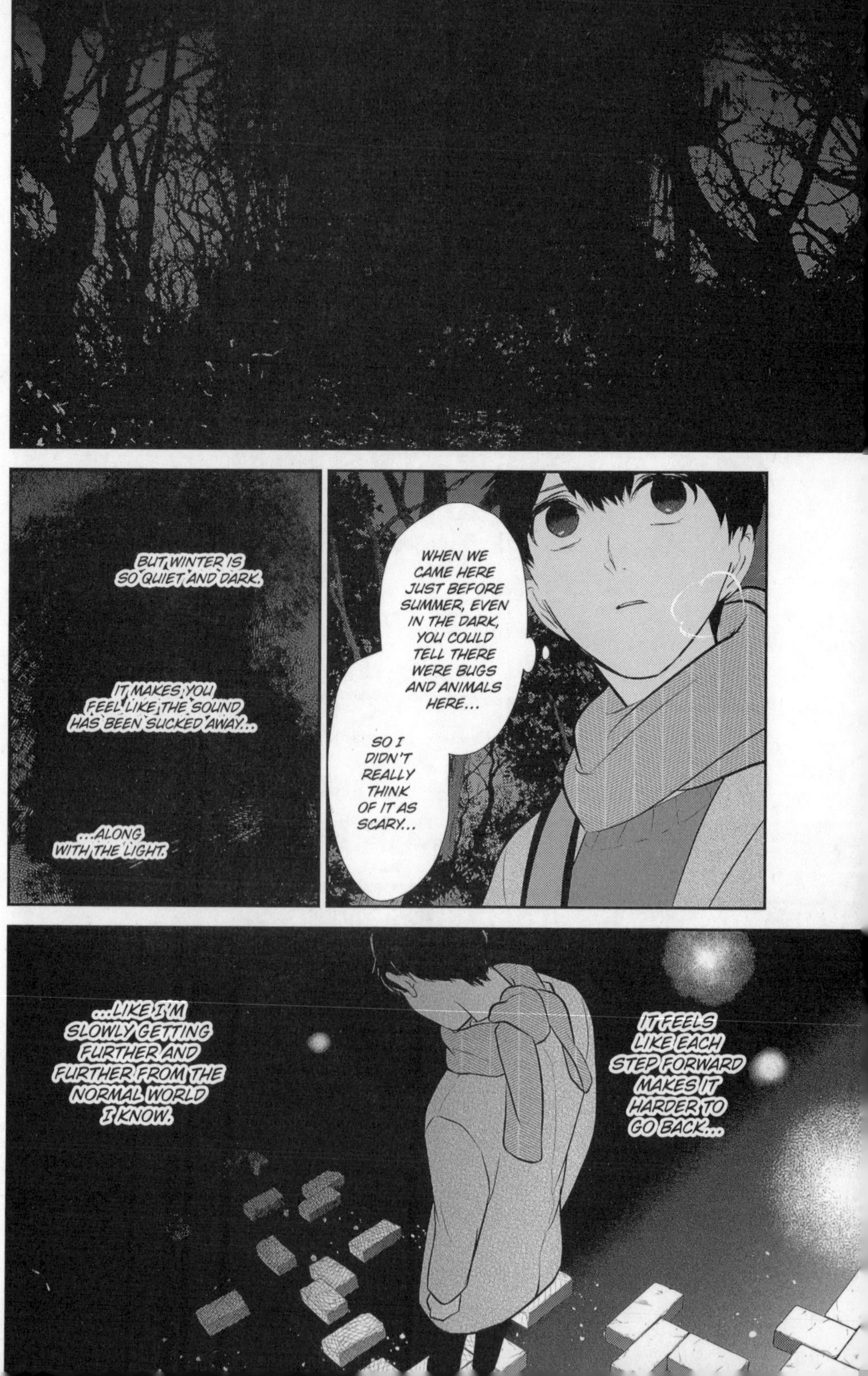
WHEN WE CAME HERE JUST BEFORE SUMMER, EVEN IN THE DARK, YOU COULD TELL THERE WERE BUGS AND ANIMALS HERE...
SO I DIDN'T REALLY THINK OF IT AS SCARY...
BUT WINTER IS SO QUIET AND DARK.
IT MAKES YOU FEEL LIKE THE SOUND HAS BEEN SUCKED AWAY...
...ALONG WITH THE LIGHT.
IT FEELS LIKE EACH STEP FORWARD MAKES IT HARDER TO GO BACK...
...LIKE I'M SLOWLY GETTING FURTHER AND FURTHER FROM THE NORMAL WORLD I KNOW.

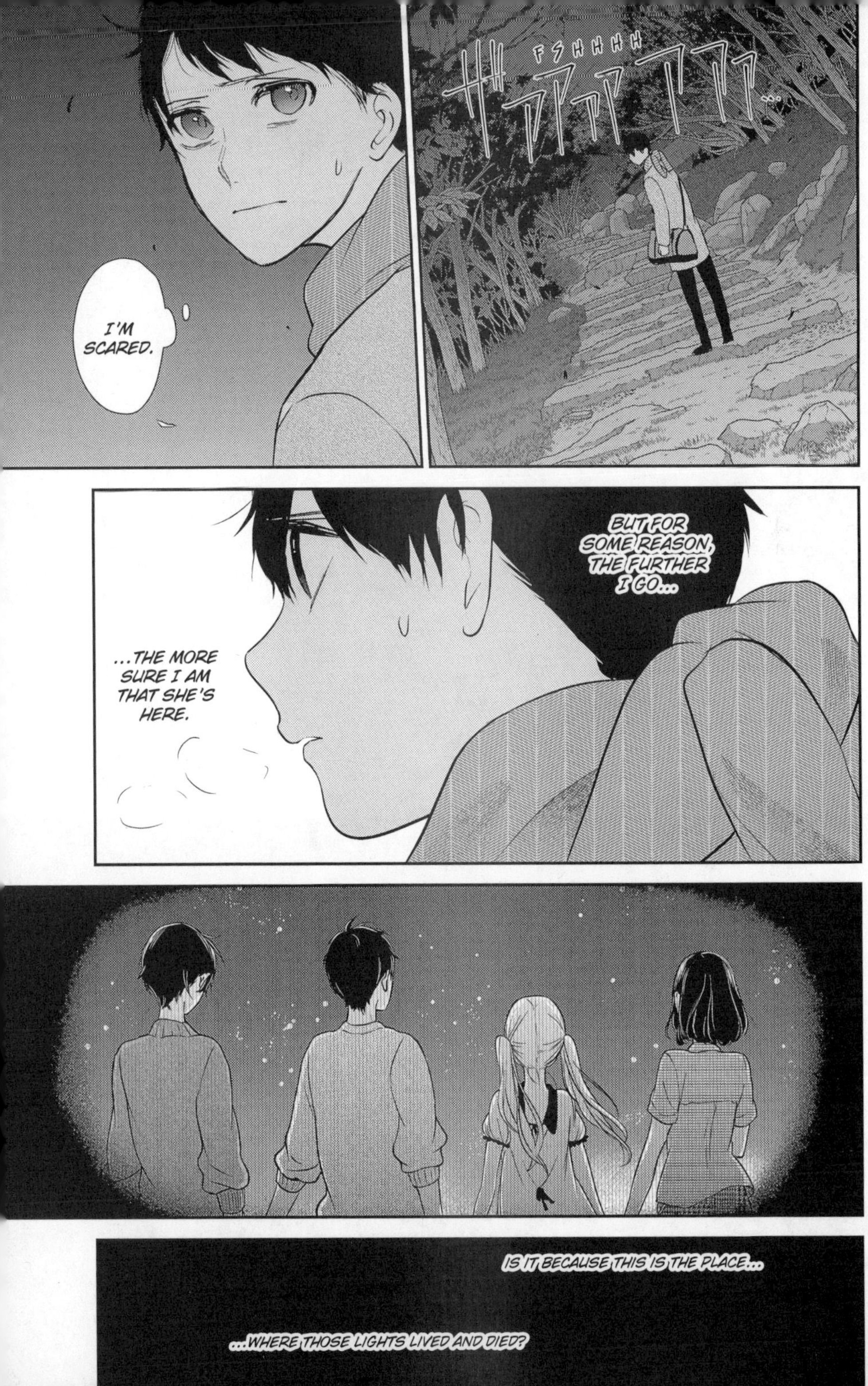
FSHHHH
I'M SCARED.
BUT FOR SOME REASON, THE FURTHER I GO...
...THE MORE SURE I AM THAT SHE'S HERE.
IS IT BECAUSE THIS IS THE PLACE...
...WHERE THOSE LIGHTS LIVED AND DIED?

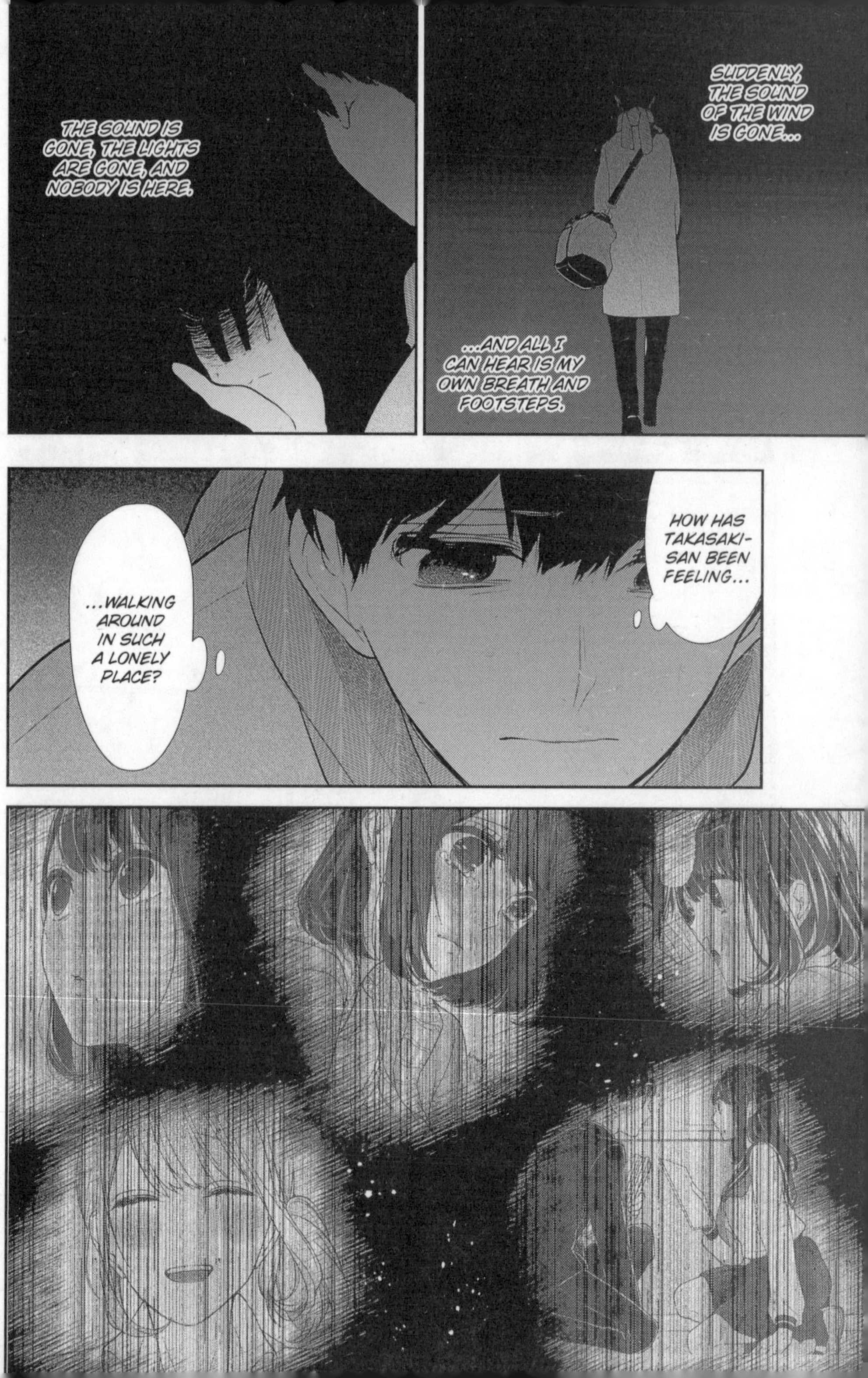
SUDDENLY, THE SOUND OF THE WIND IS GONE...
...AND ALL I CAN HEAR IS MY OWN BREATH AND FOOTSTEPS.
THE SOUND IS GONE, THE LIGHTS ARE GONE, AND NOBODY IS HERE.
HOW HAS TAKASAKI-SAN BEEN FEELING...
...WALKING AROUND IN SUCH A LONELY PLACE?

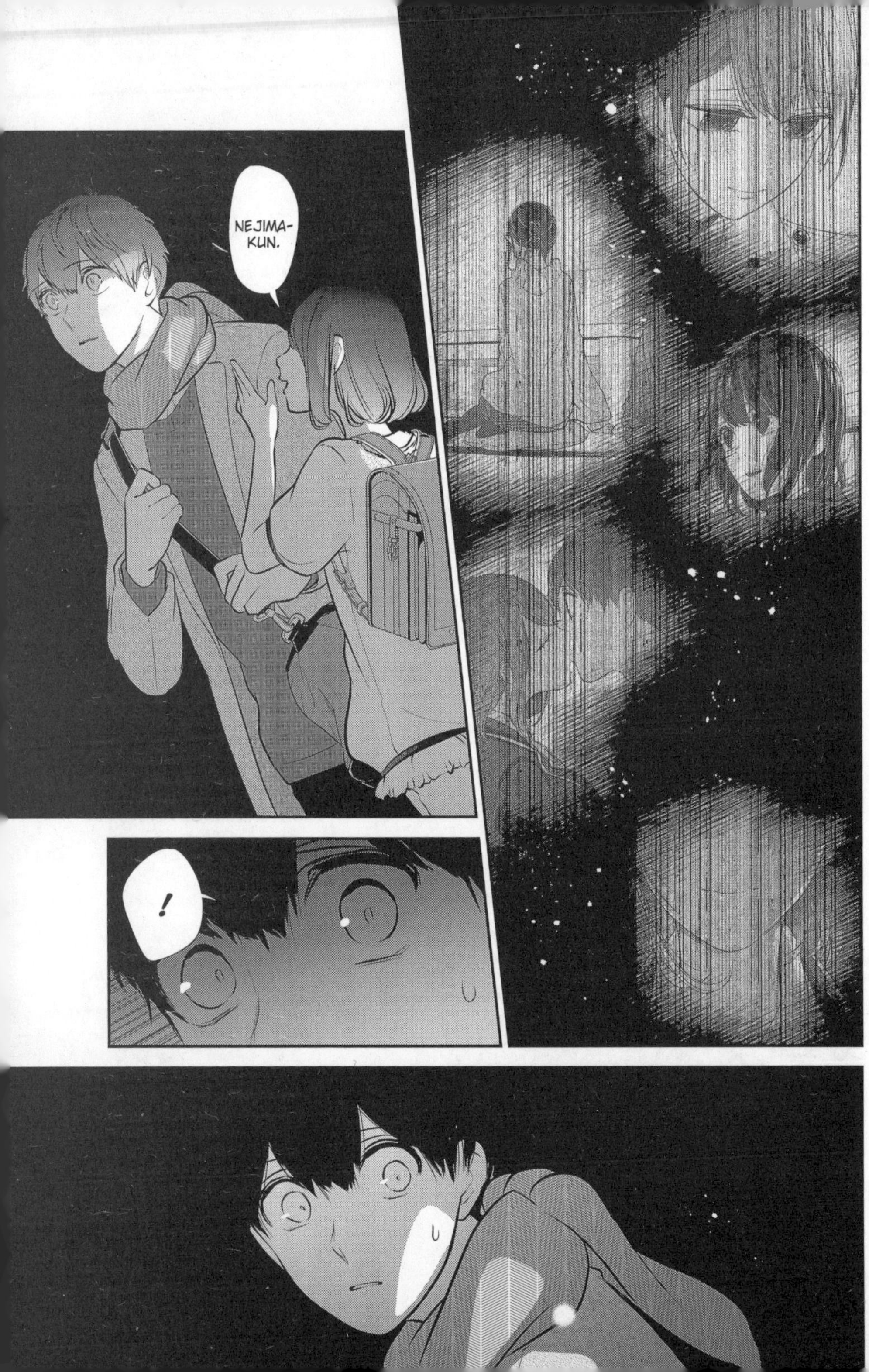
NEJIMA-KUN.
!

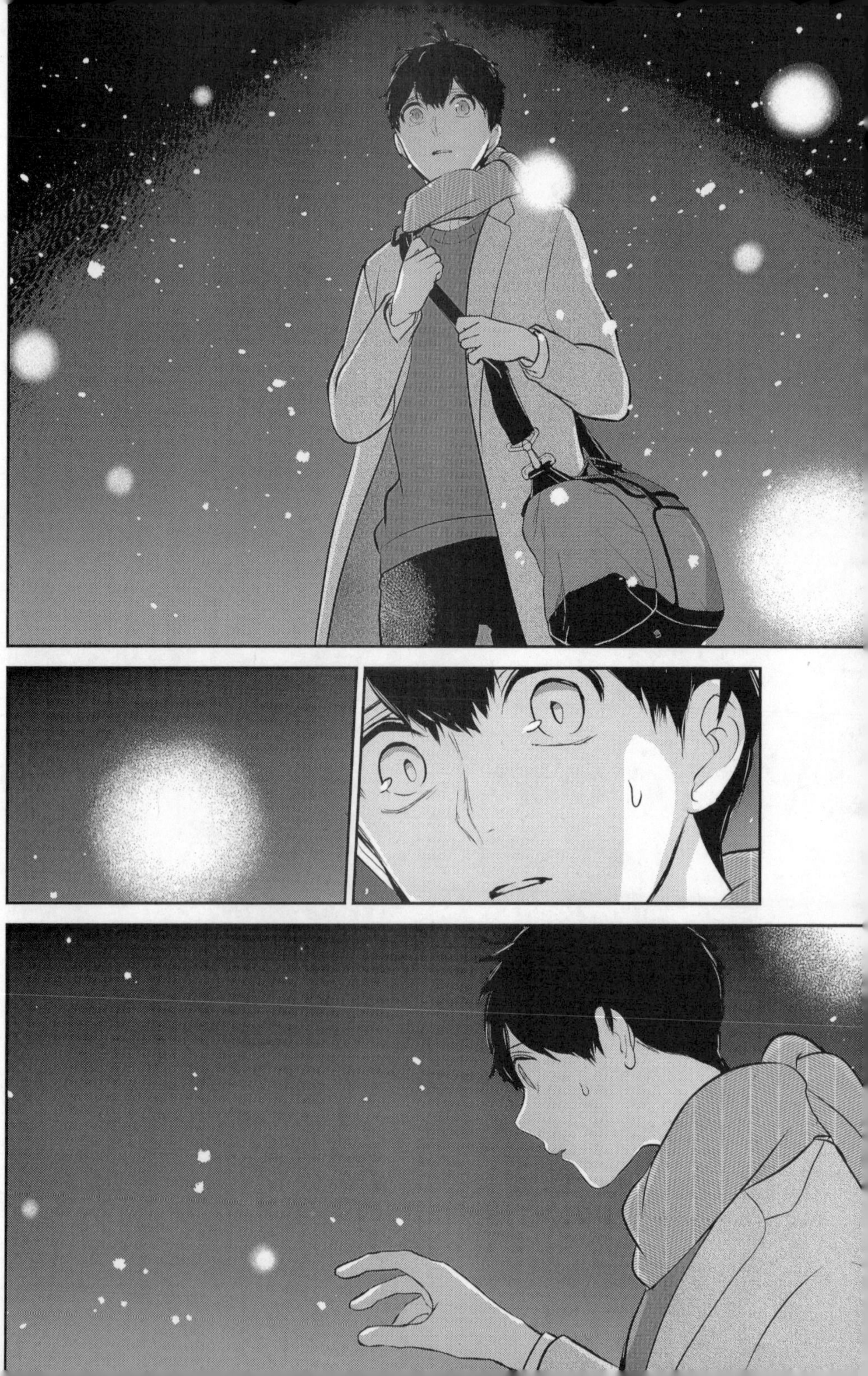

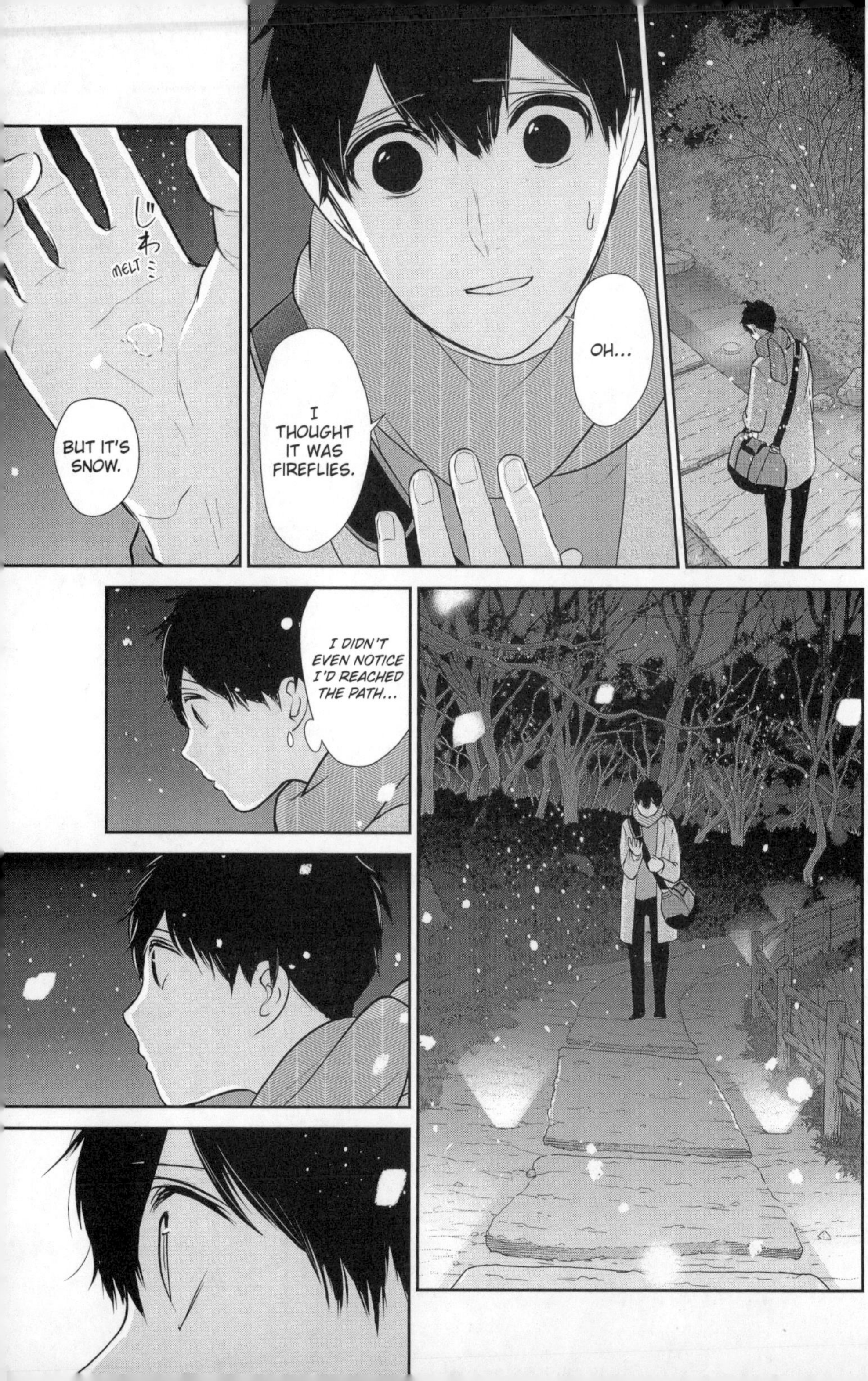
OH...
I THOUGHT IT WAS FIREFLIES.
じわ
MELT
BUT IT'S SNOW.
I DIDN'T EVEN NOTICE I'D REACHED THE PATH...

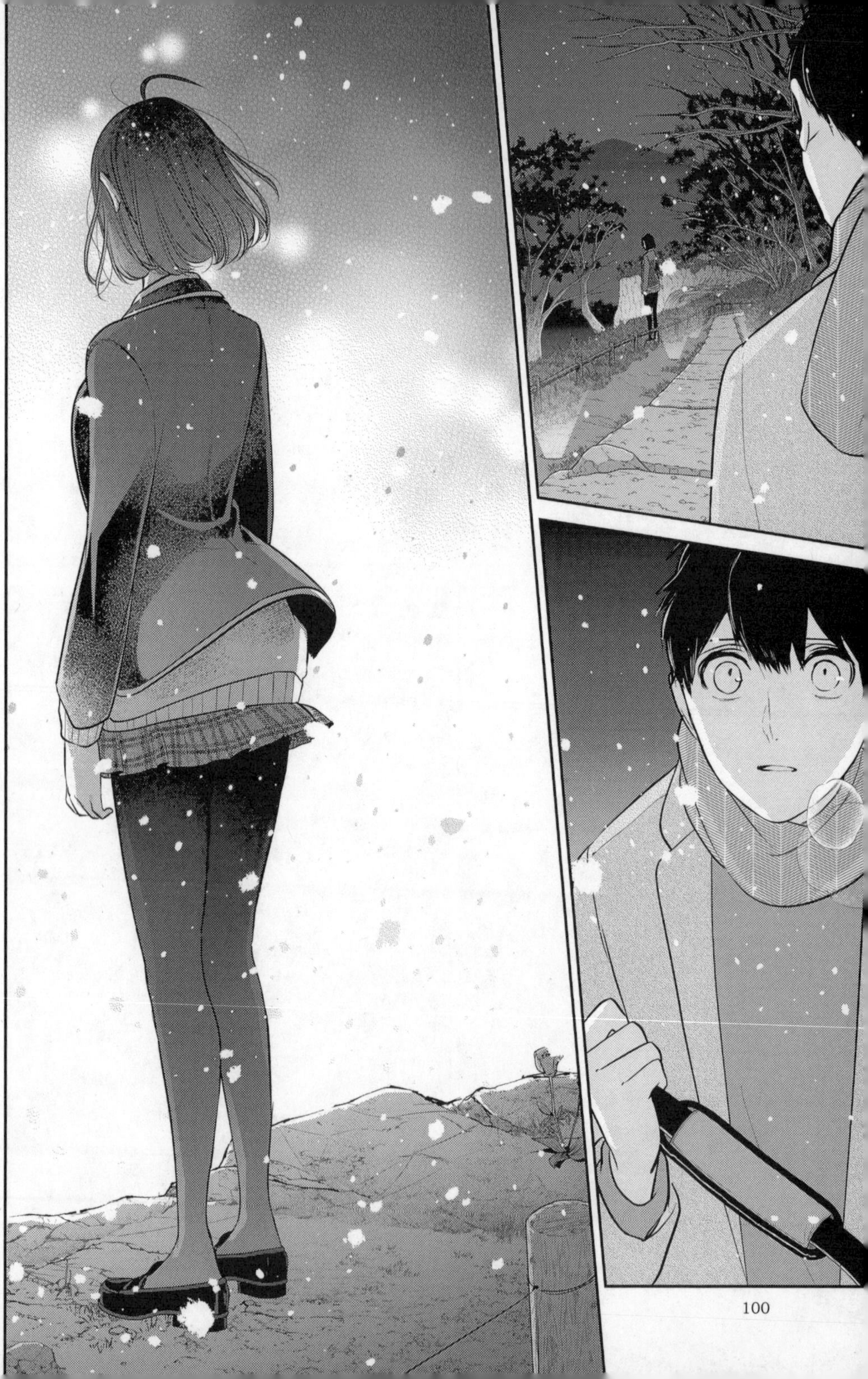

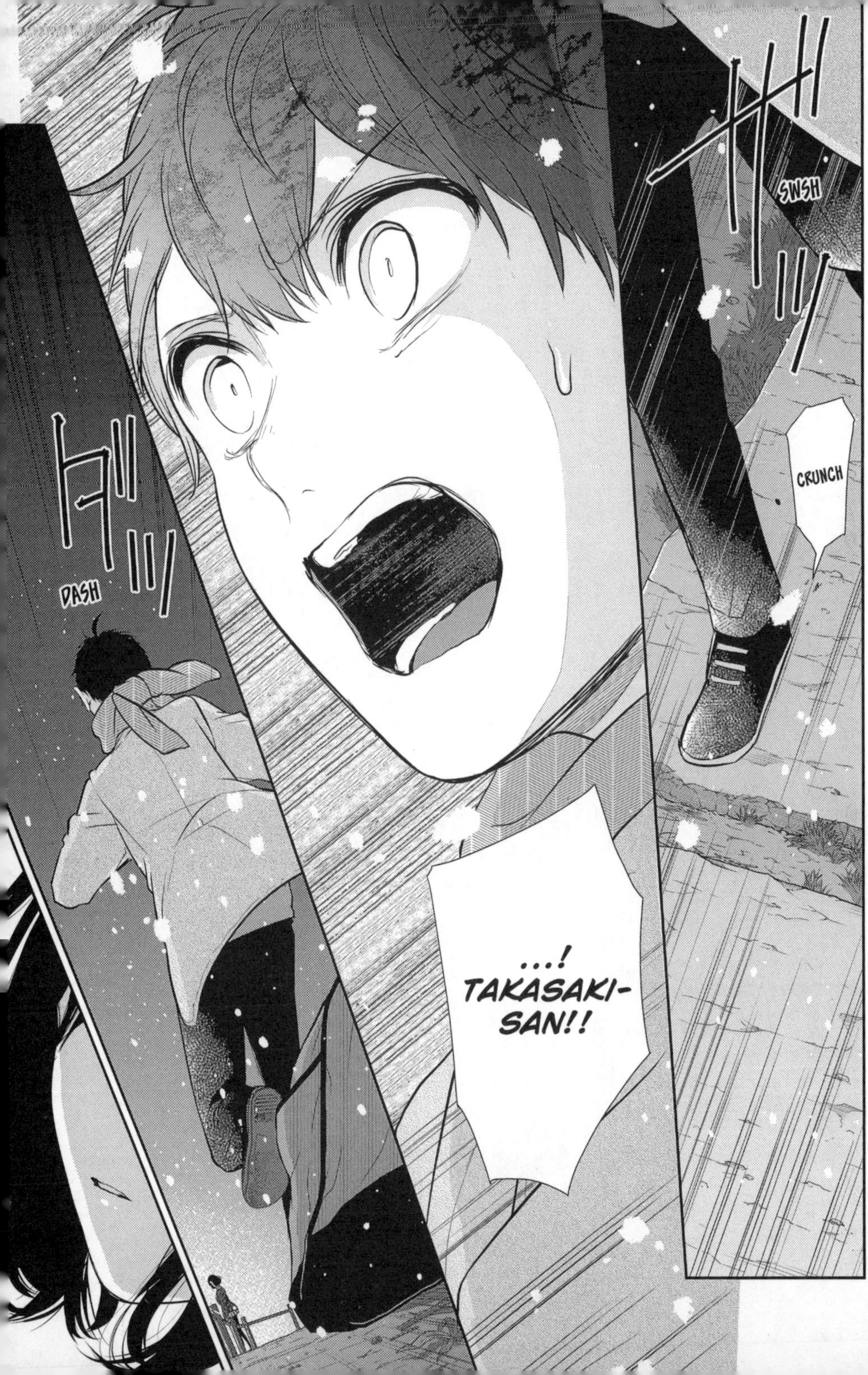
SWSH
CRUNCH
...! TAKASAKI-SAN!!
DASH

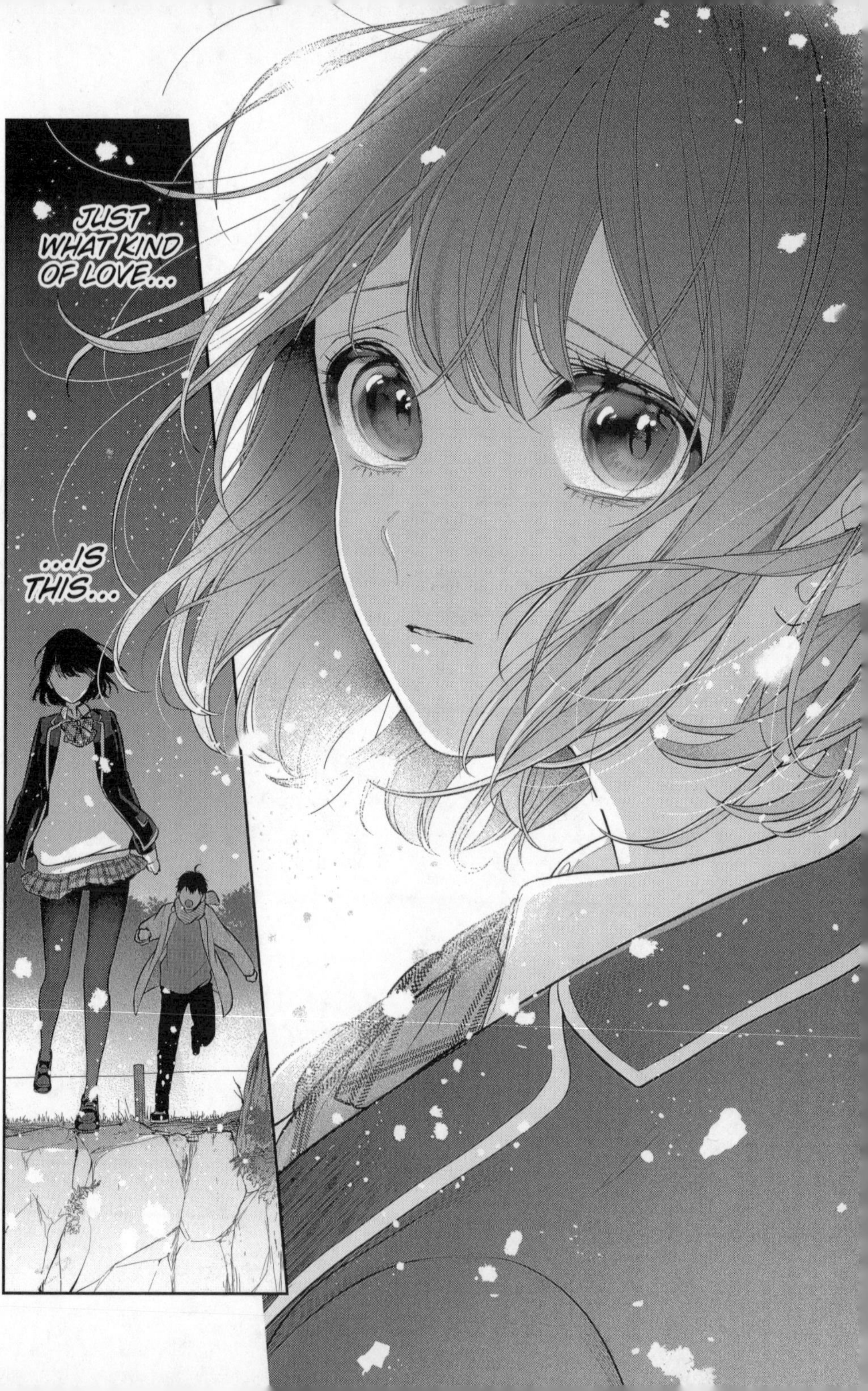
JUST WHAT KIND OF LOVE...
...IS THIS...

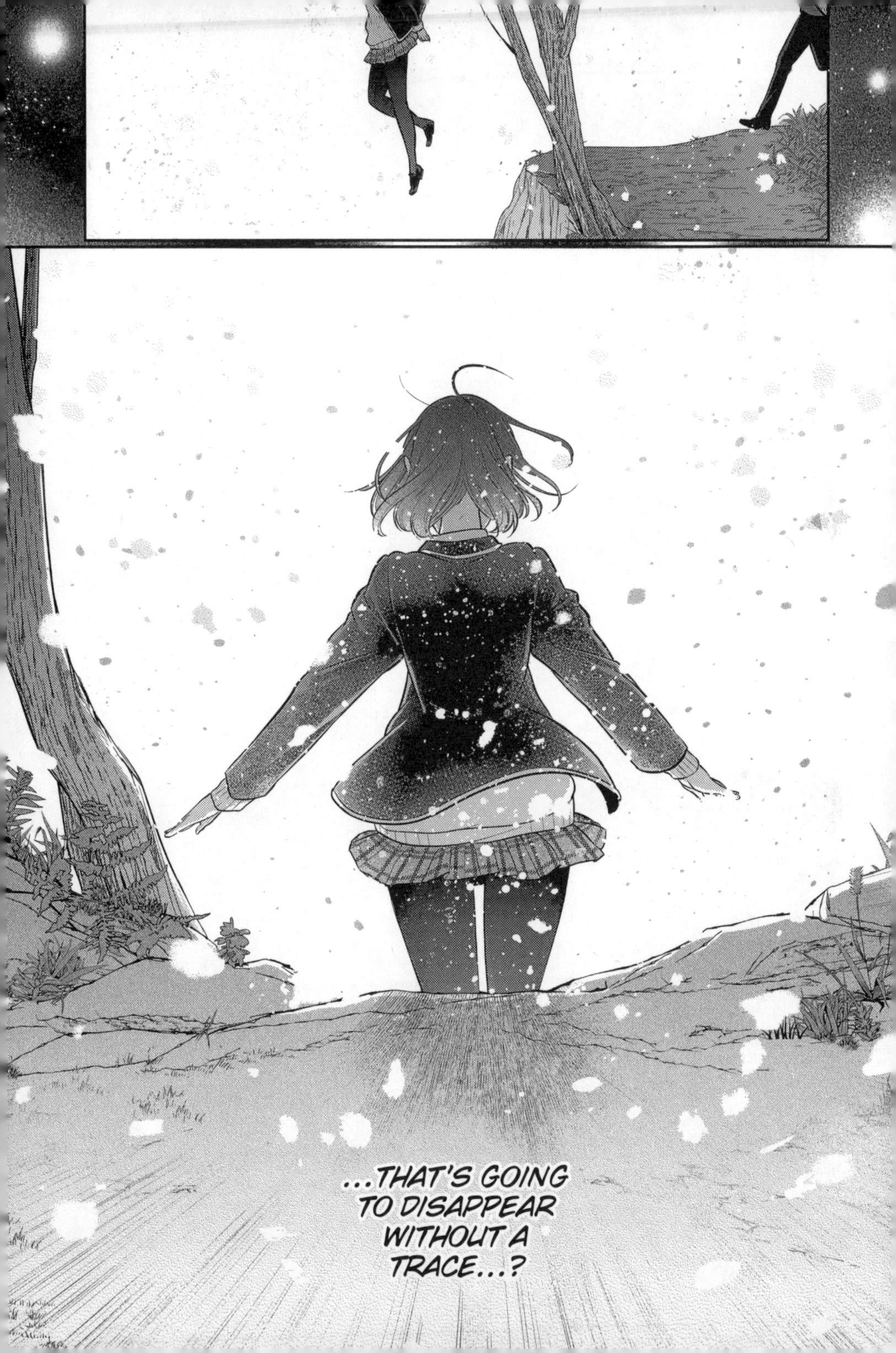
...THAT'S GOING TO DISAPPEAR WITHOUT A TRACE...?

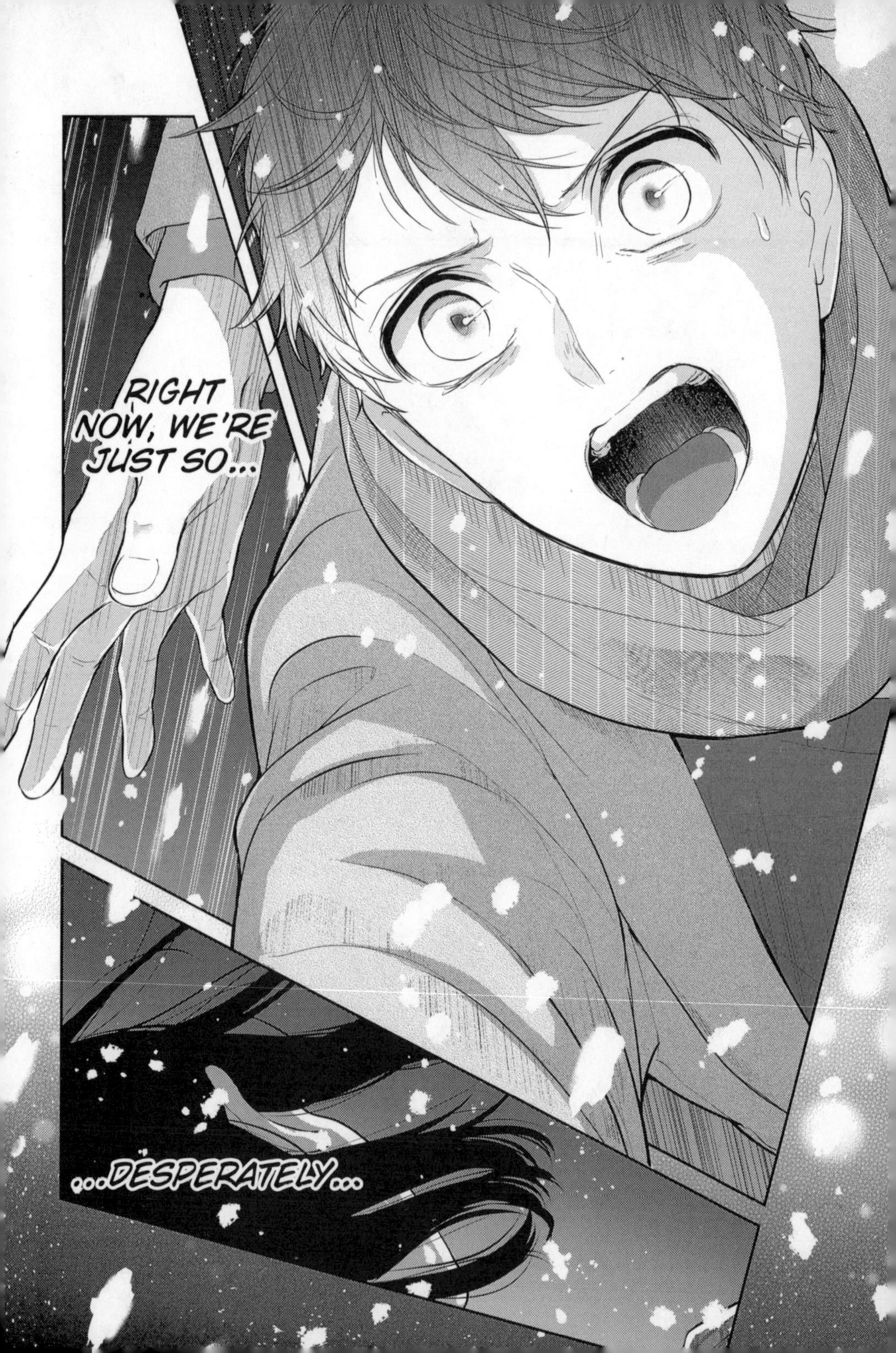
RIGHT NOW, WE'RE JUST SO...
...DESPERATELY...

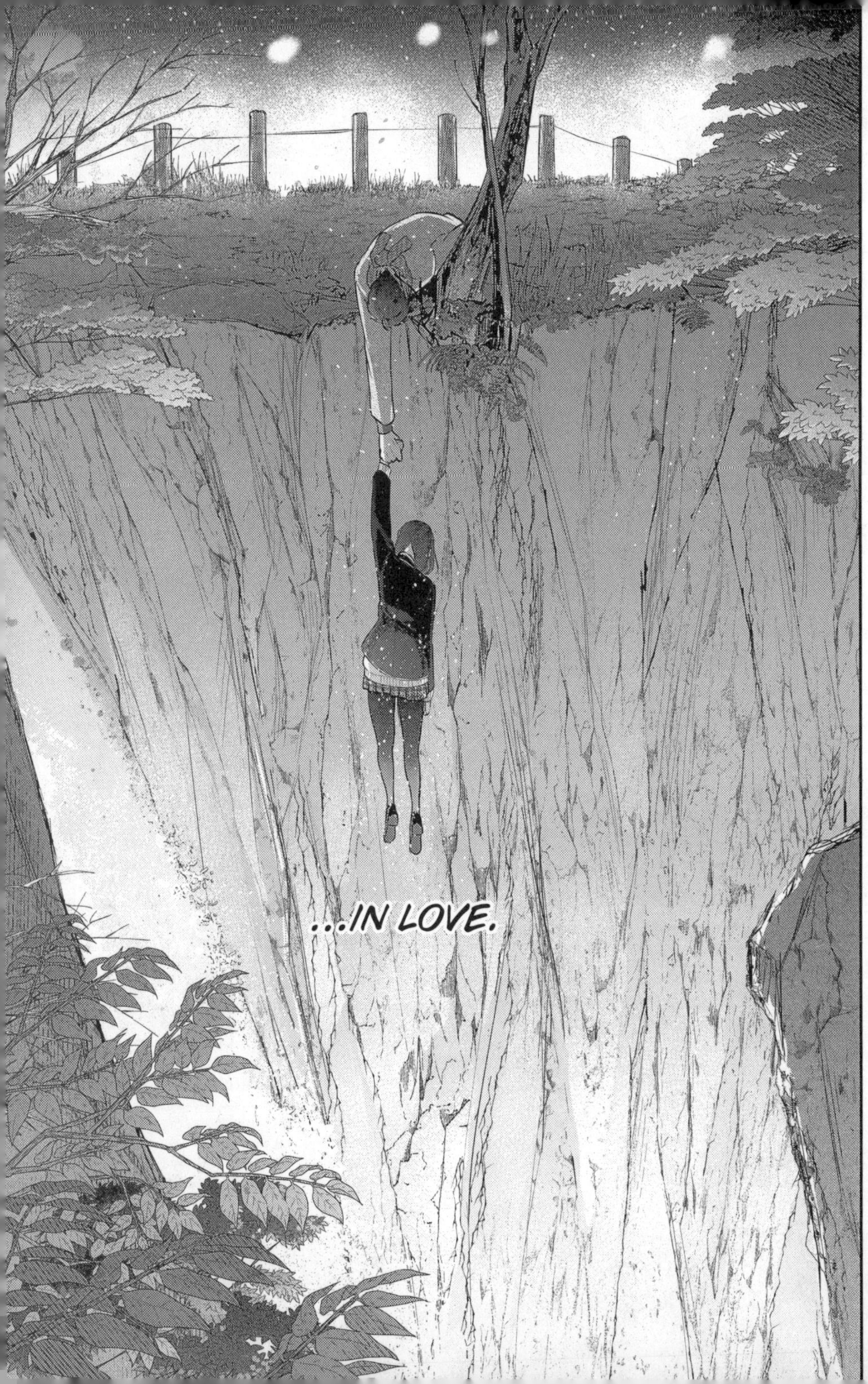
...IN LOVE.

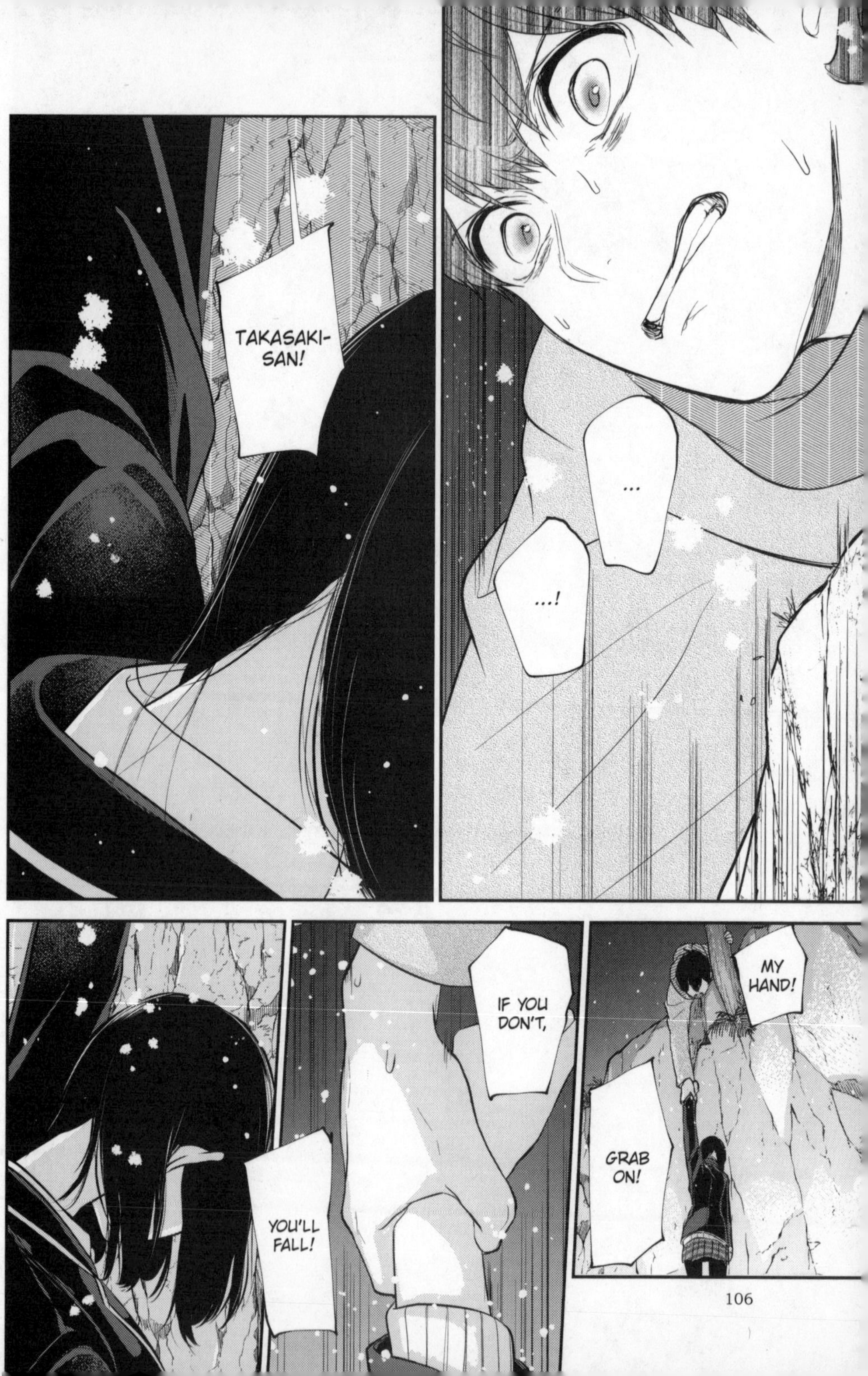
...
...!
TAKASAKI-SAN!
MY HAND!
GRAB ON!
IF YOU DON'T,
YOU'LL FALL!

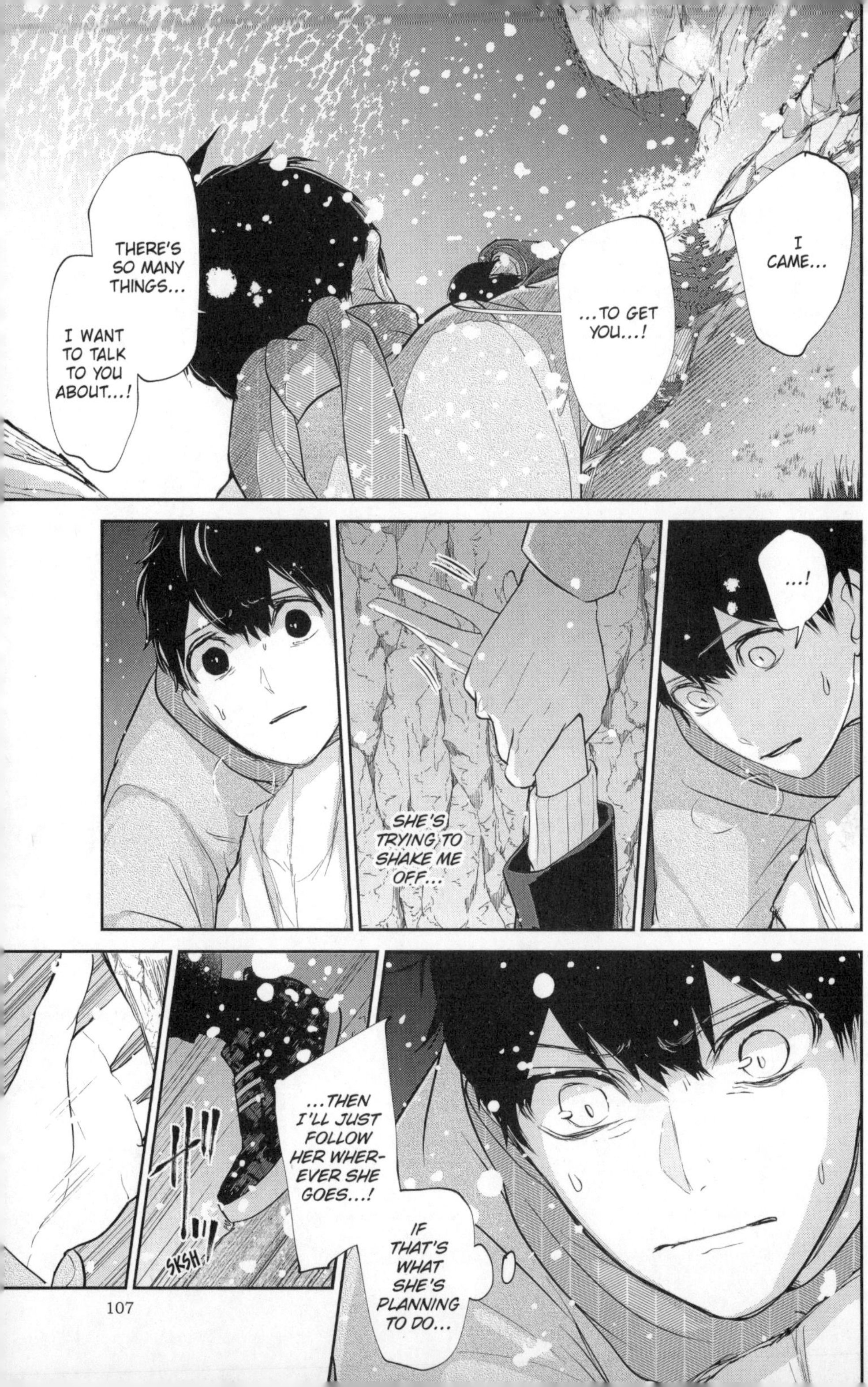

I CAME...
...TO GET YOU...!
THERE'S SO MANY THINGS...
I WANT TO TALK TO YOU ABOUT...!
...!
SHE'S TRYING TO SHAKE ME OFF...
...THEN I'LL JUST FOLLOW HER WHER-EVER SHE GOES...!
IF THAT'S WHAT SHE'S PLANNING TO DO...
SKSH

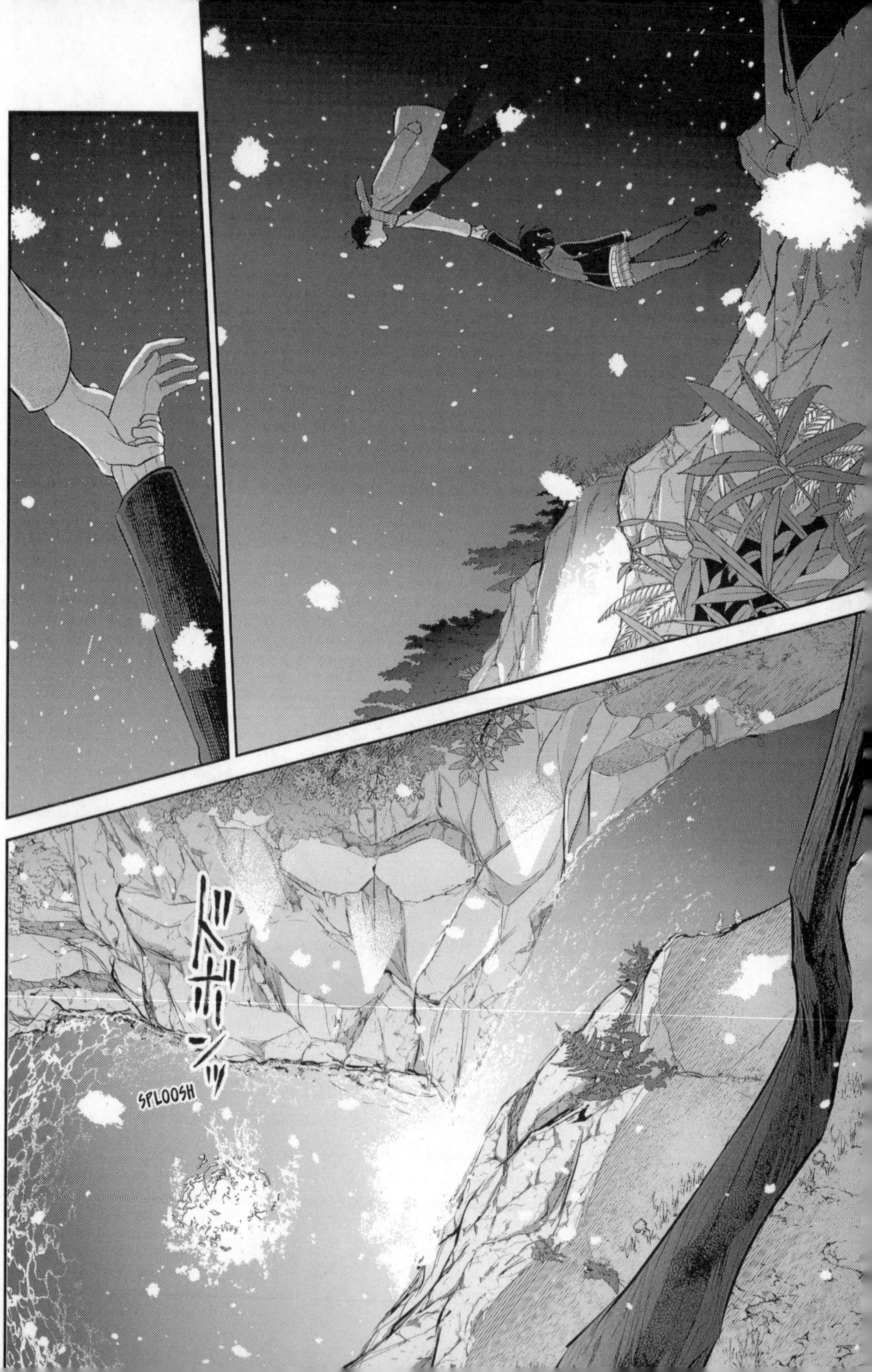
ドボンッ
SPLOOSH

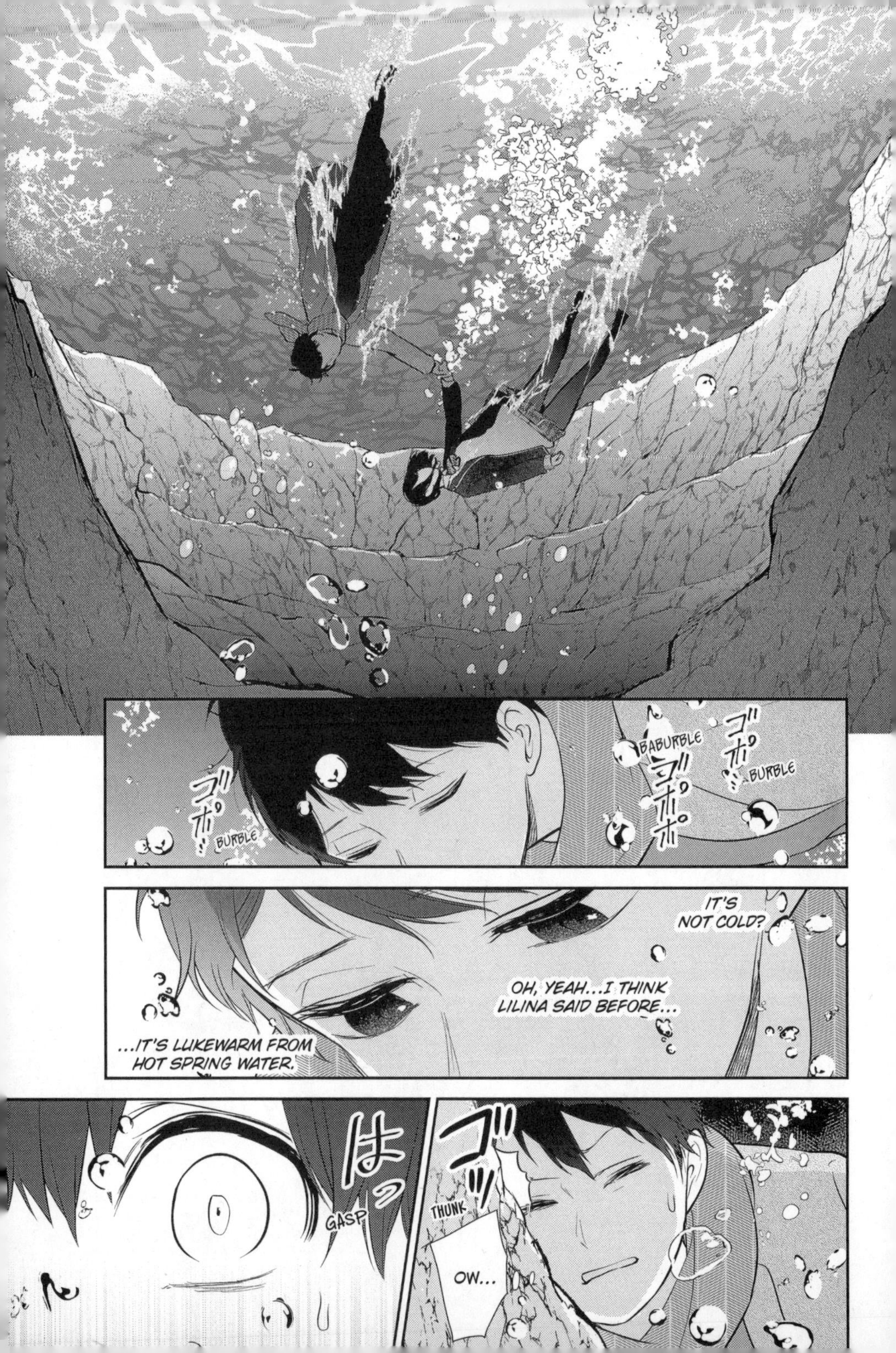
BURBLE
BABURBLE
BURBLE
IT'S NOT COLD?
OH, YEAH...I THINK LILINA SAID BEFORE...
...IT'S LUKEWARM FROM HOT SPRING WATER.
ゴッ
THUNK
OW...
はっ
GASP

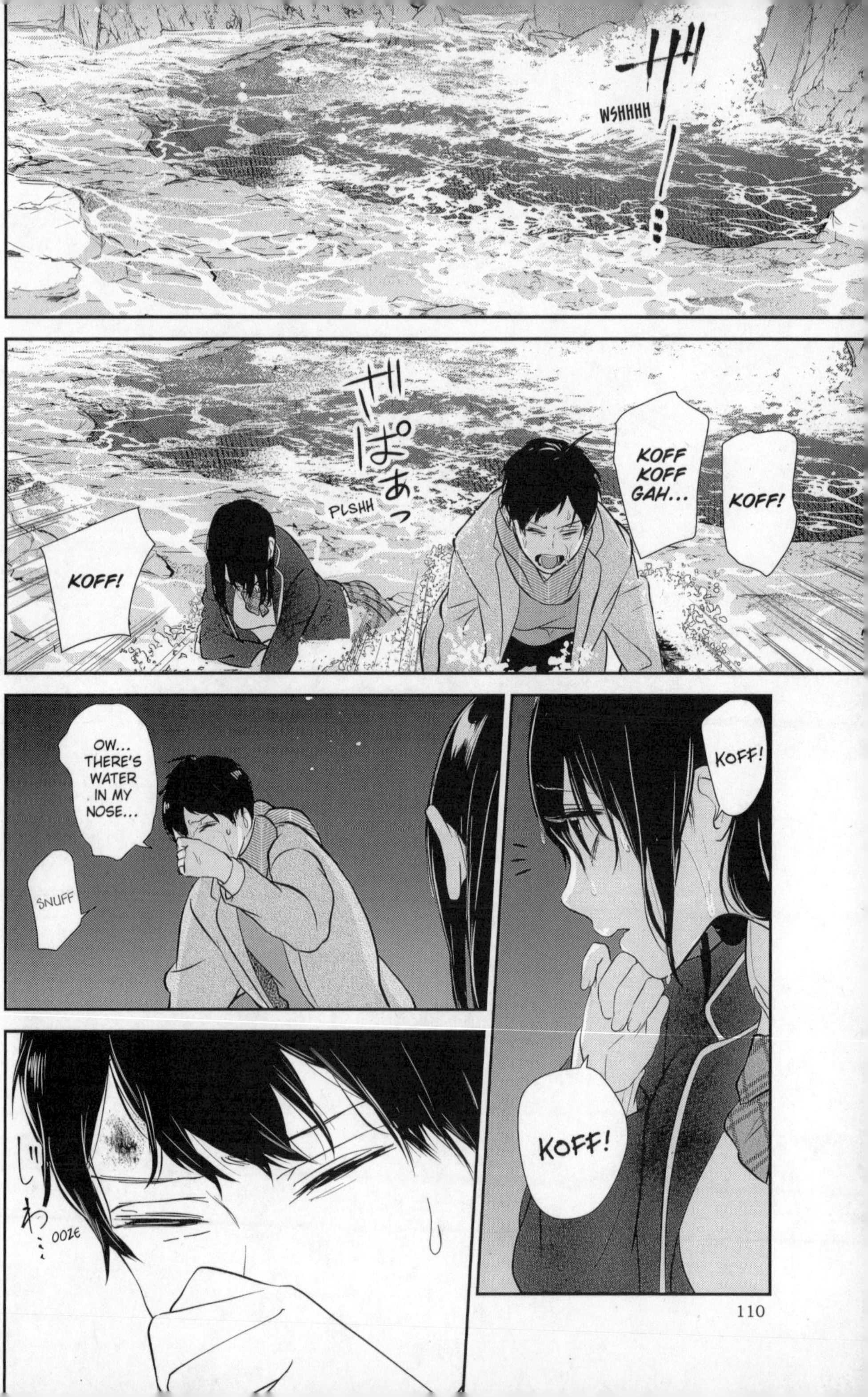

ザ
WSHHHH
KOFF!
KOFF KOFF GAH...
ざぱあっ
PLSHH
KOFF!
KOFF!
KOFF!
OW... THERE'S WATER IN MY NOSE...
SNUFF
じわ…
OOZE

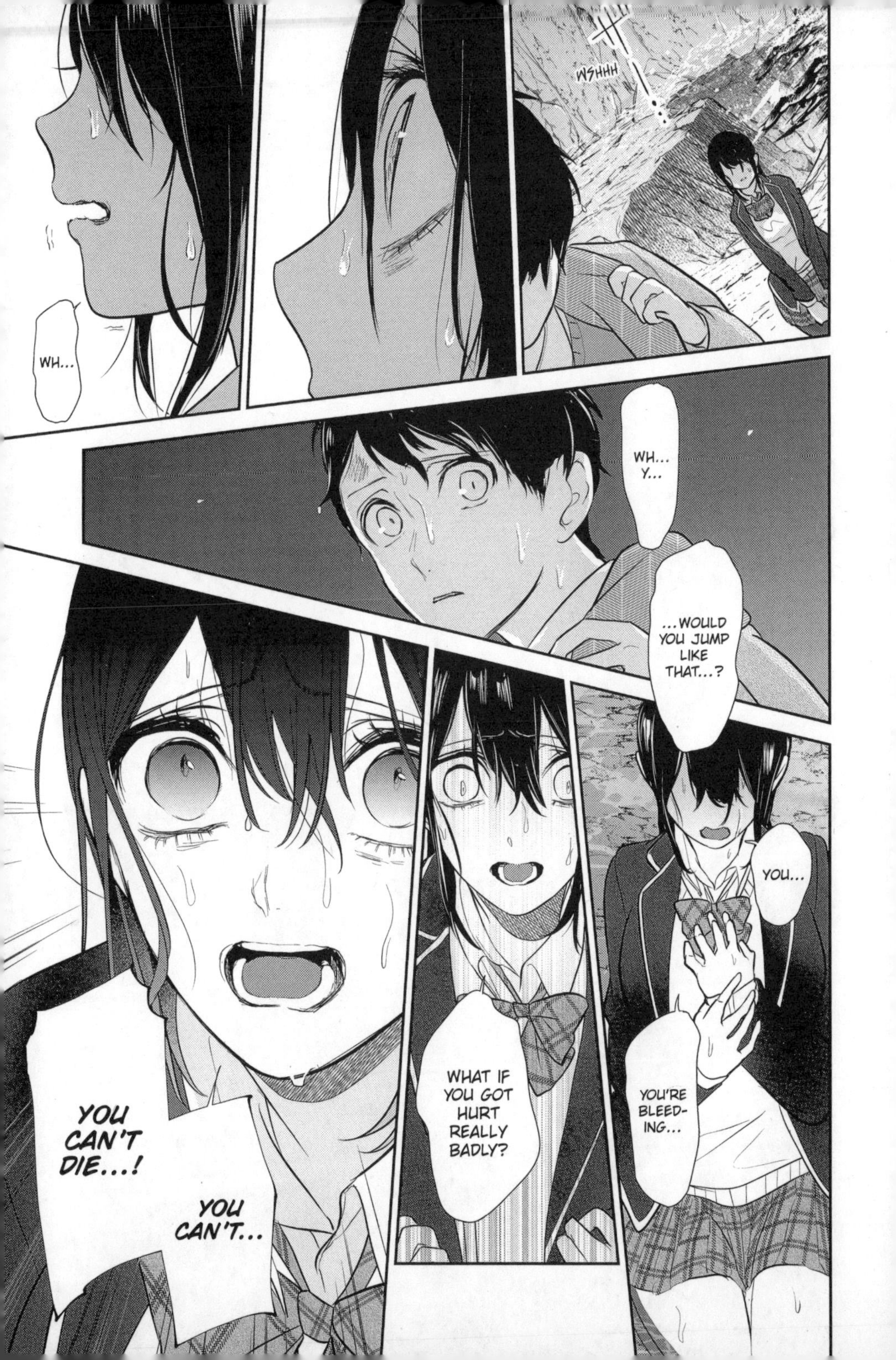
WSHHH
WH...
WH... Y...
...WOULD YOU JUMP LIKE THAT...?
YOU...
YOU'RE BLEED-ING...
WHAT IF YOU GOT HURT REALLY BADLY?
YOU CAN'T DIE...!
YOU CAN'T...

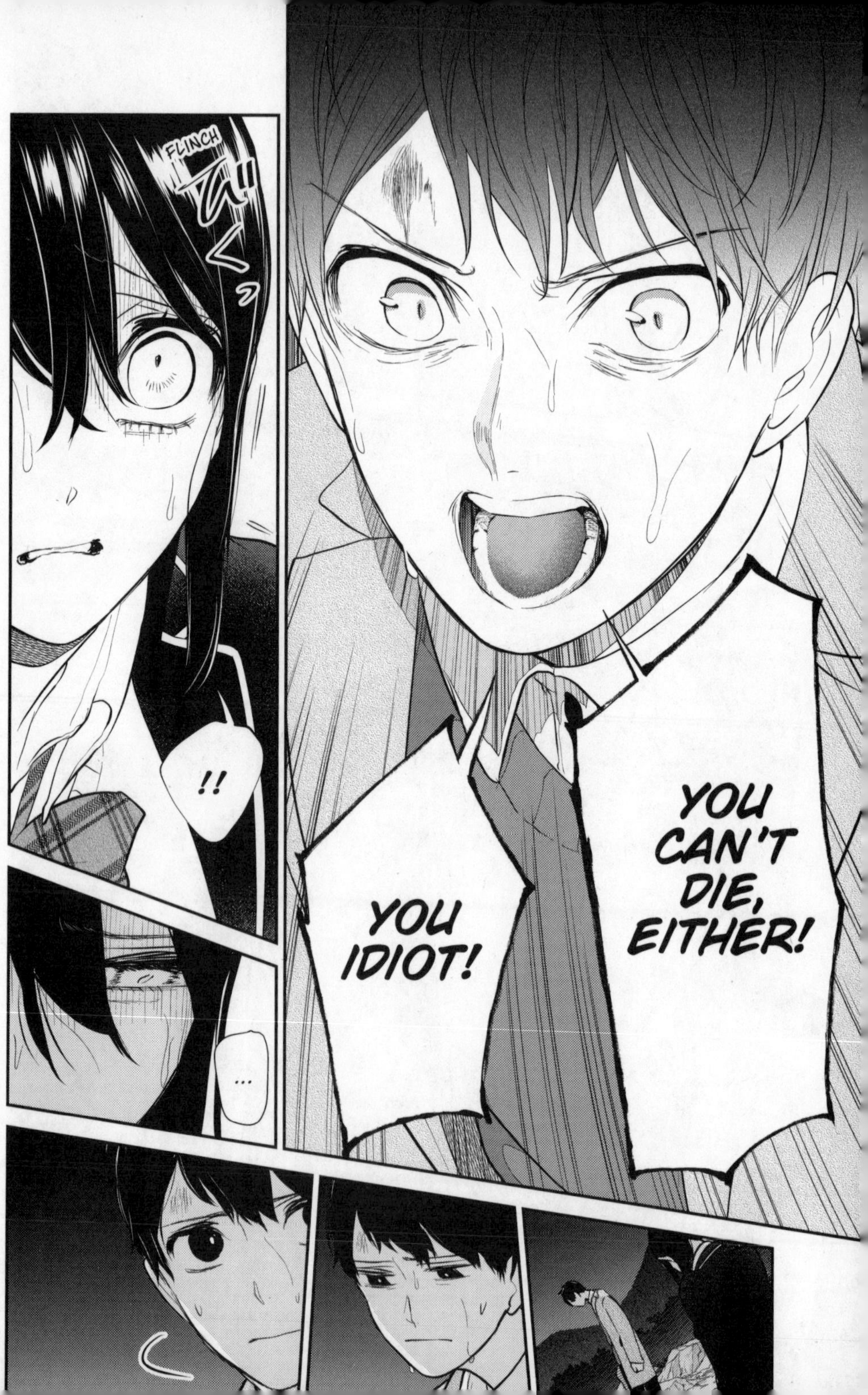

YOU CAN'T DIE, EITHER!
YOU IDIOT!
FLINCH
!!
...

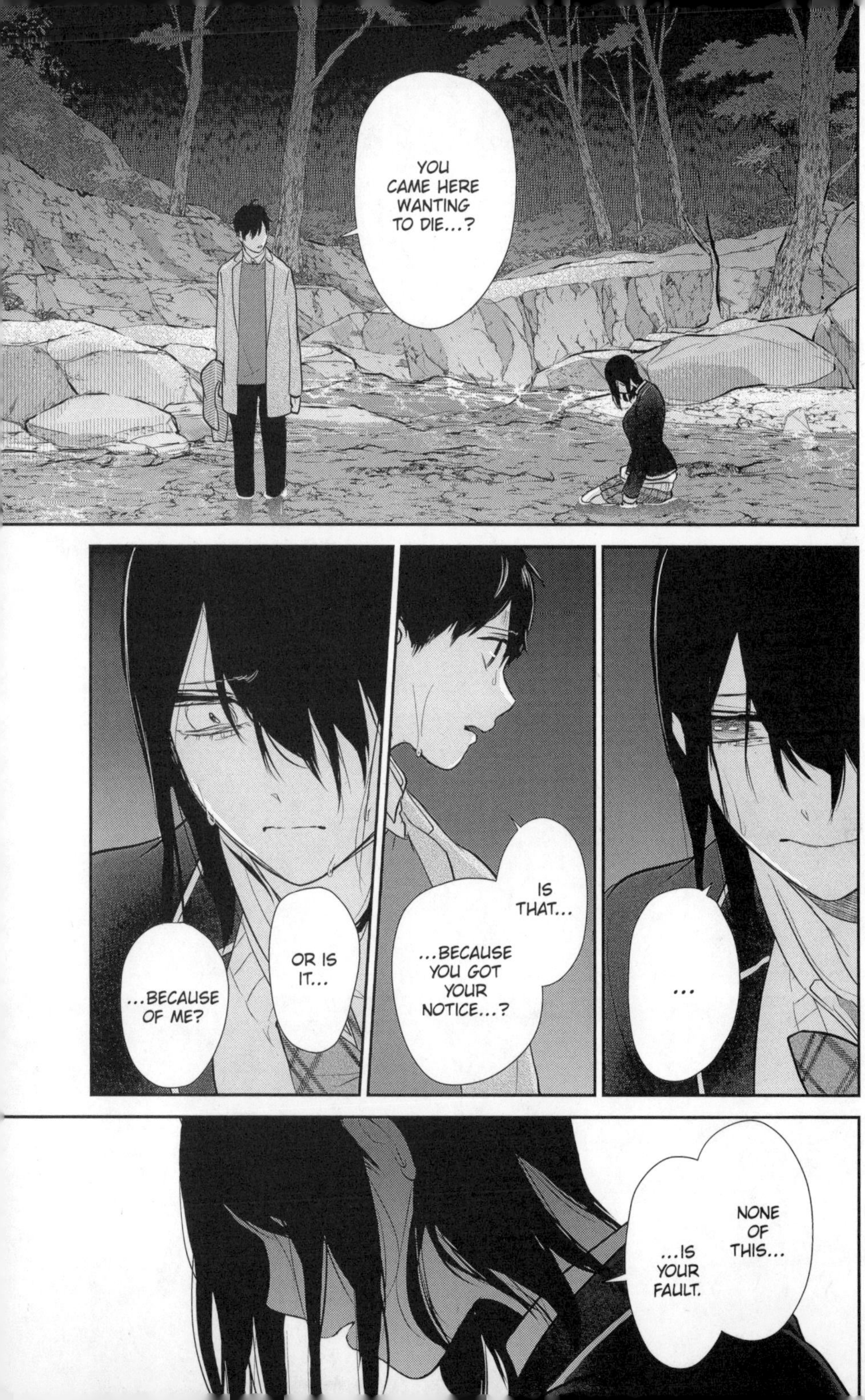
YOU CAME HERE WANTING TO DIE...?
...
IS THAT...
...BECAUSE YOU GOT YOUR NOTICE...?
OR IS IT...
...BECAUSE OF ME?
NONE OF THIS...
...IS YOUR FAULT.

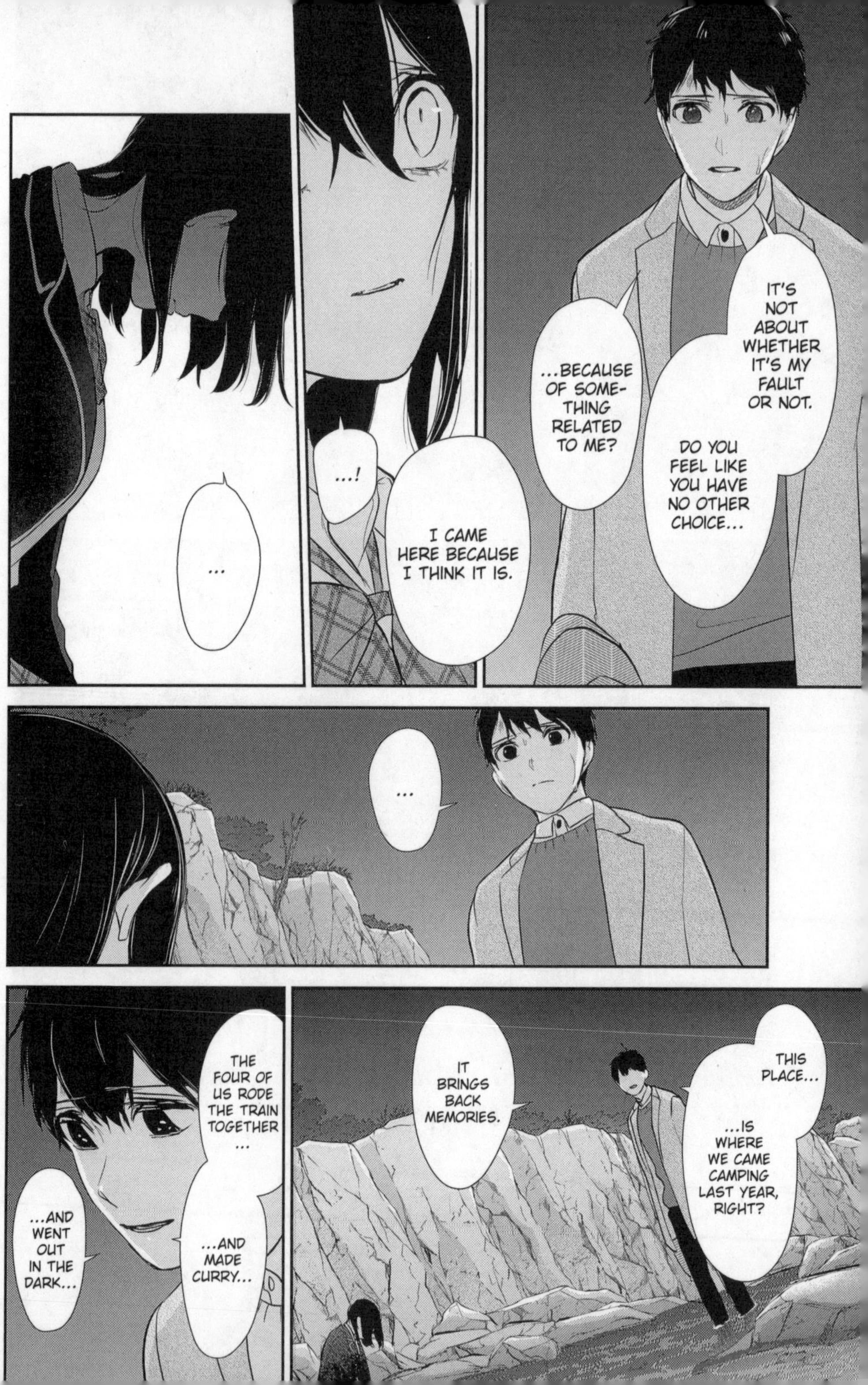
IT'S NOT ABOUT WHETHER IT'S MY FAULT OR NOT.
DO YOU FEEL LIKE YOU HAVE NO OTHER CHOICE...
...BECAUSE OF SOME-THING RELATED TO ME?
...!
I CAME HERE BECAUSE I THINK IT IS.
...
...
THIS PLACE...
...IS WHERE WE CAME CAMPING LAST YEAR, RIGHT?
IT BRINGS BACK MEMORIES.
THE FOUR OF US RODE THE TRAIN TOGETHER...
...AND MADE CURRY...
...AND WENT OUT IN THE DARK...

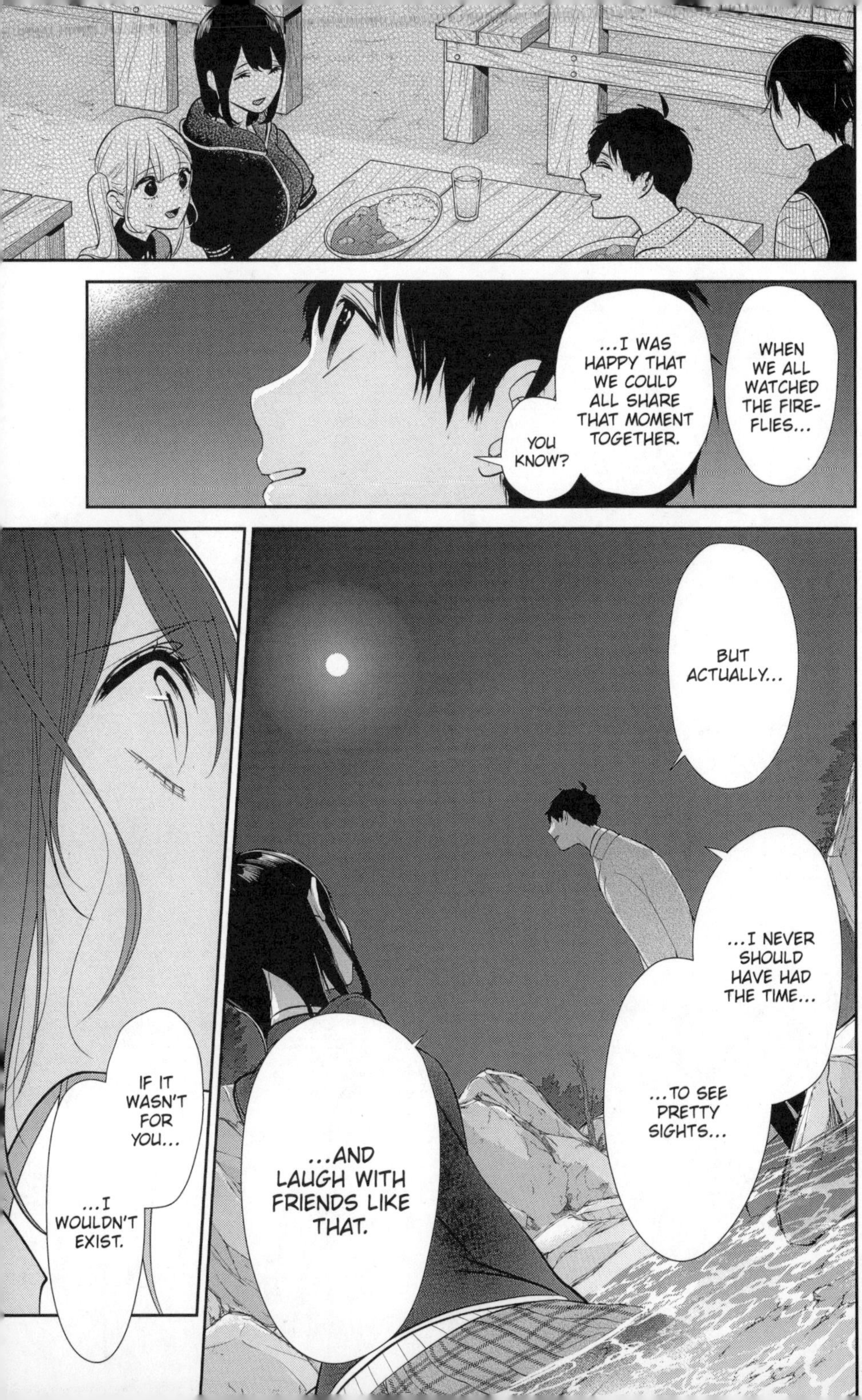
WHEN WE ALL WATCHED THE FIRE-FLIES...
...I WAS HAPPY THAT WE COULD ALL SHARE THAT MOMENT TOGETHER.
YOU KNOW?
BUT ACTUALLY...
...I NEVER SHOULD HAVE HAD THE TIME...
...TO SEE PRETTY SIGHTS...
...AND LAUGH WITH FRIENDS LIKE THAT.
IF IT WASN'T FOR YOU...
...I WOULDN'T EXIST.

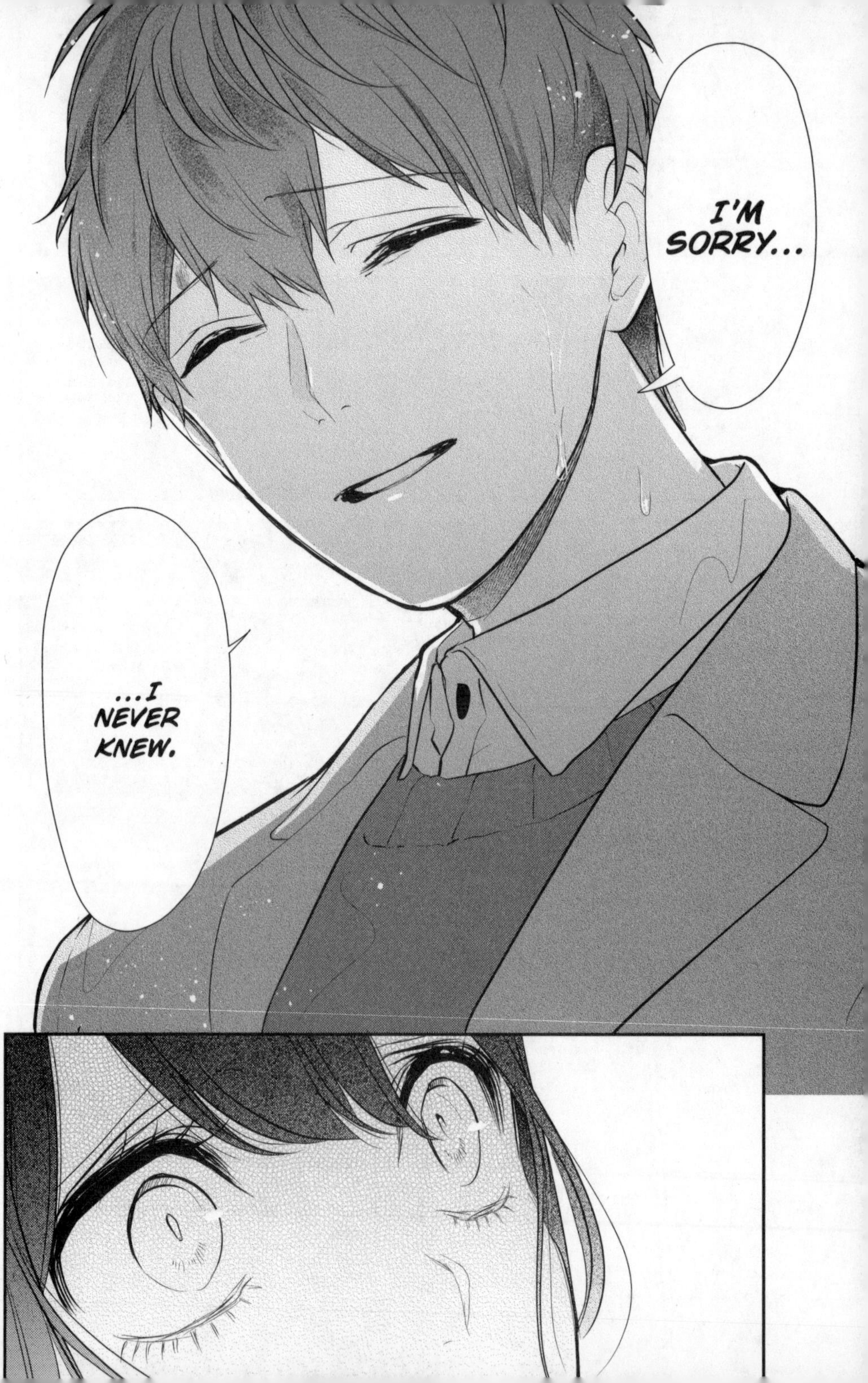
I'M SORRY...
...I NEVER KNEW.

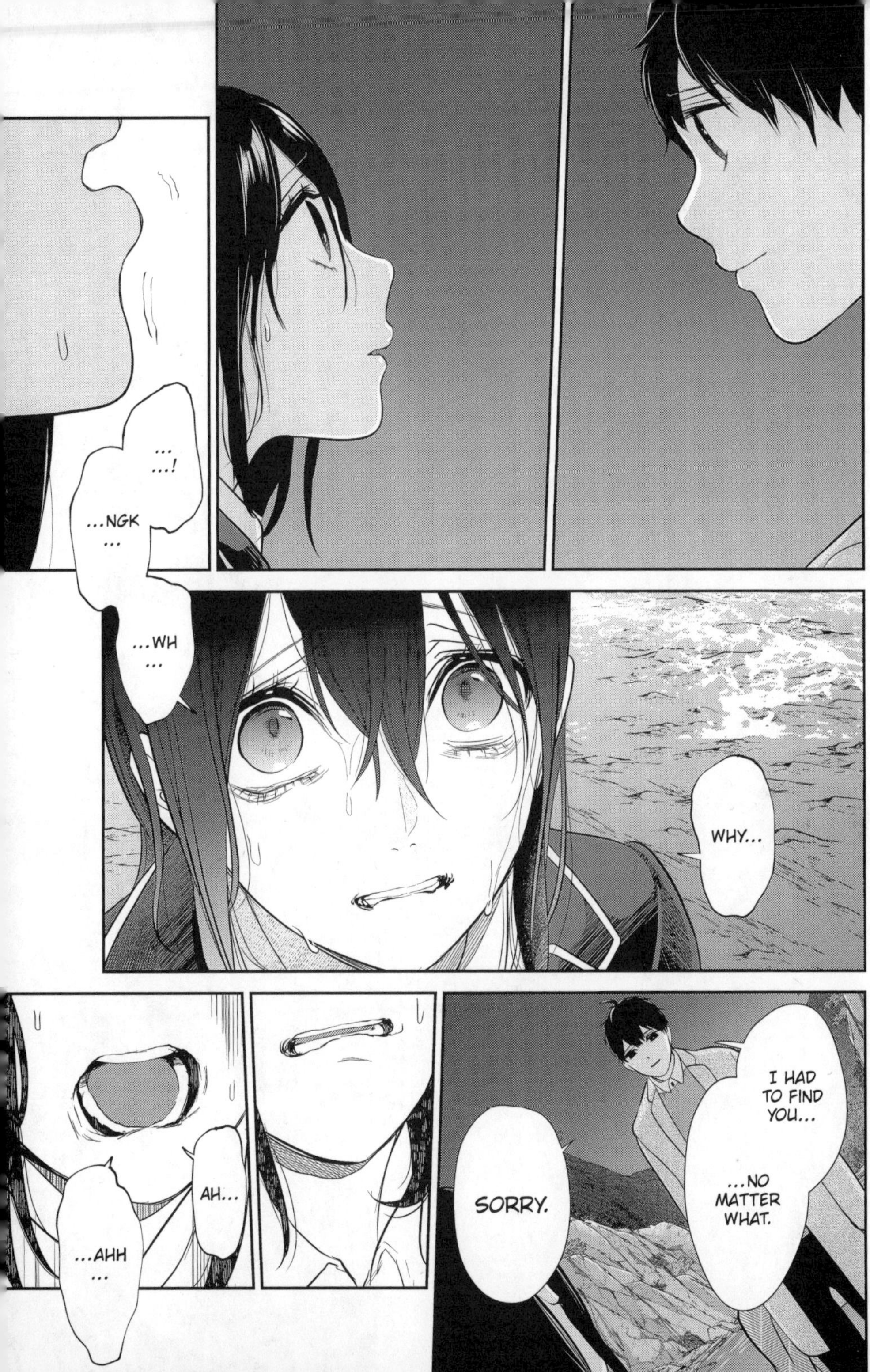
...
...!
...NGK
...
...WH
...
WHY...
I HAD TO FIND YOU...
...NO MATTER WHAT.
SORRY.
AH...
...AHH
...

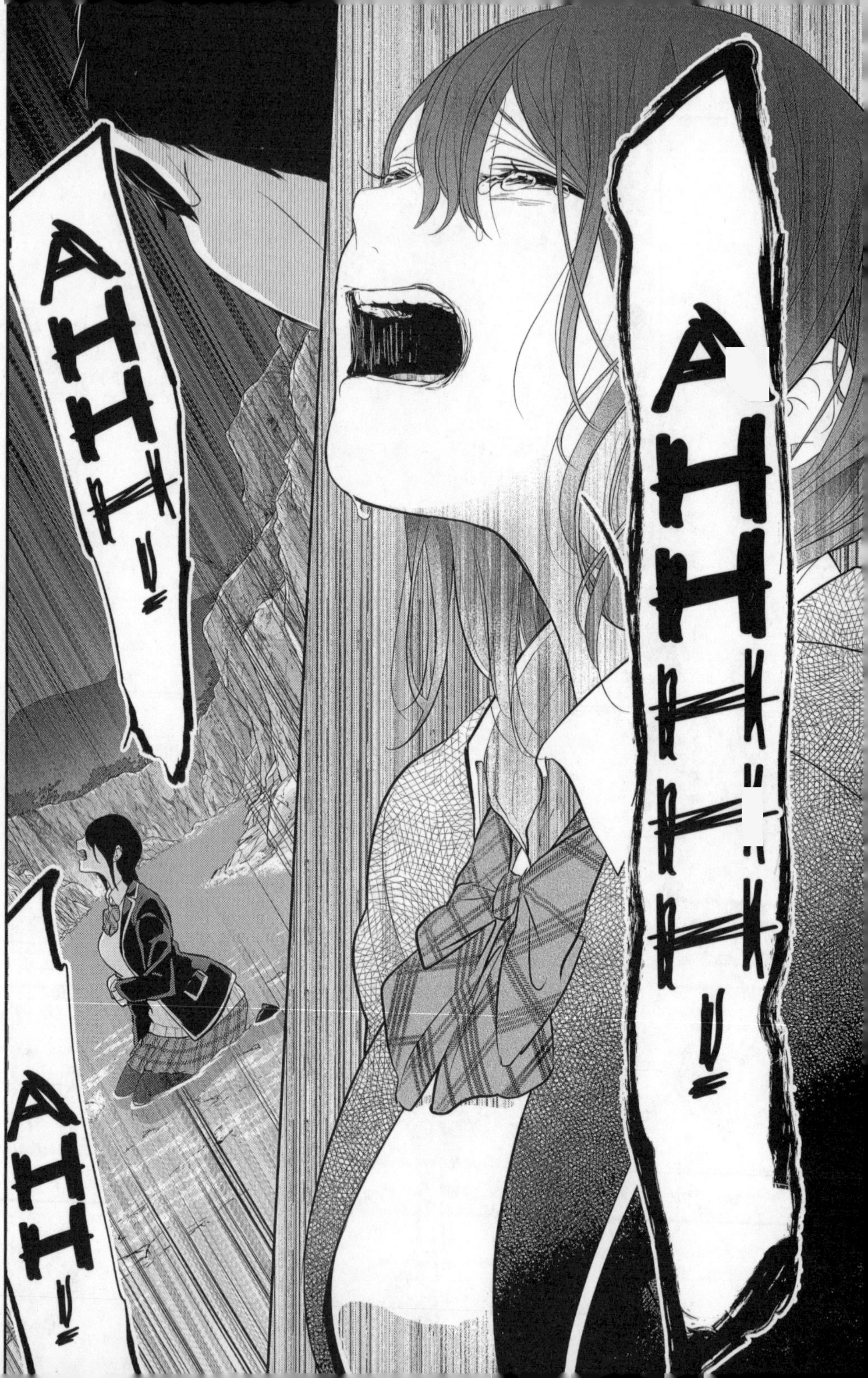
AHHHHHH!!
AHHH!!
AHH!!

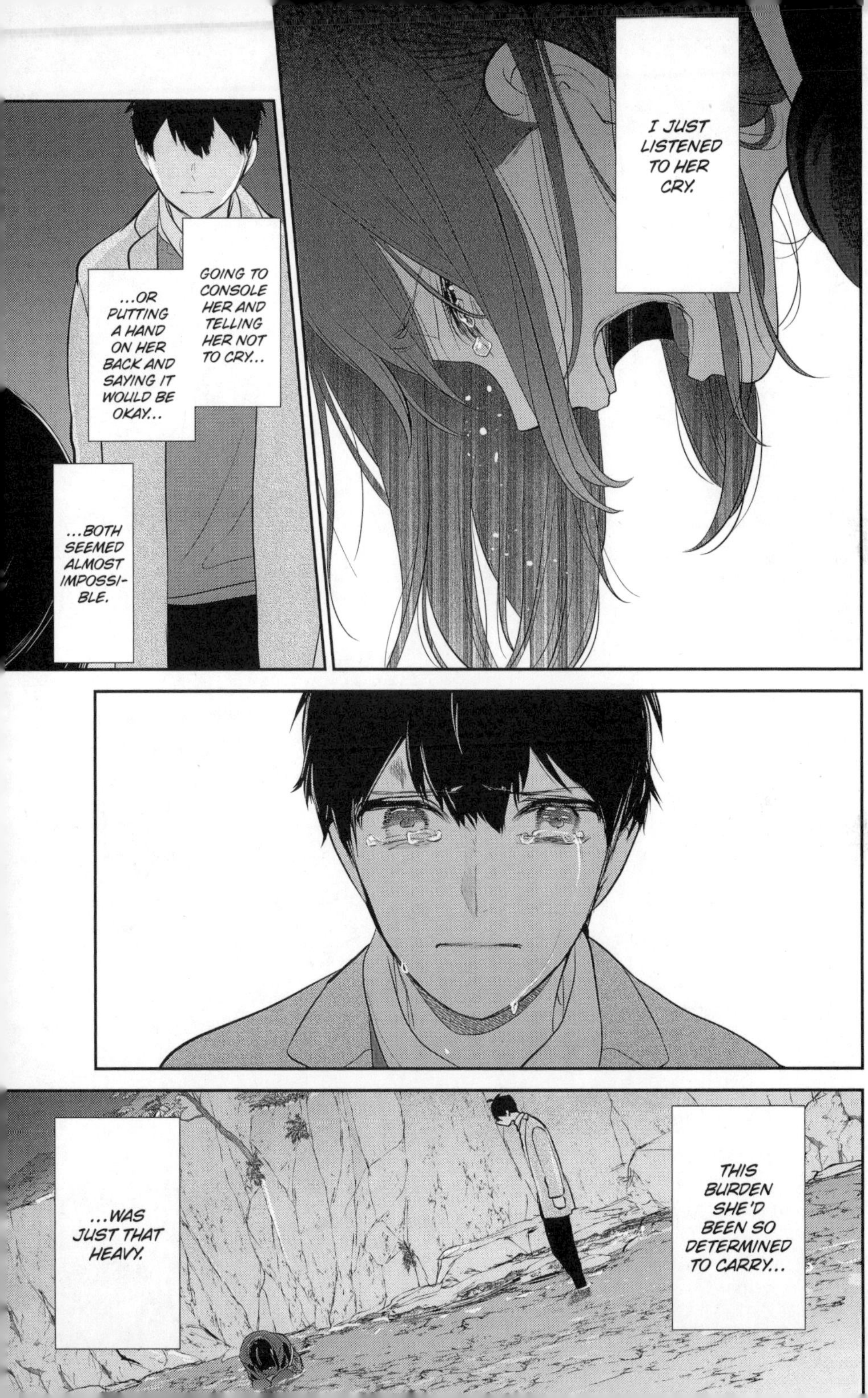
I JUST LISTENED TO HER CRY.
GOING TO CONSOLE HER AND TELLING HER NOT TO CRY...
...OR PUTTING A HAND ON HER BACK AND SAYING IT WOULD BE OKAY...
...BOTH SEEMED ALMOST IMPOSSI-BLE.
THIS BURDEN SHE'D BEEN SO DETERMINED TO CARRY...
...WAS JUST THAT HEAVY.

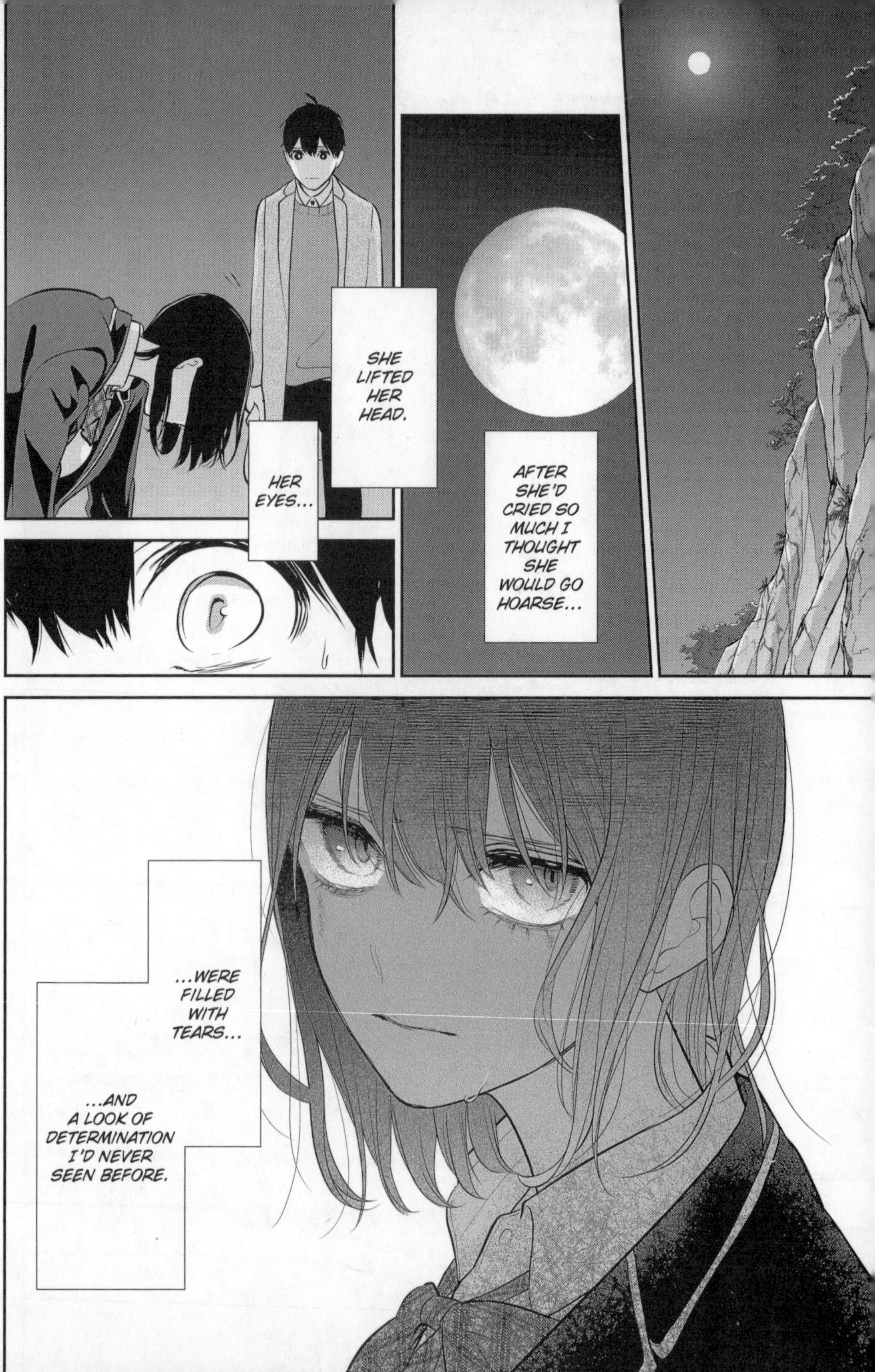
AFTER SHE'D CRIED SO MUCH I THOUGHT SHE WOULD GO HOARSE...
SHE LIFTED HER HEAD.
HER EYES...
...WERE FILLED WITH TEARS...
...AND A LOOK OF DETERMINATION I'D NEVER SEEN BEFORE.

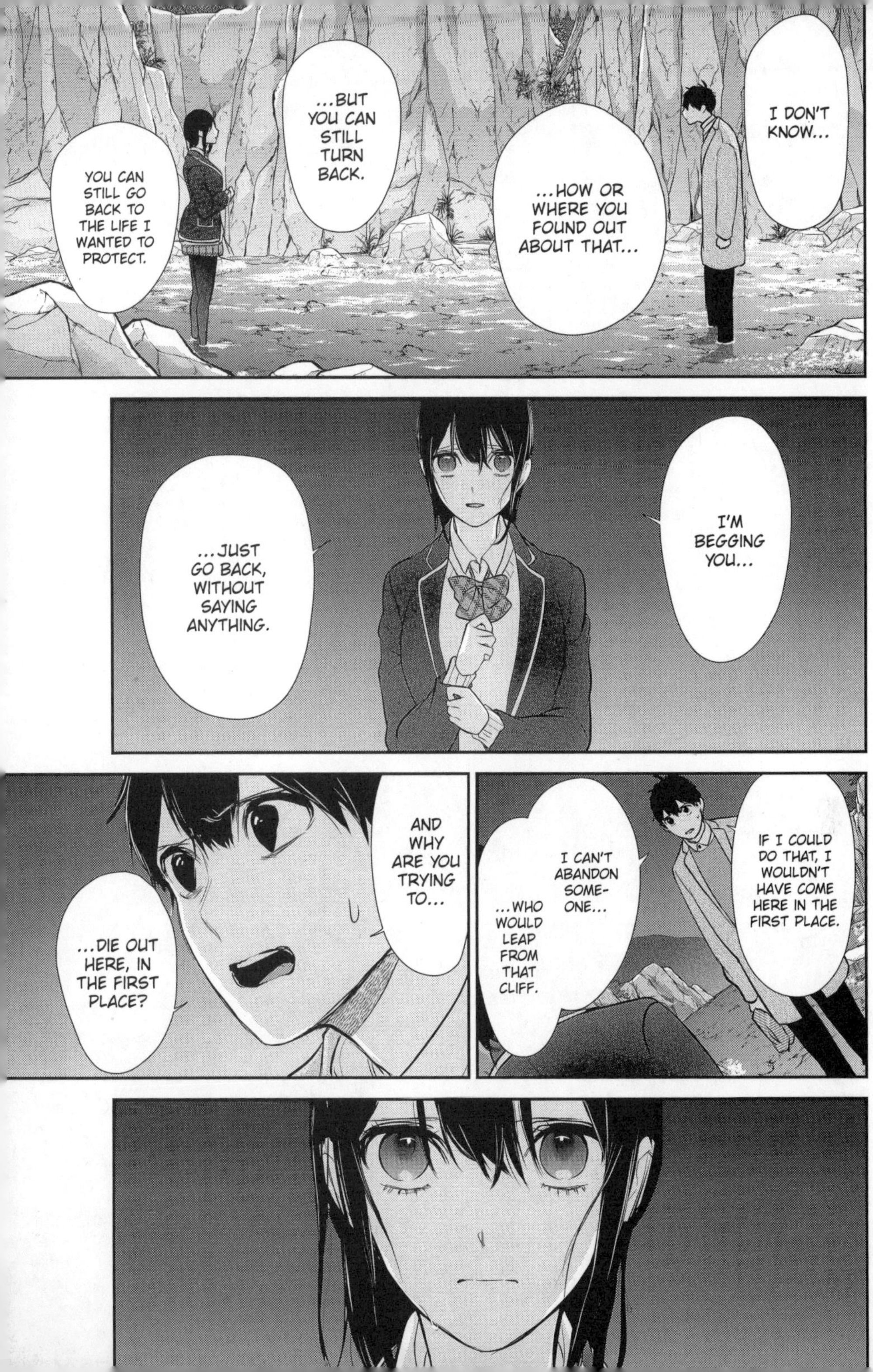
I DON'T KNOW...
...HOW OR WHERE YOU FOUND OUT ABOUT THAT...
...BUT YOU CAN STILL TURN BACK.
YOU CAN STILL GO BACK TO THE LIFE I WANTED TO PROTECT.
I'M BEGGING YOU...
...JUST GO BACK, WITHOUT SAYING ANYTHING.
IF I COULD DO THAT, I WOULDN'T HAVE COME HERE IN THE FIRST PLACE.
I CAN'T ABANDON SOME-ONE...
...WHO WOULD LEAP FROM THAT CLIFF.
AND WHY ARE YOU TRYING TO...
...DIE OUT HERE, IN THE FIRST PLACE?

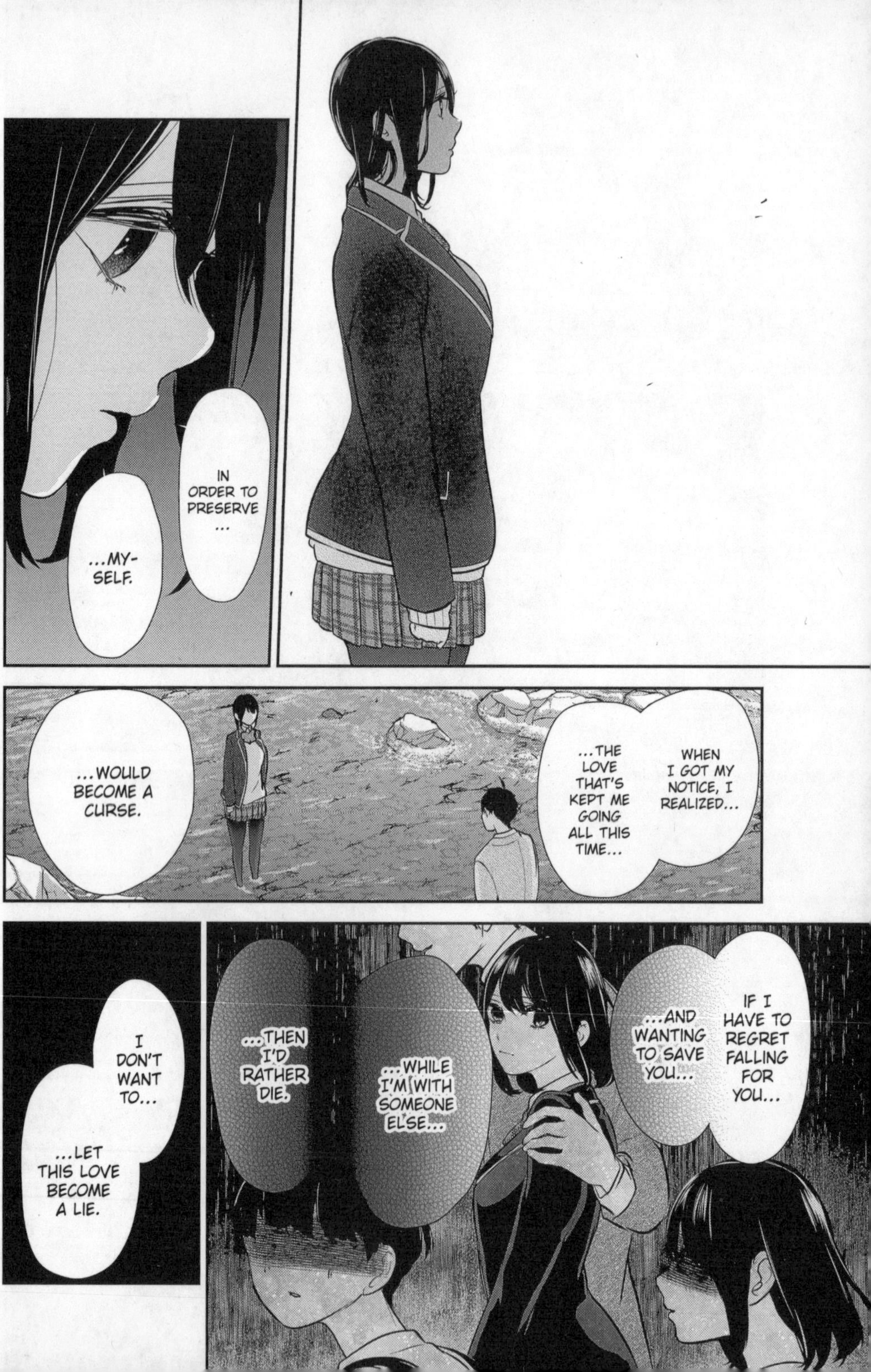
IN ORDER TO PRESERVE ...
...MY-SELF.
WHEN I GOT MY NOTICE, I REALIZED...
...THE LOVE THAT'S KEPT ME GOING ALL THIS TIME...
...WOULD BECOME A CURSE.
IF I HAVE TO REGRET FALLING FOR YOU...
...AND WANTING TO SAVE YOU...
...WHILE I'M WITH SOMEONE ELSE...
...THEN I'D RATHER DIE.
I DON'T WANT TO...
...LET THIS LOVE BECOME A LIE.

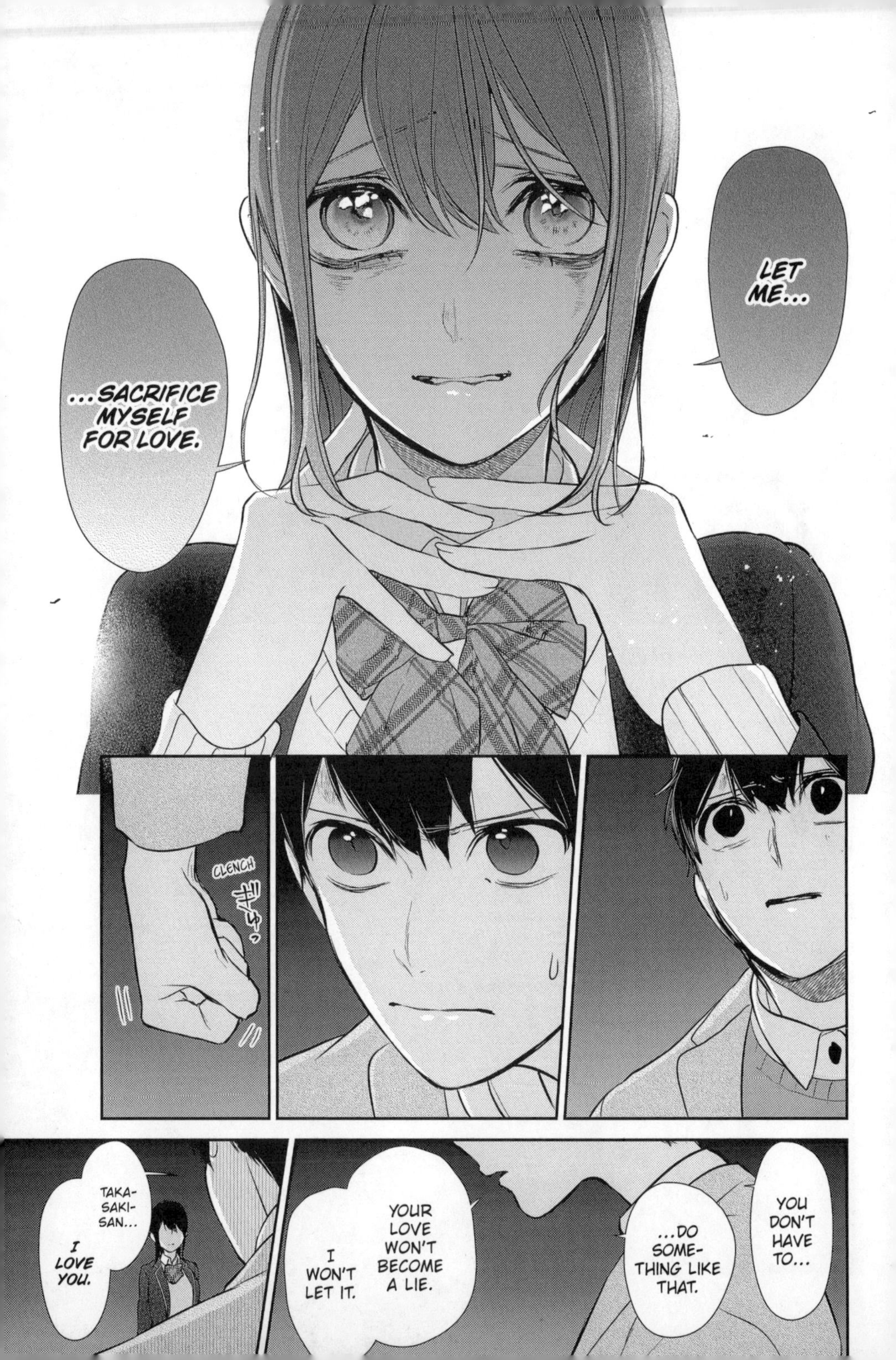
LET ME...
...SACRIFICE MYSELF FOR LOVE.
CLENCH
YOU DON'T HAVE TO...
...DO SOMETHING LIKE THAT.
YOUR LOVE WON'T BECOME A LIE.
I WON'T LET IT.
TAKASAKI-SAN...
I LOVE YOU.

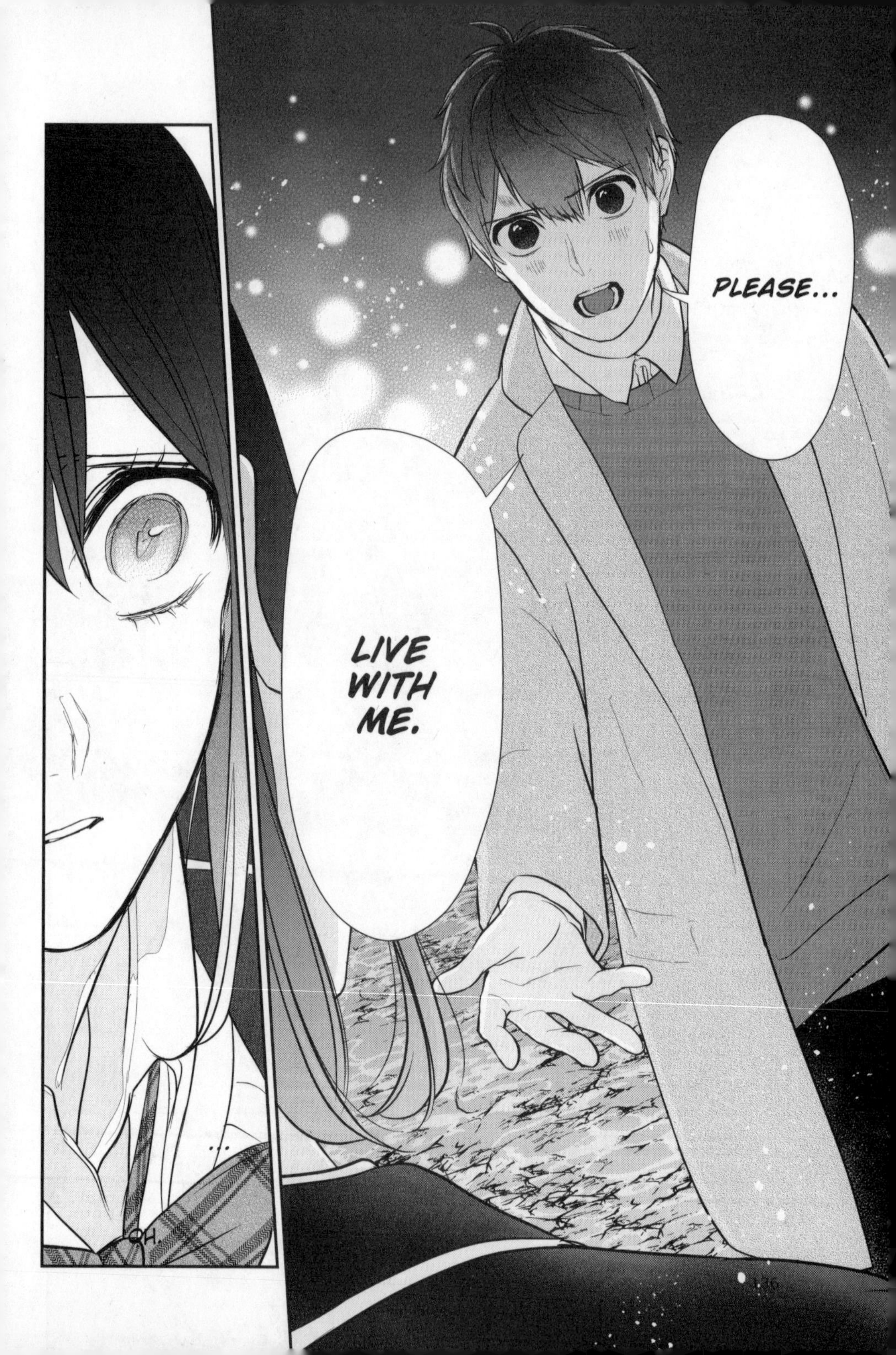
PLEASE...
LIVE WITH ME.
...
OH.

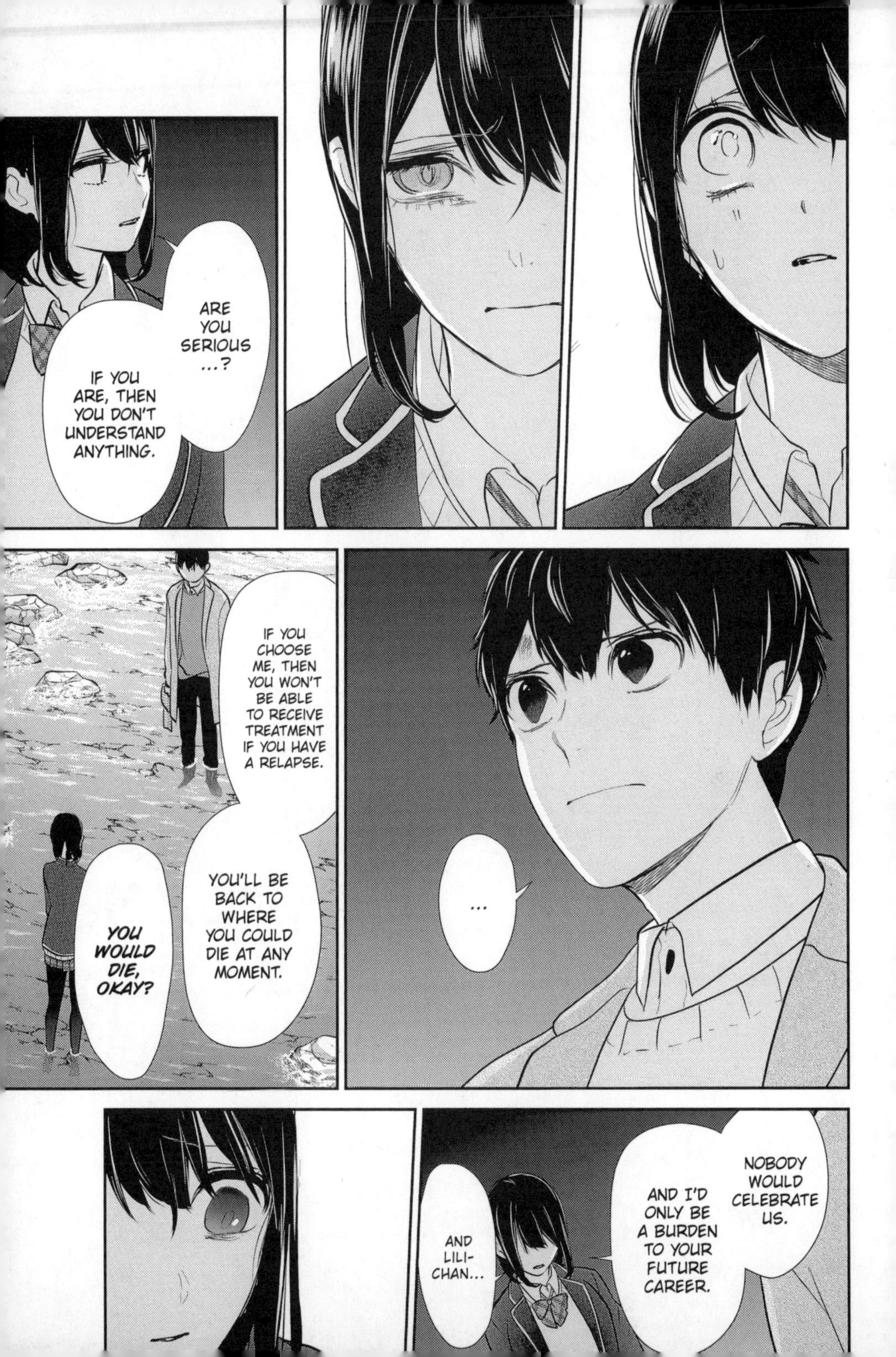
ARE YOU SERIOUS ...?
IF YOU ARE, THEN YOU DON'T UNDERSTAND ANYTHING.
...
IF YOU CHOOSE ME, THEN YOU WON'T BE ABLE TO RECEIVE TREATMENT IF YOU HAVE A RELAPSE.
YOU'LL BE BACK TO WHERE YOU COULD DIE AT ANY MOMENT.
YOU WOULD DIE, OKAY?
NOBODY WOULD CELEBRATE US.
AND I'D ONLY BE A BURDEN TO YOUR FUTURE CAREER.
AND LILI-CHAN...

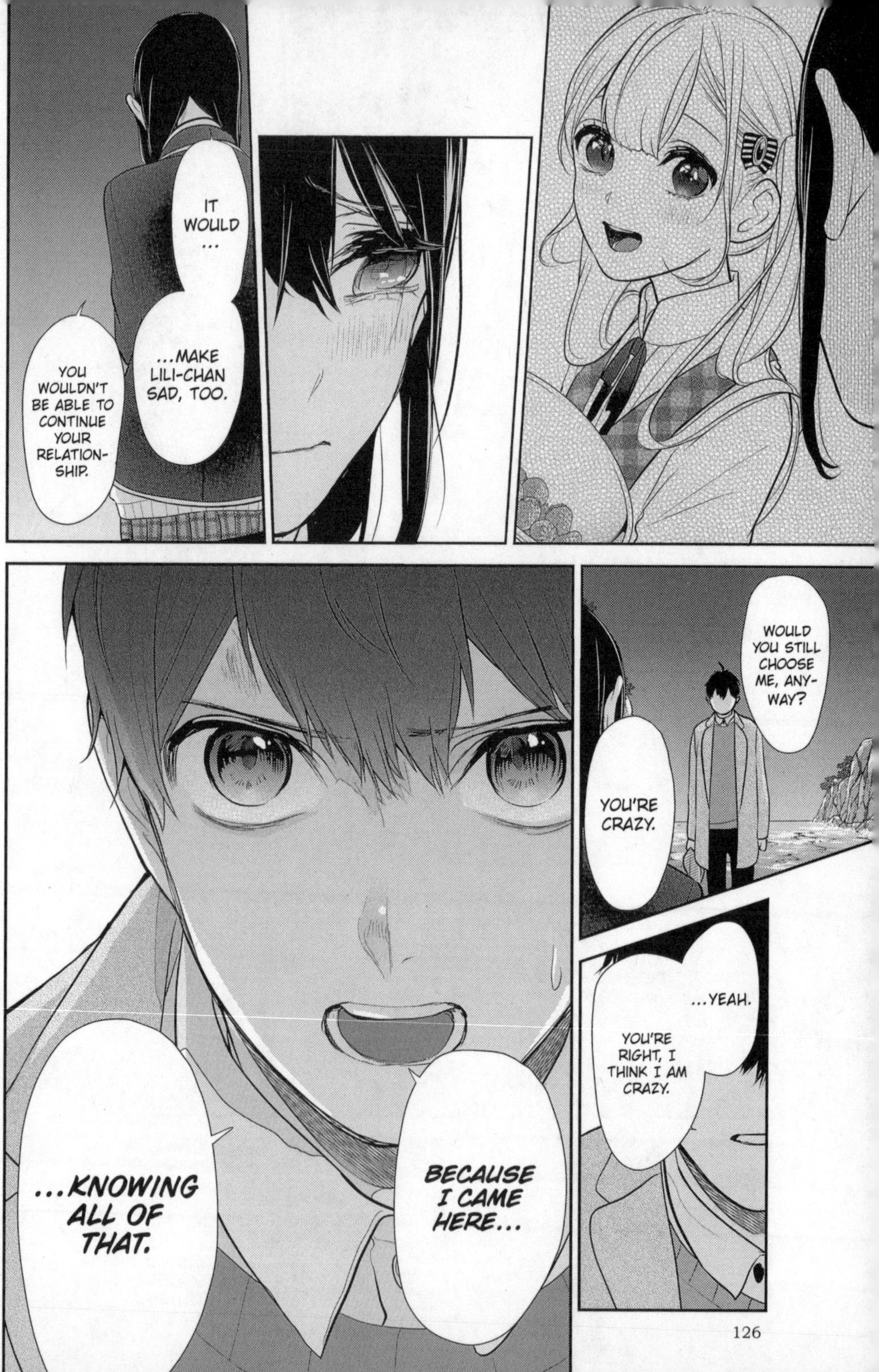
IT WOULD ...
...MAKE LILI-CHAN SAD, TOO.
YOU WOULDN'T BE ABLE TO CONTINUE YOUR RELATION-SHIP.
WOULD YOU STILL CHOOSE ME, ANY-WAY?
YOU'RE CRAZY.
...YEAH.
YOU'RE RIGHT, I THINK I AM CRAZY.
BECAUSE I CAME HERE...
...KNOWING ALL OF THAT.

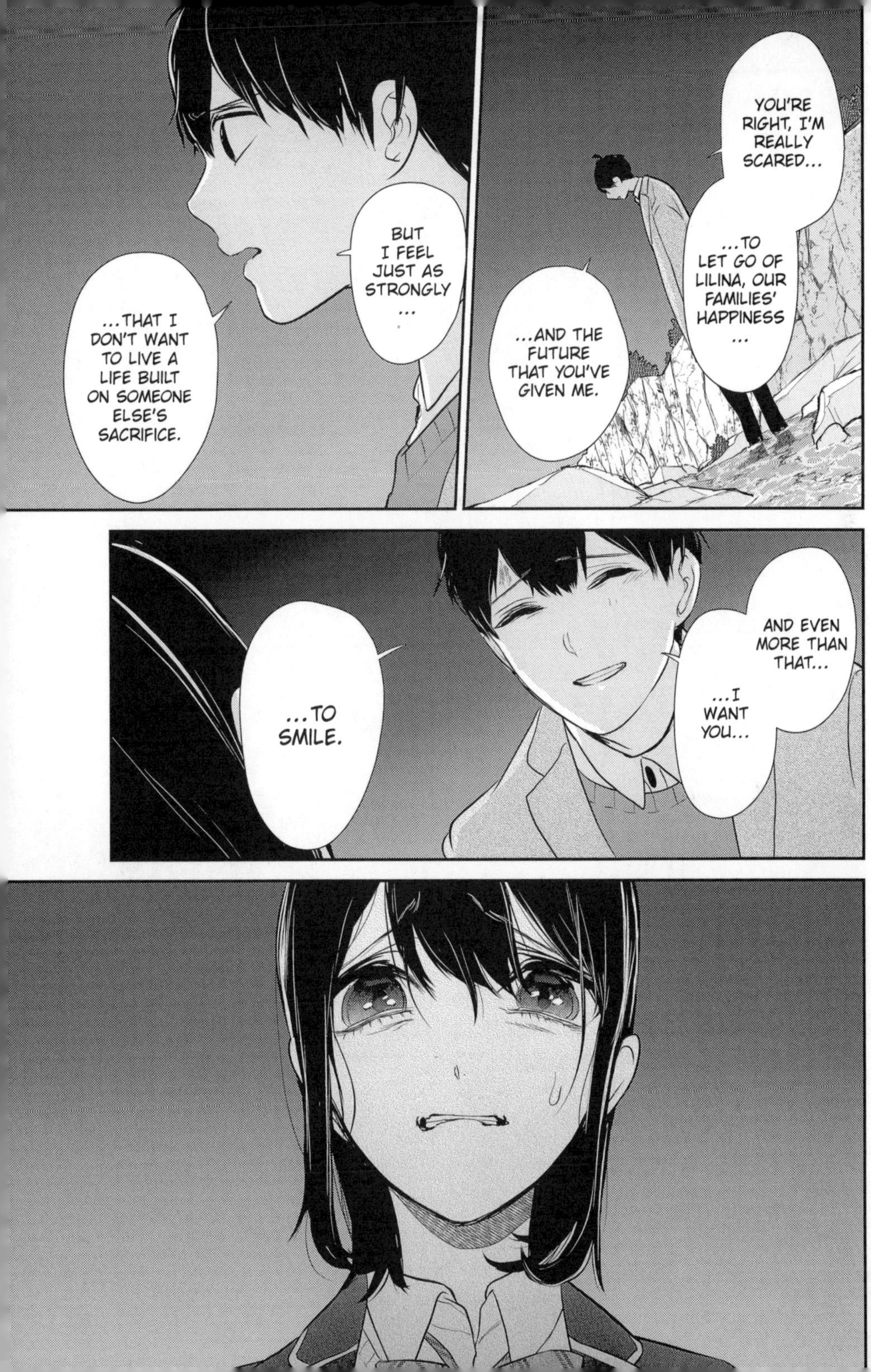
YOU'RE RIGHT, I'M REALLY SCARED...
...TO LET GO OF LILINA, OUR FAMILIES' HAPPINESS ...
...AND THE FUTURE THAT YOU'VE GIVEN ME.
BUT I FEEL JUST AS STRONGLY ...
...THAT I DON'T WANT TO LIVE A LIFE BUILT ON SOMEONE ELSE'S SACRIFICE.
AND EVEN MORE THAN THAT...
...I WANT YOU...
...TO SMILE.

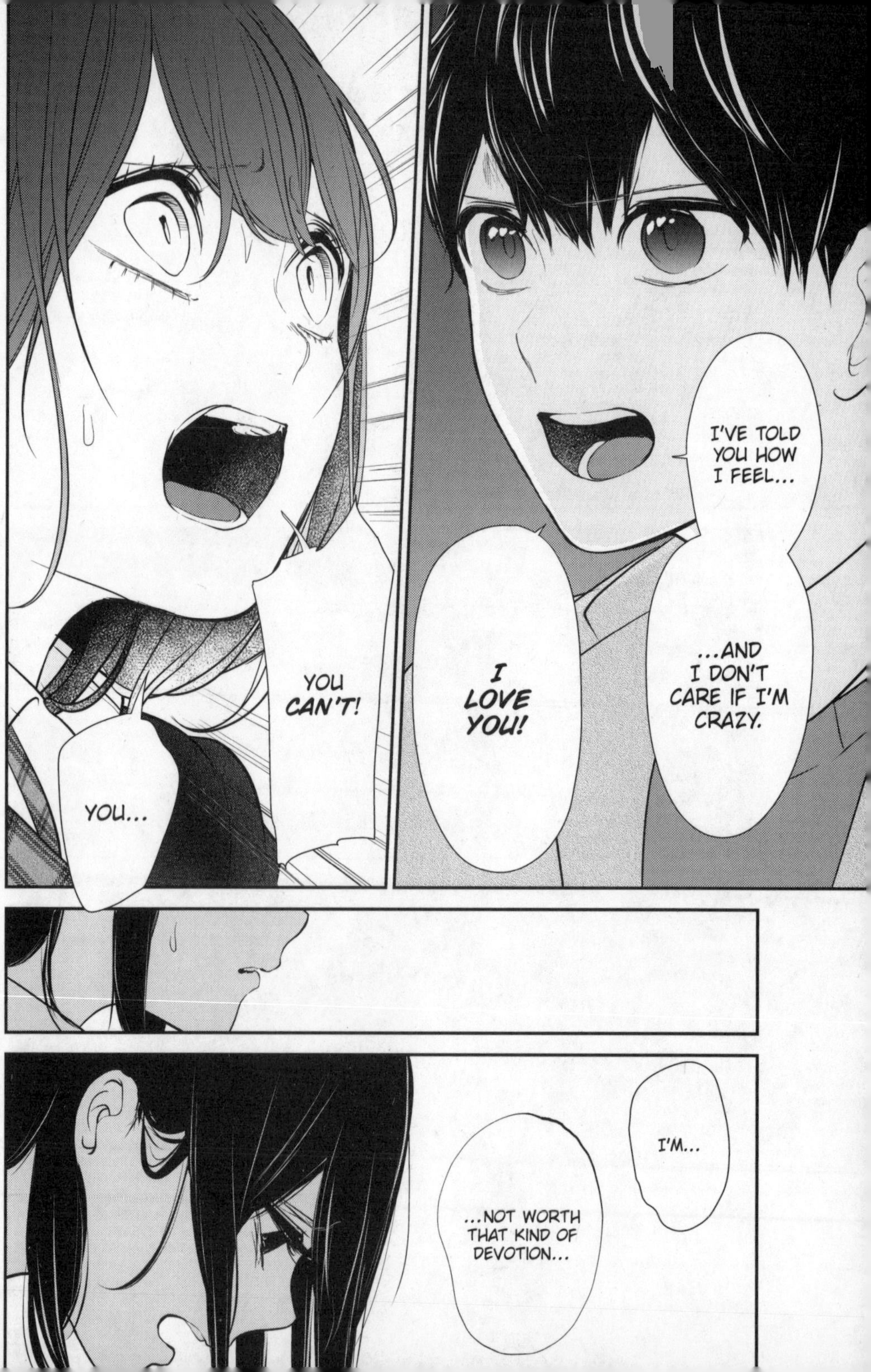
I'VE TOLD YOU HOW I FEEL...
...AND I DON'T CARE IF I'M CRAZY.
I LOVE YOU!
YOU CAN'T!
YOU...
I'M...
...NOT WORTH THAT KIND OF DEVOTION...

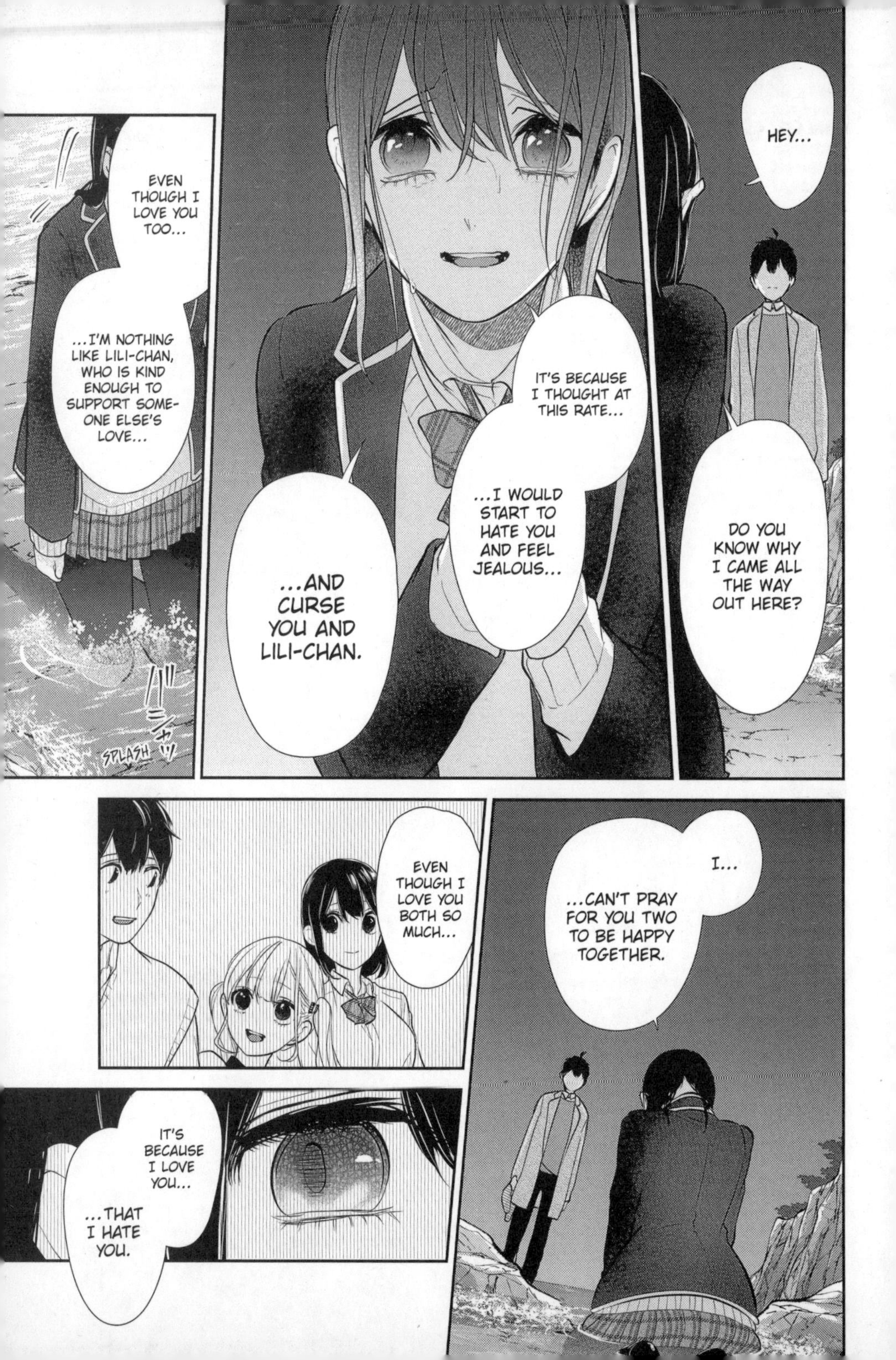
HEY...
DO YOU KNOW WHY I CAME ALL THE WAY OUT HERE?
IT'S BECAUSE I THOUGHT AT THIS RATE...
...I WOULD START TO HATE YOU AND FEEL JEALOUS...
...AND CURSE YOU AND LILI-CHAN.
EVEN THOUGH I LOVE YOU TOO...
...I'M NOTHING LIKE LILI-CHAN, WHO IS KIND ENOUGH TO SUPPORT SOME-ONE ELSE'S LOVE...
SPLASH
I...
...CAN'T PRAY FOR YOU TWO TO BE HAPPY TOGETHER.
EVEN THOUGH I LOVE YOU BOTH SO MUCH...
IT'S BECAUSE I LOVE YOU...
...THAT I HATE YOU.

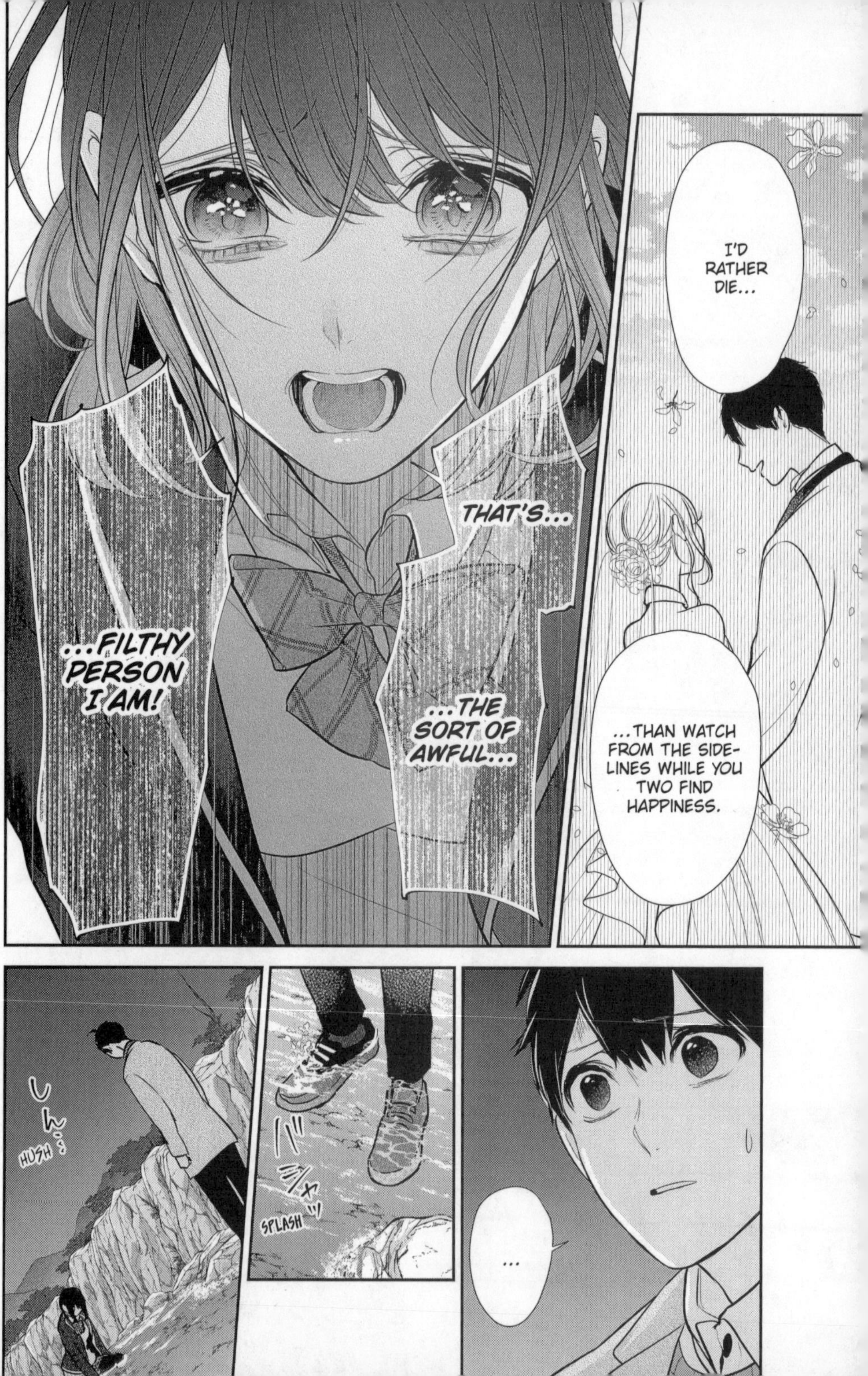
I'D RATHER DIE...
...THAN WATCH FROM THE SIDE-LINES WHILE YOU TWO FIND HAPPINESS.
THAT'S...
...THE SORT OF AWFUL...
...FILTHY PERSON I AM!
...
バシャッ
SPLASH
しん…
HUSH

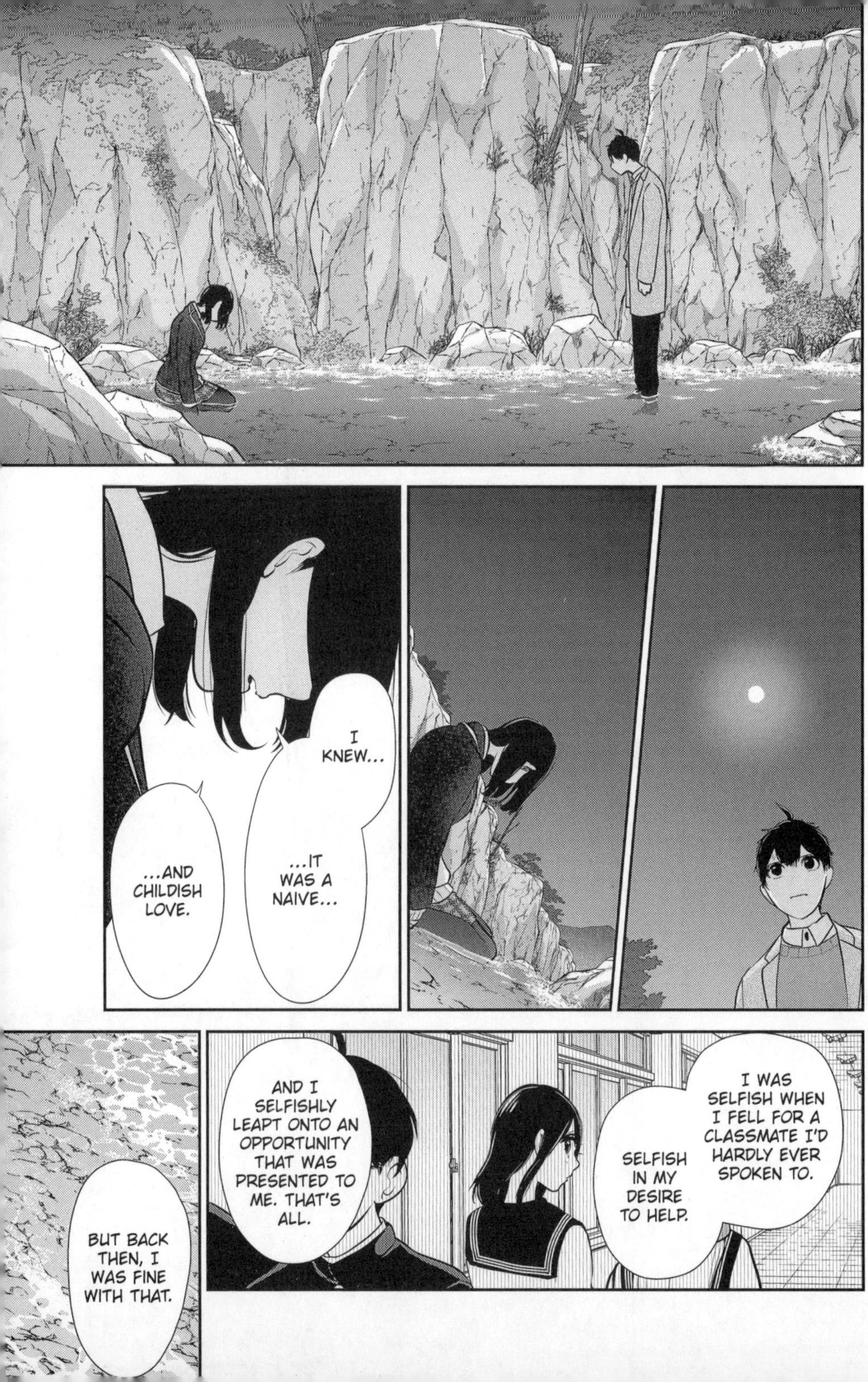
I KNEW...
...IT WAS A NAIVE...
...AND CHILDISH LOVE.
I WAS SELFISH WHEN I FELL FOR A CLASSMATE I'D HARDLY EVER SPOKEN TO.
SELFISH IN MY DESIRE TO HELP.
AND I SELFISHLY LEAPT ONTO AN OPPORTUNITY THAT WAS PRESENTED TO ME. THAT'S ALL.
BUT BACK THEN, I WAS FINE WITH THAT.

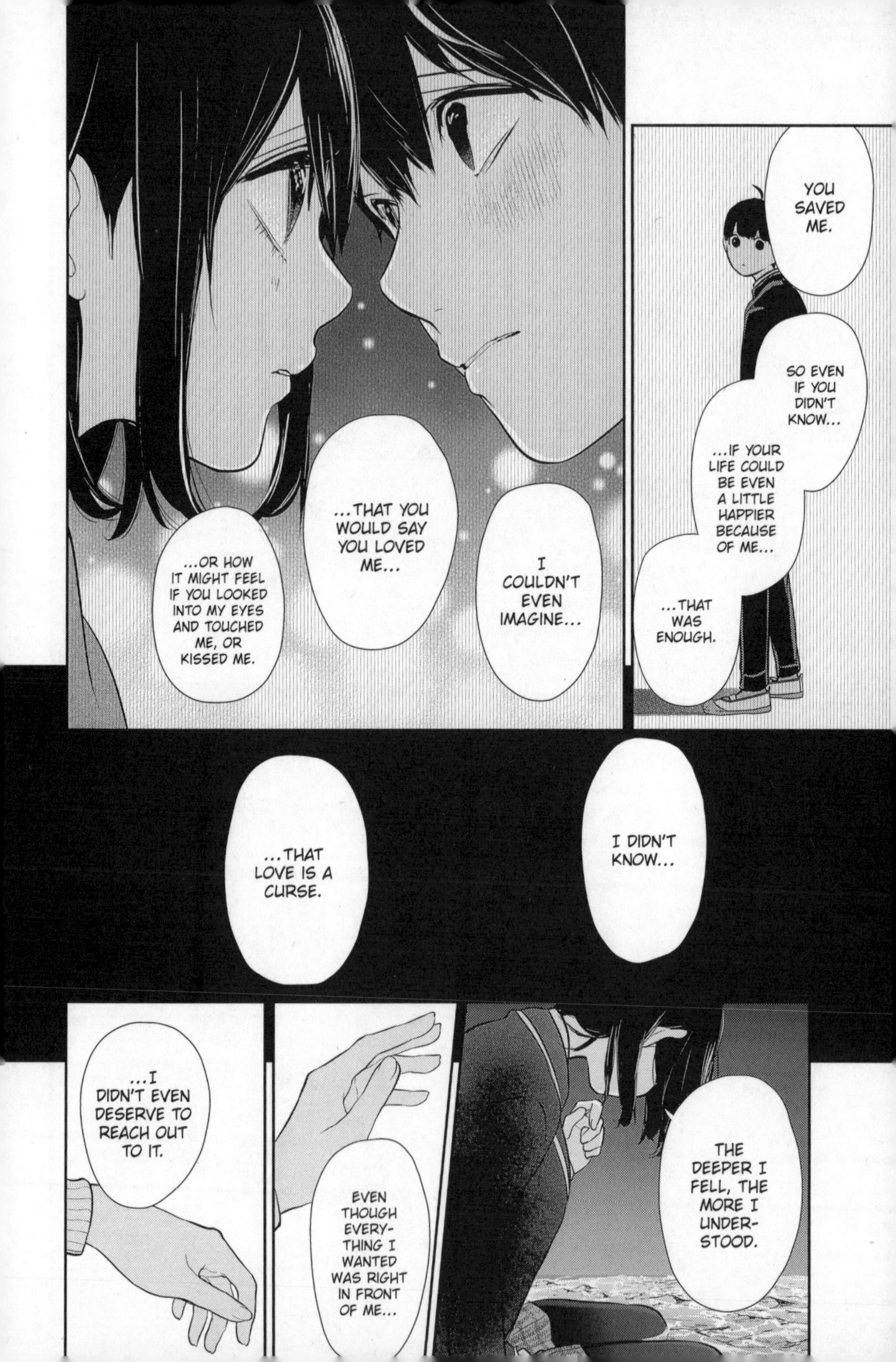
YOU SAVED ME.
SO EVEN IF YOU DIDN'T KNOW...
...IF YOUR LIFE COULD BE EVEN A LITTLE HAPPIER BECAUSE OF ME...
...THAT WAS ENOUGH.
I COULDN'T EVEN IMAGINE...
...THAT YOU WOULD SAY YOU LOVED ME...
...OR HOW IT MIGHT FEEL IF YOU LOOKED INTO MY EYES AND TOUCHED ME, OR KISSED ME.
I DIDN'T KNOW...
...THAT LOVE IS A CURSE.
THE DEEPER I FELL, THE MORE I UNDER-STOOD.
EVEN THOUGH EVERY-THING I WANTED WAS RIGHT IN FRONT OF ME...
...I DIDN'T EVEN DESERVE TO REACH OUT TO IT.

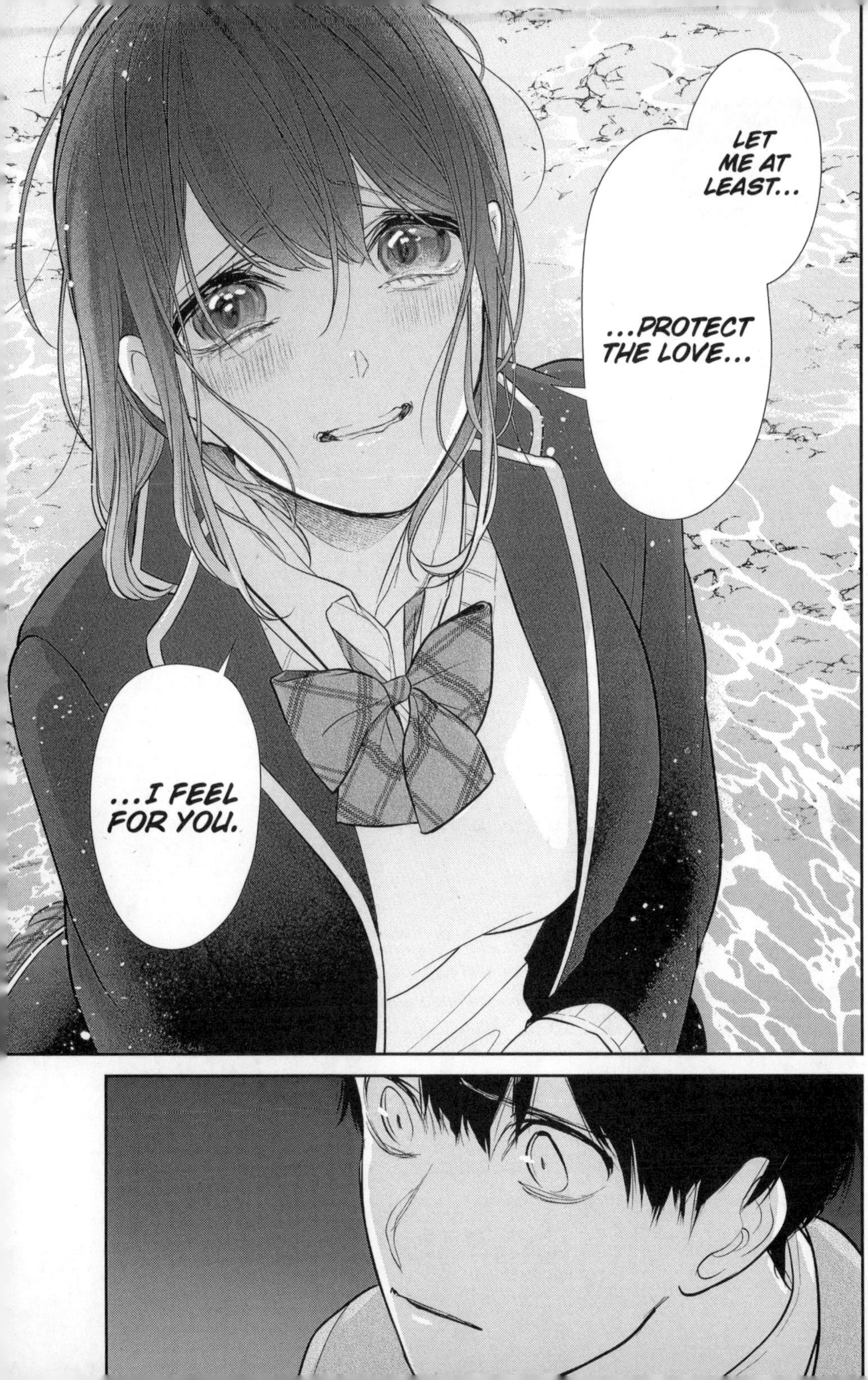
LET ME AT LEAST...
...PROTECT THE LOVE...
...I FEEL FOR YOU.

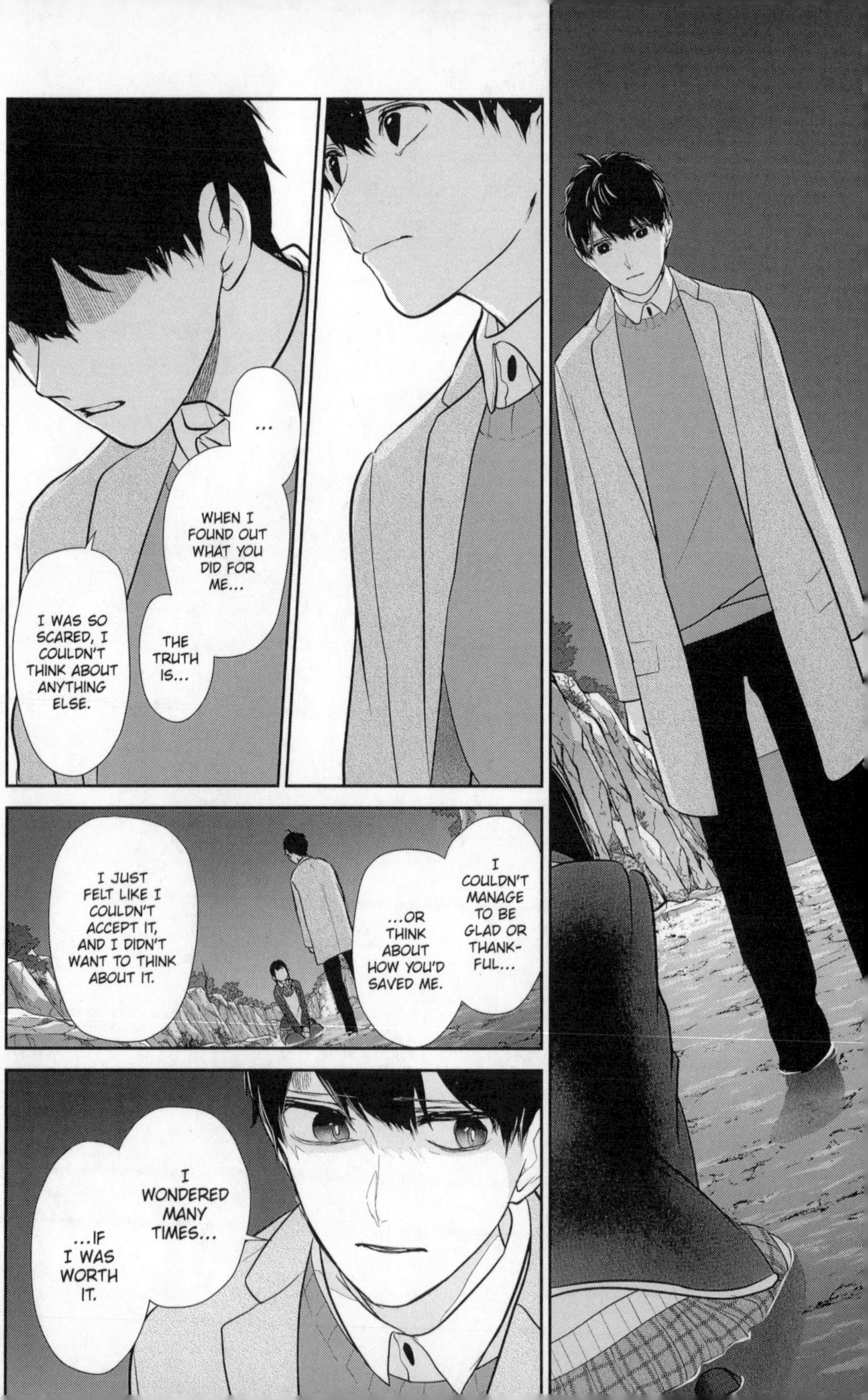
...
WHEN I FOUND OUT WHAT YOU DID FOR ME...
THE TRUTH IS...
I WAS SO SCARED, I COULDN'T THINK ABOUT ANYTHING ELSE.
I COULDN'T MANAGE TO BE GLAD OR THANK-FUL...
...OR THINK ABOUT HOW YOU'D SAVED ME.
I JUST FELT LIKE I COULDN'T ACCEPT IT, AND I DIDN'T WANT TO THINK ABOUT IT.
I WONDERED MANY TIMES...
...IF I WAS WORTH IT.

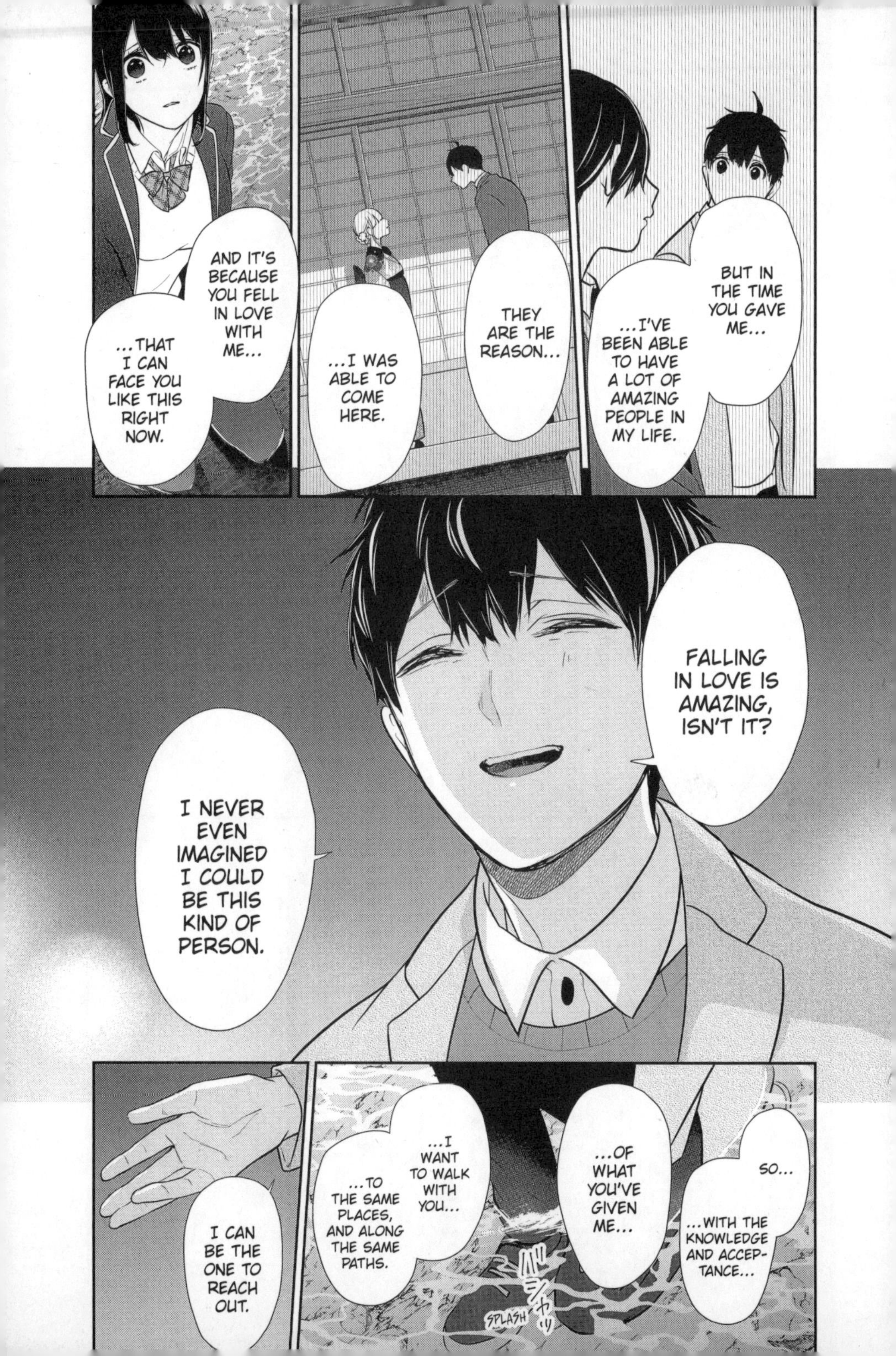
BUT IN THE TIME YOU GAVE ME...
...I'VE BEEN ABLE TO HAVE A LOT OF AMAZING PEOPLE IN MY LIFE.
THEY ARE THE REASON...
...I WAS ABLE TO COME HERE.
AND IT'S BECAUSE YOU FELL IN LOVE WITH ME...
...THAT I CAN FACE YOU LIKE THIS RIGHT NOW.
FALLING IN LOVE IS AMAZING, ISN'T IT?
I NEVER EVEN IMAGINED I COULD BE THIS KIND OF PERSON.
SO...
...WITH THE KNOWLEDGE AND ACCEPTANCE...
...OF WHAT YOU'VE GIVEN ME...
...I WANT TO WALK WITH YOU...
...TO THE SAME PLACES, AND ALONG THE SAME PATHS.
バシャッ
SPLASH
I CAN BE THE ONE TO REACH OUT.

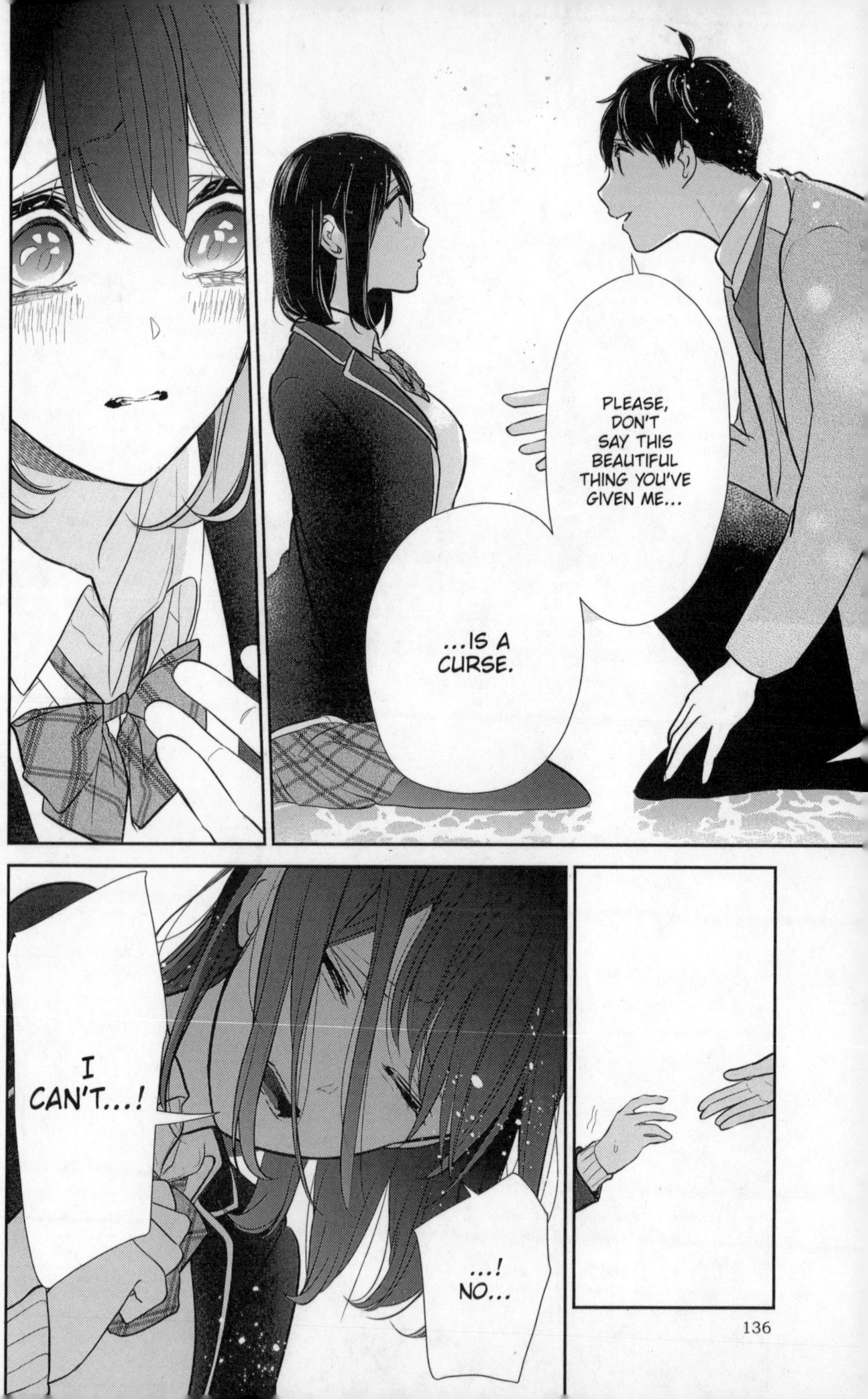
PLEASE, DON'T SAY THIS BEAUTIFUL THING YOU'VE GIVEN ME...
...IS A CURSE.
...! NO...
I CAN'T...!

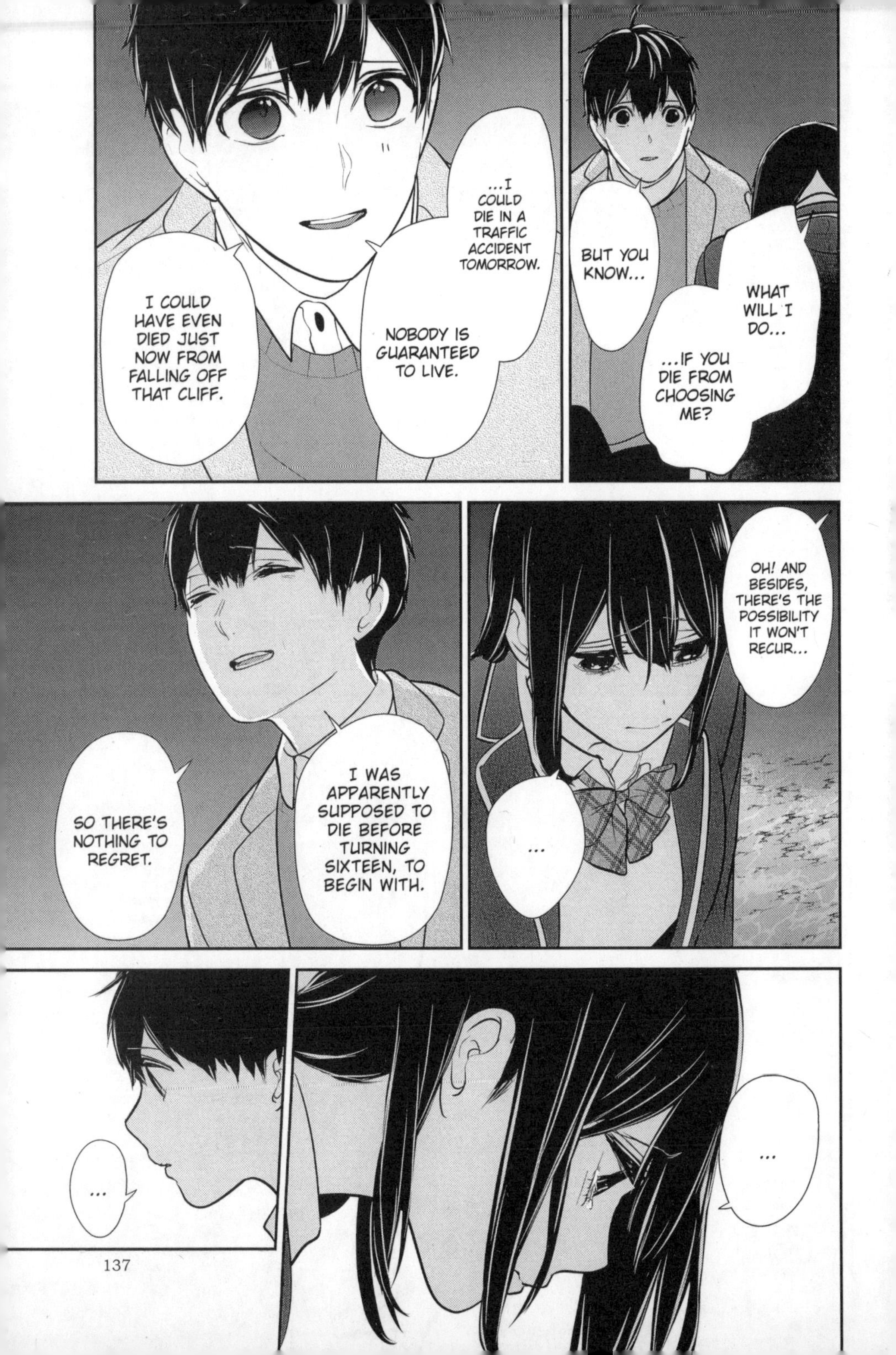
BUT YOU KNOW...
WHAT WILL I DO...
...IF YOU DIE FROM CHOOSING ME?
...I COULD DIE IN A TRAFFIC ACCIDENT TOMORROW.
NOBODY IS GUARANTEED TO LIVE.
I COULD HAVE EVEN DIED JUST NOW FROM FALLING OFF THAT CLIFF.
OH! AND BESIDES, THERE'S THE POSSIBILITY IT WON'T RECUR...
...
I WAS APPARENTLY SUPPOSED TO DIE BEFORE TURNING SIXTEEN, TO BEGIN WITH.
SO THERE'S NOTHING TO REGRET.
...
...

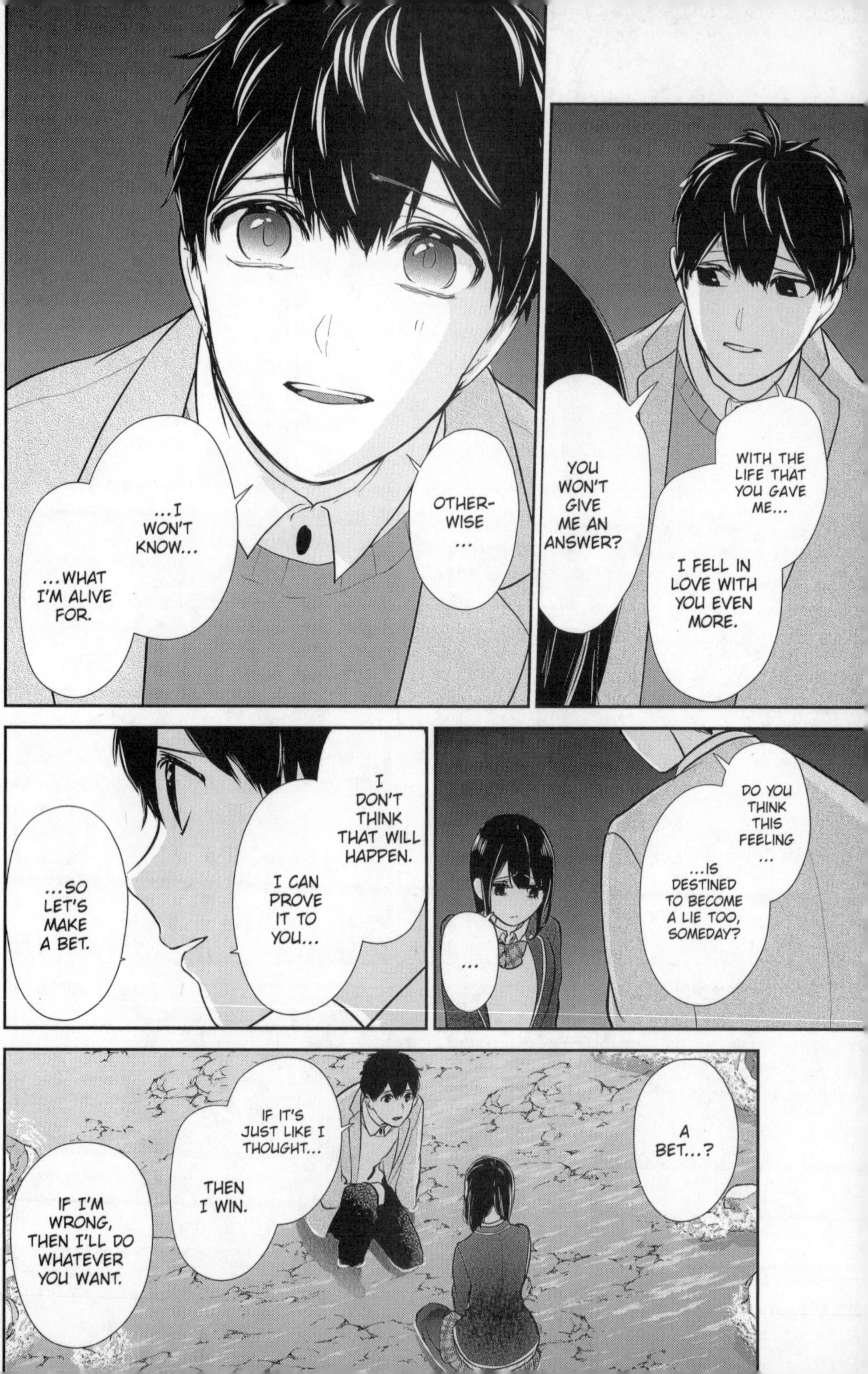
WITH THE LIFE THAT YOU GAVE ME...
I FELL IN LOVE WITH YOU EVEN MORE.
YOU WON'T GIVE ME AN ANSWER?
OTHER-WISE...
...I WON'T KNOW...
...WHAT I'M ALIVE FOR.
DO YOU THINK THIS FEELING...
...IS DESTINED TO BECOME A LIE TOO, SOMEDAY?
...
I DON'T THINK THAT WILL HAPPEN.
I CAN PROVE IT TO YOU...
...SO LET'S MAKE A BET.
A BET...?
IF IT'S JUST LIKE I THOUGHT...
THEN I WIN.
IF I'M WRONG, THEN I'LL DO WHATEVER YOU WANT.

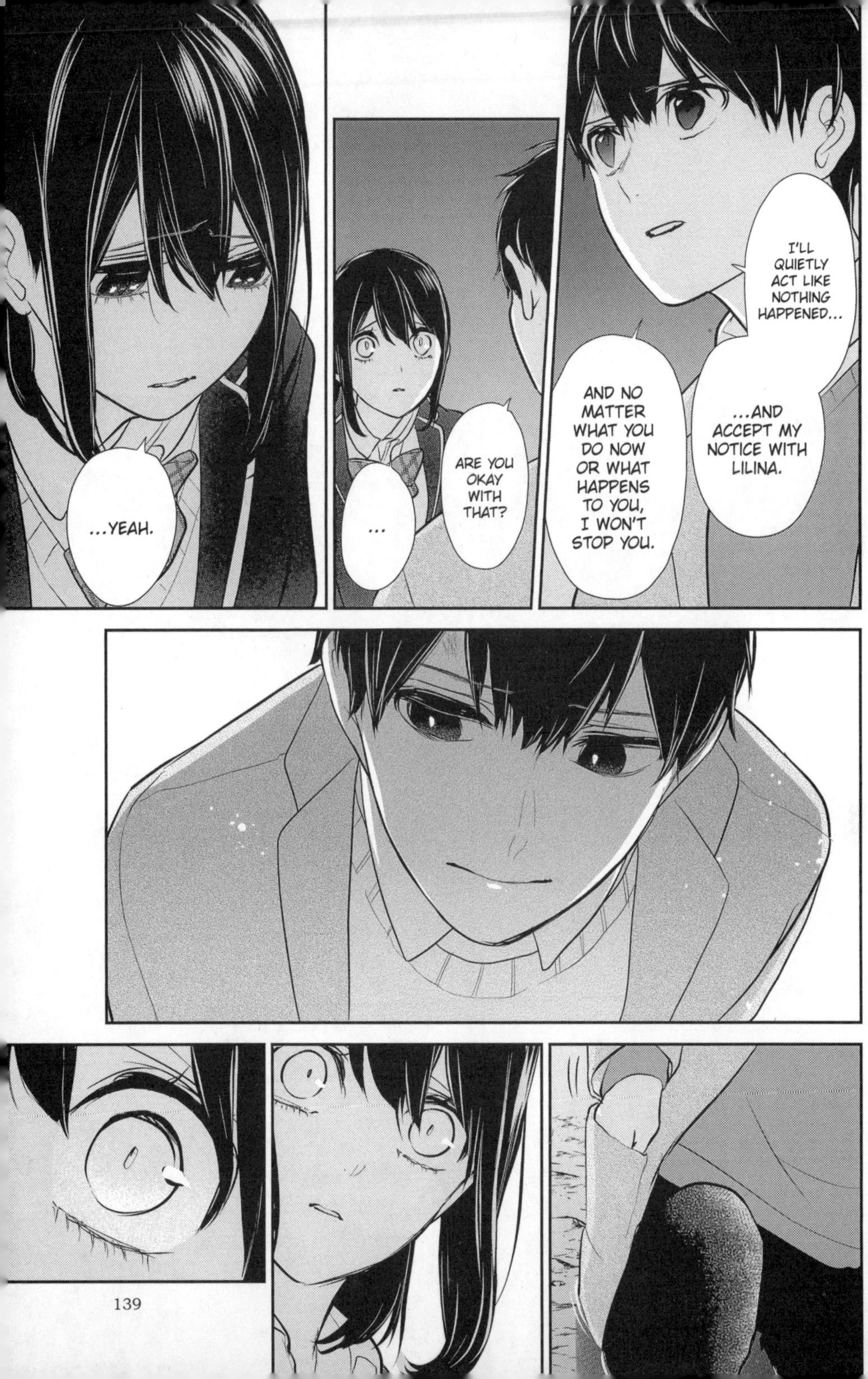
I'LL QUIETLY ACT LIKE NOTHING HAPPENED...
...AND ACCEPT MY NOTICE WITH LILINA.
AND NO MATTER WHAT YOU DO NOW OR WHAT HAPPENS TO YOU, I WON'T STOP YOU.
ARE YOU OKAY WITH THAT?
...
...YEAH.

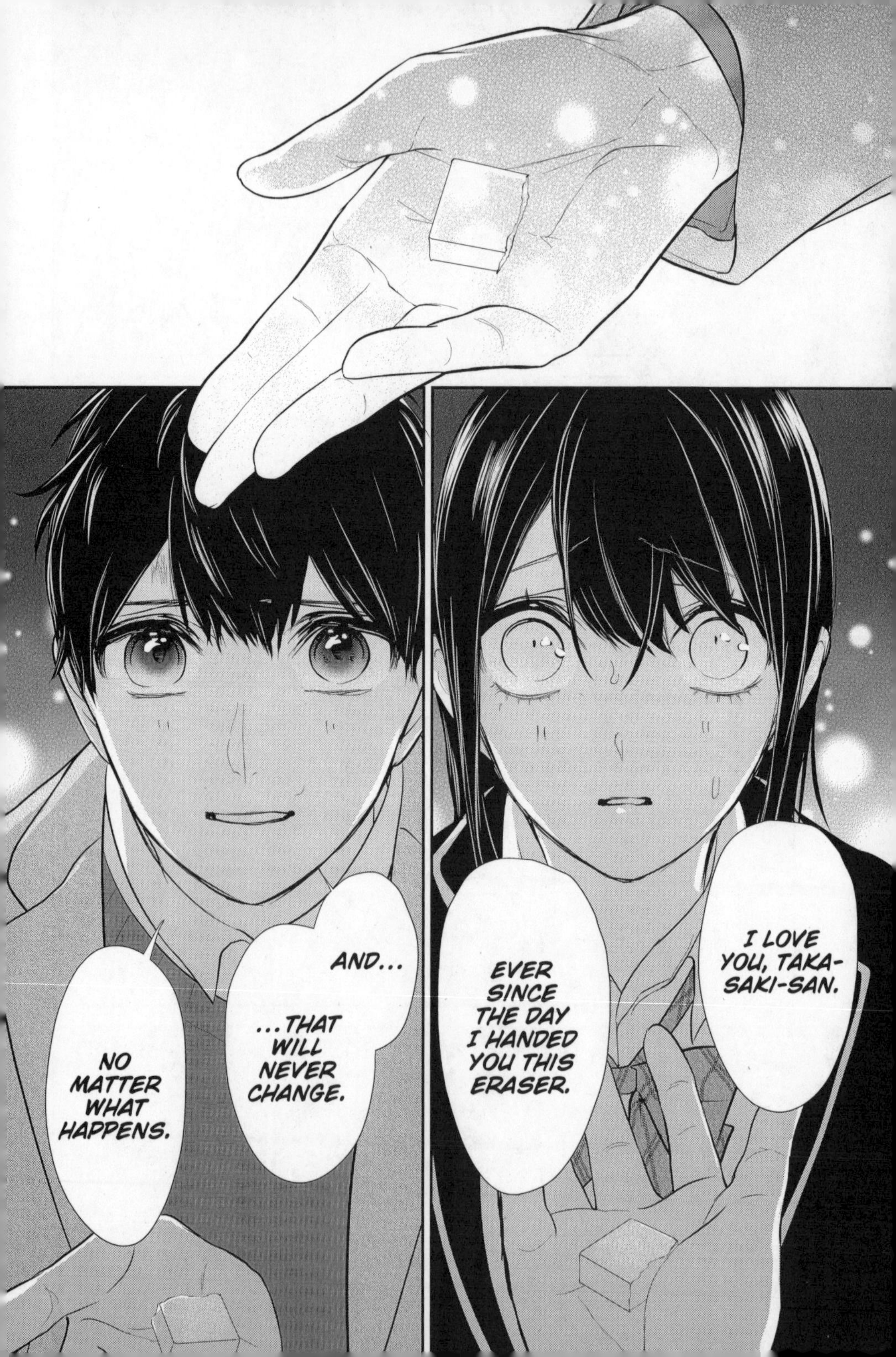
I LOVE YOU, TAKA-SAKI-SAN.
EVER SINCE THE DAY I HANDED YOU THIS ERASER.
AND...
...THAT WILL NEVER CHANGE.
NO MATTER WHAT HAPPENS.

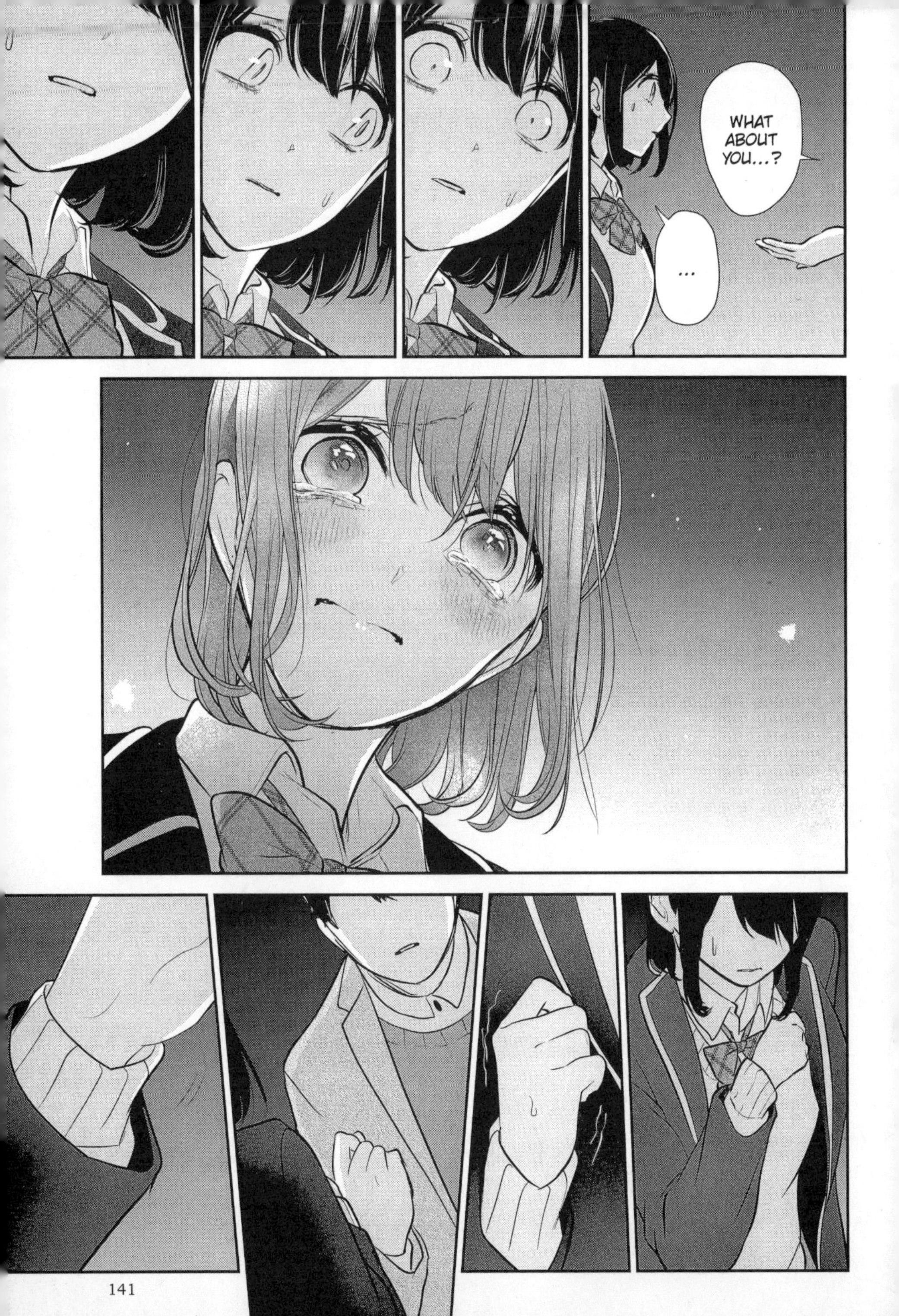
WHAT ABOUT YOU...?
...

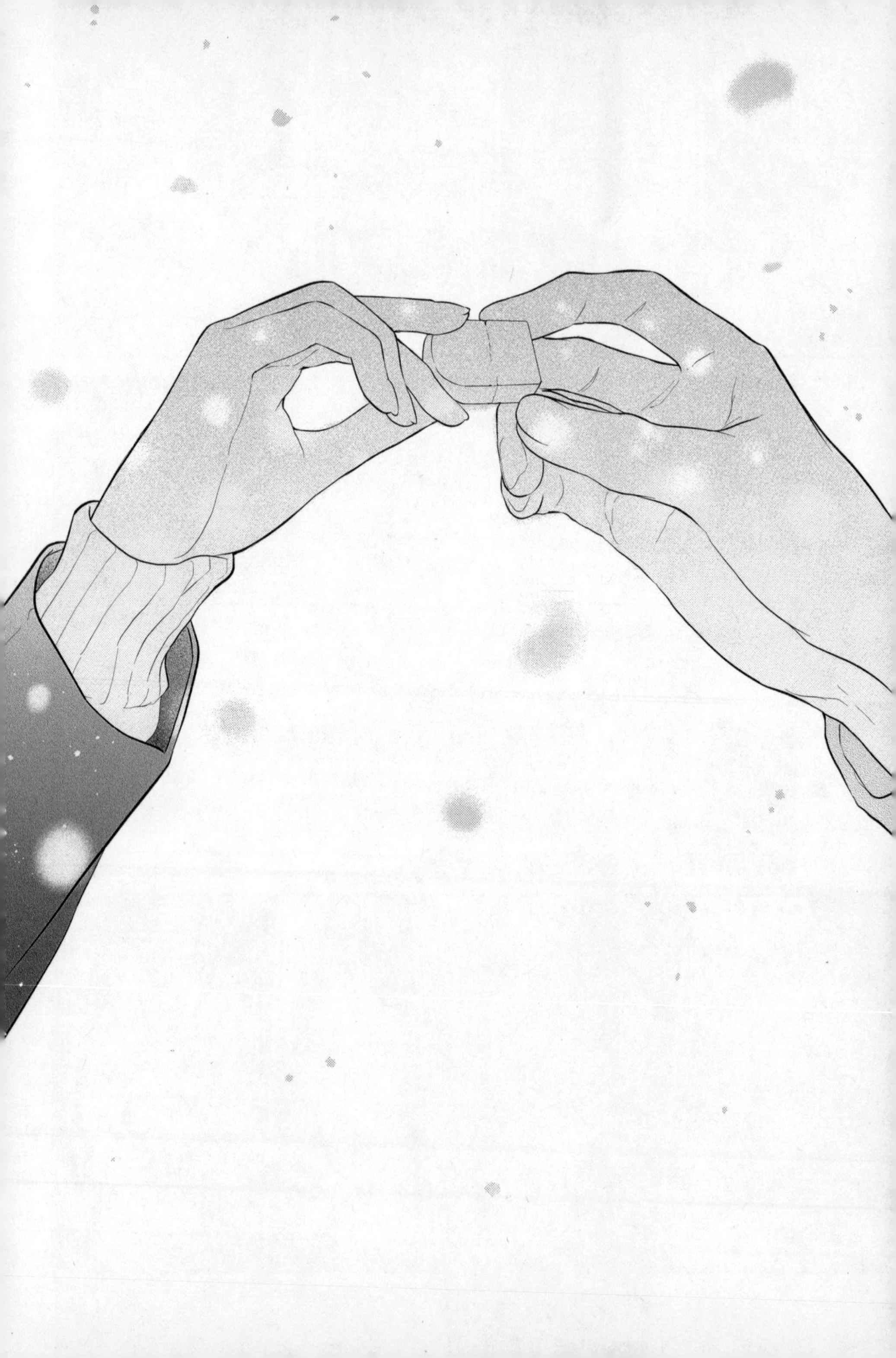

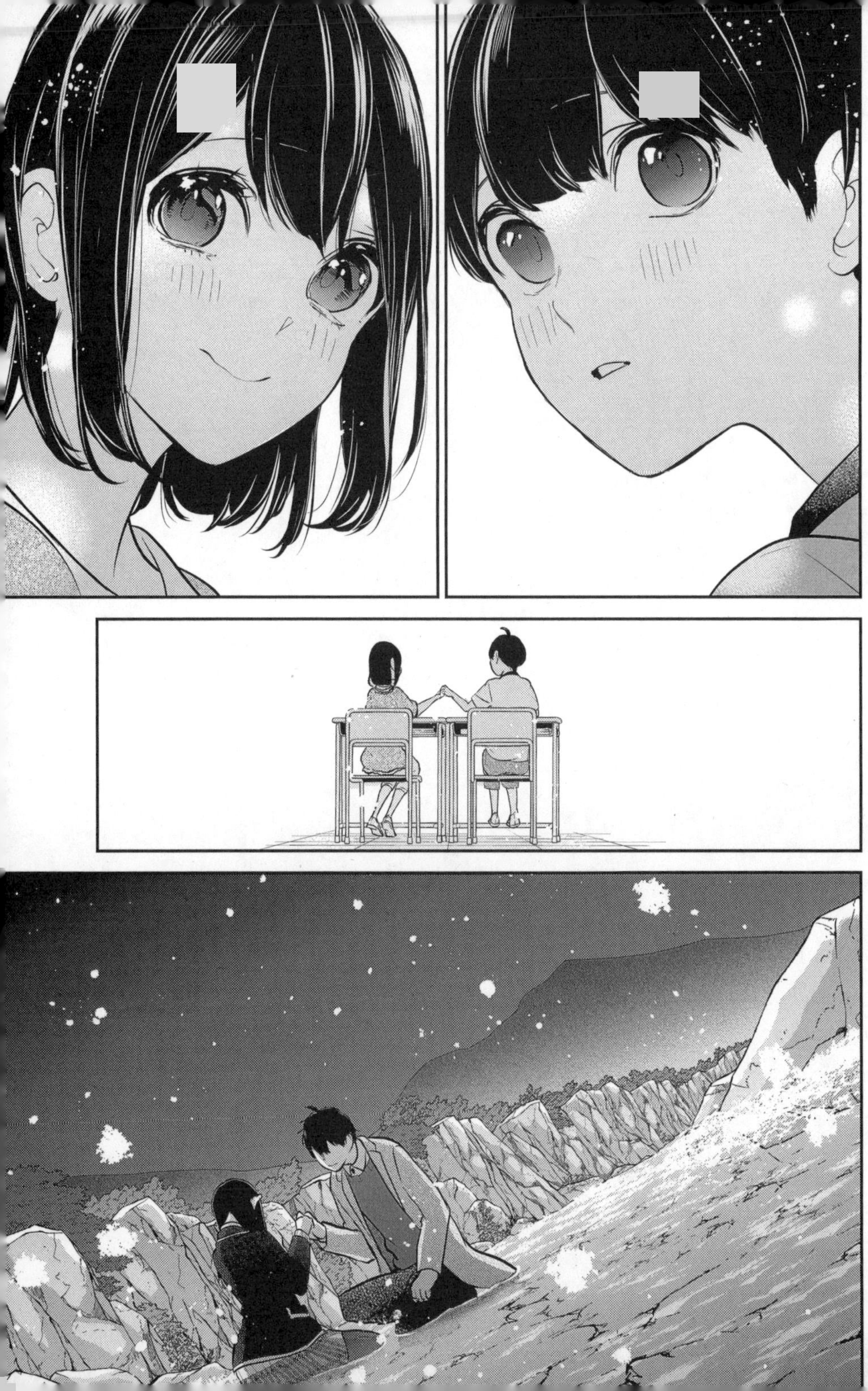

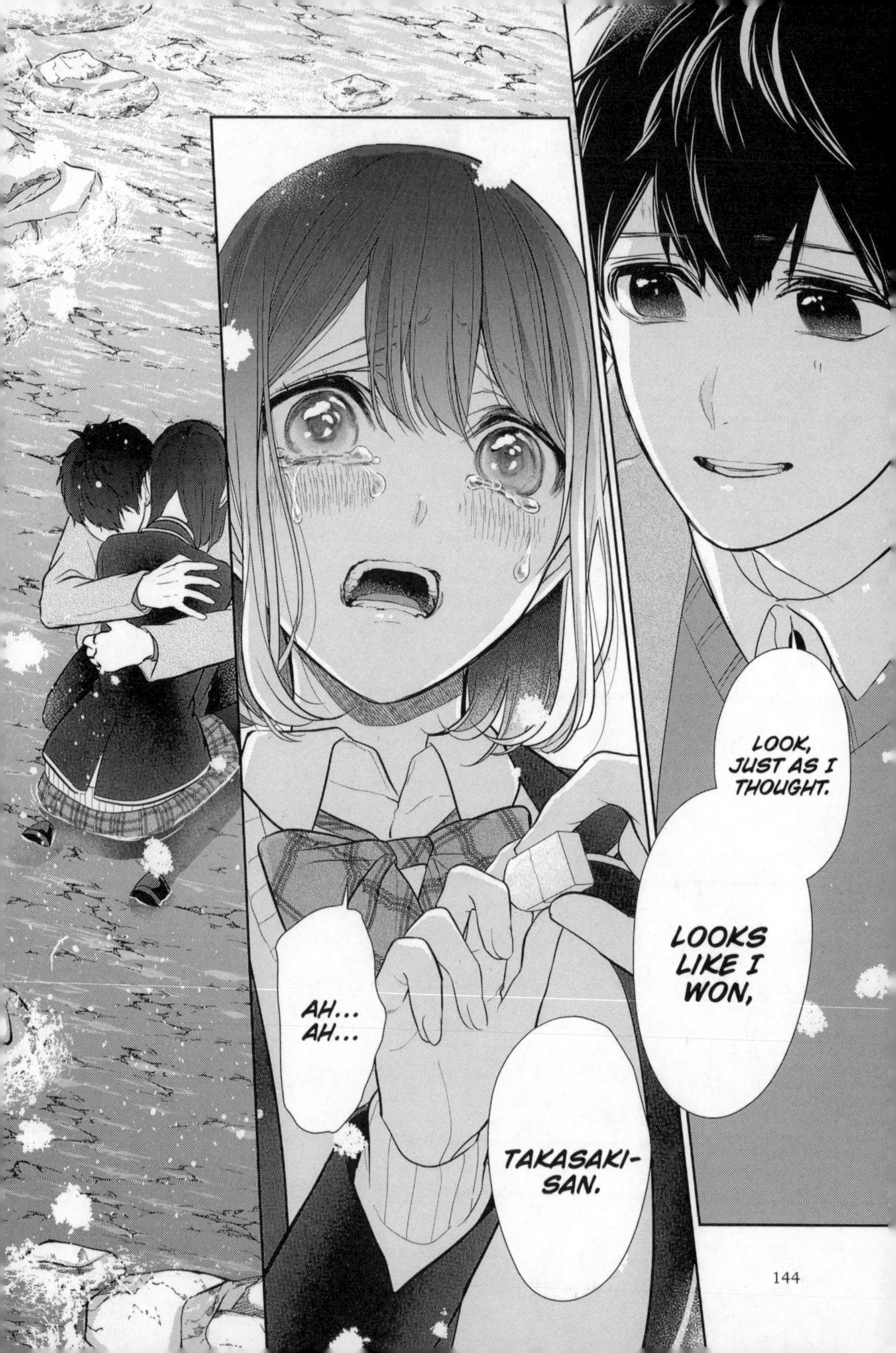
LOOK, JUST AS I THOUGHT.
LOOKS LIKE I WON,
TAKASAKI-SAN.
AH... AH...

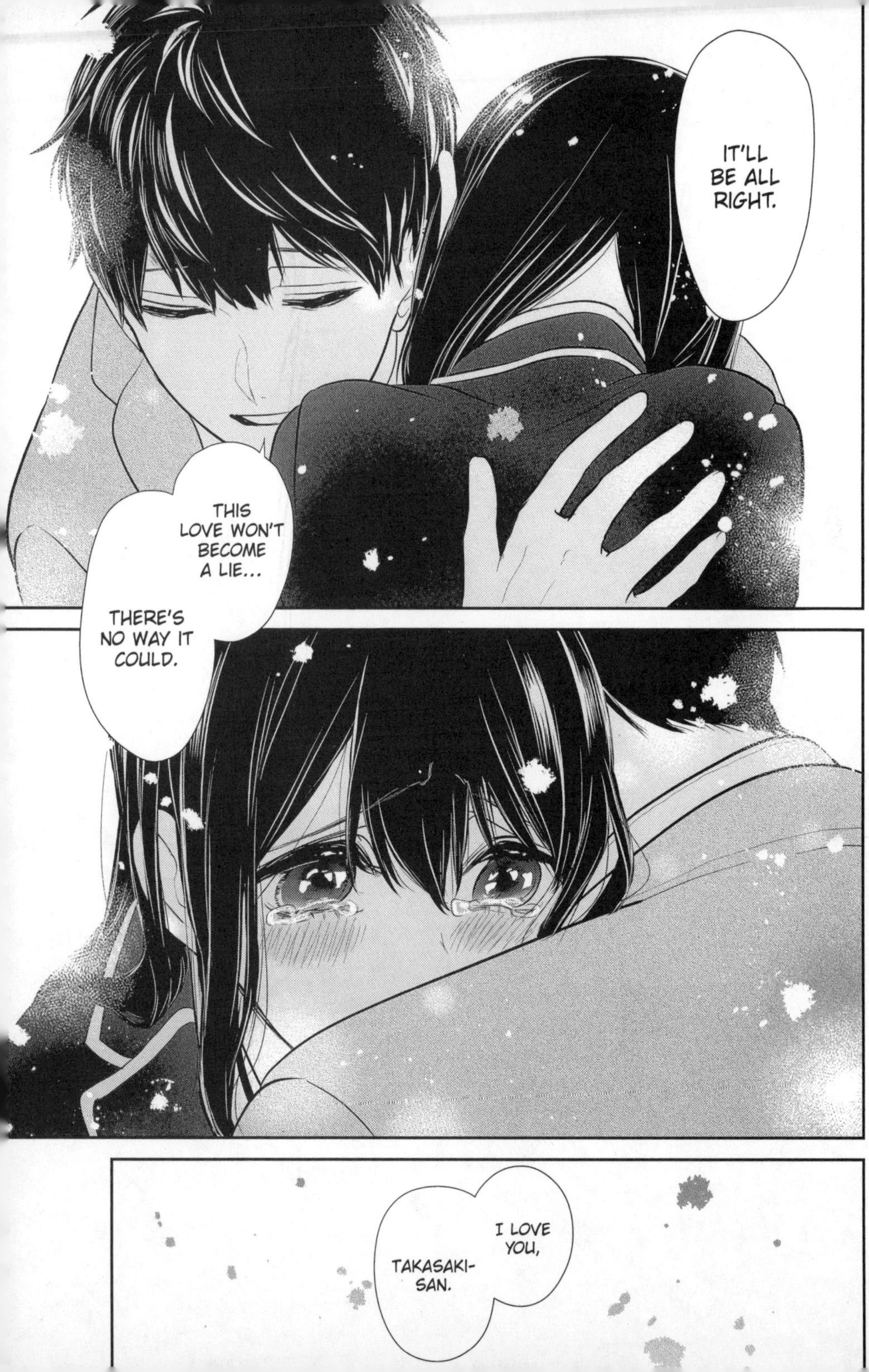
IT'LL BE ALL RIGHT.
THIS LOVE WON'T BECOME A LIE... THERE'S NO WAY IT COULD.
I LOVE YOU, TAKASAKI-SAN.

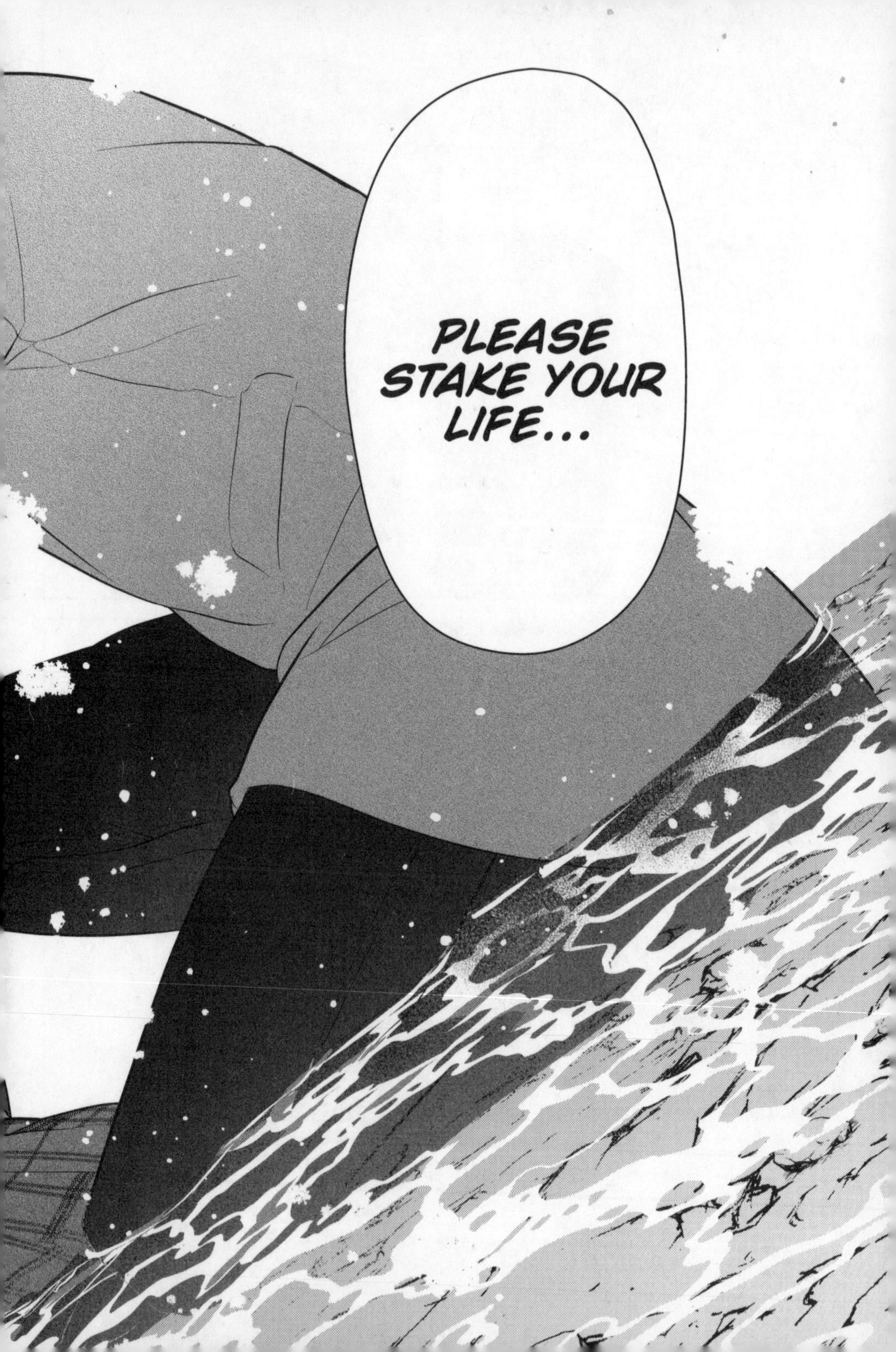
PLEASE STAKE YOUR LIFE...

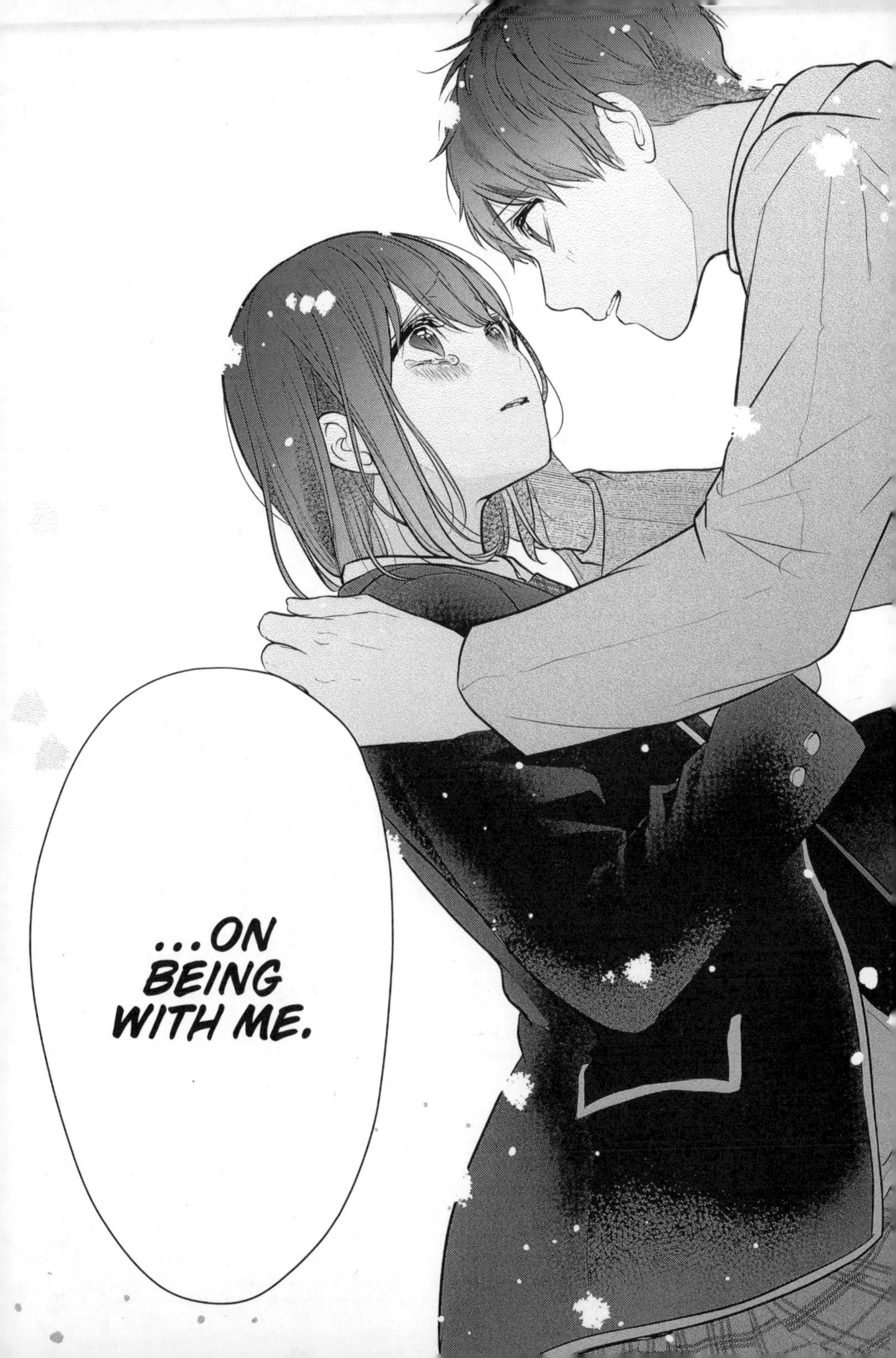
...ON BEING WITH ME.

 ★ SPECIAL THANKS ★

TAKANAGA-SAMA
YOSHIMURA-SAMA
ISHIKAWA-SAMA
SHINOHARA-SAMA   BOKU-SAMA

MANARU AMAGAWA-SAMA   FUKU-SAMA   KOUSUKE KOMATSU-SAMA
YUTAKA TACHIBANA-SAMA   KATSURAGI-SAMA   SHIDOU   HIDEKI-SAMA

WEEKLY SHONEN MAGAZINE EDITORIAL
EVERYONE FROM PROOFREADING, SALES, ADVERTISING, RIGHTS
AND MANGABOX

SHINDO KEISHODO KK   FUTABA KIKAKU KK
ALL THE BOOKSTORES ACROSS THE COUNTRY
EVERYONE INVOLVED WITH THE ANIME

COVER DESIGN
HIVE-SAMA

ALL MY FRIENDS
EVERYONE IN MY FAMILY

 ☆ AND ☆

ALL OF MY READERS

I WAS ALWAYS PUSHING MY LIMITS TRYING TO MAKE THIS MANGA AS GOOD AS IT COULD BE,
SO I STUMBLED A LOT, AND EVERY TIME, MY EDITORS SUPPORTED ME AND KEPT ME GOING.

THANKS AS WELL TO THE BOOKSELLERS WHO SHIPPED OFF THIS MANGA I WORKED ON,
AND ALL OF THE READERS WHO PICKED THEM UP. WITH THIS STORY, I WAS ABLE TO
REACH PLACES THAT I WOULD NEVER HAVE IMAGINED BEFORE THIS SERIALIZATION BEGAN.

THANK YOU VERY MUCH FOR ALWAYS STAYING WITH ME AS I'VE DONE MY BEST TO PUSH MYSELF.
I HOPE NEXT TIME I CAN SHOW YOU EVEN GREATER GROWTH!

MUSAWO

Chapter 49: Beneath the Sunrise

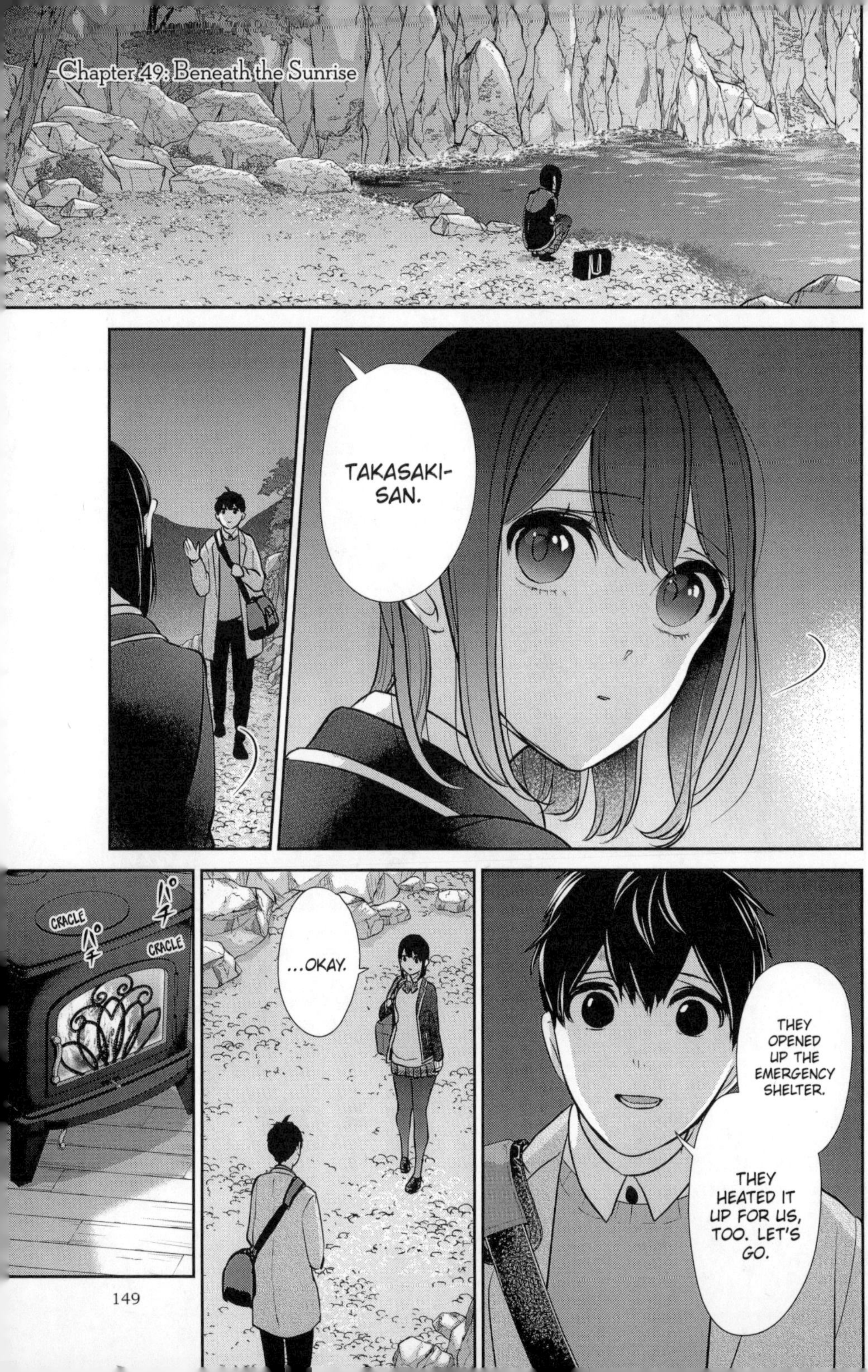
TAKASAKI-SAN.
THEY OPENED UP THE EMERGENCY SHELTER.
THEY HEATED IT UP FOR US, TOO. LET'S GO.
...OKAY.
パチ
CRACLE
パチ
CRACLE

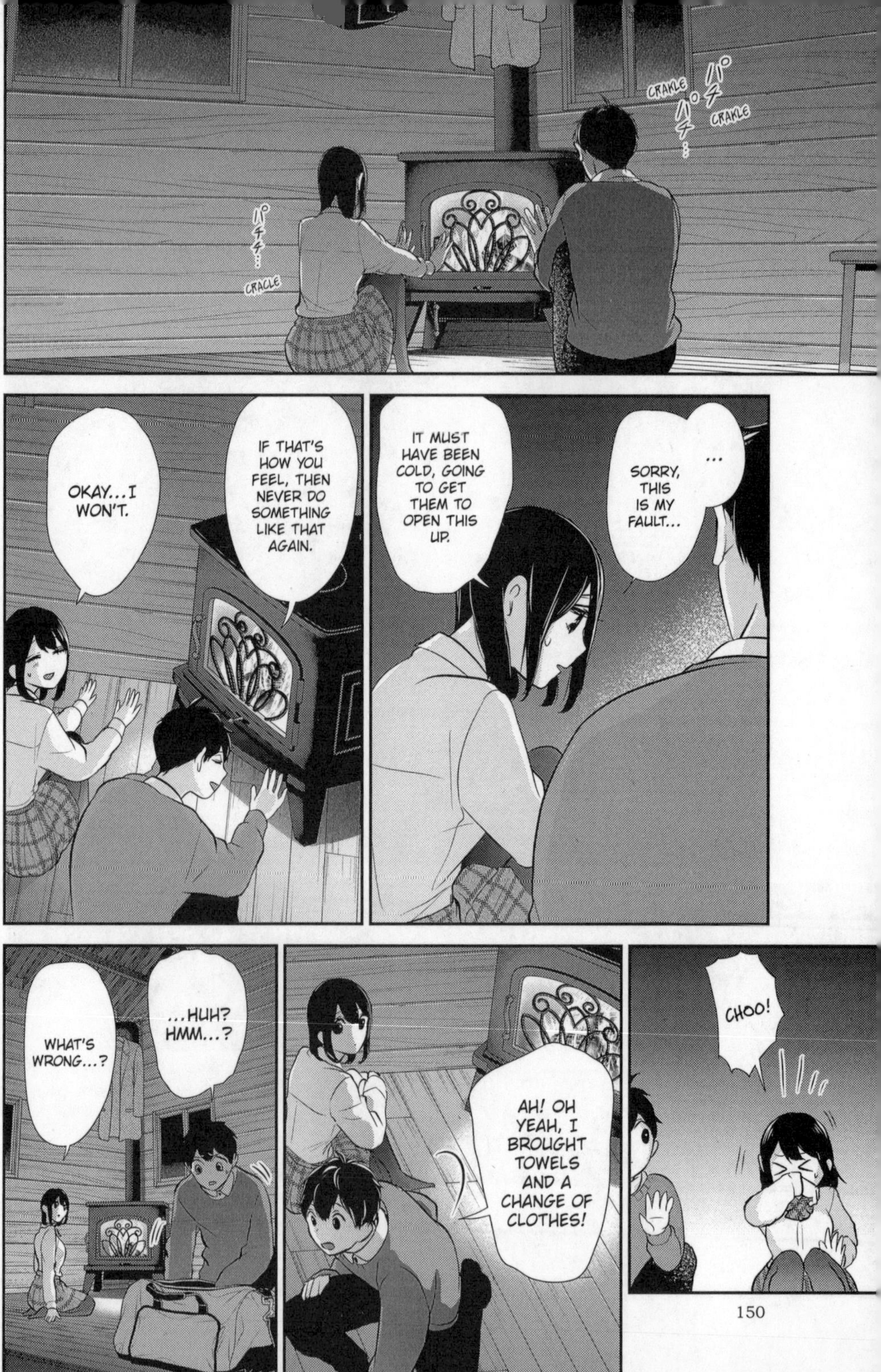
パチ
CRAKLE
パチ…
CRAKLE
パチチ…
CRACLE
...
SORRY, THIS IS MY FAULT...
IT MUST HAVE BEEN COLD, GOING TO GET THEM TO OPEN THIS UP.
IF THAT'S HOW YOU FEEL, THEN NEVER DO SOMETHING LIKE THAT AGAIN.
OKAY...I WON'T.
CHOO!
AH! OH YEAH, I BROUGHT TOWELS AND A CHANGE OF CLOTHES!
...HUH? HMM...?
WHAT'S WRONG...?

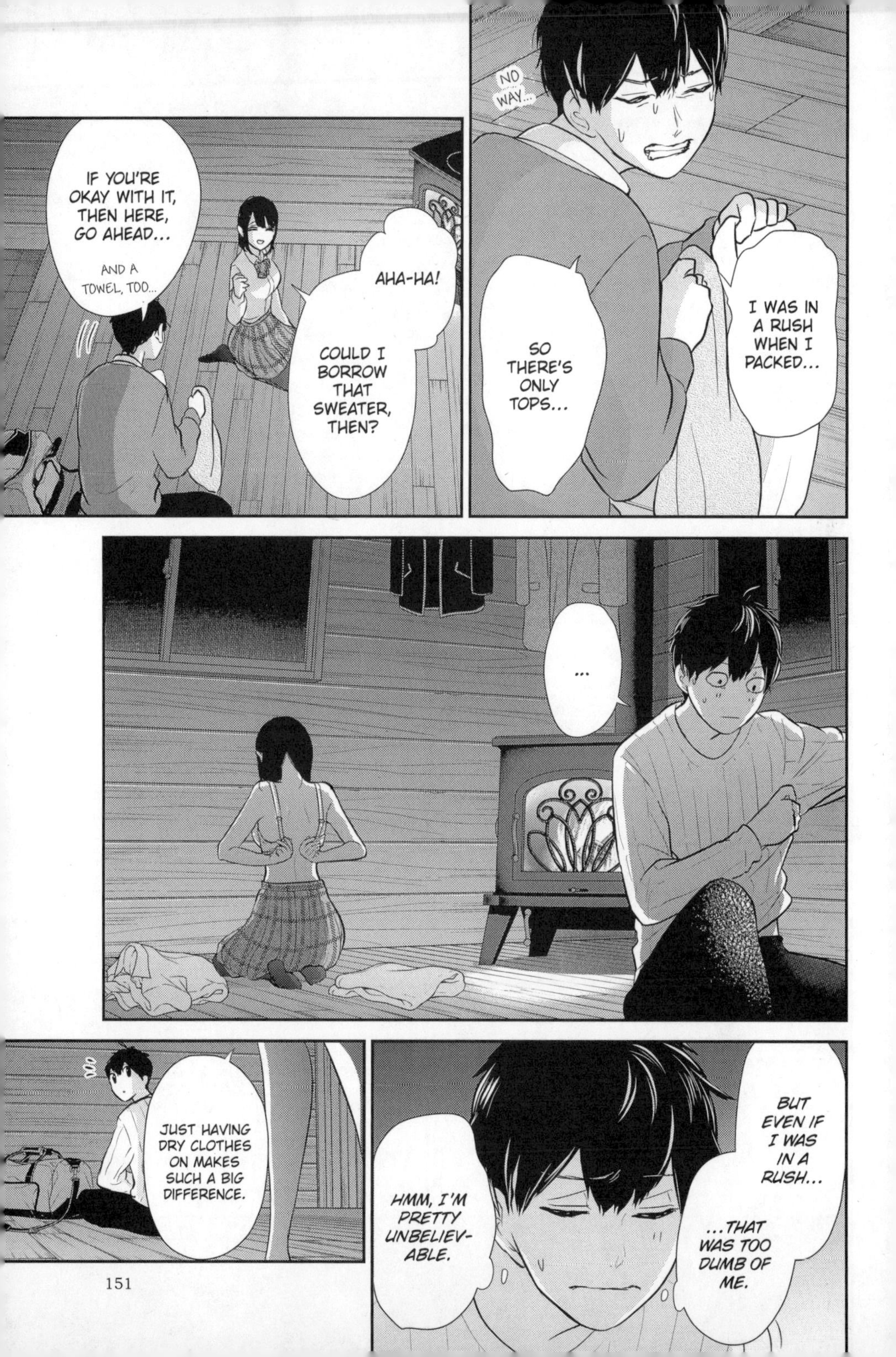
NO WAY...
I WAS IN A RUSH WHEN I PACKED...
SO THERE'S ONLY TOPS...
IF YOU'RE OKAY WITH IT, THEN HERE, GO AHEAD...
AND A TOWEL, TOO...
AHA-HA!
COULD I BORROW THAT SWEATER, THEN?
...
BUT EVEN IF I WAS IN A RUSH...
...THAT WAS TOO DUMB OF ME.
HMM, I'M PRETTY UNBELIEV-ABLE.
JUST HAVING DRY CLOTHES ON MAKES SUCH A BIG DIFFERENCE.

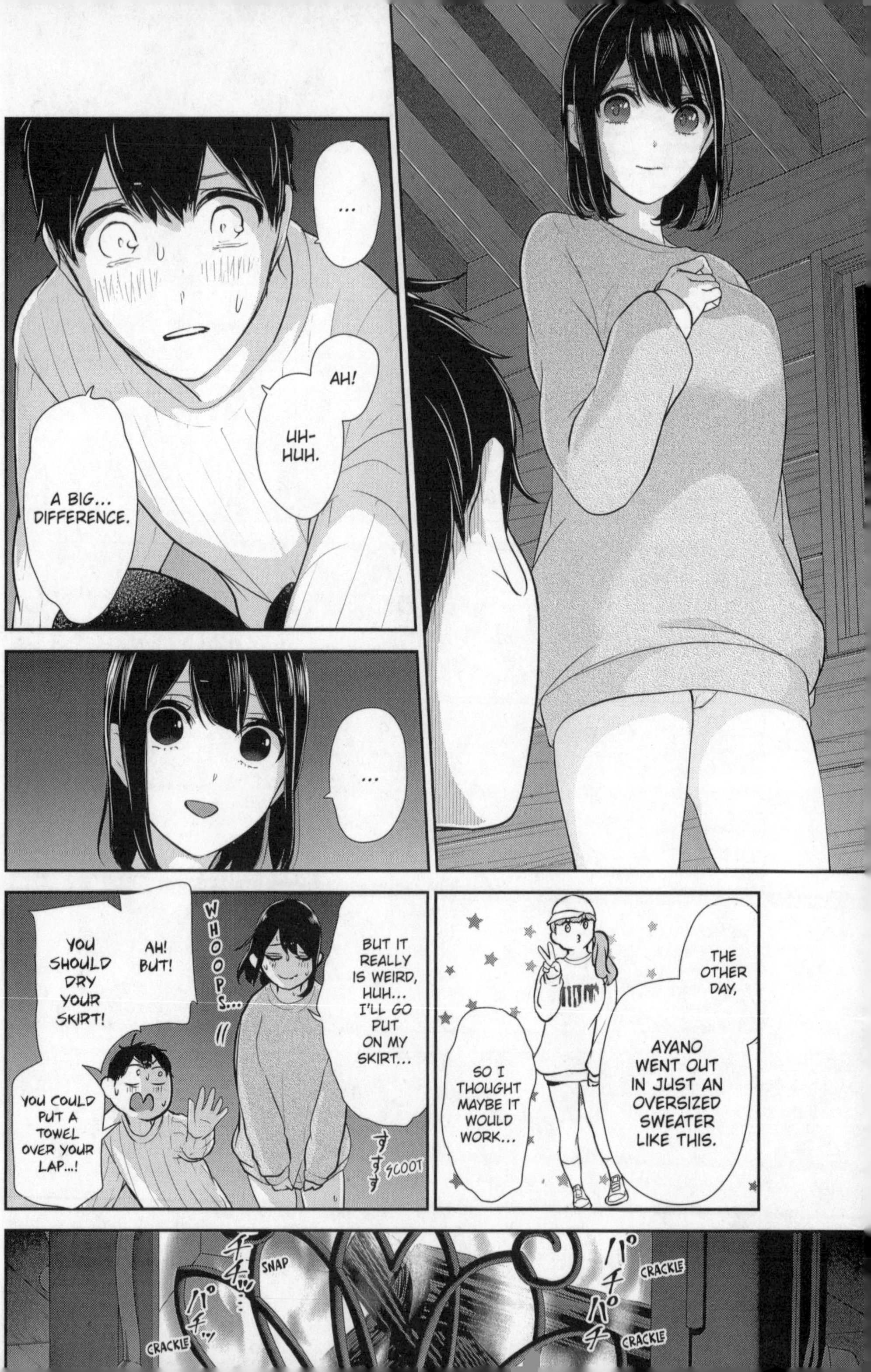
...
AH!
UH-HUH.
A BIG... DIFFERENCE.
...
THE OTHER DAY,
AYANO WENT OUT IN JUST AN OVERSIZED SWEATER LIKE THIS.
SO I THOUGHT MAYBE IT WOULD WORK...
BUT IT REALLY IS WEIRD, HUH... I'LL GO PUT ON MY SKIRT...
すすす
SCOOT
WHOOPS...!!
AH! BUT!
YOU SHOULD DRY YOUR SKIRT!
YOU COULD PUT A TOWEL OVER YOUR LAP...!
パチパチ
CRACKLE
CRACKLE
チチッ…
SNAP
パチッ
CRACKLE

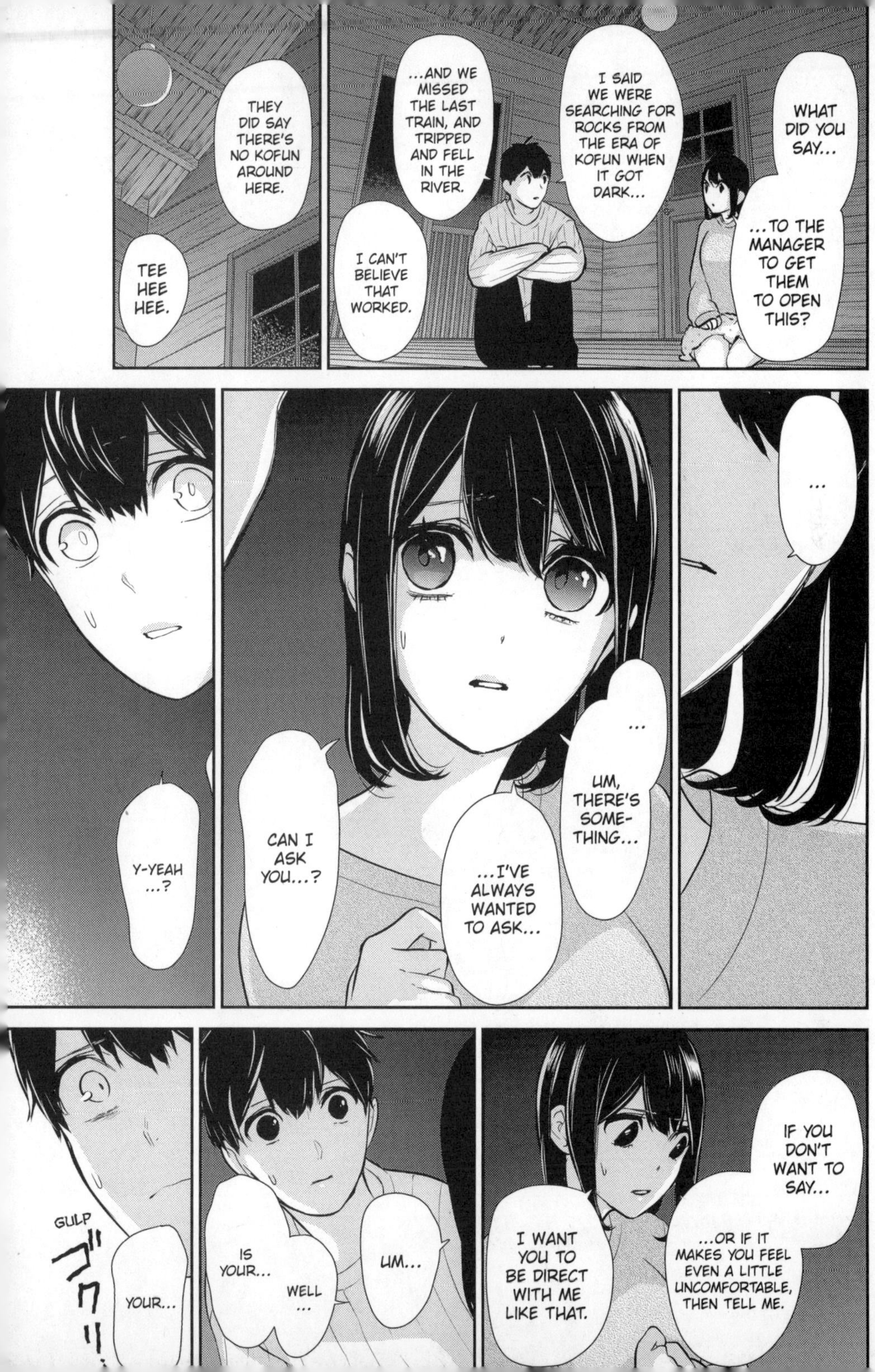
WHAT DID YOU SAY...
...TO THE MANAGER TO GET THEM TO OPEN THIS?
I SAID WE WERE SEARCHING FOR ROCKS FROM THE ERA OF KOFUN WHEN IT GOT DARK...
...AND WE MISSED THE LAST TRAIN, AND TRIPPED AND FELL IN THE RIVER.
I CAN'T BELIEVE THAT WORKED.
THEY DID SAY THERE'S NO KOFUN AROUND HERE.
TEE HEE HEE.
...
...
UM, THERE'S SOME-THING...
...I'VE ALWAYS WANTED TO ASK...
CAN I ASK YOU...?
Y-YEAH ...?
IF YOU DON'T WANT TO SAY...
...OR IF IT MAKES YOU FEEL EVEN A LITTLE UNCOMFORTABLE, THEN TELL ME.
I WANT YOU TO BE DIRECT WITH ME LIKE THAT.
UM...
IS YOUR...
WELL ...
GULP
ゴクリ
YOUR...

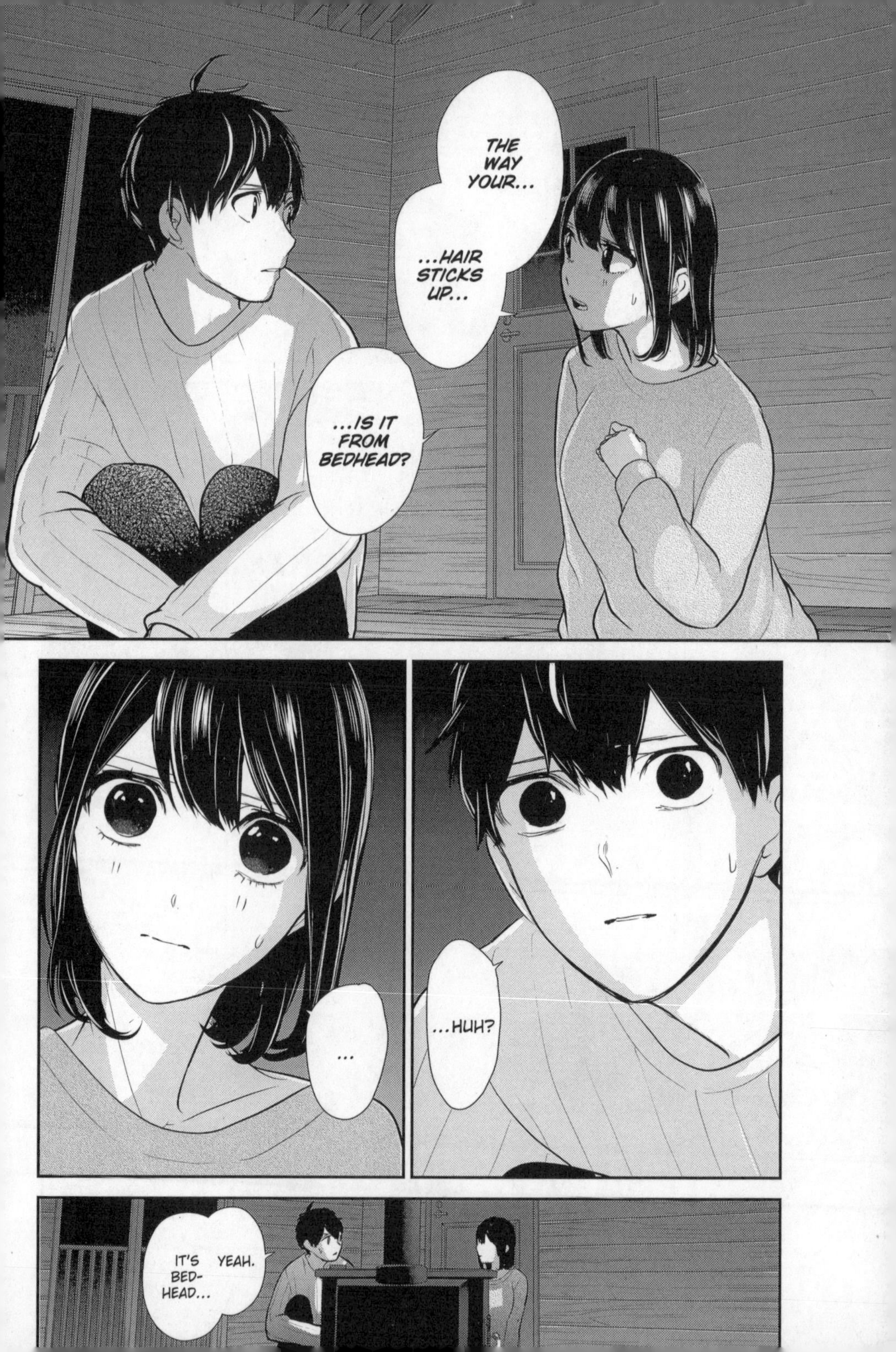
THE WAY YOUR...
...HAIR STICKS UP...
...IS IT FROM BEDHEAD?
...HUH?
...
YEAH.
IT'S BED-HEAD...

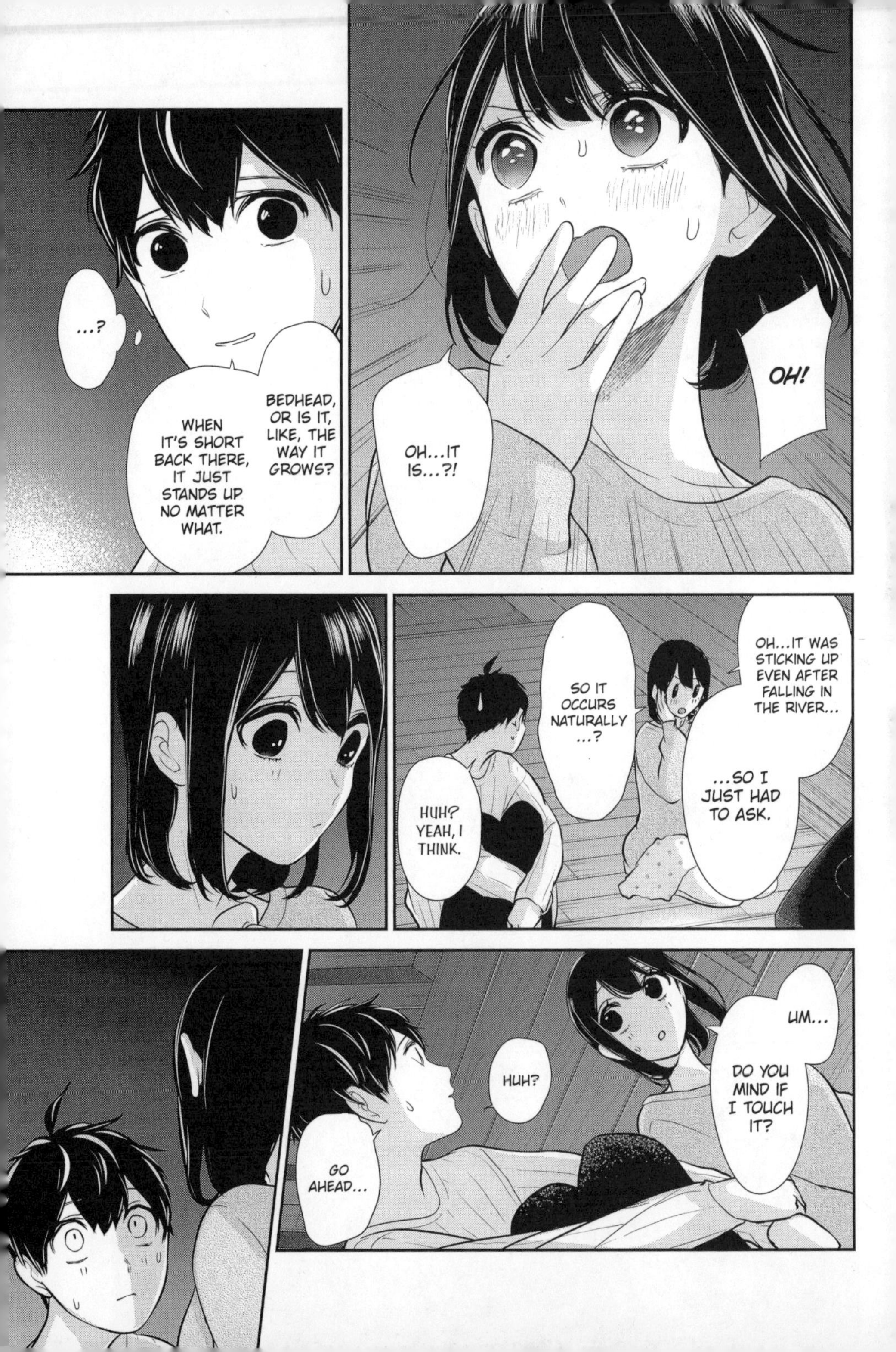
OH!
OH...IT IS...?!
...?
BEDHEAD, OR IS IT, LIKE, THE WAY IT GROWS?
WHEN IT'S SHORT BACK THERE, IT JUST STANDS UP NO MATTER WHAT.
OH...IT WAS STICKING UP EVEN AFTER FALLING IN THE RIVER...
SO IT OCCURS NATURALLY...?
...SO I JUST HAD TO ASK.
HUH? YEAH, I THINK.
UM...
DO YOU MIND IF I TOUCH IT?
HUH?
GO AHEAD...

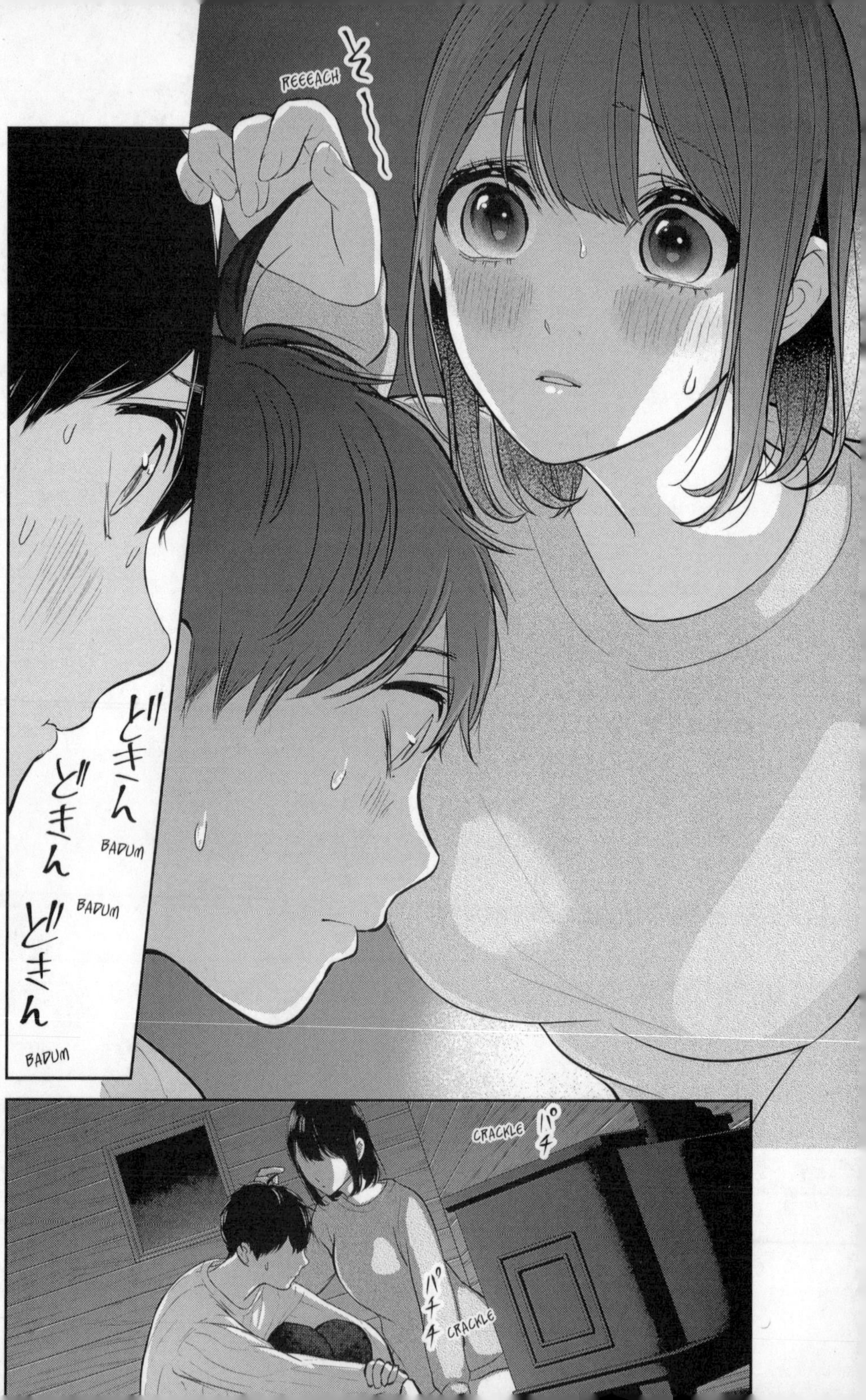
REEEACH
どきん
BADUM
どきん
BADUM
どきん
BADUM
パチ
CRACKLE
パチチ
CRACKLE

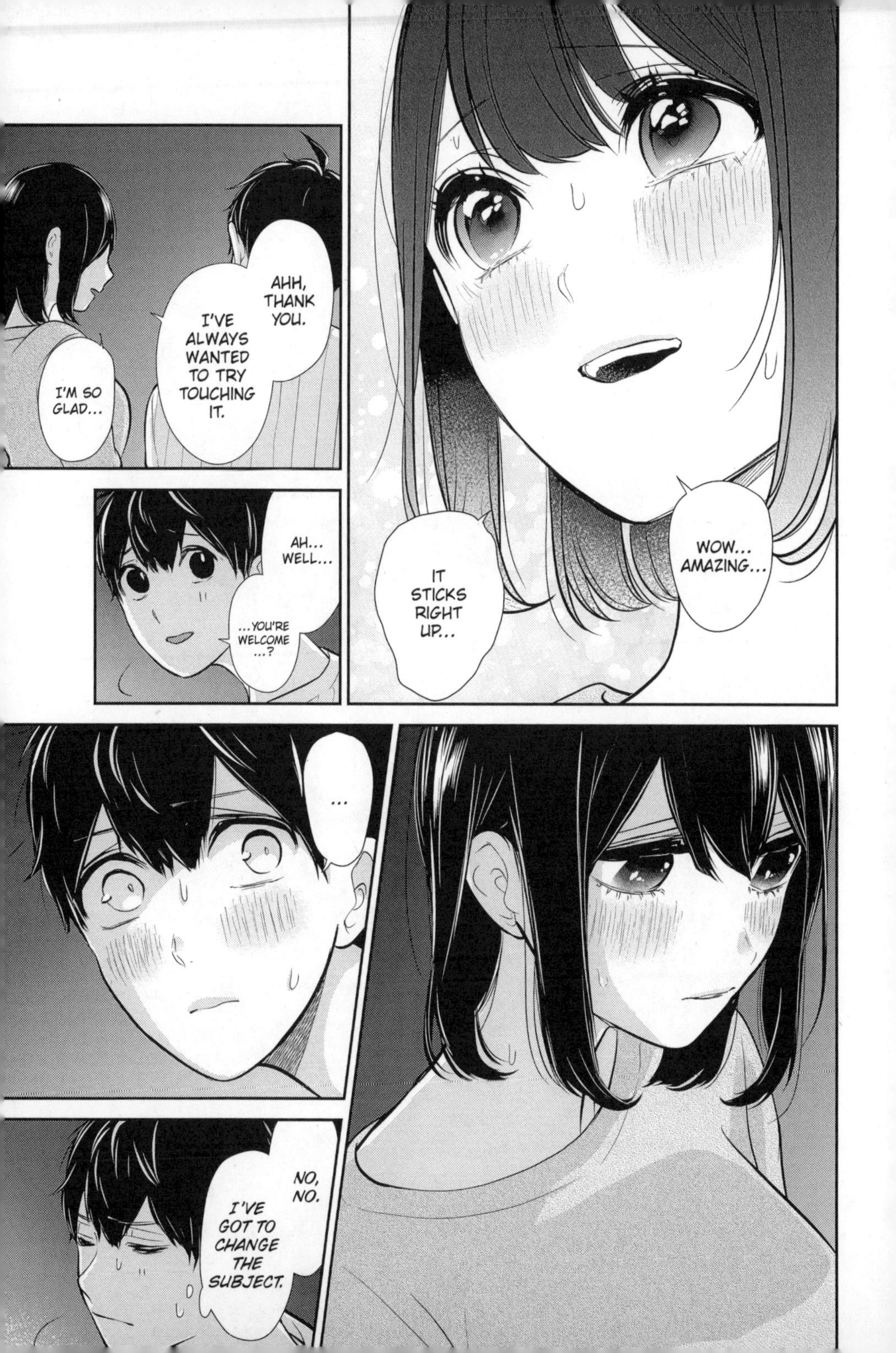
WOW... AMAZING...
IT STICKS RIGHT UP...
AHH, THANK YOU.
I'VE ALWAYS WANTED TO TRY TOUCHING IT.
I'M SO GLAD...
AH... WELL...
...YOU'RE WELCOME ...?
...
NO, NO.
I'VE GOT TO CHANGE THE SUBJECT.

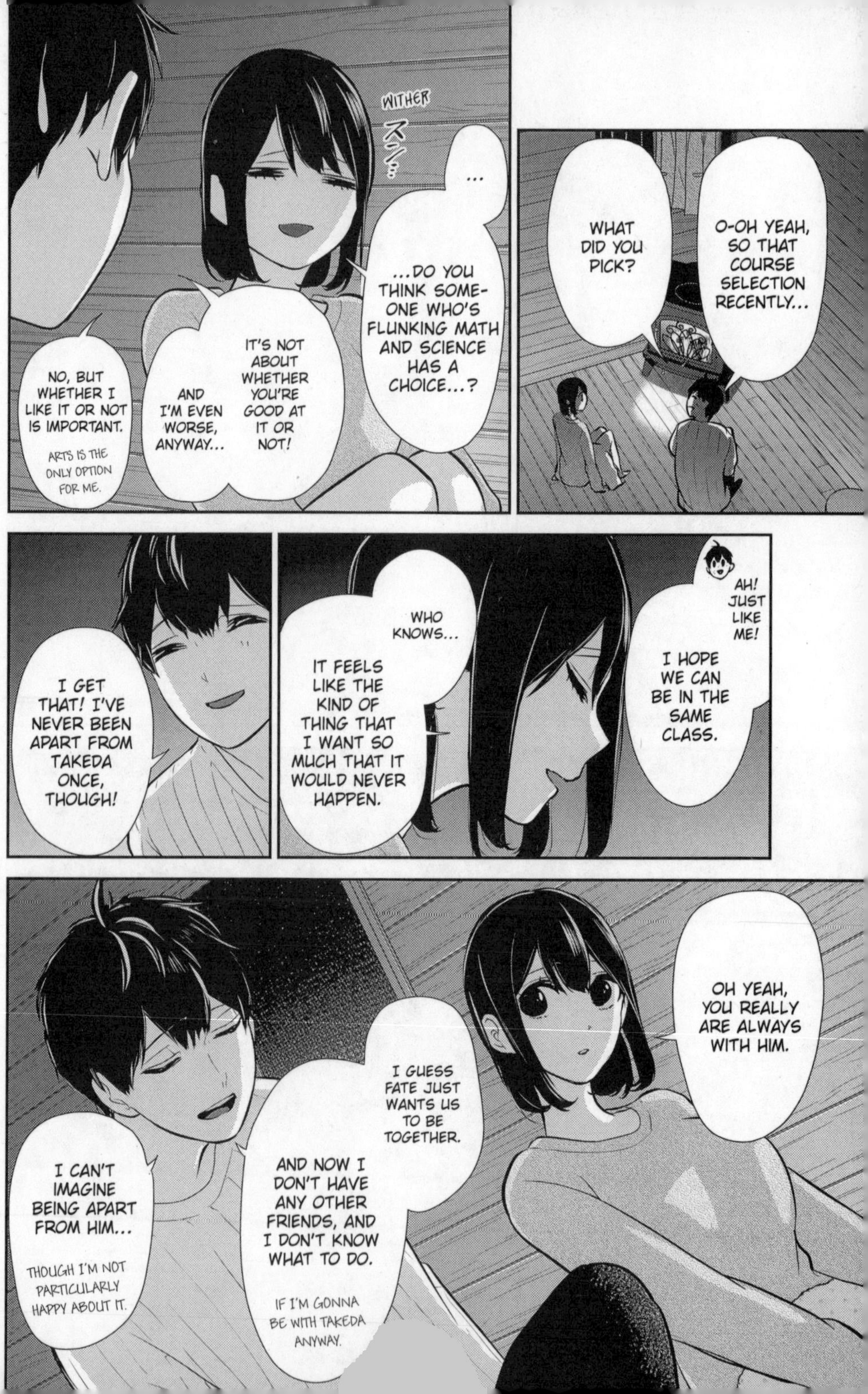
O-OH YEAH, SO THAT COURSE SELECTION RECENTLY...
WHAT DID YOU PICK?
WITHER
...
...DO YOU THINK SOME-ONE WHO'S FLUNKING MATH AND SCIENCE HAS A CHOICE...?
IT'S NOT ABOUT WHETHER YOU'RE GOOD AT IT OR NOT!
AND I'M EVEN WORSE, ANYWAY...
NO, BUT WHETHER I LIKE IT OR NOT IS IMPORTANT.
ARTS IS THE ONLY OPTION FOR ME.
AH! JUST LIKE ME!
I HOPE WE CAN BE IN THE SAME CLASS.
WHO KNOWS...
IT FEELS LIKE THE KIND OF THING THAT I WANT SO MUCH THAT IT WOULD NEVER HAPPEN.
I GET THAT! I'VE NEVER BEEN APART FROM TAKEDA ONCE, THOUGH!
OH YEAH, YOU REALLY ARE ALWAYS WITH HIM.
I GUESS FATE JUST WANTS US TO BE TOGETHER.
AND NOW I DON'T HAVE ANY OTHER FRIENDS, AND I DON'T KNOW WHAT TO DO.
IF I'M GONNA BE WITH TAKEDA ANYWAY.
I CAN'T IMAGINE BEING APART FROM HIM...
THOUGH I'M NOT PARTICULARLY HAPPY ABOUT IT.

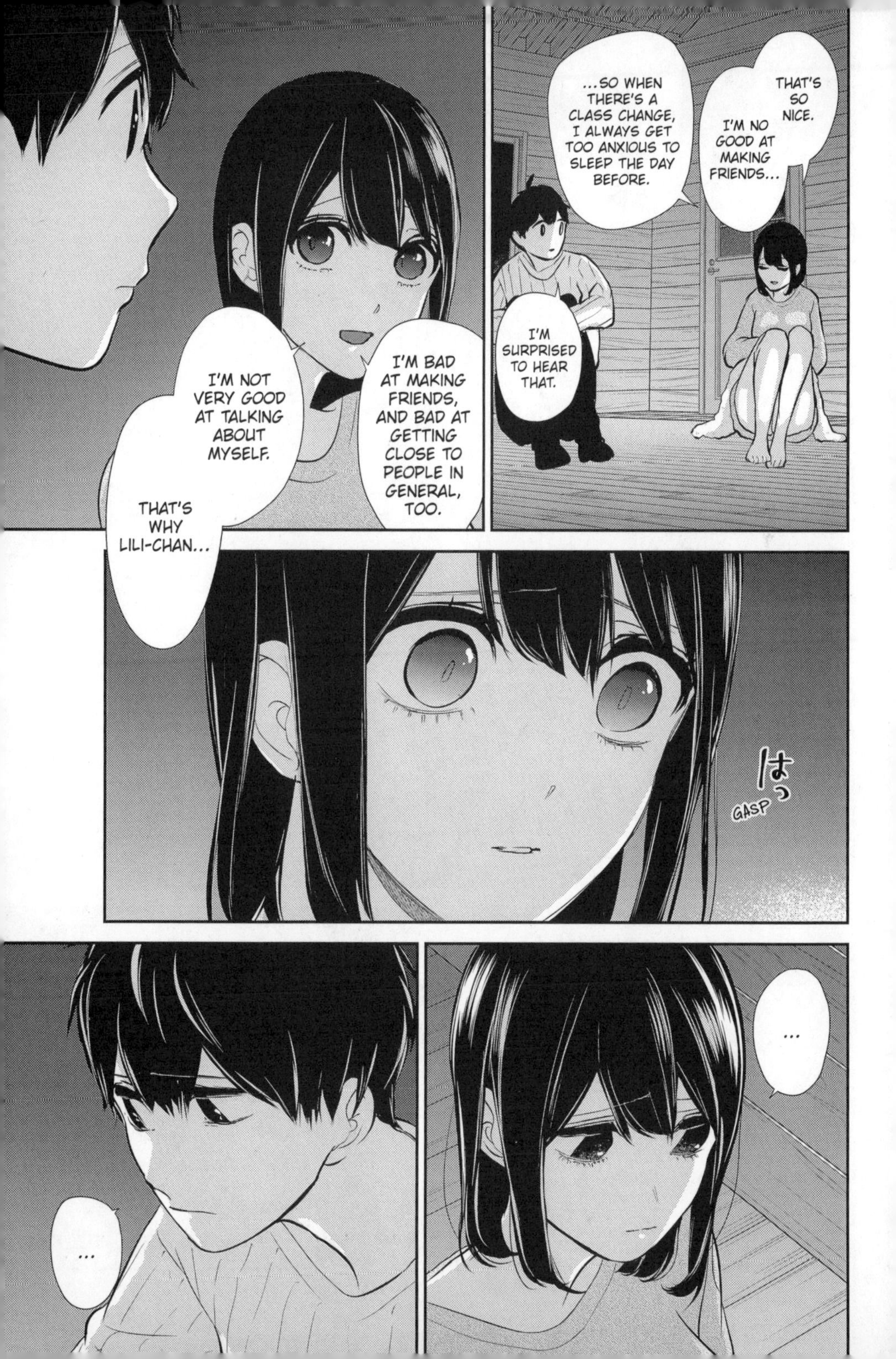
...SO WHEN THERE'S A CLASS CHANGE, I ALWAYS GET TOO ANXIOUS TO SLEEP THE DAY BEFORE.
THAT'S SO NICE.
I'M NO GOOD AT MAKING FRIENDS...
I'M SURPRISED TO HEAR THAT.
I'M BAD AT MAKING FRIENDS, AND BAD AT GETTING CLOSE TO PEOPLE IN GENERAL, TOO.
I'M NOT VERY GOOD AT TALKING ABOUT MYSELF.
THAT'S WHY LILI-CHAN...
はっ
GASP
...
...

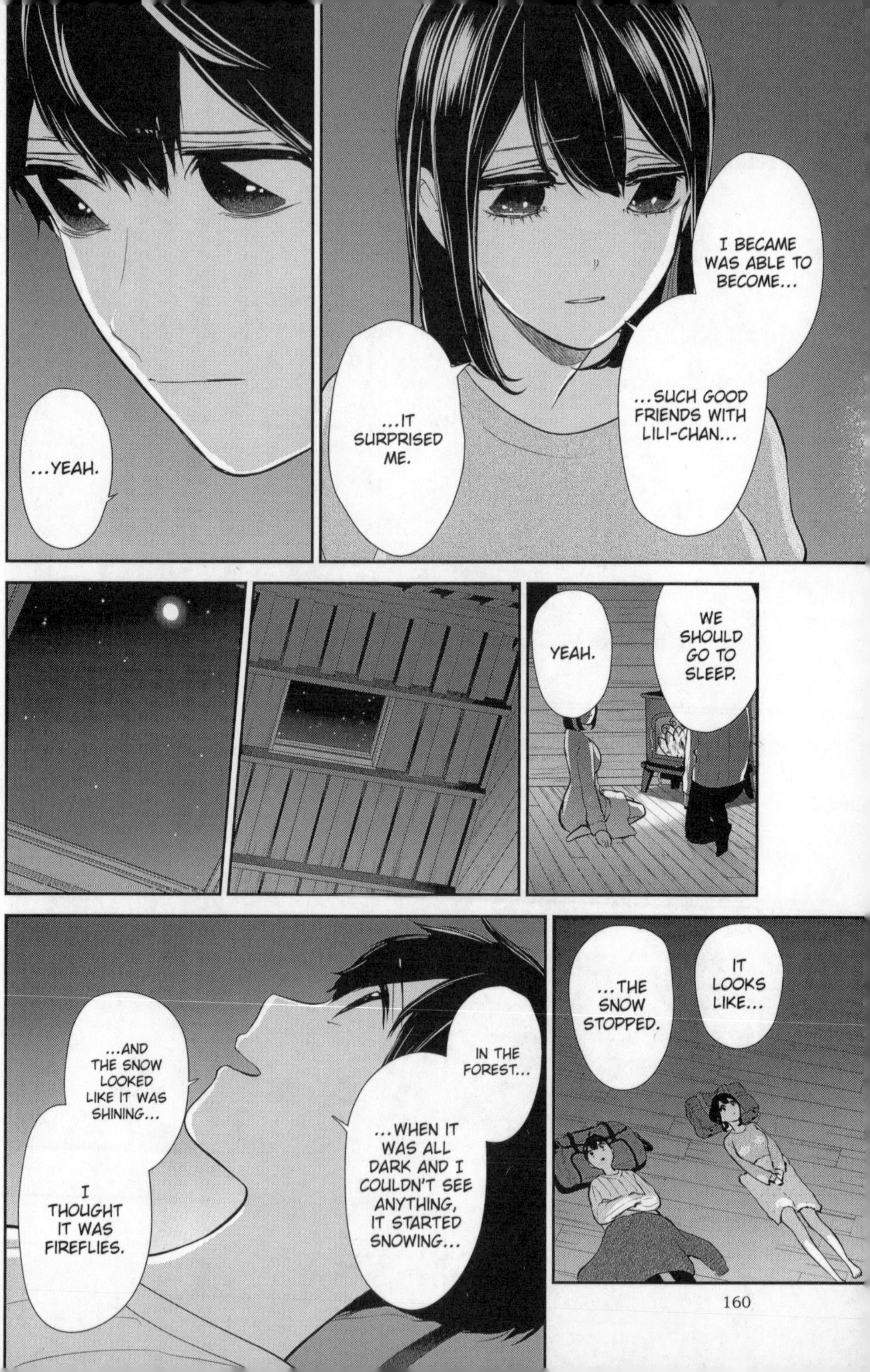
I BECAME WAS ABLE TO BECOME...
...SUCH GOOD FRIENDS WITH LILI-CHAN...
...IT SURPRISED ME.
...YEAH.
WE SHOULD GO TO SLEEP.
YEAH.
IT LOOKS LIKE...
...THE SNOW STOPPED.
IN THE FOREST...
...WHEN IT WAS ALL DARK AND I COULDN'T SEE ANYTHING, IT STARTED SNOWING...
...AND THE SNOW LOOKED LIKE IT WAS SHINING...
I THOUGHT IT WAS FIREFLIES.

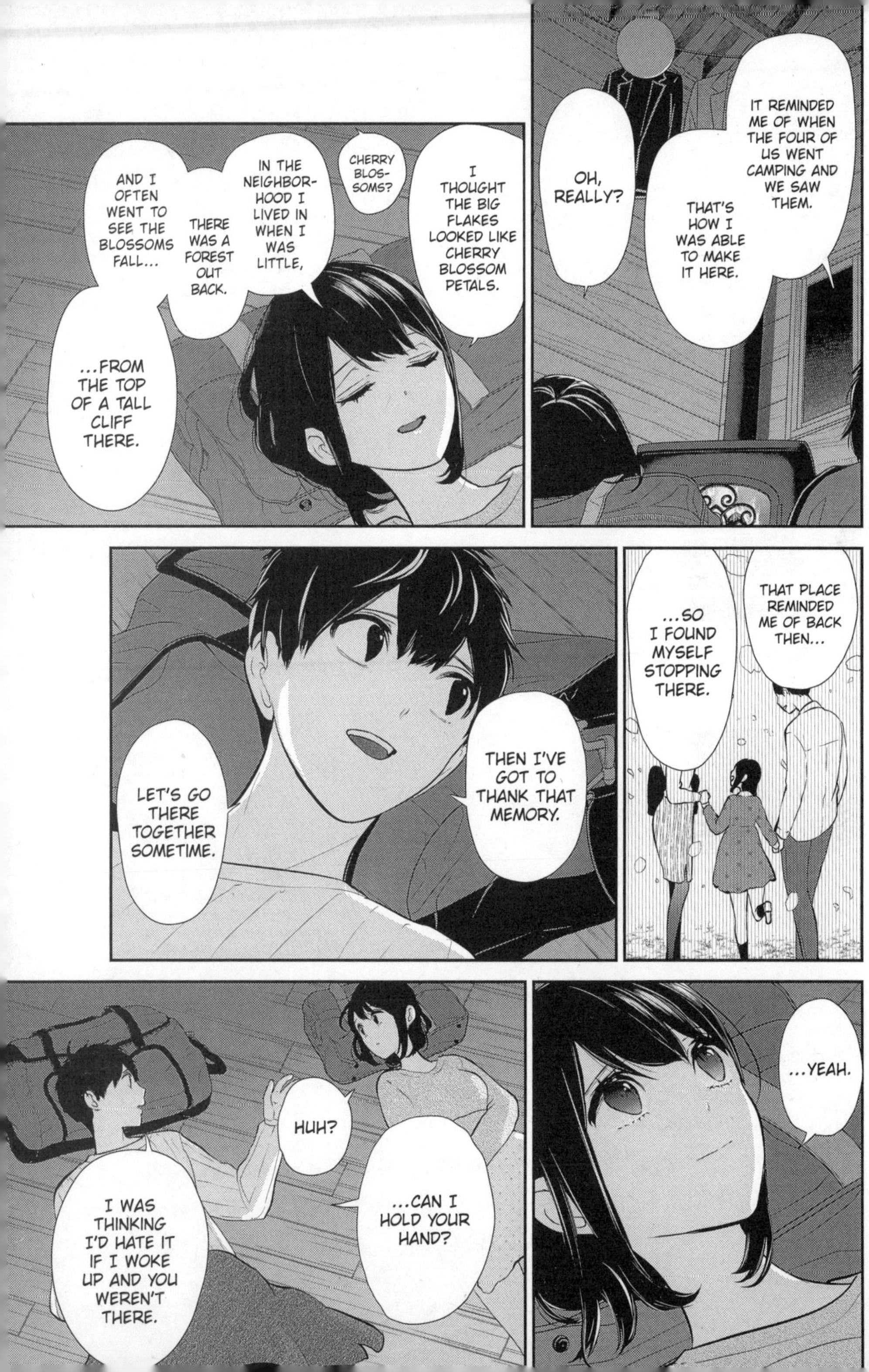
IT REMINDED ME OF WHEN THE FOUR OF US WENT CAMPING AND WE SAW THEM.
THAT'S HOW I WAS ABLE TO MAKE IT HERE.
OH, REALLY?
I THOUGHT THE BIG FLAKES LOOKED LIKE CHERRY BLOSSOM PETALS.
CHERRY BLOSSOMS?
IN THE NEIGHBORHOOD I LIVED IN WHEN I WAS LITTLE,
THERE WAS A FOREST OUT BACK.
AND I OFTEN WENT TO SEE THE BLOSSOMS FALL...
...FROM THE TOP OF A TALL CLIFF THERE.
THAT PLACE REMINDED ME OF BACK THEN...
...SO I FOUND MYSELF STOPPING THERE.
THEN I'VE GOT TO THANK THAT MEMORY.
LET'S GO THERE TOGETHER SOMETIME.
...YEAH.
...CAN I HOLD YOUR HAND?
HUH?
I WAS THINKING I'D HATE IT IF I WOKE UP AND YOU WEREN'T THERE.

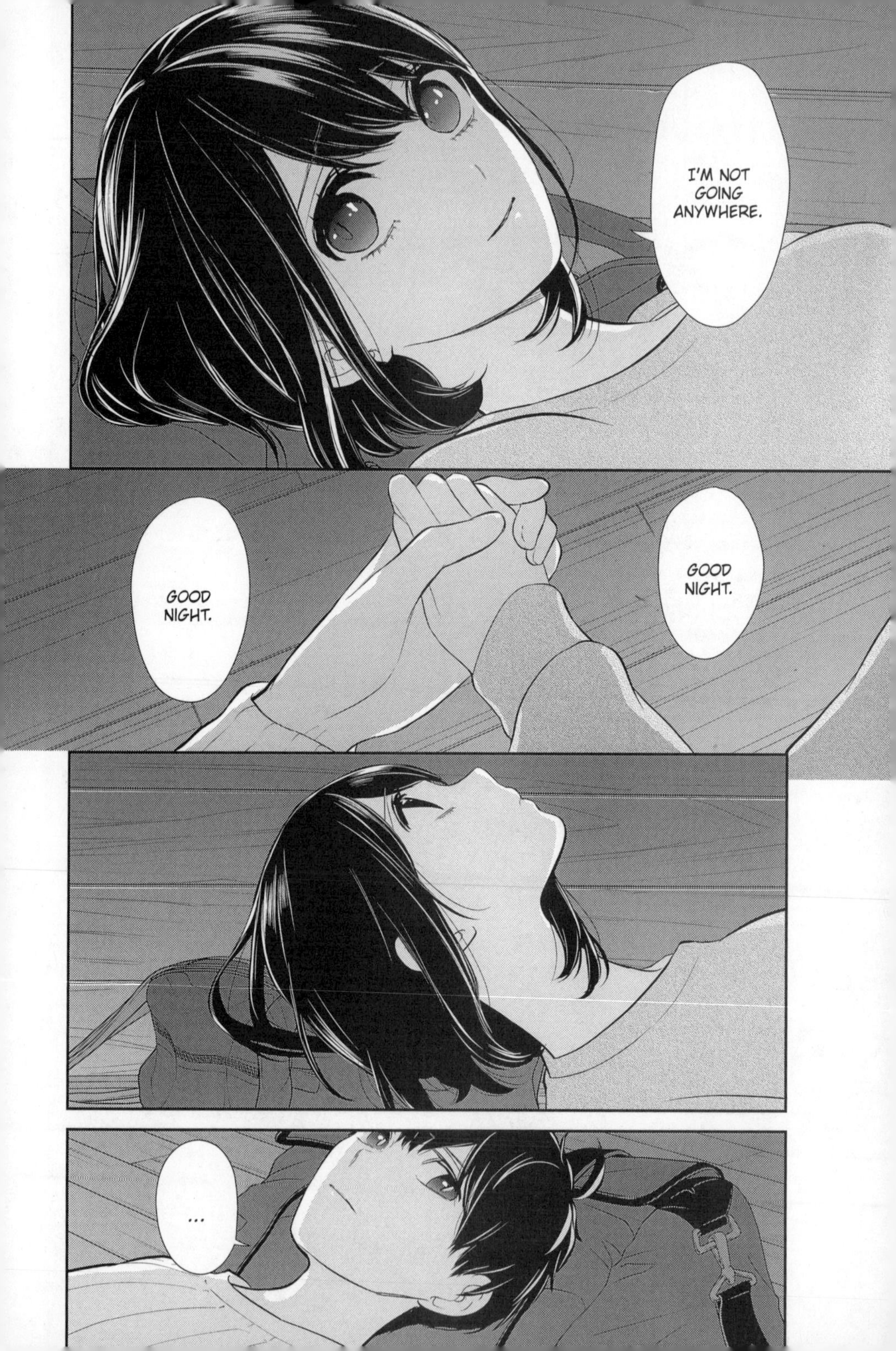
I'M NOT GOING ANYWHERE.
GOOD NIGHT.
GOOD NIGHT.
...

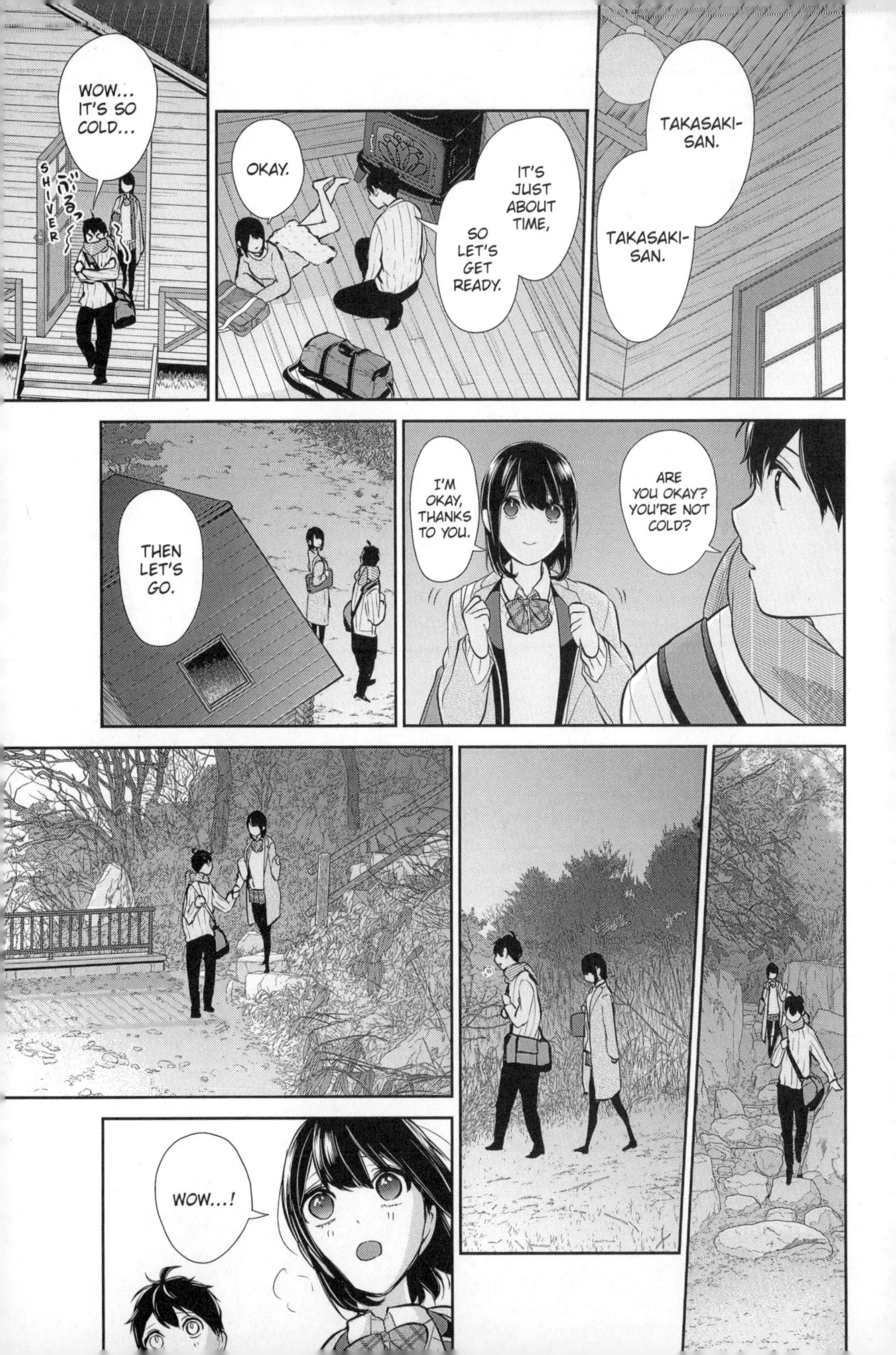
TAKASAKI-SAN.
TAKASAKI-SAN.
IT'S JUST ABOUT TIME,
SO LET'S GET READY.
OKAY.
WOW... IT'S SO COLD...
SHIVER
ぶるっ
ARE YOU OKAY? YOU'RE NOT COLD?
I'M OKAY, THANKS TO YOU.
THEN LET'S GO.
WOW...!

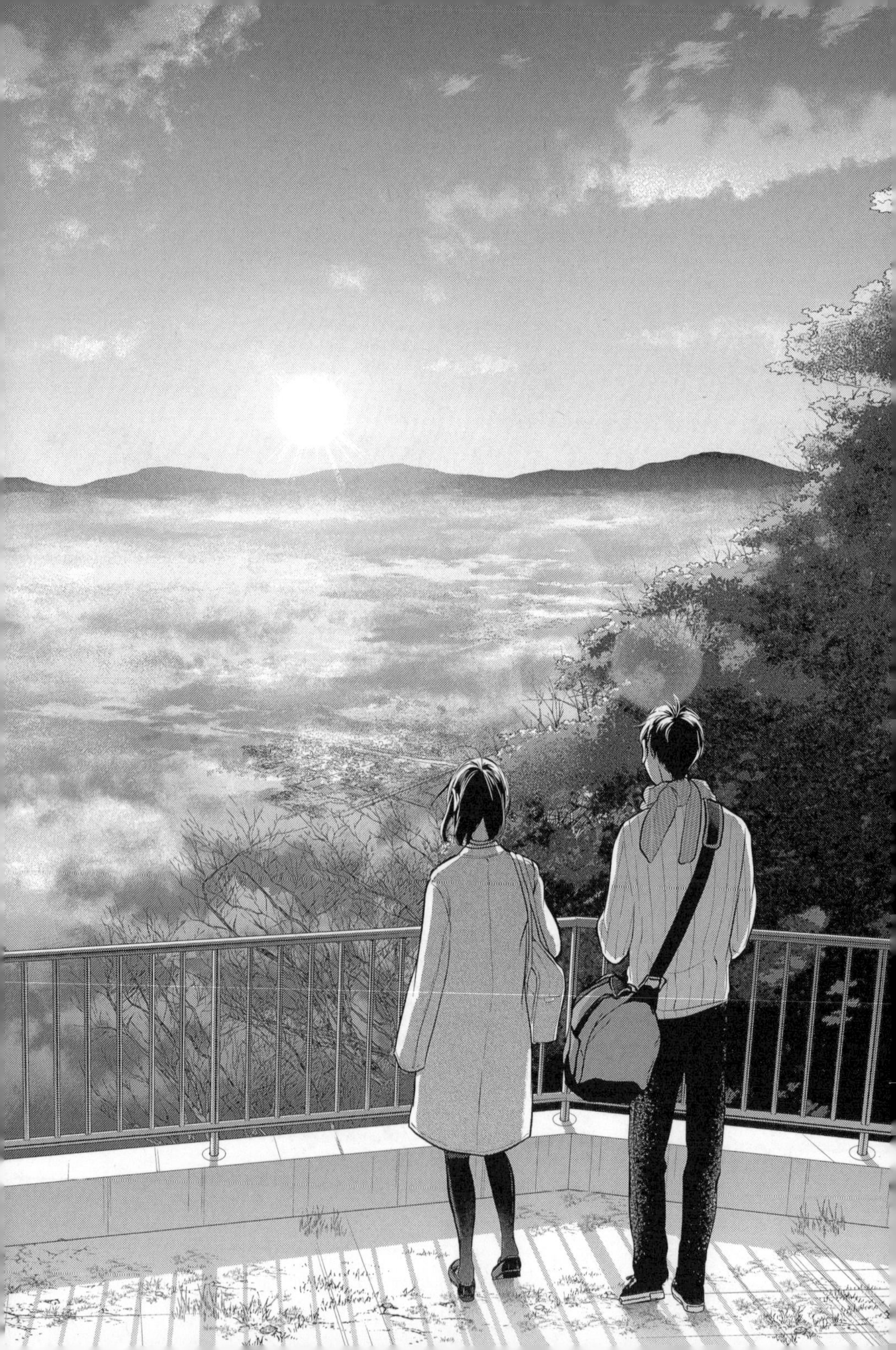

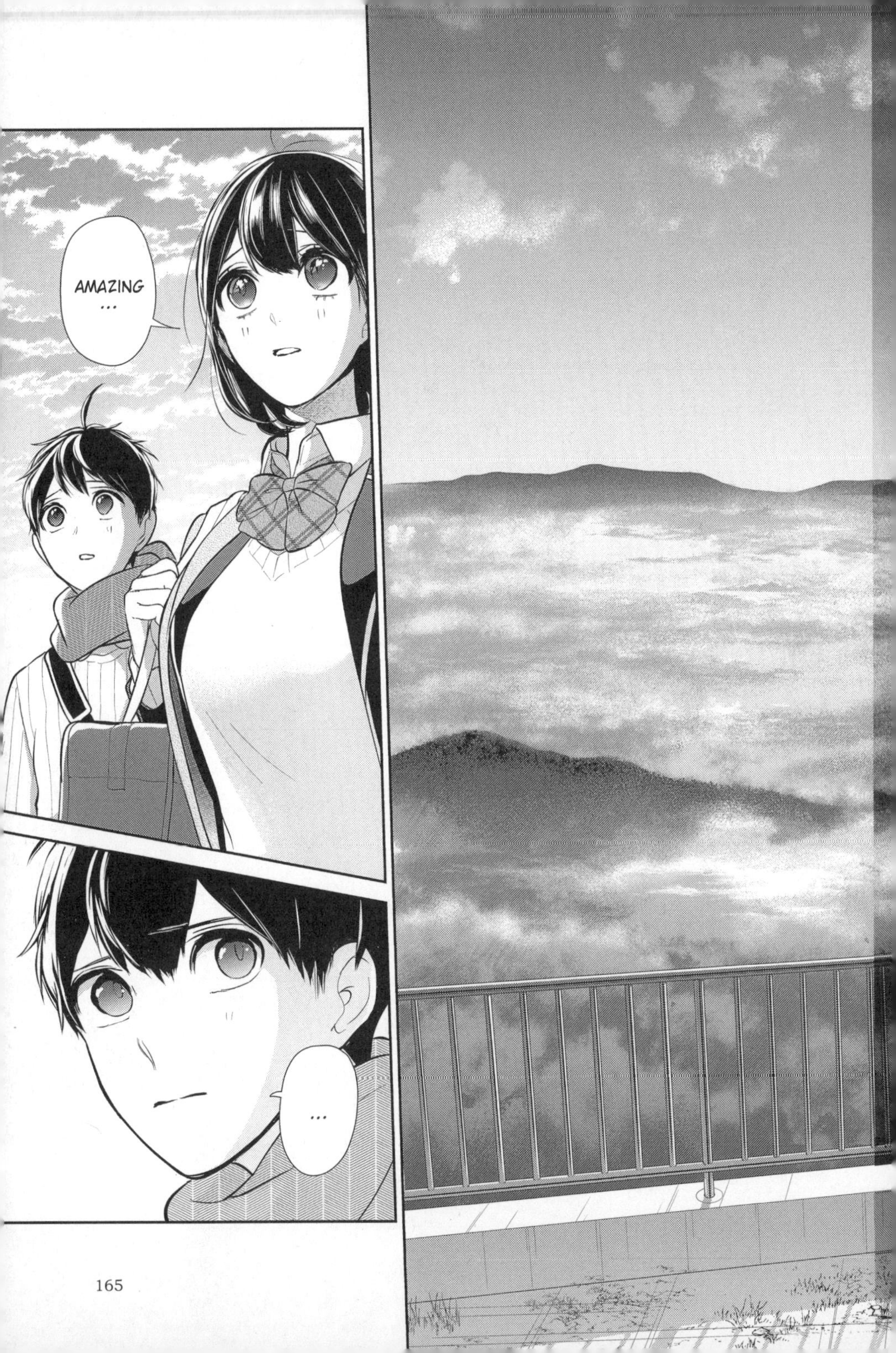
AMAZING ...
...

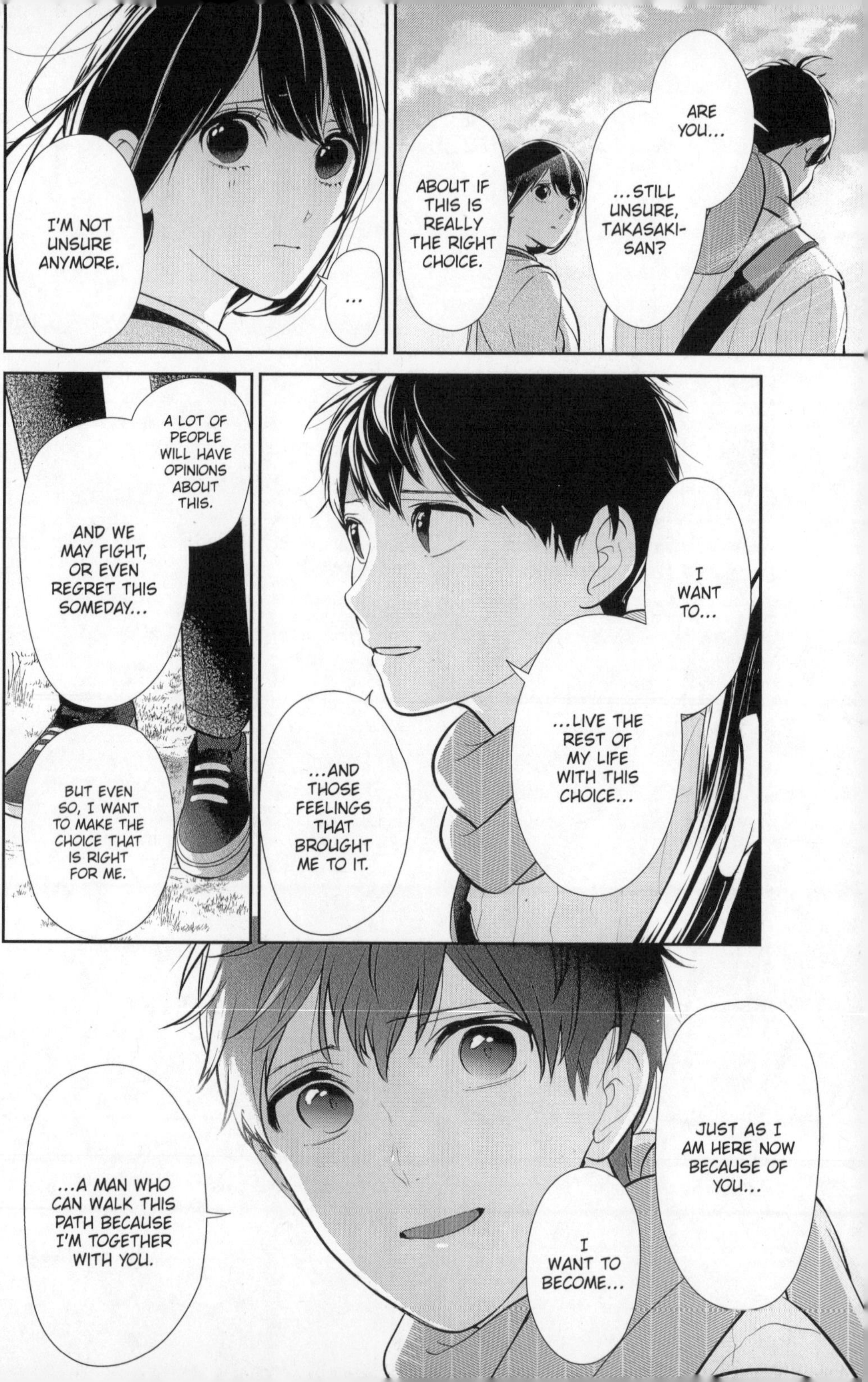
ARE YOU...
...STILL UNSURE, TAKASAKI-SAN?
ABOUT IF THIS IS REALLY THE RIGHT CHOICE.
...
I'M NOT UNSURE ANYMORE.
I WANT TO...
...LIVE THE REST OF MY LIFE WITH THIS CHOICE...
...AND THOSE FEELINGS THAT BROUGHT ME TO IT.
A LOT OF PEOPLE WILL HAVE OPINIONS ABOUT THIS.
AND WE MAY FIGHT, OR EVEN REGRET THIS SOMEDAY...
BUT EVEN SO, I WANT TO MAKE THE CHOICE THAT IS RIGHT FOR ME.
JUST AS I AM HERE NOW BECAUSE OF YOU...
I WANT TO BECOME...
...A MAN WHO CAN WALK THIS PATH BECAUSE I'M TOGETHER WITH YOU.

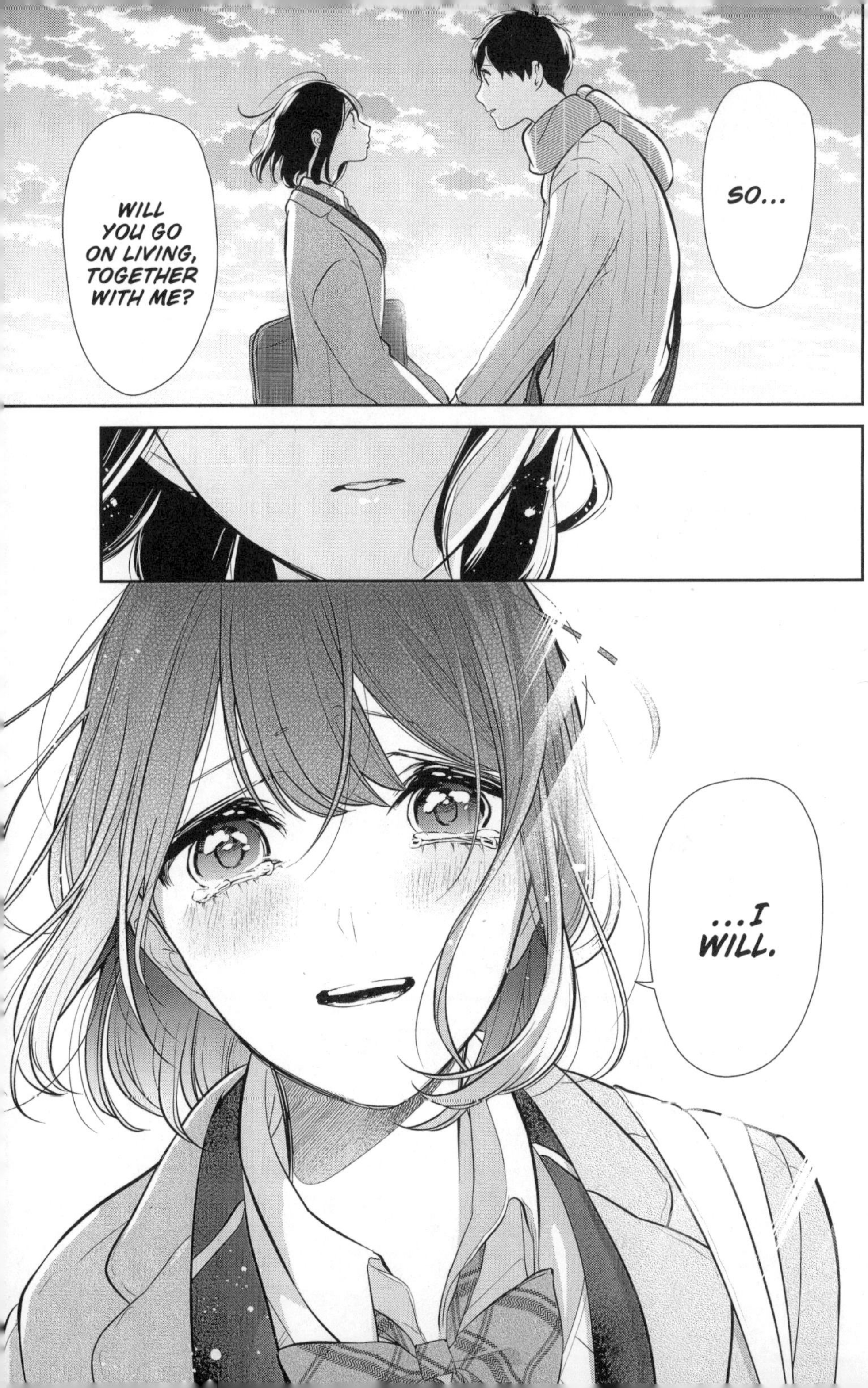
SO...
WILL YOU GO ON LIVING, TOGETHER WITH ME?
...I WILL.

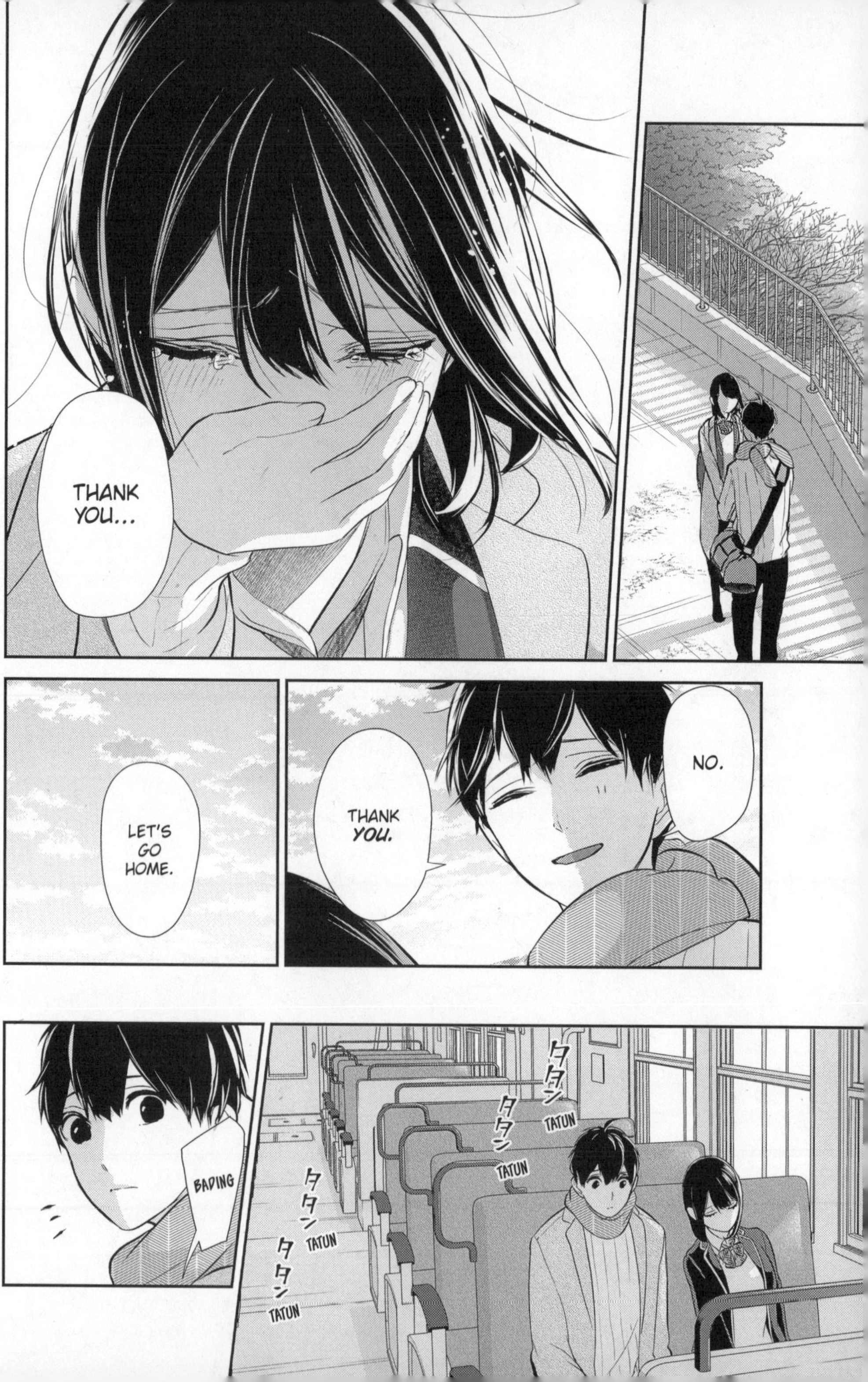
THANK YOU...
NO.
THANK YOU.
LET'S GO HOME.
タタン TATUN
タタン TATUN
タタン TATUN
タタン TATUN
BADING

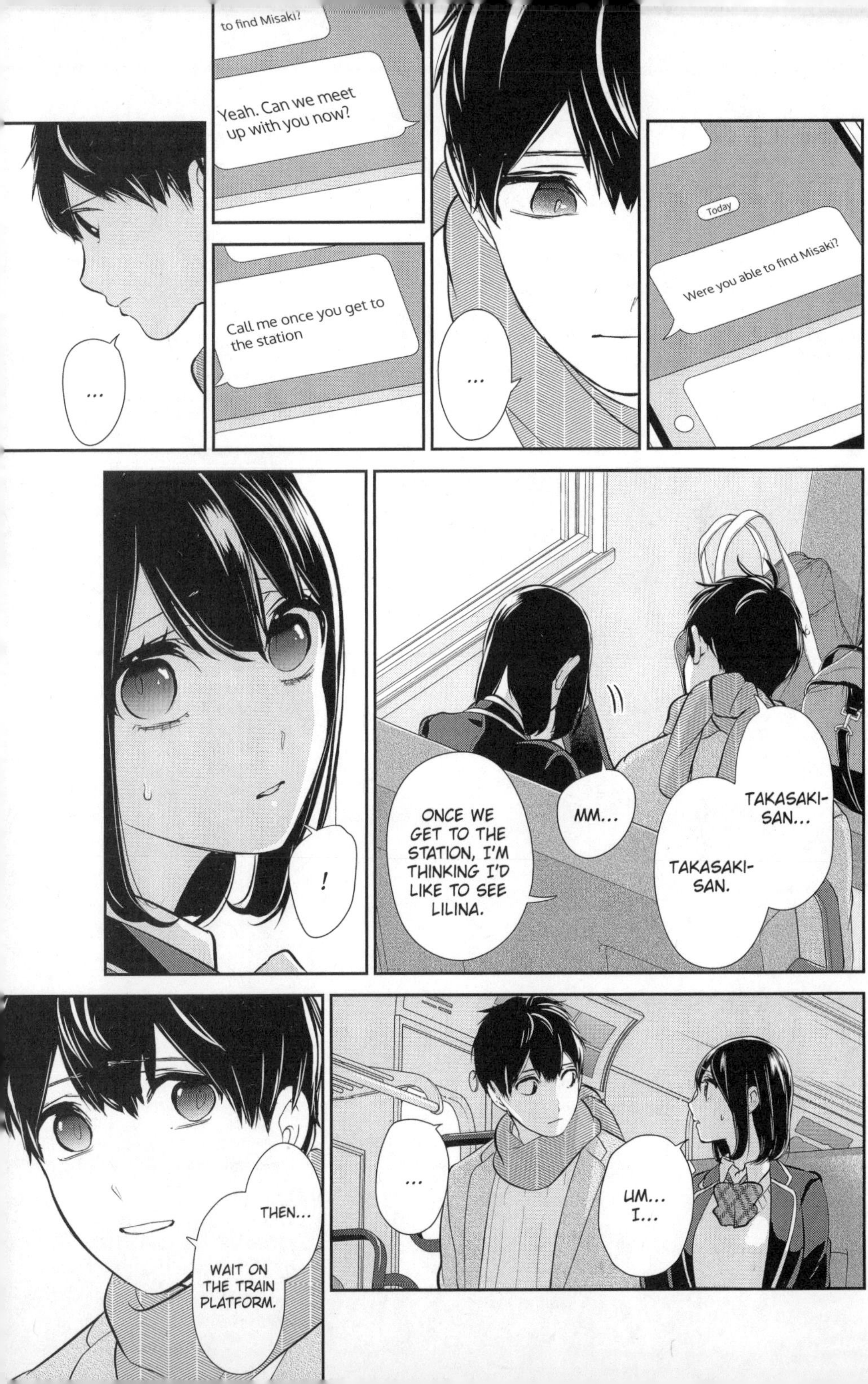
Today
Were you able to find Misaki?
...
to find Misaki?
Yeah. Can we meet up with you now?
Call me once you get to the station
...
TAKASAKI-SAN...
TAKASAKI-SAN.
MM...
ONCE WE GET TO THE STATION, I'M THINKING I'D LIKE TO SEE LILINA.
!
UM... I...
...
THEN...
WAIT ON THE TRAIN PLATFORM.

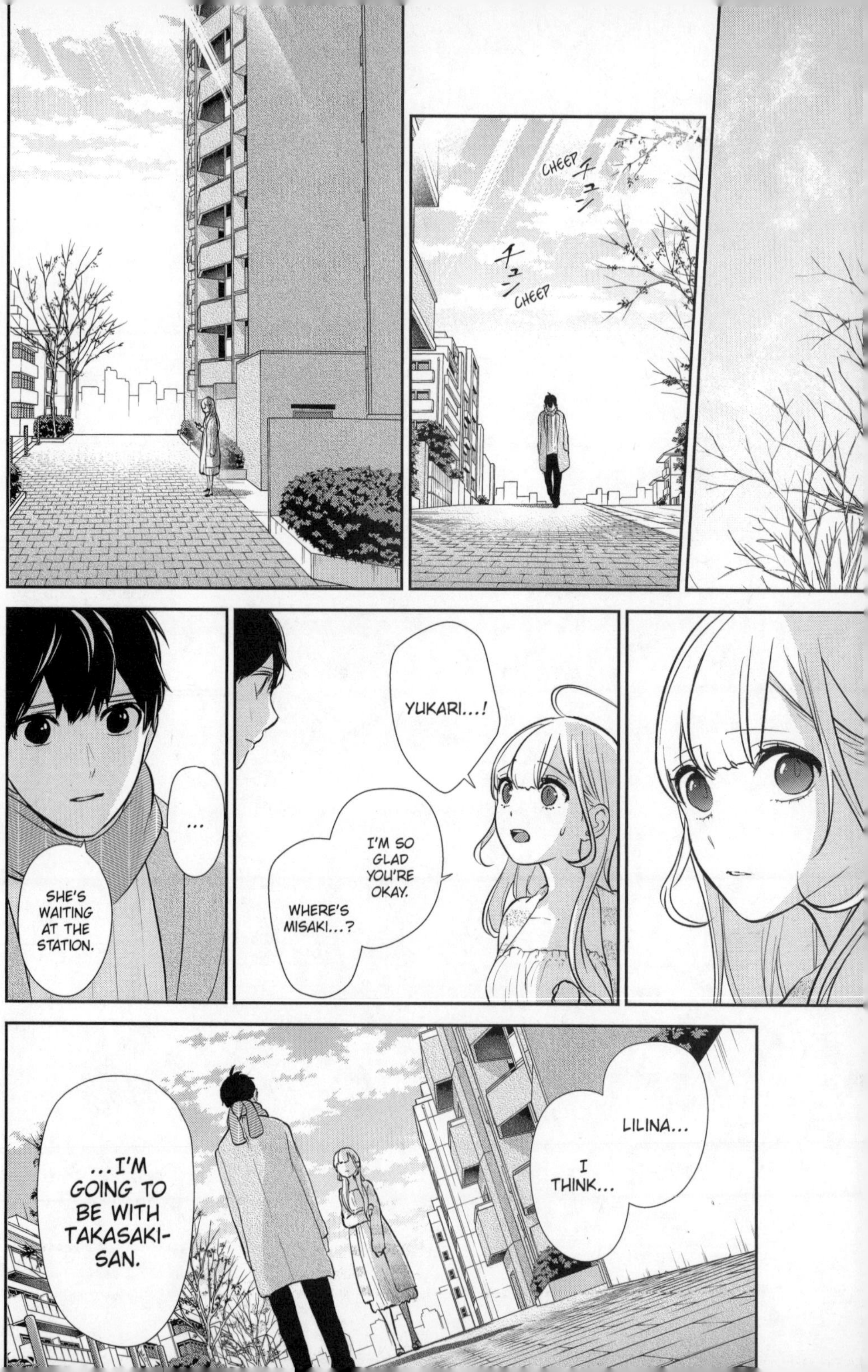
CHEEP チュン
チュン CHEEP
YUKARI...!
I'M SO GLAD YOU'RE OKAY.
WHERE'S MISAKI...?
...
SHE'S WAITING AT THE STATION.
LILINA...
I THINK...
...I'M GOING TO BE WITH TAKASAKI-SAN.

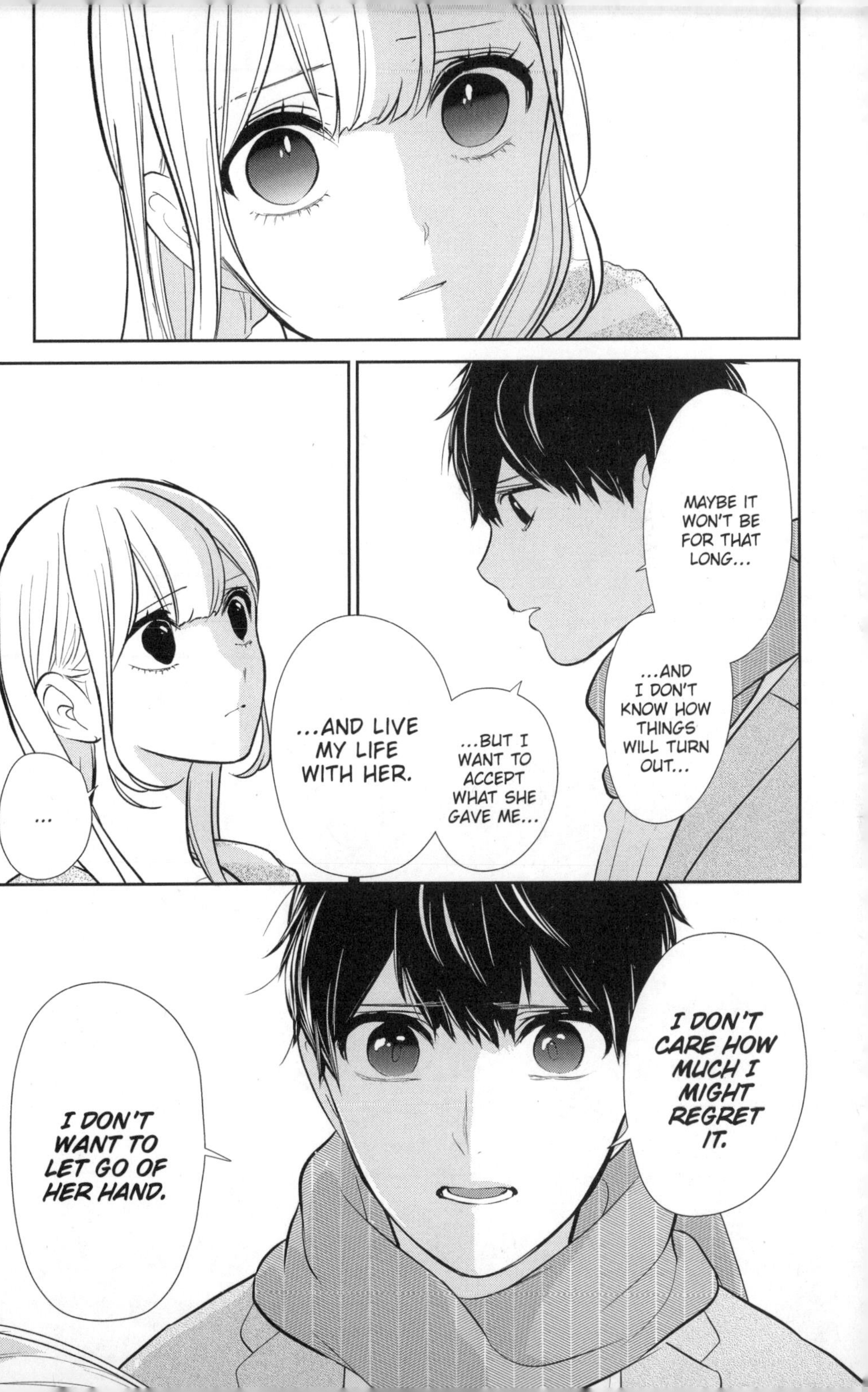

MAYBE IT WON'T BE FOR THAT LONG...
...AND I DON'T KNOW HOW THINGS WILL TURN OUT...
...BUT I WANT TO ACCEPT WHAT SHE GAVE ME...
...AND LIVE MY LIFE WITH HER.
...
I DON'T CARE HOW MUCH I MIGHT REGRET IT.
I DON'T WANT TO LET GO OF HER HAND.

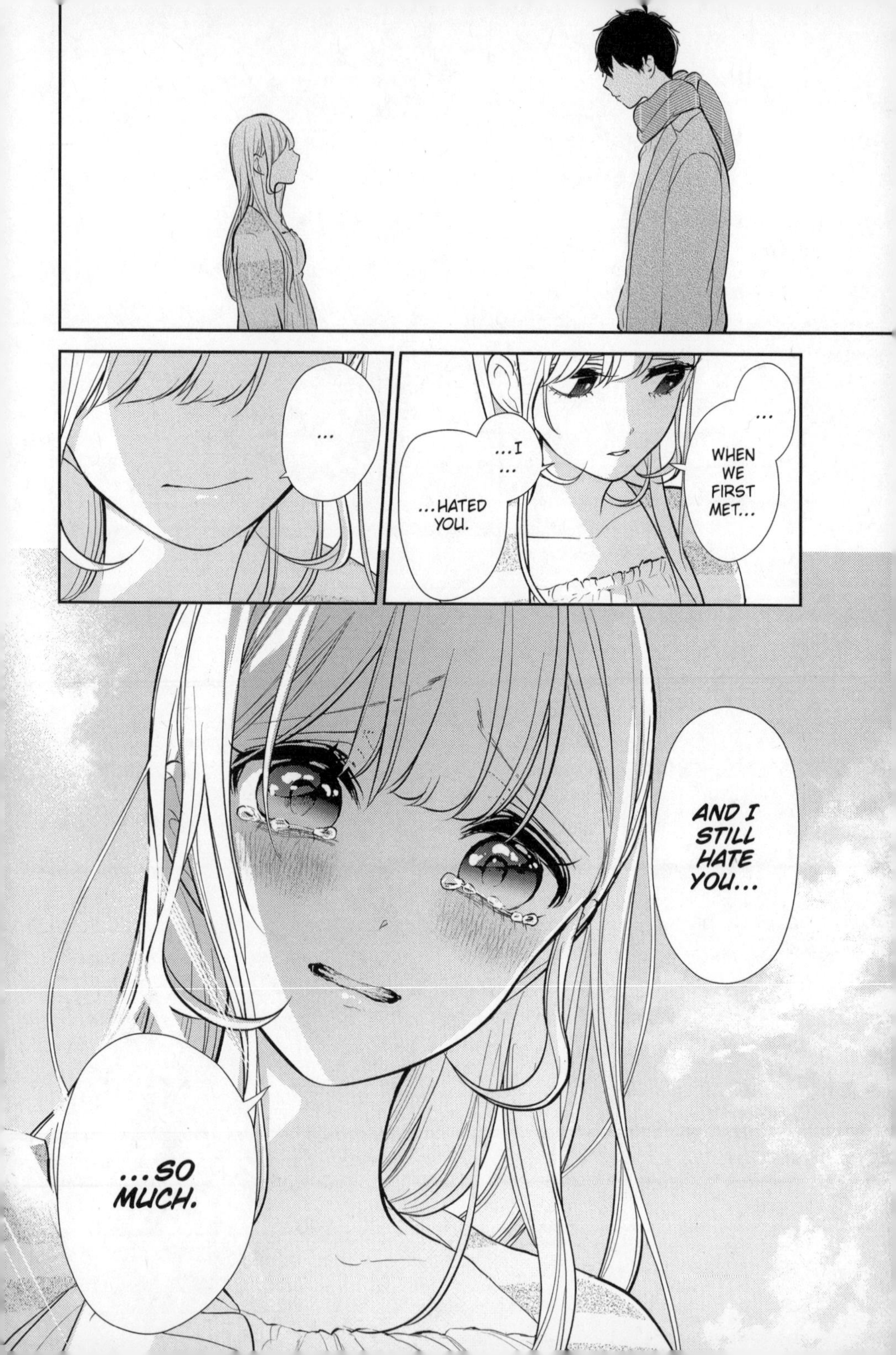

... WHEN WE FIRST MET...
...I ... ...HATED YOU.
...
AND I STILL HATE YOU...
...SO MUCH.

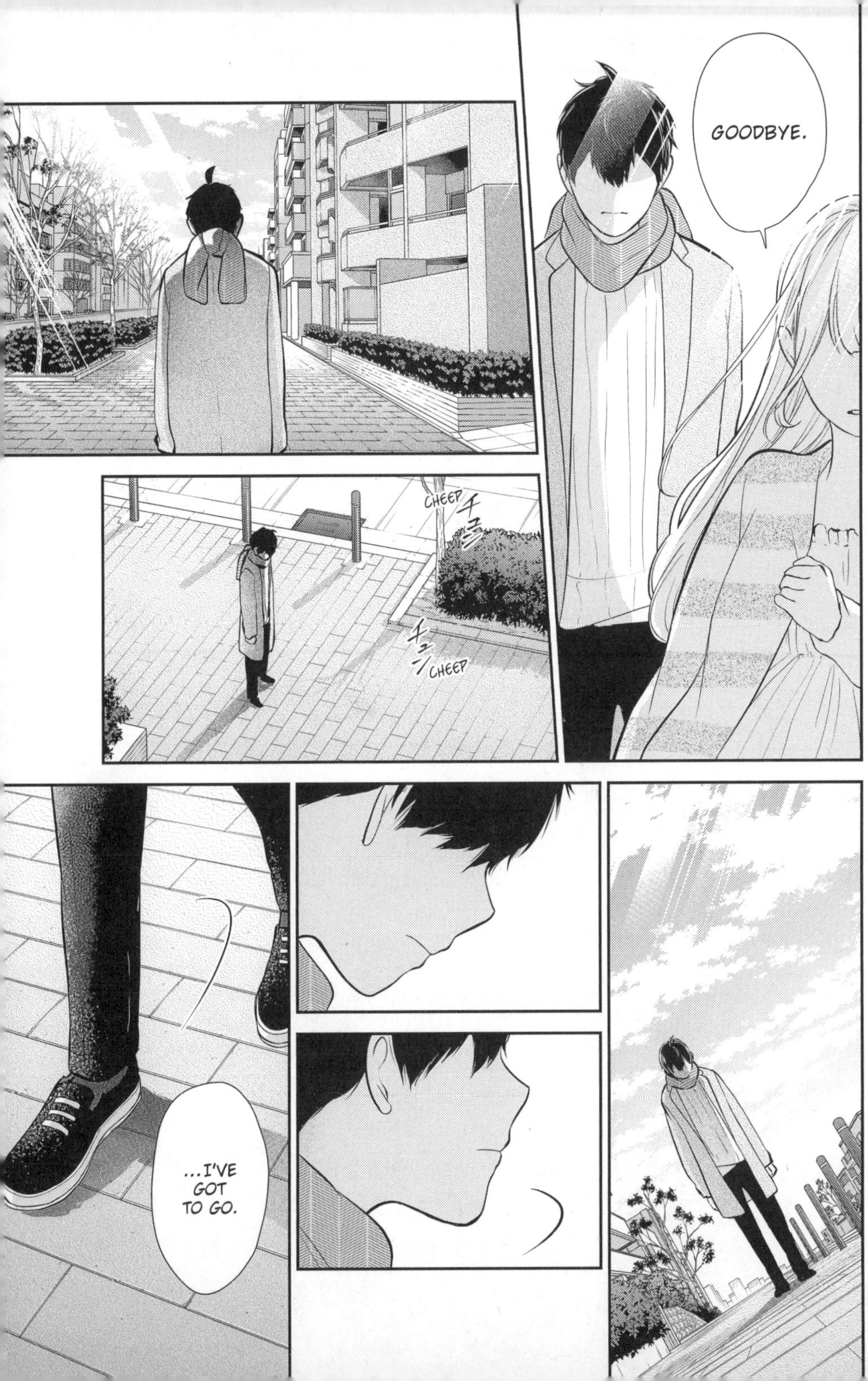
GOODBYE.
CHEEP
CHEEP
...I'VE GOT TO GO.

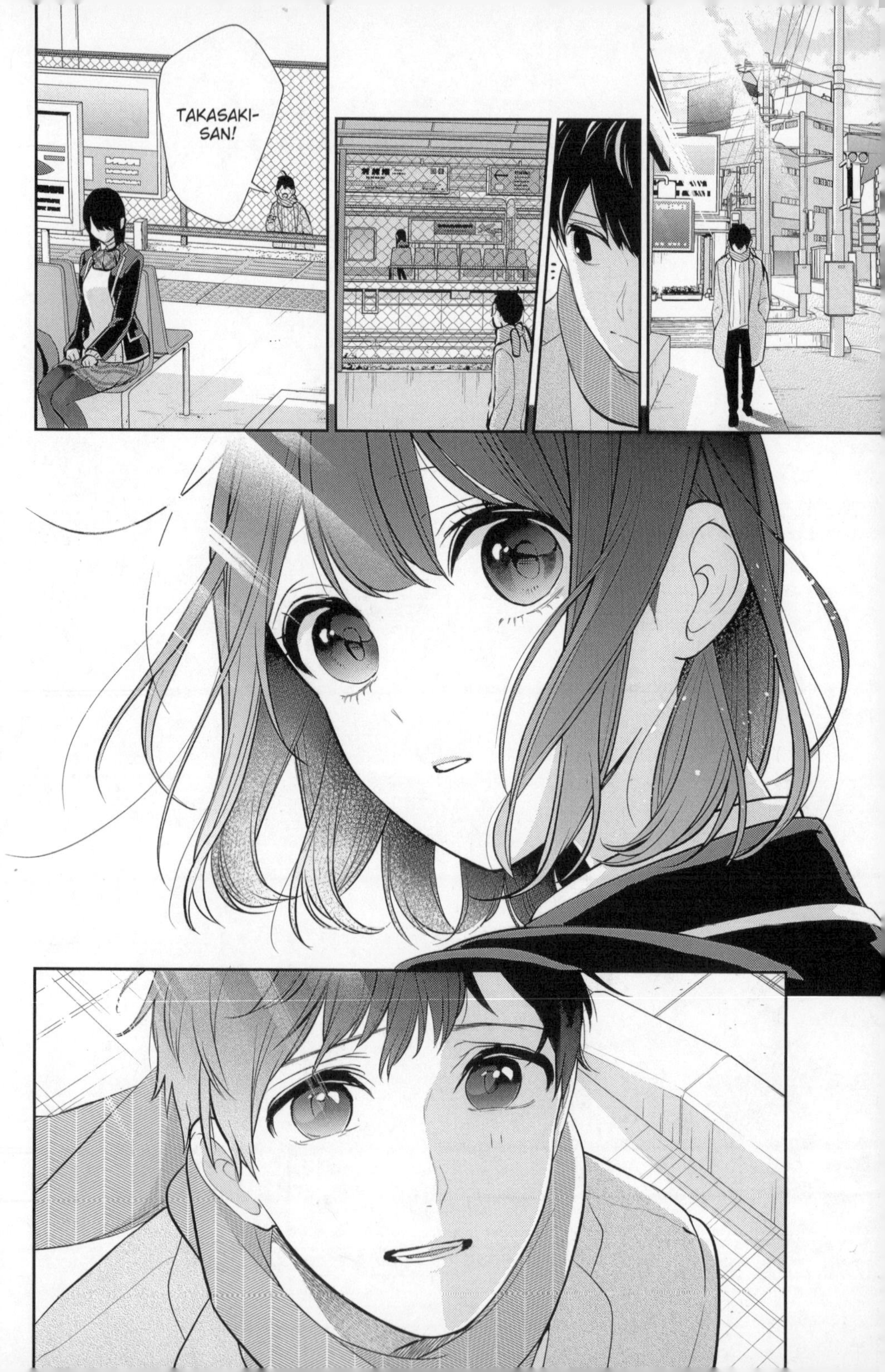
TAKASAKI-SAN!

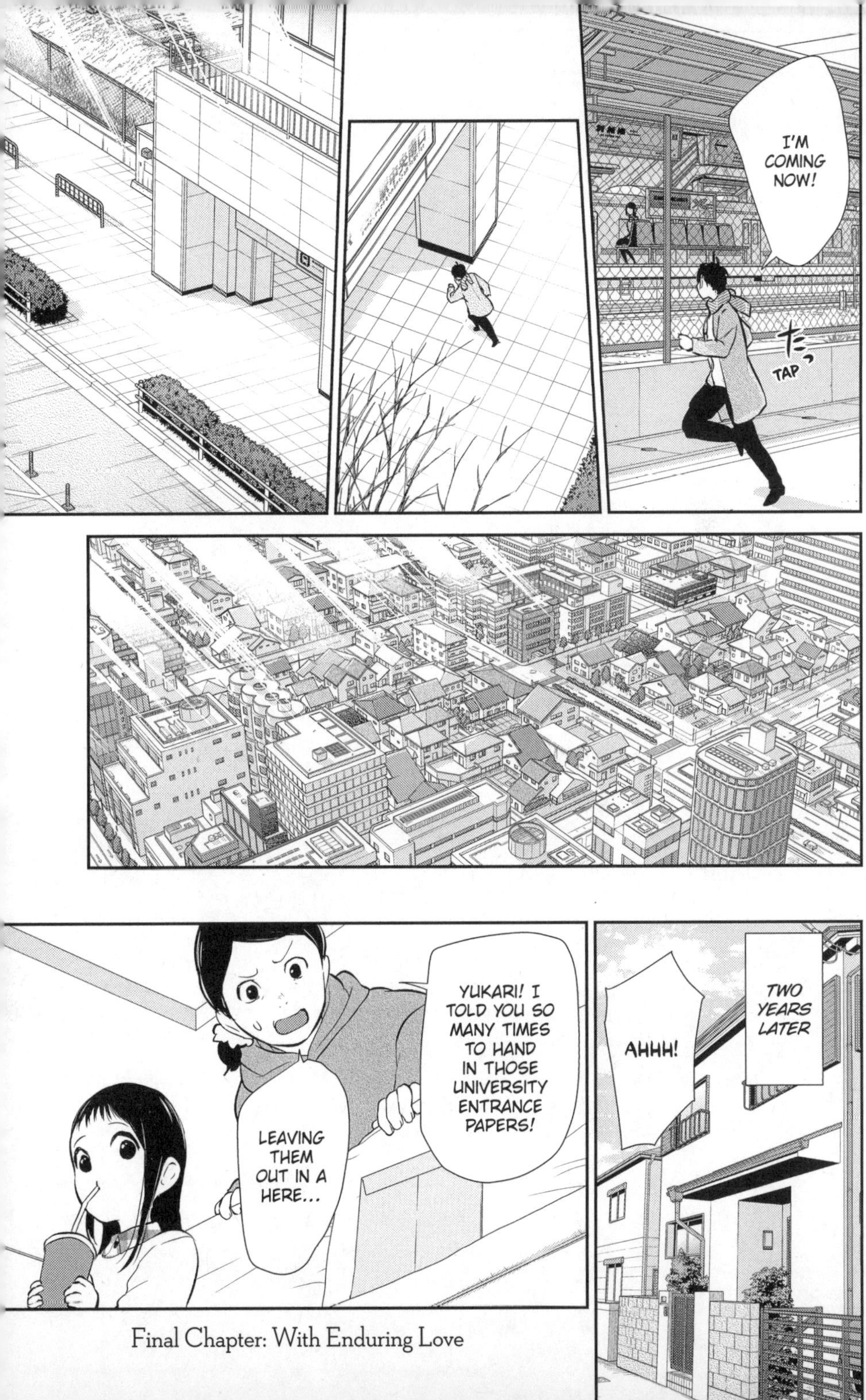
I'M COMING NOW!
TAP
TWO YEARS LATER
AHHH!
YUKARI! I TOLD YOU SO MANY TIMES TO HAND IN THOSE UNIVERSITY ENTRANCE PAPERS!
LEAVING THEM OUT IN A HERE...

Final Chapter: With Enduring Love

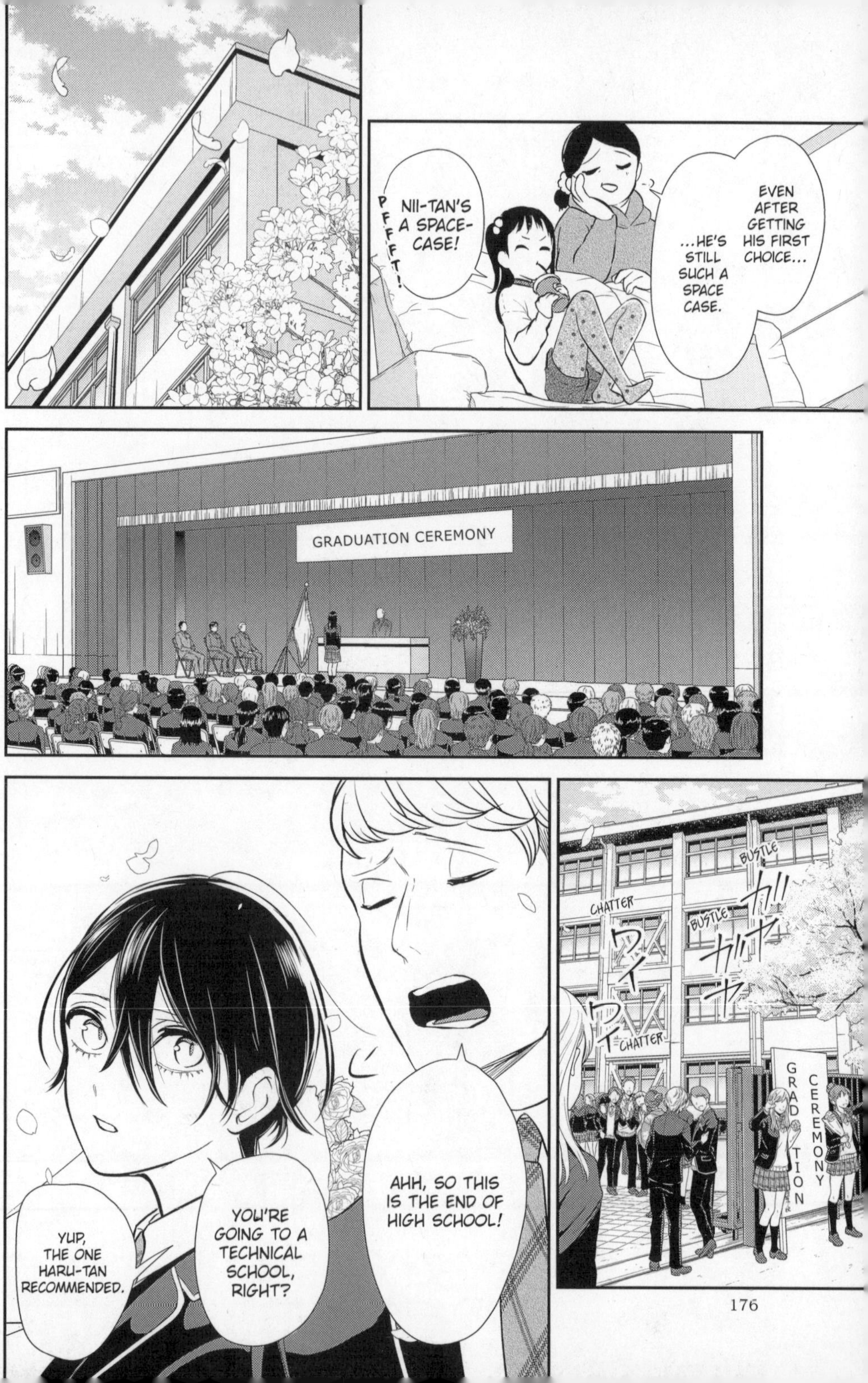
EVEN AFTER GETTING HIS FIRST CHOICE...
...HE'S STILL SUCH A SPACE CASE.
PFFFT!
NII-TAN'S A SPACE-CASE!
GRADUATION CEREMONY
BUSTLE
BUSTLE
CHATTER
CHATTER
GRADUATION CEREMONY
AHH, SO THIS IS THE END OF HIGH SCHOOL!
YOU'RE GOING TO A TECHNICAL SCHOOL, RIGHT?
YUP, THE ONE HARU-TAN RECOMMENDED.

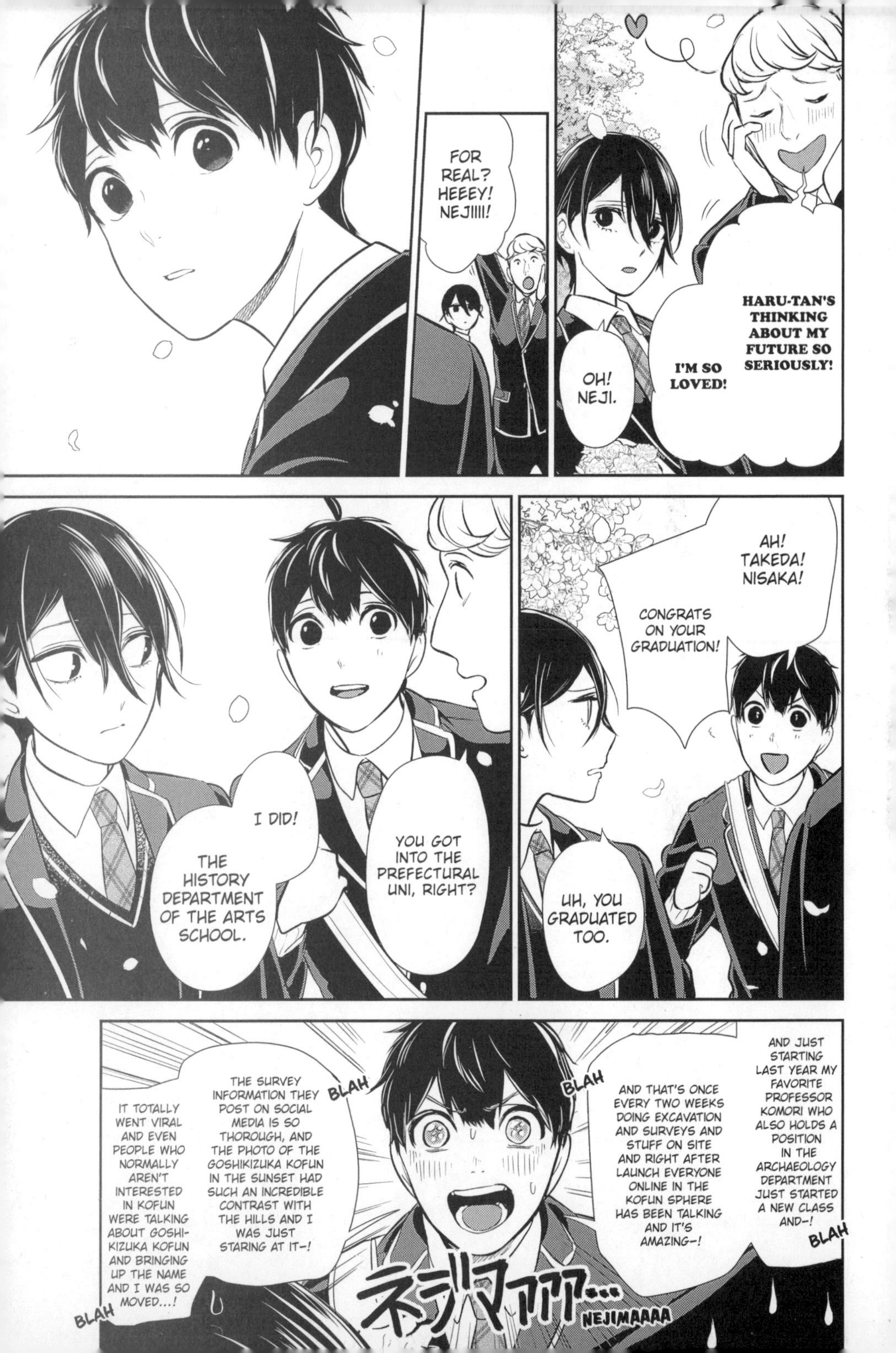
HARU-TAN'S THINKING ABOUT MY FUTURE SO SERIOUSLY!
I'M SO LOVED!
OH! NEJI.
FOR REAL? HEEEY! NEJIIII!
AH! TAKEDA! NISAKA!
CONGRATS ON YOUR GRADUATION!
UH, YOU GRADUATED TOO.
YOU GOT INTO THE PREFECTURAL UNI, RIGHT?
I DID!
THE HISTORY DEPARTMENT OF THE ARTS SCHOOL.
AND JUST STARTING LAST YEAR MY FAVORITE PROFESSOR KOMORI WHO ALSO HOLDS A POSITION IN THE ARCHAEOLOGY DEPARTMENT JUST STARTED A NEW CLASS AND–!
BLAH
AND THAT'S ONCE EVERY TWO WEEKS DOING EXCAVATION AND SURVEYS AND STUFF ON SITE AND RIGHT AFTER LAUNCH EVERYONE ONLINE IN THE KOFUN SPHERE HAS BEEN TALKING AND IT'S AMAZING–!
BLAH
THE SURVEY INFORMATION THEY POST ON SOCIAL MEDIA IS SO THOROUGH, AND THE PHOTO OF THE GOSHIKIZUKA KOFUN IN THE SUNSET HAD SUCH AN INCREDIBLE CONTRAST WITH THE HILLS AND I WAS JUST STARING AT IT–!
BLAH
IT TOTALLY WENT VIRAL AND EVEN PEOPLE WHO NORMALLY AREN'T INTERESTED IN KOFUN WERE TALKING ABOUT GOSHIKIZUKA KOFUN AND BRINGING UP THE NAME AND I WAS SO MOVED...!
BLAH
ネジマアアア…
NEJIMAAAA

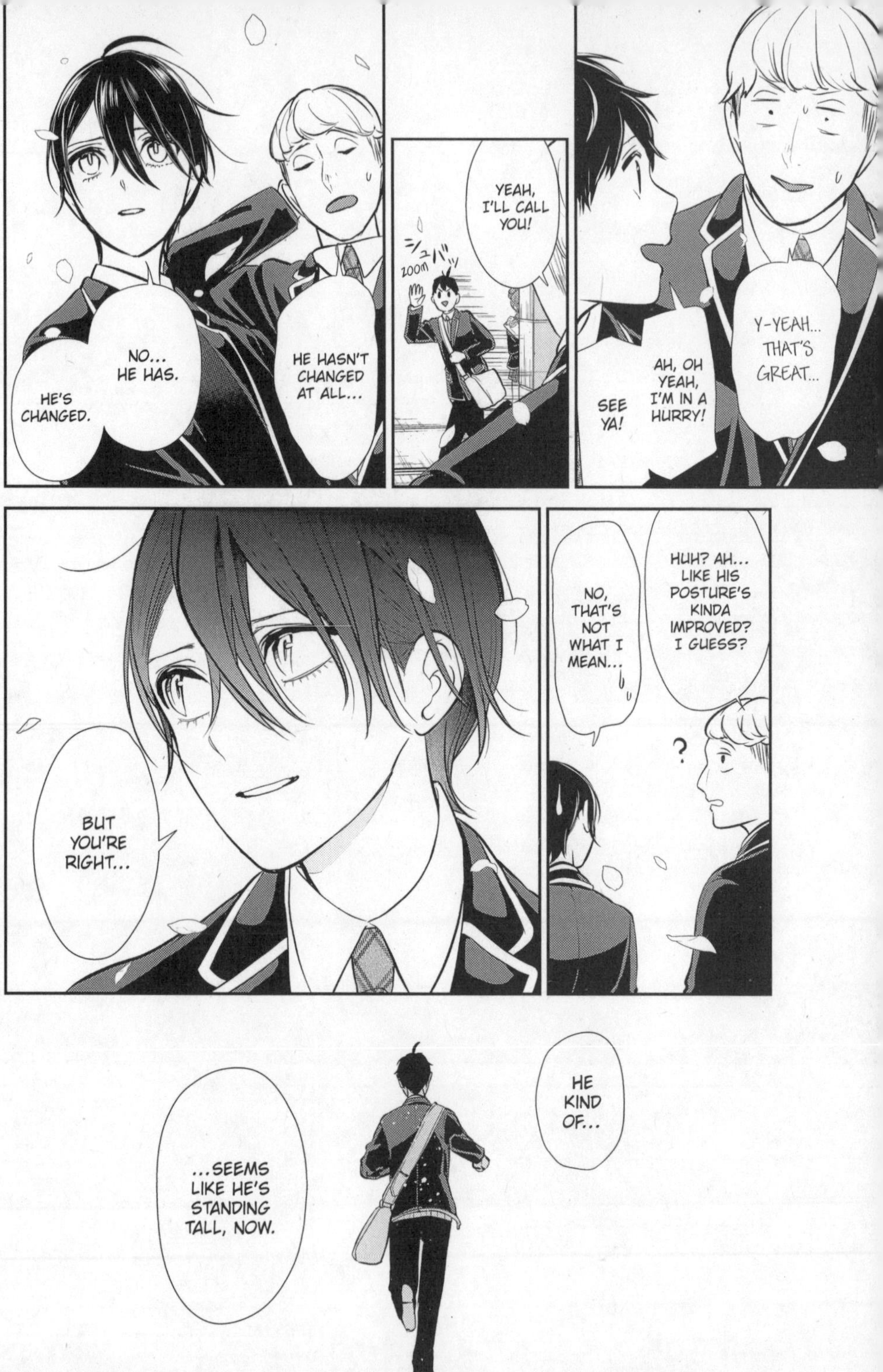
Y-YEAH... THAT'S GREAT...
AH, OH YEAH, I'M IN A HURRY!
SEE YA!
YEAH, I'LL CALL YOU!
シュバッ
ZOOM
HE HASN'T CHANGED AT ALL...
NO... HE HAS.
HE'S CHANGED.
HUH? AH... LIKE HIS POSTURE'S KINDA IMPROVED? I GUESS?
NO, THAT'S NOT WHAT I MEAN...
?
BUT YOU'RE RIGHT...
HE KIND OF...
...SEEMS LIKE HE'S STANDING TALL, NOW.

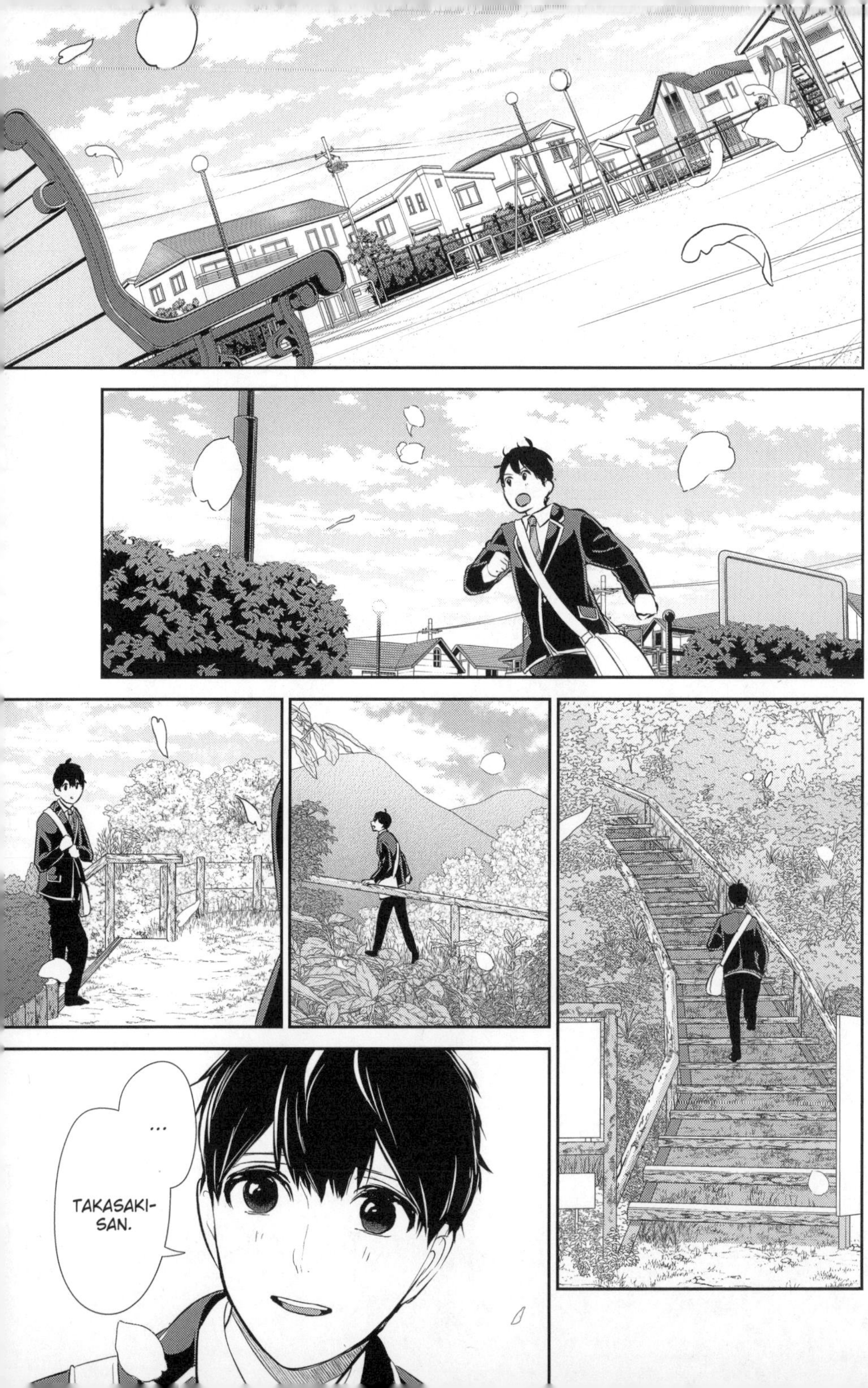
...
TAKASAKI-SAN.

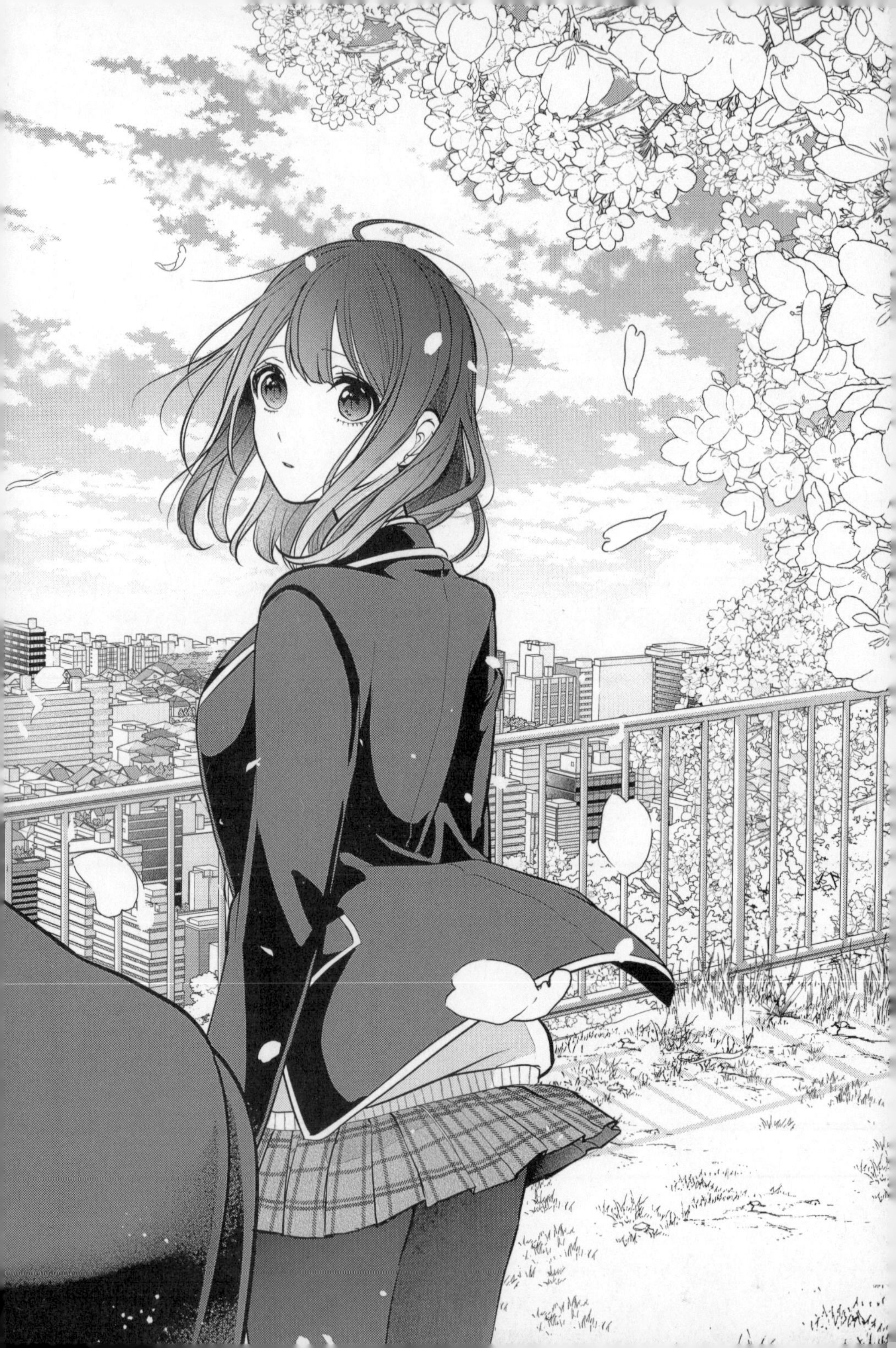

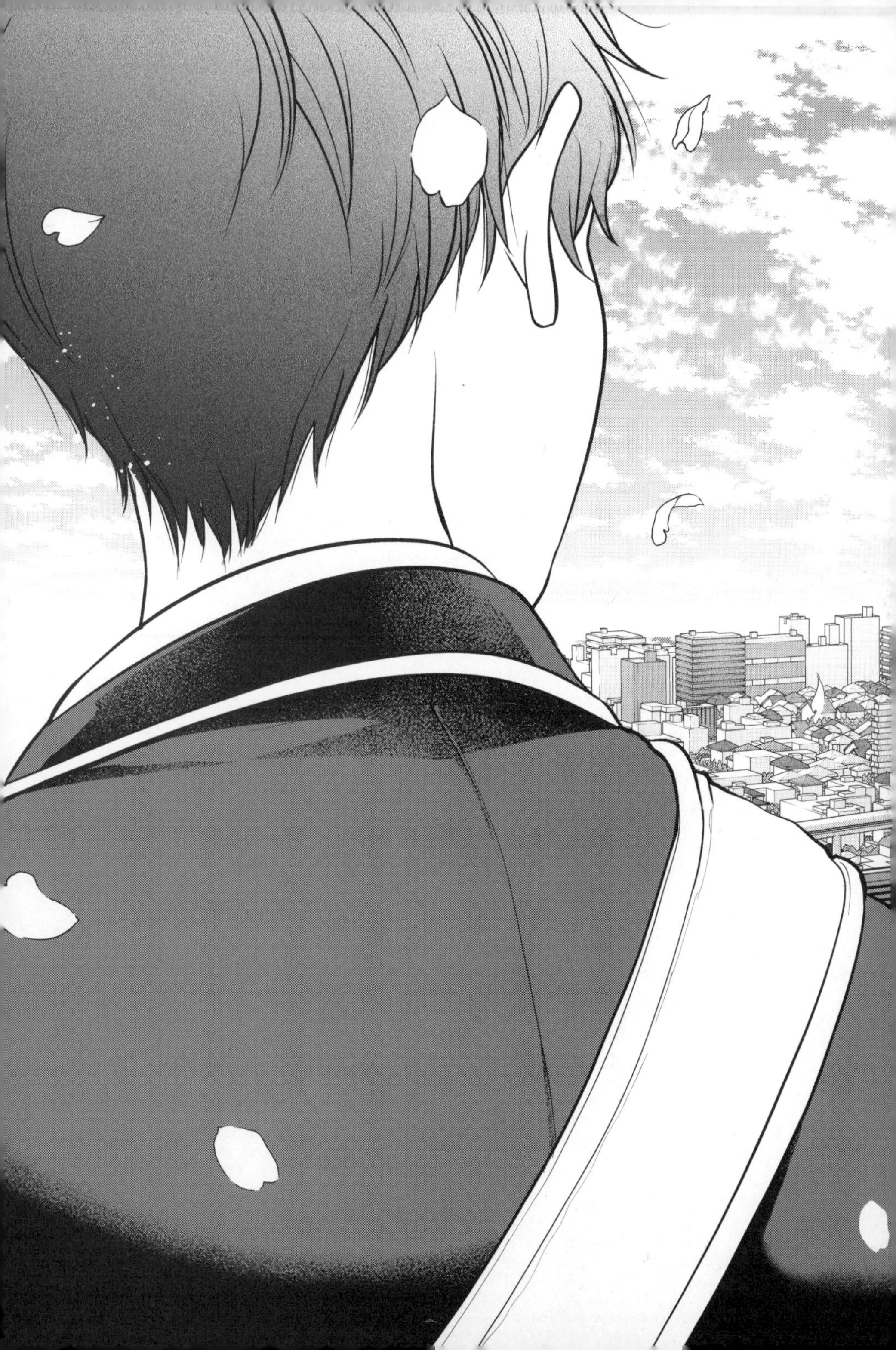

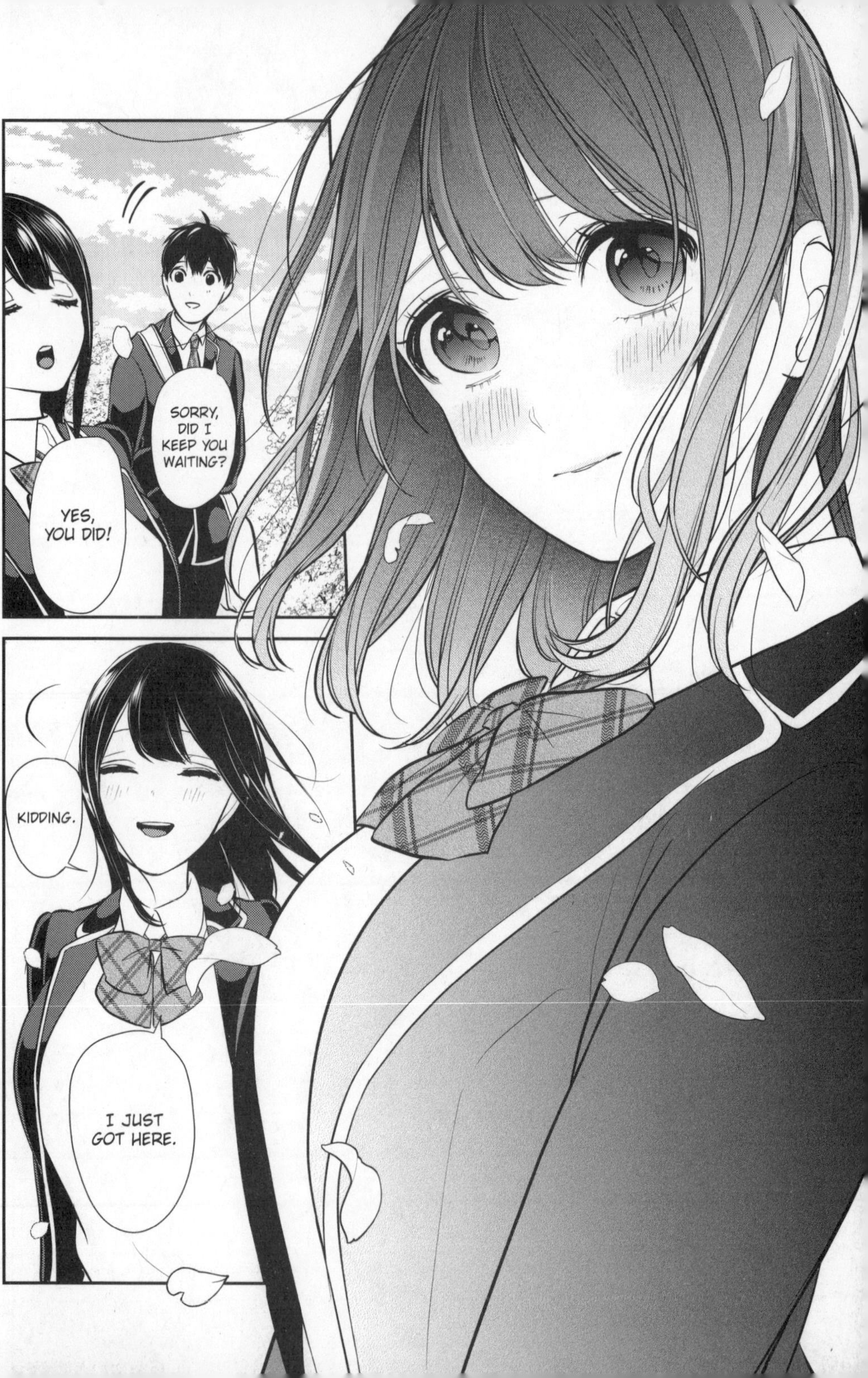
SORRY, DID I KEEP YOU WAITING?
YES, YOU DID!
KIDDING.
I JUST GOT HERE.

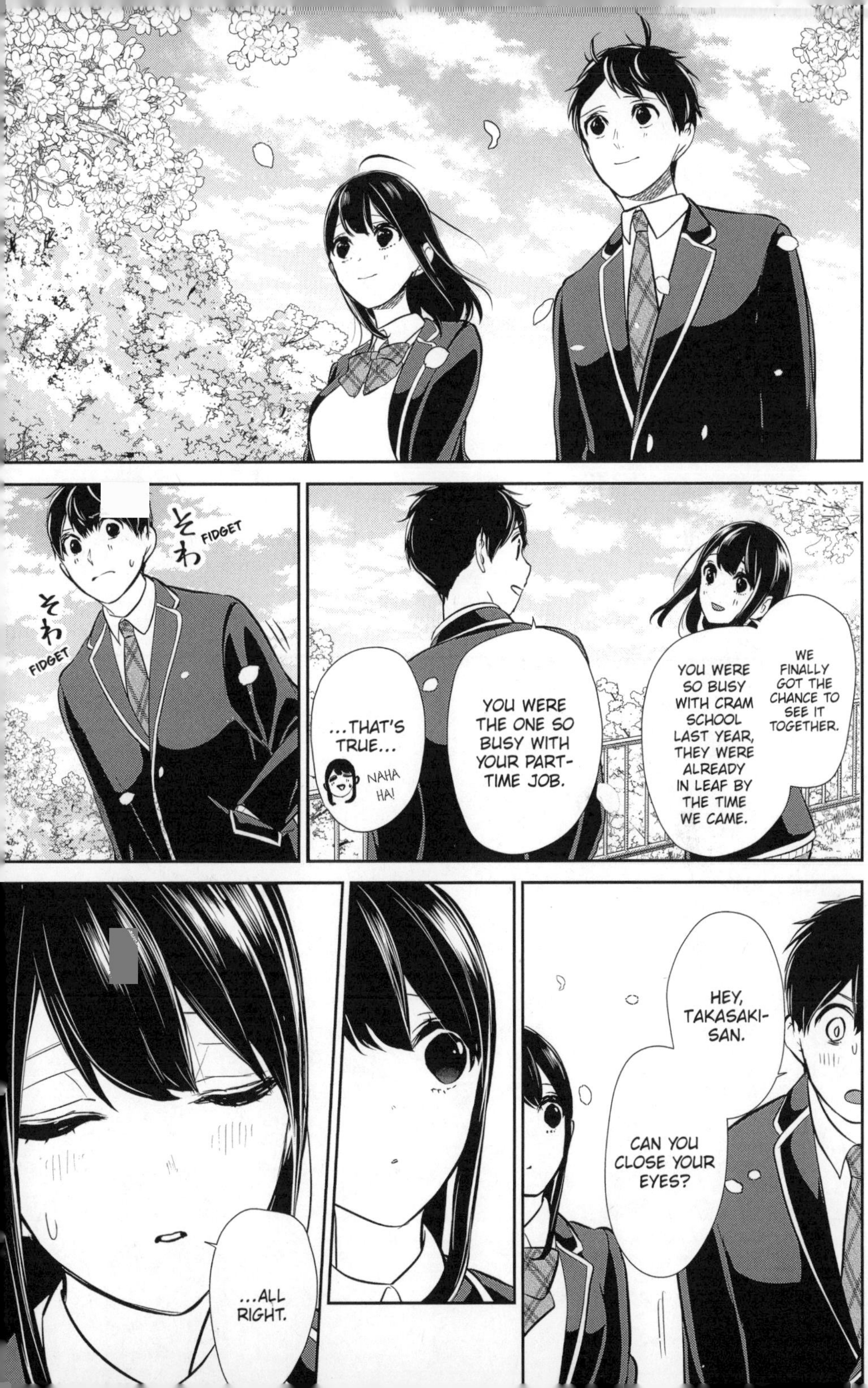
WE FINALLY GOT THE CHANCE TO SEE IT TOGETHER.
YOU WERE SO BUSY WITH CRAM SCHOOL LAST YEAR, THEY WERE ALREADY IN LEAF BY THE TIME WE CAME.
YOU WERE THE ONE SO BUSY WITH YOUR PART-TIME JOB.
...THAT'S TRUE...
NAHA HA!
そわ FIDGET
そわ FIDGET
HEY, TAKASAKI-SAN.
CAN YOU CLOSE YOUR EYES?
...ALL RIGHT.

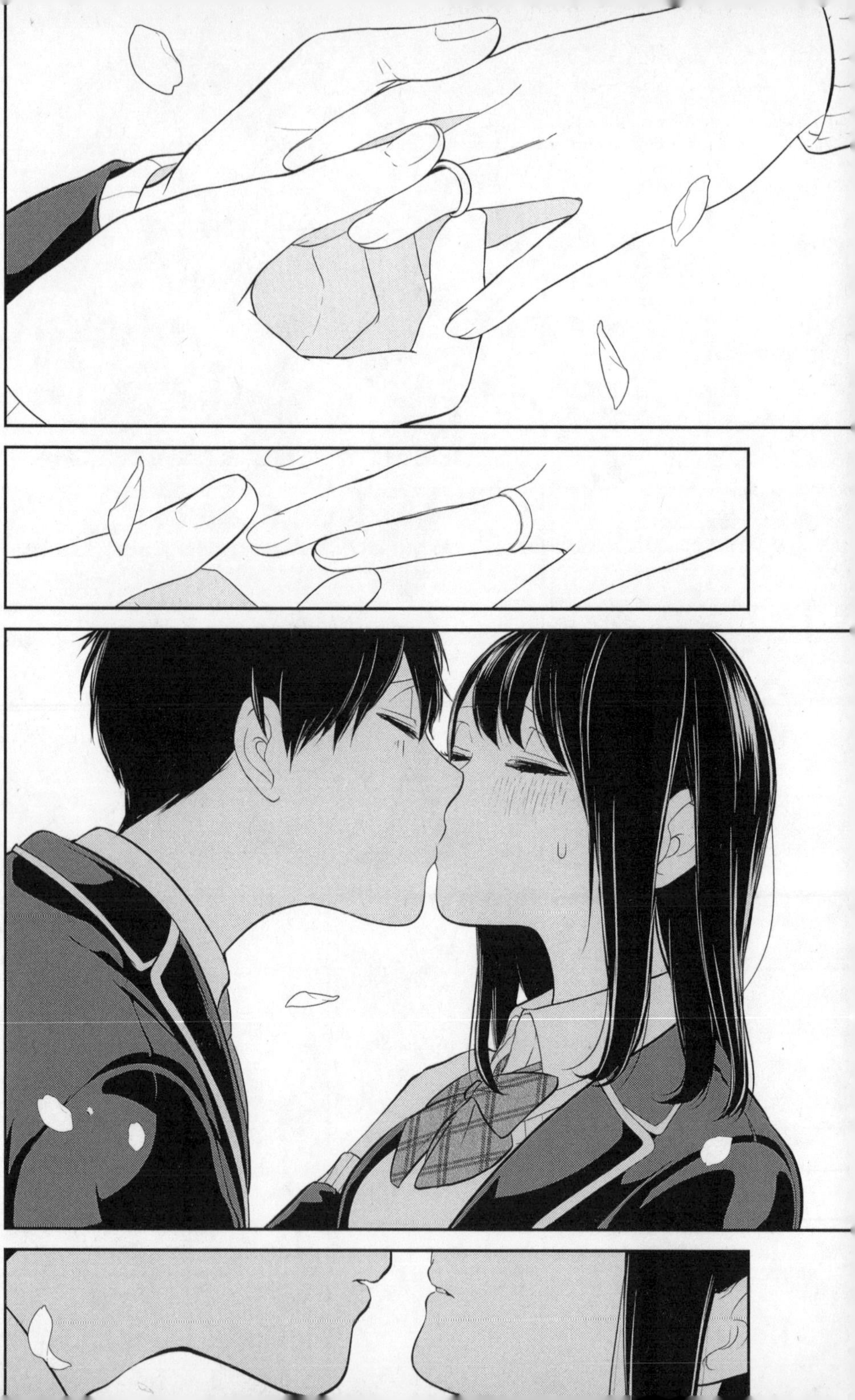

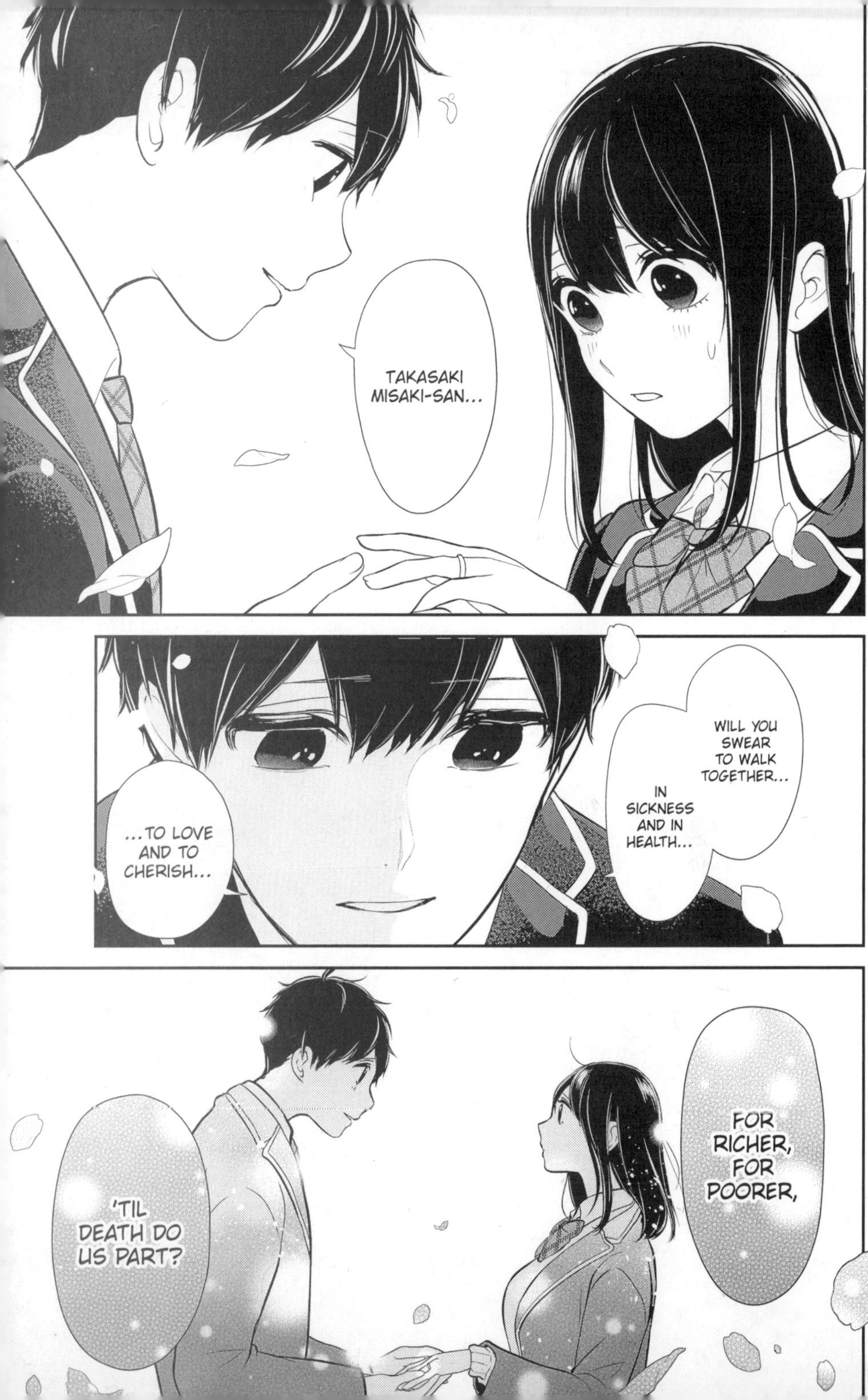
TAKASAKI MISAKI-SAN...
WILL YOU SWEAR TO WALK TOGETHER...
IN SICKNESS AND IN HEALTH...
...TO LOVE AND TO CHERISH...
FOR RICHER, FOR POORER,
'TIL DEATH DO US PART?

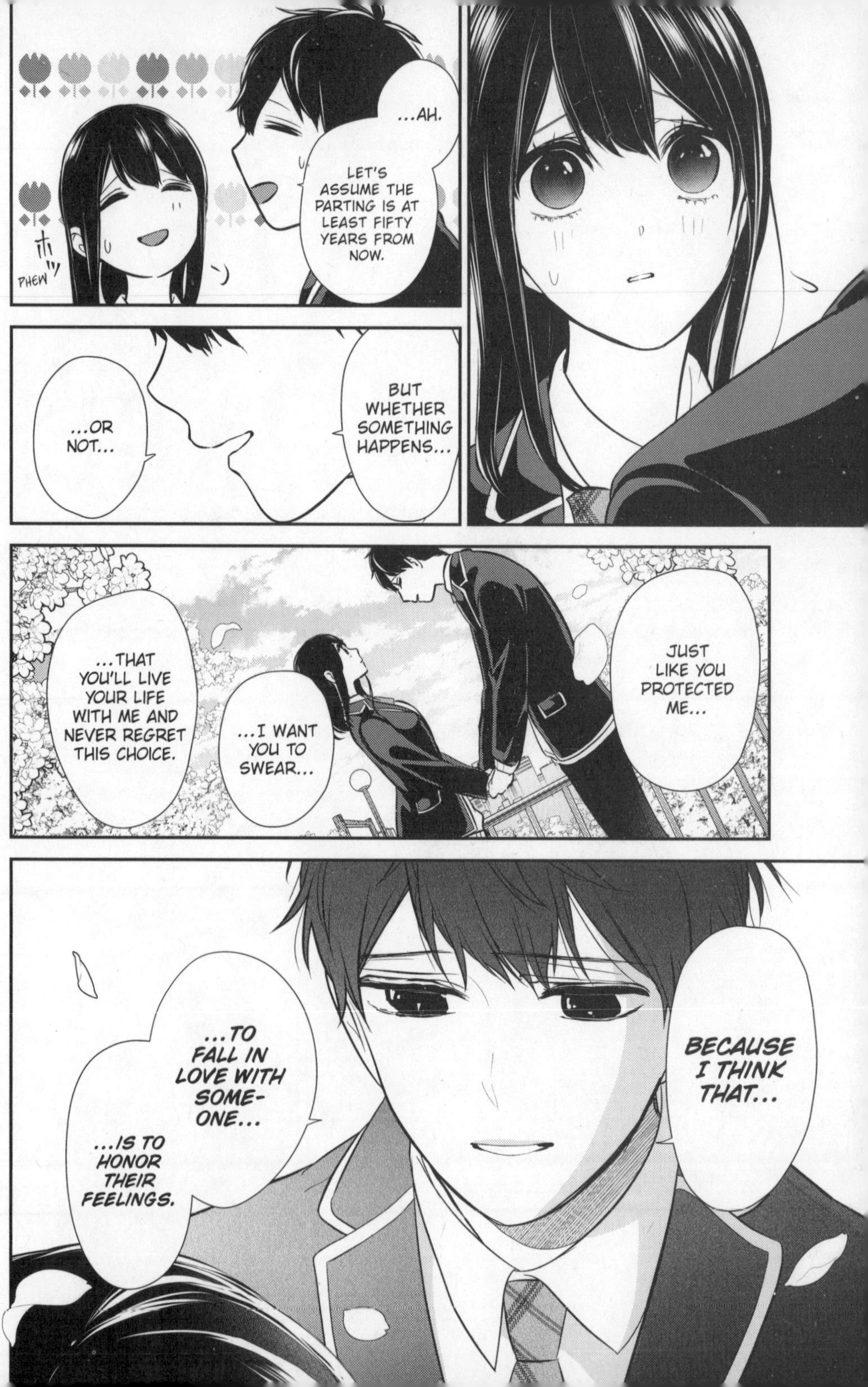
...AH.
LET'S ASSUME THE PARTING IS AT LEAST FIFTY YEARS FROM NOW.
ホッ
PHEW
BUT WHETHER SOMETHING HAPPENS...
...OR NOT...
JUST LIKE YOU PROTECTED ME...
...I WANT YOU TO SWEAR...
...THAT YOU'LL LIVE YOUR LIFE WITH ME AND NEVER REGRET THIS CHOICE.
BECAUSE I THINK THAT...
...TO FALL IN LOVE WITH SOME-ONE...
...IS TO HONOR THEIR FEELINGS.

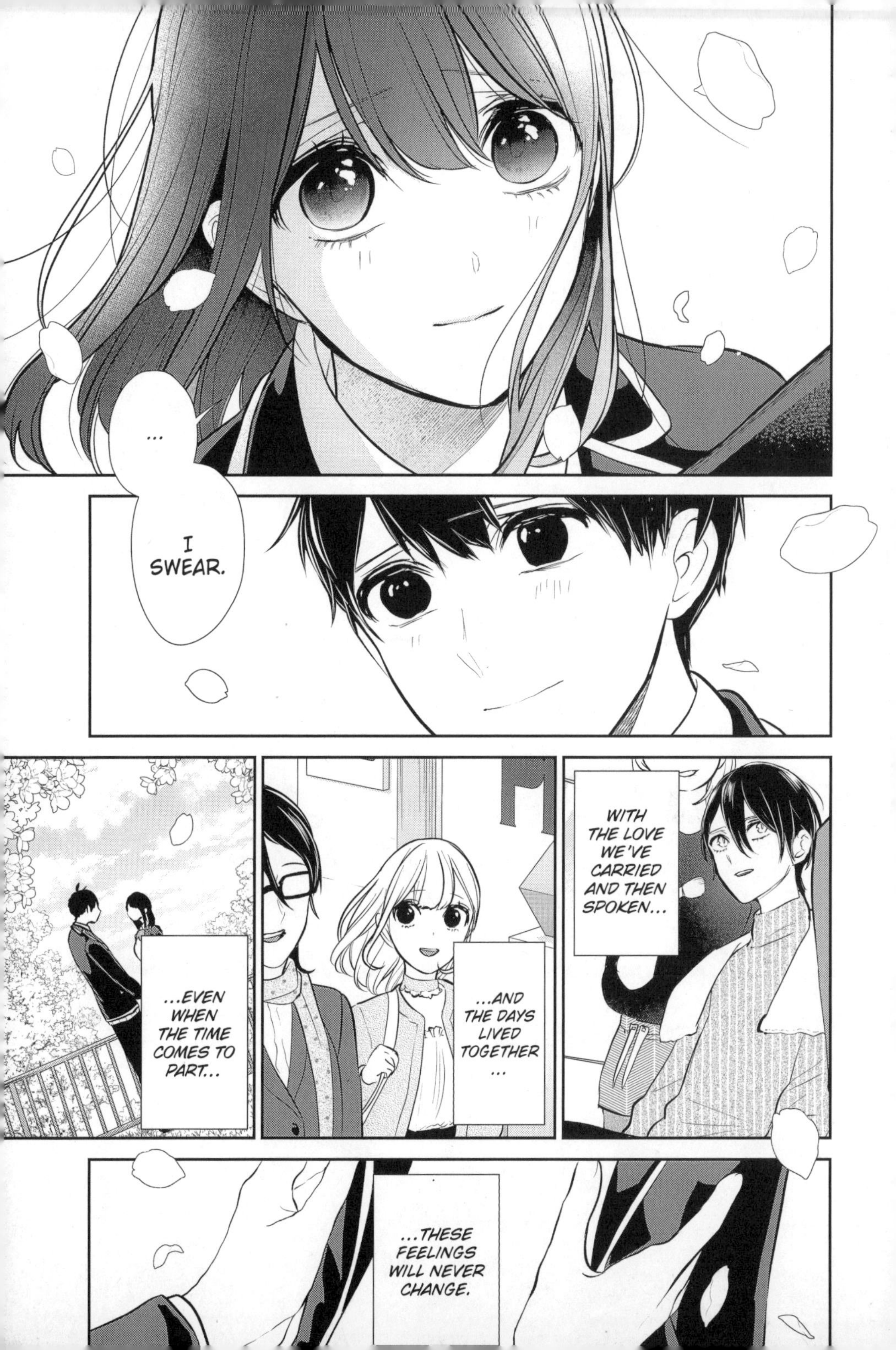
...
I SWEAR.
WITH THE LOVE WE'VE CARRIED AND THEN SPOKEN...
...AND THE DAYS LIVED TOGETHER...
...EVEN WHEN THE TIME COMES TO PART...
...THESE FEELINGS WILL NEVER CHANGE.

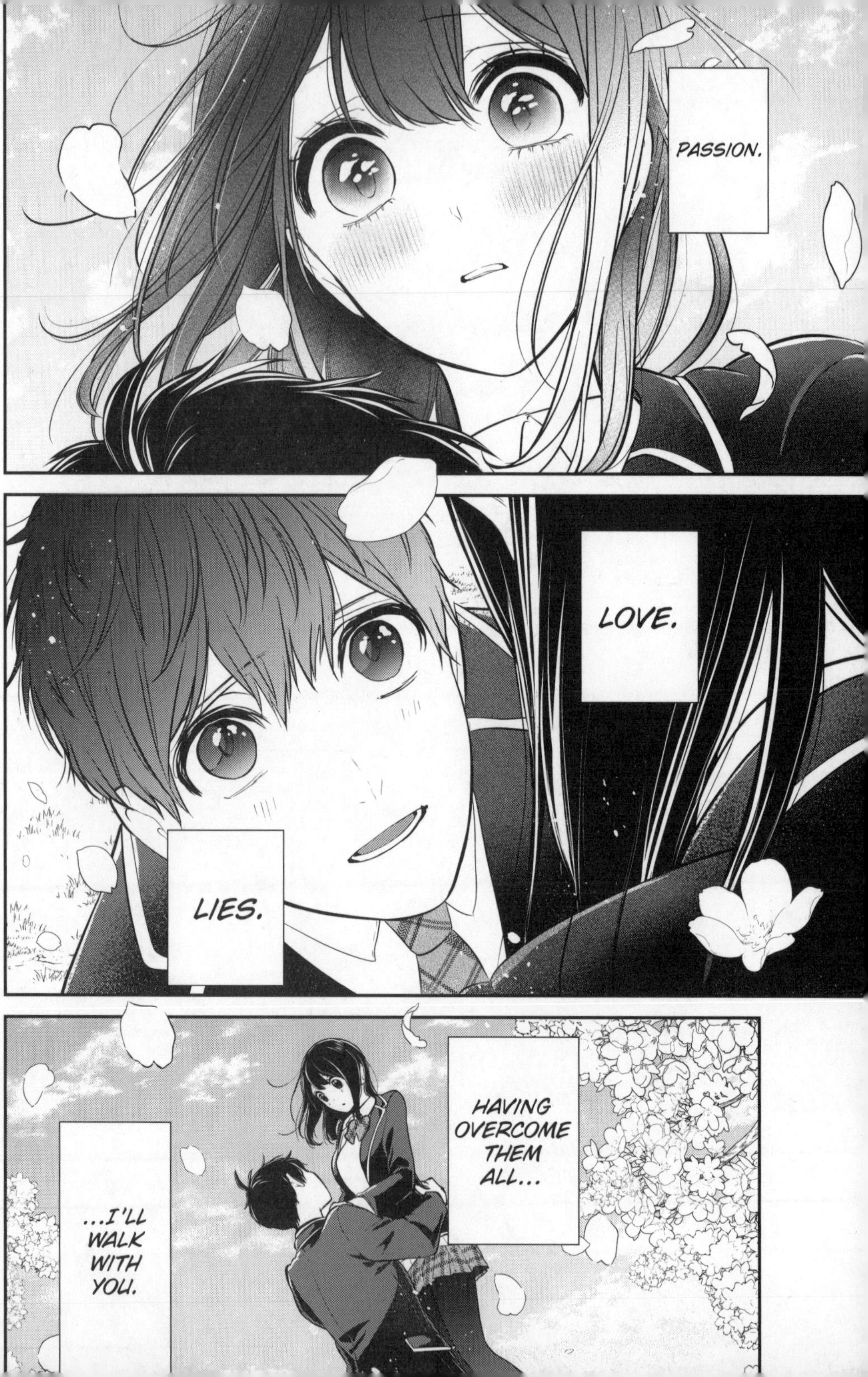
PASSION.
LOVE.
LIES.
HAVING OVERCOME THEM ALL...
...I'LL WALK WITH YOU.

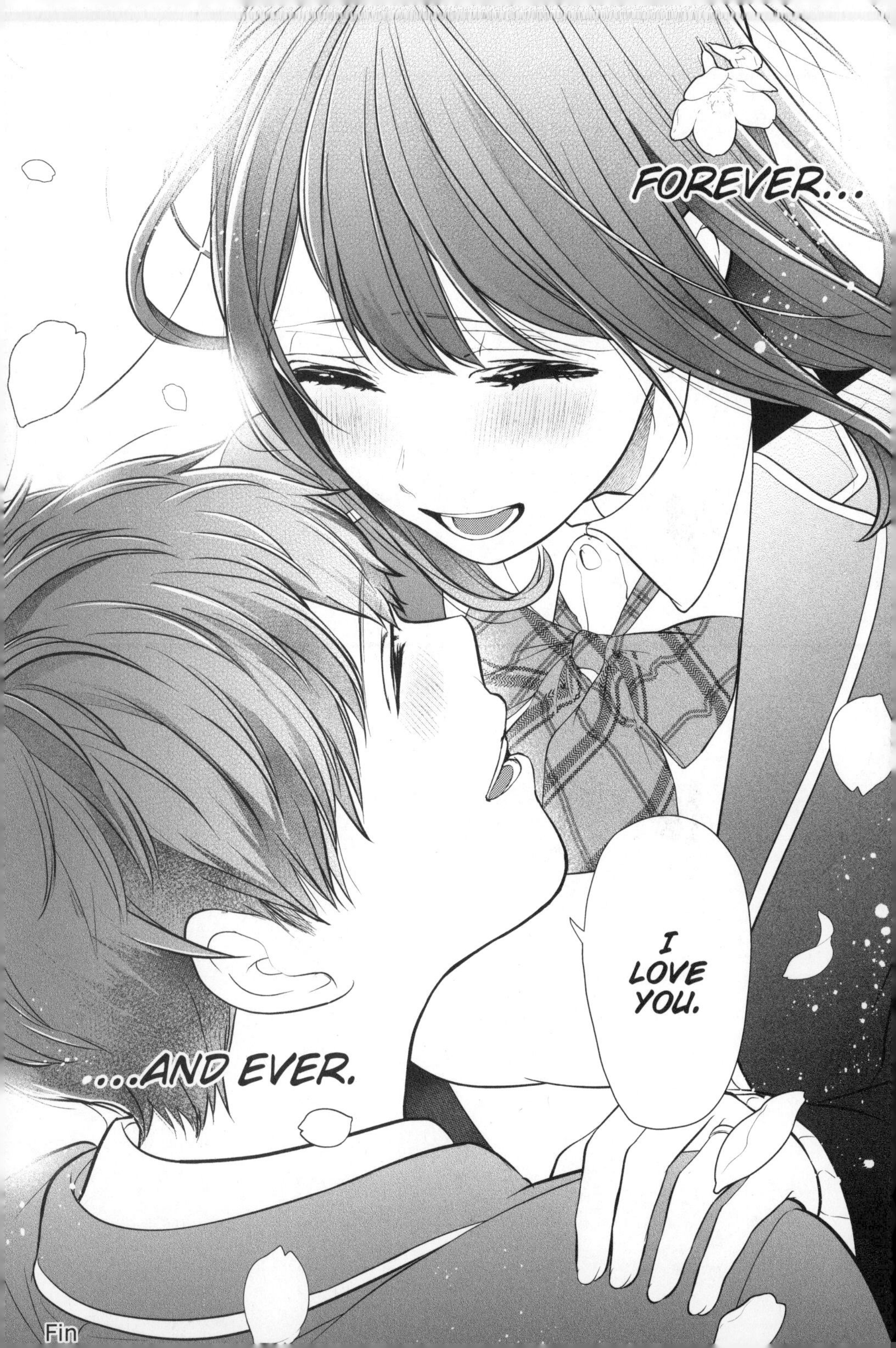
FOREVER...
I LOVE YOU.
...AND EVER.
Fin

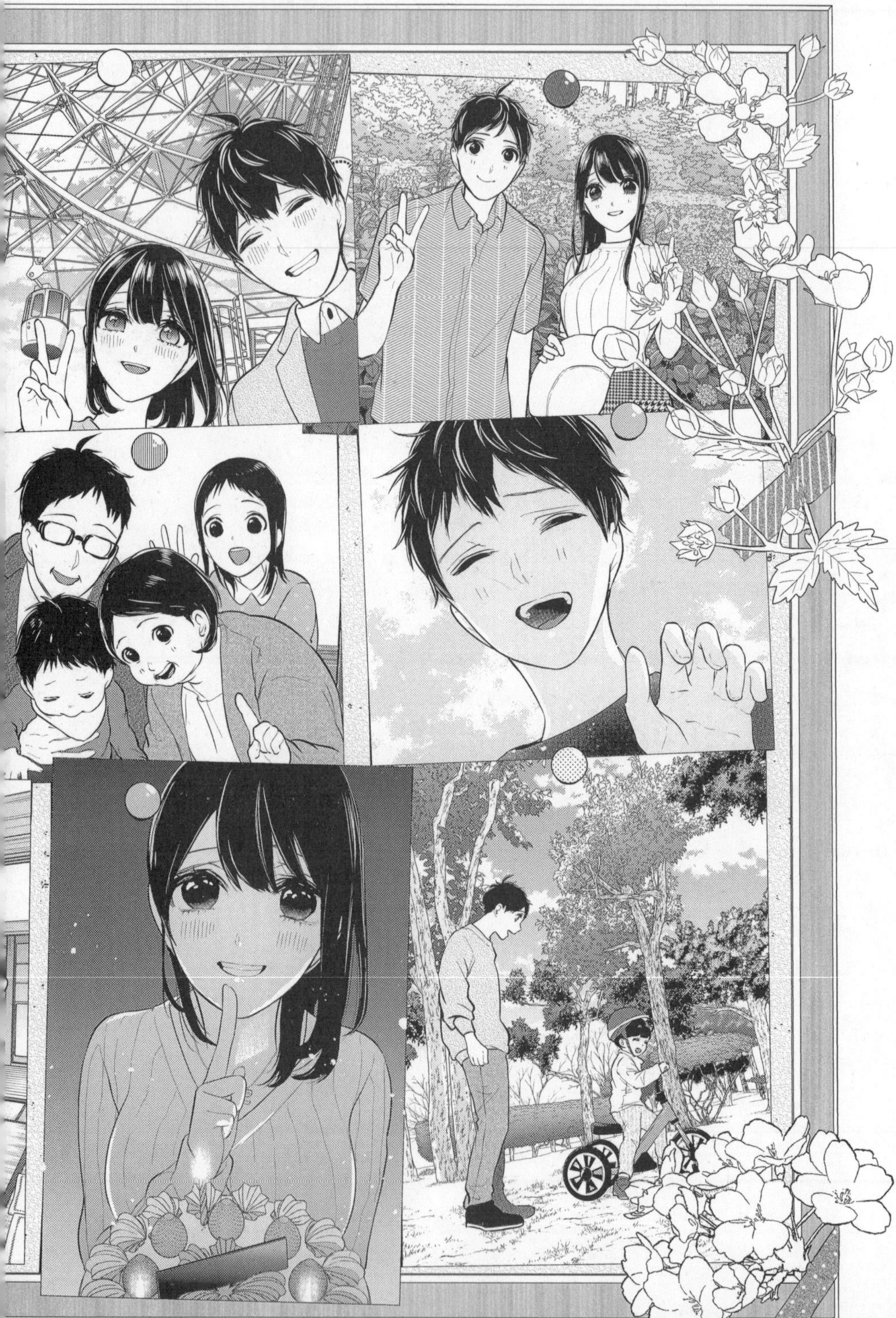

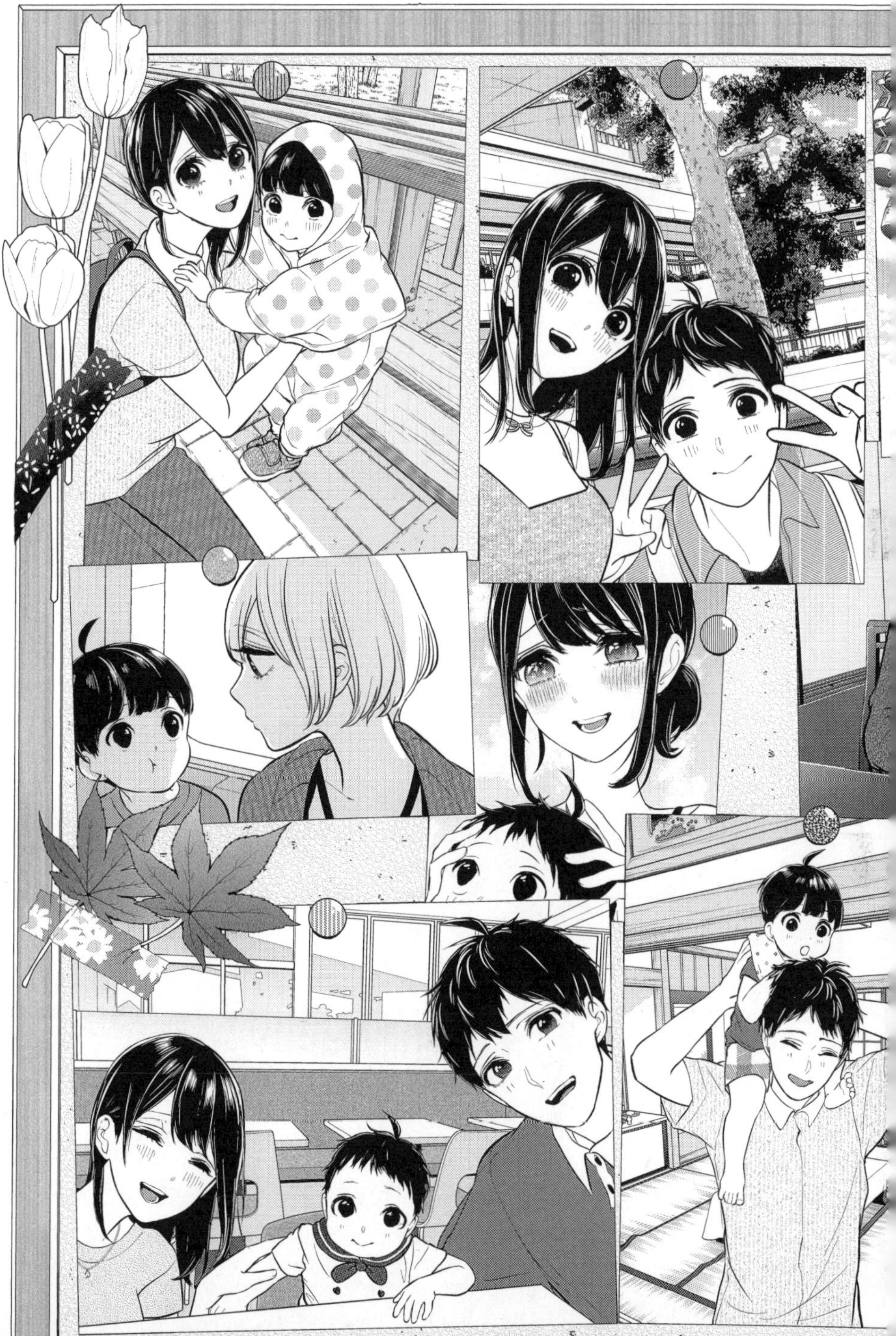

A Kodansha Comics Trade Paperback Original
Love and Lies 12: *The Misaki Ending* copyright © 2022 Musawo
English translation copyright © 2022 Musawo

All rights reserved.

Published in the United States by Kodansha Comics, an imprint of
Kodansha USA Publishing, LLC, New York.

Publication rights for this English edition arranged through
Kodansha Ltd., Tokyo.

First published in Japan in 2022 by Kodansha Ltd., Tokyo
as *Koi to uso*, volume 12, Misaki ver.

ISBN 978-1-64651-581-3

Original cover design by Tadashi Hisamochi (hive & co., Ltd.)

Printed in the United States of America.

www.kodansha.us

9 8 7 6 5 4 3 2 1
Translation: Jennifer Ward
Lettering: Daniel CY
Editing: Aimee Zink
Kodansha Comics edition cover design by Phil Balsman

Publisher: Kiichiro Sugawara

Director of publishing services: Ben Applegate
Director of publishing operations: Dave Barrett
Associate director of publishing operations: Stephen Pakula
Publishing services managing editors: Alanna Ruse, Madison Salters, with Grace Chen
Senior production manager: Angela Zurlo